CULTURAL HERITAGE LAW AND POLICY

Cultural Objects and Reparative Justice

CULTURAL HERITAGE LAW AND POLICY

The aim of this series is to publish significant and original research on and scholarly analysis of all aspects of cultural heritage law through the lens of international law, private international law, and comparative law. The series is wide in scope, traversing disciplines, regions, and viewpoints. Topics given particular prominence are those which, while of interest to academic lawyers, have significant bearing on policymaking and current public discourse on the interaction between art, heritage, and the law.

Cultural Objects and Reparative Justice

A Legal and Historical Analysis

PATTY GERSTENBLITH

OXFORD
UNIVERSITY PRESS

OXFORD
UNIVERSITY PRESS

Great Clarendon Street, Oxford, OX2 6DP,
United Kingdom

Oxford University Press is a department of the University of Oxford.
It furthers the University's objective of excellence in research, scholarship,
and education by publishing worldwide. Oxford is a registered trade mark of
Oxford University Press in the UK and in certain other countries

First Edition published in 2023

Published in the United States of America by Oxford University Press
198 Madison Avenue, New York, NY 10016, United States of America

British Library Cataloguing in Publication Data

Data available

Library of Congress Control Number: 2023943120

ISBN 978–0–19–287210–4

DOI: 10.1093/oso/9780192872104.001.0001

Printed and bound by
CPI Group (UK) Ltd, Croydon, CR0 4YY

Preface

I started thinking about this project close to fifteen years ago. During this time, it evolved through numerous stages, but I kept returning to particular issues. One was the formative time period between the mid-eighteenth century and early part of the nineteenth century when the strands of the cultural heritage debate developed. This formative period set the groundwork for the questions of why cultural objects were appropriated during colonialism, imperialism and armed conflict and under what circumstances they should be returned.

Cultural heritage and cultural heritage law have received increasing attention in the past several decades. Much of this attention has expanded in two directions: first, to give greater consideration to intangible heritage, and, second, with respect to tangible heritage, to focus on the destruction of historic structures, looting of archaeological sites, and thefts from institutions, often in the context of armed conflict. This volume focuses not on destruction and the means of preservation but what I call the cultural heritage debate—the question of where movable tangible cultural objects that were taken without consent both recently and in the further past should be located. Such objects have often been appropriated through armed conflict, theft, colonialism, and different forms of imperialism. These different methods of appropriation in different time periods implicate different legal responses and the search for other answers when the law, as currently configured, gives an inadequate response. In particular, focus has turned to what may be termed 'historic appropriations'—those that occurred beyond the reach of contemporary law and therefore require other solutions.

This volume attempts to bridge legal approaches and non-legal approaches in an interdisciplinary manner. Any attempt to provide a comprehensive answer to the question of where cultural objects should be located depends on the use of three interdisciplinary methodologies. The first requires us to look at cultural heritage from three perspectives: the universal or global, the State (or national), and the local community. The second methodology is interdisciplinary within the fields of law and ethics, combining international and domestic law, international humanitarian law, and international human rights law. The third methodology includes the several disciplines of history, art history, archaeology, and anthropology. This volume also attempts to interrelate within tangible cultural heritage three areas that are often analysed independently: Holocaust-looted art, Indigenous cultural heritage and human remains, and archaeological artefacts. Distinct legal responses have evolved around these, but each can learn from the solutions and challenges that restitution in the context of the other two has posed.

In an innovative approach, the work analyses several examples of appropriation cutting across time and geography to consider the Parthenon Sculptures, the Yuanmingyuan Palace, the Benin objects, Indigenous human remains and cultural items, archaeological artefacts, and artworks looted during the Holocaust. These types of cultural objects and different circumstances of their appropriation inform the work's proposal of a paradigm for reparations. Acknowledging that the foundations of our modern laws and ethical guidelines with respect to cultural heritage are built on a history of imperialism and colonialism, this work advocates for a new structure based on reparation, restitution, repatriation, compensation, and market regulation in order to no longer perpetuate past harms while disincentivizing new harms. Finally, it sets out a paradigm based on process and defined principles for the restitution of human remains and cultural objects that were removed from their communities and States as a result of colonialism, armed conflict, or imperialism. It is in proposing this paradigm and set of principles for reparations that this volume hopes to make its contribution to the debate concerning the location of cultural objects.

July 2023

Series Editors' Preface

The complex legal and moral questions surrounding the return of 'historically removed' cultural objects have increasingly enlivened the imagination of lawyers, scholars, and the general public in the last decade. The fraught circumstances surrounding the removal, display, and possible restitution of cultural objects during foreign occupation, especially colonial occupation has come to the fore again, some half century or more since the formal commencement of decolonization by the United Nations. The current iteration of these debates reveals, once again, that these processes are incomplete, and its legacies ongoing.

Patty Gerstenblith's book is the first volume in this series which focuses on the fate of movable heritage as defined in national and international law. Professor Gerstenblith zeroes in on the perennial issues around removal, protection, and return in an all-encompassing way, drawing on veins of scholarship from multiple disciplines and legal and policy practice across several continents. The first half of this important monograph lays out the key conceptual and historical concerns which have come to define this field. For it is impossible to truly appreciate the constructs (legal and linguistic) which define the legal and scholarly debates and blockages (real and perceived) which hinder confrontation and resolution of restitution claims without a detailed, nuanced, and critical understanding of the historical context. The second half is equally meticulous in its forensic and systematic examination of the national and international legal and non-legal frameworks which define responses to restitution claims. Mirroring the ambition of the first part, Professor Gerstenblith draws on important recent developments from a broad swath of sources to emphasize the perennial nature of legal and ethical concerns across time and space. For the circumstances which gave rise to 'historic' removals continue to inform cultural losses in the same communities today. And lessons learned in respect of successful restitution of human remains or Holocaust-related claims may inform responses to other restitution requests. Satisfyingly, the author brings all these threads together to distil the major modalities for the resolution of restitution claims.

From beginning to end—from its framing of the conceptual and historic issues, to its all-encompassing treatment of the legal and ethical concerns, to its enunciation of a way forward for resolving claims—this volume provides a vital and rich contribution to one of the most important issues in cultural heritage law today.

Francesco Francioni and Ana Filipa Vrdoljak

Acknowledgements

This project evolved over many years, attempting to keep pace with the many changing facets of the issues involved in determining where cultural objects should be located. The project benefited from conversations, both serious and casual, with many colleagues and mentors in this field. While I risk omitting someone from this list, I want to thank especially Professor Francesco Francioni and Professor Ana Vrdoljak, the editors of the Oxford University Press Cultural Heritage Law and Policy series, for their wisdom, guidance, encouragement, and friendship. Among my peers, colleagues, and friends to whom I am much indebted, I include Neil Brodie, Brian Daniels, Holly Flora, Morag Kersel, Laetitia La Follette, Richard Leventhal, Jane Levine, Claire Lyons, Victoria Reed, and Nancy Wilkie. I owe much to my mentors including Willard Boyd, Norman Palmer, Lyndel Prott, and Patrick O'Keefe. I am grateful to the Dartmouth Montgomery Fellowship Program, which gave me the opportunity to spend two weeks at Dartmouth in the autumn of 2021. There I was able to present some of this research and to discuss issues of colonialism and imperialism with several members of the Dartmouth faculty. I also presented segments of this work at the University of Pennsylvania Cultural Heritage Center and at Cardozo Law School. I appreciate the feedback I received that helped to improve this endeavour. I also want to thank the anonymous reviewers whose critiques contributed to improvement of the volume.

Much as I have learned from my teachers and colleagues, I have also learned from my students. Many have helped me with this project over the years, including Lauren Bursey, Kahlia Halpern, and Meghan Jackson. I want to thank the Dean of the College of Law Jennifer Rosato Perea for her encouragement of this endeavour over the past several years. The DePaul University Research Council supported my work on the volume through a research leave and funding for illustration permissions.

Above all, I want to thank my family and especially my husband, Sam Gordon, for their love, patience, guidance, and support.

Contents

List of Illustrations

Table of Cases

INTERNATIONAL

REGIONAL

NATIONAL

Canada

France

Germany

Netherlands

United Kingdom

United States

Table of Instruments

NATIONAL INSTRUMENTS

Australia

Canada

Egypt

France

Germany

Greece

Italy

Iraq

Jordan

Netherlands

Switzerland

Turkey

United Kingdom

United States

List of Abbreviations

AAL	Art Antiquity and Law
AAM	American Alliance of Museums
AAMD	Association of Art Museum Directors
AHR	American Historical Review
AIA	Archaeological Institute of America
AJIL	American Journal of International Law
ASOR	American Society of Overseas Research
ATADA	Authentic Tribal Art Dealers Association
BJIL	Brooklyn Journal of International Law
CAELJ	Cardozo Arts and Entertainment Law Journal
CINOA	Confédération Internationale des Négociants en Oeuvres d'Art
CJIL	Chinese Journal of International Law
CTS	Consolidated Treaty Series
DCMS	Department of Culture, Media and Sport
EJCPR	European Journal on Criminal Policy and Research
EJIL	European Journal of International Law
ERR	Einsatzstab Reichsleiter Rosenberg
FSIA	Foreign Sovereign Immunities Act of 1976
HEAR	Holocaust Expropriated Art Recovery Act
HHRJ	Harvard Human Rights Journal
HLR	Harvard Law Review
HRC	Human Rights Council
IACtHR	Inter-American Court of Human Rights
ICC	International Criminal Court
ICCPR	International Covenant on Civil and Political Rights
ICESCR	International Covenant on Economic, Social and Cultural Rights
ICJ	International Court of Justice
ICJ Rep	International Court of Justice Reports of Judgments, Advisory Opinions and Orders
ICLQ	International and Comparative Law Quarterly
ICOM	International Council of Museums
IJCP	International Journal of Cultural Property
ILM	International Legal Materials
IRRC	International Review of the Red Cross
IS	International Spectator
JEMAHS	Journal of Eastern Mediterranean Archaeology and Heritage
JICJ	Journal of International Criminal Justice
JIPITEC	Journal of Intellectual Property, Information Technology and Electronic Commerce Law

JIPL	Journal of Intellectual Property Law
MFA&A	Monuments, Fine Arts and Archives
MiJIL	Michigan Journal of International Law
MJIL	Melbourne Journal of International Law
NAGPRA	Native American Graves Protection and Repatriation Act
NEA	Near Eastern Archaeology
NYUJILP	New York University Journal of International Law & Policy
PPICPA	Protect and Preserve International Cultural Property Act
SAACLR	Santander Art and Culture Law Review
SBL	Society of Biblical Literature
SCJ	Sixteenth Century Journal
TEFAF	Maastricht Code of Conduct for The European Fine Art Fair
UDHR	Universal Declaration of Human Rights (1948)
UNDRIP	United Nations Declaration on the Rights of Indigenous Peoples
UNESCO	United Nations Educational, Scientific and Cultural Organization
UNGA	United Nations General Assembly
UNHCR	United Nations High Commissioner for Refugees
UNSC	United Nations Security Counsel
UNTS	United Nations Treaty Series
USC	United States Code
YLJ	Yale Law Journal

1
Introduction

1.1 Introduction

This is a study of the question of whether those tangible movable cultural objects that have been removed in the past from their original contexts should be returned to the places from which they were taken or whether current possessors have the right to continue to maintain their possession of these cultural objects. We look to cultural heritage to help us define our identities, our communities, our place in the world, our past, and also our future. As a result, many aspects of cultural heritage are imbued with fraught meanings. One of the most contentious of these aspects centres on the debate as to where movable cultural objects should be located and under what circumstances removed objects should be returned to the contexts from which they were taken. In examining the law that has developed over the past two centuries concerning cultural heritage and the debates that are engendered, this study is distinctive in focusing exclusively on movable tangible objects. It is also distinctive in recognizing that the law concerning the location of cultural objects is inadequate to answer the question of location and contexts and is relatively meagre in comparison to that which addresses immovable heritage. Although some cultural objects were always intended to circulate, the movement of cultural objects has often been, and still is today, the result of armed conflict, colonialism, imperialism, economic exploitation, and other types of violence. This makes the question of return not only about the location of cultural objects and the contexts in which they should be held but also about achieving reparative justice through return.

Removal and return are forms of movement. Cultural objects are itinerant. They moved from place-to-place in the past, continue to move in the present, and will move in the future, thereby encompassing a broad range of social and other networks.[1] 'Treating things as active in transit puts even partial and collective object histories into context as segments of potentially unending itineraries that shape space and enable action.'[2] Each of these places gives contexts and new meanings to

[1] Rosemary A Joyce, 'Things in Motion: Itineraries of Ulua Marble Vases' in Rosemary A Joyce and Susan D Gillespie (eds), *Things in Motion: Object Itineraries in Anthropological Practice* (SAR Press 2015) 21, 29.

[2] ibid; Alexander A Bauer, 'The *Kula* of Long Term Loans: Cultural Object Itineraries and the Promise of the Postcolonial "Universal" Museum' in Rosemary A Joyce and Susan D Gillespie (eds), *Things in Motion: Object Itineraries in Anthropological Practice* (SAR Press 2015) 147, 148–49 (describing how

Cultural Objects and Reparative Justice. Patty Gerstenblith, Oxford University Press. © Patty Gerstenblith 2023.
DOI: 10.1093/oso/9780192872104.003.0001

the object, and the status of the object as legal or illegal or its possession as ethical or unethical also changes with this movement over time and space.

Movement of cultural objects inevitably raises questions of time and location—we must decide at what point in time we make determinations of legitimacy, to what points of reference in the past we give meaning, and which claims of heritage are privileged in making these determinations. The movement of cultural objects and the means by which movement is achieved are fundamental to the debate concerning the disposition of cultural objects: whether cultural objects found or produced in one part of the world should move to other parts of the world or whether they should remain within or be returned to their original context from which these objects derive much of their meaning. In addressing the questions of location and movement, it is necessary to recognize that much of the past movement of cultural objects was not and is still not free. The means by which object movement occurred, the tension between movement and original contexts, and the means of determining where objects should be located or to which communities and other contexts they should be returned form central elements in the debate concerning the location of cultural objects.

1.2 Defining Culture and Cultural Objects

Culture is often defined in 'either of the two ways established in the nineteenth century—as the universal heritage of humankind—culture with a capital C—or in the plural anthropological sense, in which different cultures lay claim to different properties'.[3] This distinction sets up the tension between a universal value of cultural objects and their communal and contextual values. In the former, culture indicates the high arts in an art historical and aesthetic sense—objects that are placed in art museums and become part of a global heritage that is presumed to have universal and perpetual value. This universal heritage is characterized as cutting across national boundaries and belonging to an amorphous everyone who wishes to have an interest in the physical manifestation. As such, universalism means that we care less about the location of cultural objects, but, in fact, it also becomes a justification for their removal and retention. The designation of a cultural object as 'art' is a method of conferring value, both monetary and aesthetic, within a system of what Rosemary Coombe describes as a nineteenth-century 'way of categorizing expressive works of aesthetic value in a context of European imperialism and colonialism

the concept of 'object itineraries' is useful in understanding the movement of objects and correcting for misperceptions around the repatriation of artefacts).

[3] Rosemary J Coombe, 'The Properties of Culture and the Politics of Possessing Identity: Native Claims in the Cultural Appropriation Controversy' (1993) 6 Canadian Journal of Law and Jurisprudence 249, 258 (hereafter Coombe, 'The Properties of Culture').

and the collection of objects in imperialist forays around the globe'.[4] Art objects are 'examples of a human creative ability that transcend the limitations of time and place to speak to us about the "human" condition; representing the highest point of human achievement, they are regarded as testaments to the greatness of their individual creators'.[5]

In the anthropological sense, a culture is the external manifestation of a particular group or segment of a population. A group may at times be predominately defined by its ethnicity, language, religion, or particular history, but often it represents an amalgam of these characteristics. A cultural group may be coterminous with a particular nation-State, is often smaller than a State, or may extend over more than one State. Cultural objects that are the products of such a group are valued 'as the authentic works of a distinct collectivity, as integral to the harmonious life of an ahistorical community and incomprehensible outside of "cultural context"—the defining features of authentic artifacts'.[6]

A cultural object may be taken out of its specific context and, as a result, transformed into a work of art. It acquires a universal value and is considered to be a part of the broad development of human civilization. The legal treatment of such objects may change, and the object becomes more easily viewed as a subject of monetary exchange. Further, when a cultural object is transformed into a work of art, the ability to access the object and the uses to which it may be put change radically. The object is placed within a glass case or on a pedestal, or sometimes in storage, to be admired and appreciated from afar, but not touched or used other than in very restricted ways, even by those to whom the object has spiritual, cultural, and other humanistic connections. The cultural object also changes meaning as it is enclosed within different 'parerga' and is presented differently as the result of curatorial taste.[7] Western culture thereby appropriates the physical embodiments of other peoples' cultures and determines which values and aspects will receive protection, both in the physical sense and as part of our legal system. As Coombe wrote, 'the domains of authentic masterpieces and authentic artifacts to which they relate, are mirrored in our legal categories for the valuation and protection of expressive objects. Laws of . . . cultural property reflect and secure the logic of the European art/culture system. . . .'[8] The legal system then determines who can possess and own these cultural objects and itself reflects the hierarchy of cultures developed in early cultural anthropology.[9]

4 ibid, 257.

5 ibid, 257–58.

6 ibid, 258.

7 Khadija von Zinnenburg Carroll, 'The Inbetweenness of the Vitrine: Three *Parerga* of a Feather Headdress' in Paul Basu (ed), *The Inbetweenness of Things: Materializing Mediation and Movement between Worlds* (Bloomsbury Academic 2016) 23.

8 Coombe, 'The Properties of Culture' (n 3) 258.

9 Andrezj Jakubowski, 'Cultural Rights and Cultural Heritage as a Global Concern' in Marie-Claire Foblets and others (eds), *The Oxford Handbook of Law and Anthropology* (online edn, Oxford Academic 2020) <https://doi.org/10.1093/oxfordhb/9780198840534.013.29> accessed 15 August 2022.

The legal system perpetuates the dichotomy between the way such objects are viewed in Western legal systems and the way they are viewed in other parts of the world, particularly in their original contexts. As a result of these differences, at times it is difficult to achieve recognition of non-pecuniary values inherent in cultural objects, even though these are respected by non-Western and Indigenous groups. Despite the desirability of analysing the disposition of cultural objects from the perspective of numerous legal systems, this study focuses on the status of these objects in the legal systems of Western Europe and North America. Cultural objects have tended to move in a unidirectional flow from other parts of the world first to the earlier colonial powers and today to the economic centres. In addressing whether objects should be returned, it is therefore necessary to analyse the status of these cultural objects and the potential for return from the legal perspective of where they are currently located.

1.3 Defining Cultural Property and Cultural Heritage

Relevant international conventions address movable cultural objects to varying degrees, but they tend to focus more on immovable heritage. The exceptions are the 1970 UNESCO Convention[10] and the 1995 Unidroit Convention,[11] which address contemporary trade and movement of cultural objects. The earliest legal instruments use neither the term cultural property nor cultural heritage, instead enumerating the types of structures and objects that merit special protection. For example, Article 27 of the Regulations of the 1907 Convention refers to 'buildings dedicated to religion, art, science or charitable purposes, [and] historic monuments'.[12] Adopted almost a century later, the Rome Statute of the International Criminal Court echoes this terminology, prohibiting attacks directed 'against buildings dedicated to religion, education, art, science or charitable purposes, [and] historic monuments'. Further, it provides no protection specifically for movable cultural objects aside from that granted to all civilian objects.[13]

The term 'cultural property' appears in the international instruments of the 1954 Hague Convention on the Protection of Cultural Property in the Event of Armed

[10] Convention on the Means of Prohibiting and Preventing the Illicit Import, Export and Transfer of Ownership of Cultural Property (opened for signature 14 November 1970, entered into force 24 April 1972) 823 UNTS 231 (hereafter 1970 UNESCO Convention)

[11] Unidroit Convention on Stolen or Illegally Exported Cultural Objects (adopted 24 June 1995, entered into force 1 July 1998) 34 ILM 1322.

[12] Convention (IV) Respecting the Laws and Customs of War on Land and its Annex: Regulations concerning the Laws and Customs of War on Land (open for signature 18 October 1907, entered into force 26 January 1910) 187 CTS 227.

[13] Rome Statute of the International Criminal Court, UN Doc A/Conf 183/9, 37 ILM 999 (17 July 1998) Article 8(b)(ix) (applying to international armed conflicts) and Article 8(e)(iv) (applying to non-international armed conflicts). See Lucas Lixinski, *International Heritage Law for Communities* (OUP 2019) 29–50 (hereafter Lixinski, *International Heritage Law*).

Conflict[14] and the 1970 UNESCO Convention. The 1954 Hague Convention defines 'cultural property' as 'movable or immovable property of great importance to the cultural heritage of every people'.[15] This means that the cultural property protected under the Convention is the subset of the larger universe of cultural heritage that is of great importance to the larger whole.[16] It is sometimes interpreted as requiring that the protected cultural property must bear some significance beyond its significance to the particular community or State. The 1970 UNESCO Convention omits reference to cultural heritage and gives a more specific definition of cultural property as 'property which, on religious or secular grounds, is specifically designated by each State as being of importance for archaeology, prehistory, history, literature, art or science' and belongs to one of eleven specific categories which are, in the aggregate, extensive.[17] However, subsequent conventions more consistently use the term cultural heritage.[18]

The dichotomy between the terms 'cultural heritage' and 'cultural property' can signify different meanings and positions, depending on the context. The distinction is also theoretically relevant to questions of a framework for determining retention or return. The term 'cultural property' is used more often in the United States or when ownership aspects are emphasized, leading to the critique that the term places too much emphasis on ownership and property rights. As Lyndel Prott noted, the term cultural property brings with it 'a whole baggage of associations and implications, in particular, the view in the common law ... that property and ownership rights clearly authorize exploitation, alienation ... and exclusion of others from access—all elements that, in modern heritage law, may well be restricted'.[19] Denominating cultural objects as 'property' thus emphasizes their pecuniary value, marketability, and the exclusive rights granted to the owner and protected by the legal system. However, even 'property' may be defined less in terms of such rights and more in terms of the relationship of individuals with respect to a thing,[20] which demonstrates overlap with the term 'cultural heritage'.

The term 'heritage' moves past ownership and instead emphasizes the relationship to and among people and the obligation to pass culture on to future generations

[14] Convention for the Protection of Cultural Property in the Event of Armed Conflict (adopted 14 May 1954, entered into force 7 August 1956) 249 UNTS 240 (hereafter 1954 Hague Convention).

[15] ibid, Article 1(a).

[16] A similar point is made in the Preamble to the Convention, which states that 'damage to cultural property belonging to any people whatsoever means damage to the cultural heritage of all mankind'.

[17] 1970 UNESCO Convention (n 10) Article 1.

[18] Convention concerning the Protection of the World Cultural and Natural Heritage (adopted 16 November 1972, entered into force 17 December 1975) 1037 UNTS 151 (hereafter 1972 UNESCO World Heritage Convention); Convention on the Protection of Underwater Cultural Heritage (adopted 2 November 2001, entered into force 2 January 2009) 2562 UNTS 1; Convention for the Safeguarding of the Intangible Cultural Heritage (adopted 17 October 2003, entered into force 20 April 2006) 2368 UNTS 1.

[19] Lyndel V Prott, 'The International Movement of Cultural Objects' (2005) 12 IJCP 225, 226.

[20] See Joan C Williams, 'The Rhetoric of Property' (1998) 83 Iowa Law Review 277, 296–304.

in the form of an 'inheritance' or 'heritage'.[21] The term 'cultural heritage' emphasizes notions of stewardship and responsibility. Cultural heritage encompasses immovable tangible heritage (standing structures, monuments, and sites), movable tangible heritage (portable objects, such as works of art), and intangible heritage (such as traditional knowledge, oral history, languages, cultural practices, and folklore). Natural features may be considered cultural heritage when they take on significance to people and communities and thereby constitute cultural landscapes. The intersection of tangible and intangible heritage is often located within cultural or sacred landscapes and historic structures, but the intersection is, in fact, broader. The intangible is what gives meaning to tangible cultural objects, as in the examples of archaeological context giving understanding to the artefacts found within a particular site or language giving meaning to a written text. Blake further posits that the attempt to distinguish between tangible and intangible heritage is 'artificial' and that 'the two are inextricably linked and have such a close mutual relationship that to separate them is counter-intuitive'.[22]

Lixinski casts the cultural property/cultural heritage terminology debate in terms of the dichotomy between international and domestic law. He associates the term 'cultural heritage' with international law and cosmopolitanism, while the term 'cultural property' is linked to State sovereignty and domestic law, including the domestic implementation of international law. He characterizes 'cultural property' as a legal concept and 'cultural heritage' as a non-legal, and therefore less clear, term.[23] From this he draws the conclusion that use of the term 'cultural heritage' serves to disempower national and community actors from engaging with the subject:

> Cultural property internationalism, therefore, and the move to the concept of 'heritage' it embodies, has the effect of creating disincentives for the inclusion of certain stakeholders. Instead, it privileges others that can speak the uniform language of cultural heritage, which tend to be states and experts.[24]

As a result, he advocates maintaining the term 'cultural property' as being more inclusive of a range of stakeholders. The fundamental flaw to which Lixinski points is that, for the most part, the only entities that international treaty law acknowledges

[21] Lyndel V Prott and Patrick O'Keefe, 'Cultural Heritage or Cultural Property' (1992) 1 IJCP 307, 309–12. Blake describes cultural heritage as 'an inheritance received from the past, to be held "in trust" by the current generation (that may enjoy its value in the present) to be handed down in at least as good a state as it was received to the next generation'. Janet Blake, *International Cultural Heritage Law* (OUP 2015) 7. Blake also links this broader perspective to current concerns with sustainable development, inter-generational equity, and a duty to safeguard and protect cultural heritage. ibid, 8–9.

[22] ibid, 10.

[23] Lucas Lixinski, 'A Third Way of Thinking about Cultural Property' (2019) 44 BJIL 563, 580–84 (hereafter Lixinski, 'A Third Way'); Lixinski, *International Heritage Law* (n 13) 28.

[24] Lixinski, 'A Third Way' (n 23) 583–84.

are States and their interests in location of and access to cultural objects. Cultural heritage is linked to both the community and to territory. However, as Peters noted, focusing on the State does not solve the problem of disposition of movable cultural objects because the State may take account of competing interests and claims only to the extent that it wishes or not at all.[25]

Hafstein and Skrydstrup view the terms 'cultural property' and 'cultural heritage' as complementary, rather than in tension, and as such they coexist. The cultural property regime focuses on legal rights and the settlement of disputes as to ownership. Cultural heritage, on the other hand, focuses on cooperation and the preservation and care of cultural objects so that they can be passed on, regardless of where the objects are situated. They conclude that the term 'cultural heritage' is a 'technology of reformation' in contrast to 'cultural property', which they view as a 'technology of sovereignty'.[26] In this volume, although the subject is movable tangible objects, the term 'cultural heritage' will also be used because it is all-encompassing and because it incorporates more clearly human-related values and links to people.

1.4 Interests and Authority

Questions of the proper location of cultural objects were often reduced in earlier literature to a binary approach of an internationalist and a nationalist perspective. This dichotomy is 'ultimately dangerous' and has 'outlived its utility'.[27] Francioni questioned whether this binary approach was ever an accurate depiction of law and policy with respect to cultural heritage.[28] He pointed out several ways in which the law with respect to cultural heritage has evolved past a binary approach: the intersection of cultural property law with human rights law; cross-influences between international humanitarian law and specific rules with respect to cultural property that apply during armed conflict; cross-over between the law of armed conflict and international criminal law; and the intersection of public international law and private international law with the adoption of the 1970 UNESCO Convention and the 1995 Unidroit Convention.

[25] Robert Peters, 'New Perspectives Beyond State Sovereignty and Territoriality in the Protection of Cultural Heritage' in Anne-Marie Carstens and Elizabeth Varner (eds), *Intersections in International Cultural Heritage Law* (OUP 2020) 364 (hereafter Peters 'New Perspectives').

[26] Valdimar Tr Hafstein and Martin Skrydstrup, 'Heritage vs Property: Contrasting Regimes and Rationalities in the Patrimonial Field' in Jane Anderson and Haidy Geismar (eds), *The Routledge Companion to Cultural Property* (Routledge 2017) 38, 40, 43–44.

[27] Lixinski, 'A Third Way' (n 23) 564.

[28] Francesco Francioni, 'Plurality and Interaction of Legal Orders in the Enforcement of Cultural Heritage Law' in Francesco Francioni and James Gordley (eds), *Enforcing International Cultural Heritage Law* (OUP 2013) 9, 11, 13–14 (hereafter Francioni, 'Plurality and Interaction of Legal Orders').

Emphasis on binary approaches eliminates nuances and prevents consideration of complexities and ambiguities. With the significant developments in the cultural heritage field of the past several decades, we can see that a more complex and nuanced approach is needed, one that takes into account the multiple overlapping and sometimes contradictory interests and centres of authority that determine the disposition and location of cultural objects. This multi-layered approach focuses on analysing the significance of cultural objects from the contextual, international, national, and local or community perspectives.

We can identify at least three relatively formal centres or communities,[29] each of which can be considered from the perspectives of their interests, their legal authority, and the terminology that allows for expression of their interests and authority. While the interests of these communities are often stated rhetorically as similar, their relative degrees of authority and some of their motivations may be in conflict. As David Lowenthal noted: 'Too much is now asked of heritage. In the same breath we commend national patrimony, regional and ethnic legacies, and a global heritage shared and sheltered in common. We forget that these aims are often incompatible.'[30] Further, the relative balance of power among these different communities is very unequal, particularly from a legal perspective. A fourth perspective, that of contextualism, may help to create a more even balance among these different centres of authority and power.

1.4.1 International Community

In the past, an analytical approach based on internationalism privileged an understanding of culture as an international phenomenon, regardless of an object's place of origin, original context, and current location.[31] In this view, most cultural objects should be free to circulate throughout the world, primarily through market mechanisms and with minimum legal regulation.[32] In centring on decontextualized

[29] An amorphous fourth set of 'communities' often consists of experts or scholars. Terms such as the 'preservation community', the 'museum community', the 'scholarly community', the 'expert community', and the 'archaeological community' may be used. Their interests do not necessarily align but are often seen as transcending national boundaries and therefore linked to universalism. Their location within a hierarchy of legal or other authority is often unclear. In a few instances, they are given a specific role, as with the International Council on Monuments and Sites and the World Conservation Union, which serve as technical advisors to the World Heritage Committee in recommending which cultural and natural sites (respectively) qualify for inscription on the World Heritage List. World Heritage List Nominations, para 3 <https://whc.unesco.org/en/nominations> accessed 18 March 2021.

[30] David Lowenthal, *The Heritage Crusade and the Spoils of History* (CUP 1998) 227.

[31] John Henry Merryman, 'Two Ways of Thinking about Cultural Property' (1986) 80 AJIL 831; 'The Free International Movement of Cultural Property' (1998) 31 NYUJLP 1. Although in the latter article Merryman expanded the perspectives from two to five, these five perspectives were in fact a rearrangement of the same two perspectives of internationalism and nationalism that he originally proposed.

[32] John Henry Merryman, 'Cultural Property Internationalism' (2005) 12 IJCP 11, 28–29 (hereafter Merryman, 'Cultural Property Internationalism').

objects, this approach undermined claims of States and communities within States to maintain their cultural objects and to reclaim those that were removed, either in the recent or longer ago past, regardless of the method by which they were taken. As will be discussed in chapters 2 and 7, this type of internationalist approach perpetuates the mantras of the universal and encyclopedic museum and the rescue narrative that originated in the eighteenth and nineteenth centuries.

The underlying rationales for this earlier understanding of internationalism can be traced back at least into the eighteenth century, and they persist still today when the question of return arises. These rationales are embedded in such earlier concepts as the encyclopedic or universal museum, the right to claim booty during armed conflict, and the 'rescue narrative' that developed in conjunction with the exposure of Western Europeans to non-European contemporary societies. The essence of the rescue narrative is that the current possessors of cultural objects are not capable of protecting, understanding, or appreciating them and are therefore not deserving of possessing or owning cultural objects. Finding the current possessors to be inferior provided justification for Western Europeans to remove these objects, retain them, and thereby 'rescue' them through nonconsensual appropriation. The flow of cultural objects in this internationalist paradigm consists primarily of a flow to Western Europe and North America and away from many of the communities of origin in the larger population centres in Asia and Africa. This approach denies the more fundamental connection of a descendant community or the connection between living local communities and the heritage in their midst.[33] This understanding of internationalism is today largely, although not entirely, rejected.[34]

Cultural heritage continues to often be described as a shared world, global, or universal heritage. The three earlier international conventions in this field, the 1954 Hague Convention, the 1970 UNESCO Convention, and the 1972 World Heritage Convention, all invoke the concept of a universal or shared heritage. The 1972 World Heritage Convention goes further in requiring that any cultural and natural heritage protected under the Convention be of 'outstanding universal value'.[35] The universality underlying the interests of the international community shares some elements of the older internationalist perspective in that the precise location of objects is less important than other considerations. The phrase 'shared global or universal heritage' may also be used rhetorically, as a means to galvanize the international community to take action to preserve cultural heritage.

[33] See Lixinski, 'A Third Way' (n 23) 564.

[34] Lixinski, 'A Third Way' (n 23) 572–74. Peters criticizes this characterization of internationalism because its primary purpose seems to be to justify a free-trade approach. He describes it as a 'contrived dichotomy' and 'unidimensional'. Peters 'New Perspectives' (n 25) 368. For a dissenting view, see Eric A Posner, 'The International Protection of Cultural Property: Some Skeptical Observations' (2007) 8(1) Chicago Journal of International Law 231.

[35] 1972 UNESCO World Heritage Convention (n 18) arts 1 and 2.

The international community in the cultural sphere is represented primarily by the United Nations Educational, Scientific and Cultural Organization (UNESCO), although other inter-governmental organizations, including the United Nations, wield legal and soft power authority. All of these organizations cut across national boundaries, but, because their members are States, they defer to the interests of their Member States. Some of their authority is based on consciousness-raising efforts, media, public, and educational campaigns, and other types of outreach.[36] But much of their authority derives from their ability to adopt international conventions, Security Council resolutions (in the case of the United Nations), and other standard-setting instruments. Non-governmental organizations, such as the International Committee of the Red Cross and Blue Shield International, also operate in the international sphere. These typically are restricted to the realm of soft power, although in some cases their influence is significant.

Although conventions and treaties are subject to sovereign decisions through the ratification and implementation processes, international treaties also involve some ceding of sovereign authority. With respect to movable cultural objects, we see an example in the States that have adopted reciprocal import restrictions based on their implementation of the 1970 UNESCO Convention.[37] These States allow a change in one country's laws to become automatically embedded in another country's laws. If one State Party adds a category of cultural property that is subject to export restriction, that category becomes subject to import restriction in a second State Party, if the second country has adopted the reciprocal method of implementation. Peters commented that 'true internationalism should be based on one simple rule: illegally exported cultural property from one State should be considered as illegally imported into another State'.[38]

1.4.2 States

Although described as a relative newcomer as a centre of authority within the cultural heritage debate, the State is today probably the centre of the greatest authority. Sovereigns have the ability to adopt and enforce the laws within their territories. As Peters notes, sovereignty 'establishes the link between a State's territory, its people, and the cultural heritage located within its territory. Consequently, a general assumption exists under international law that (tangible) cultural heritage is a resource that States have a right to control—similarly to any natural resource

[36] For example UNESCO's 'Unite4Heritage' campaign <https://en.unesco.org/news/join-unesco-s-unite4heritage-campaign> accessed 27 July 2023.

[37] Patty Gerstenblith, 'Theft and Illegal Excavation: Legal Principles for Protection of Archaeological Heritage' in Francesco Francioni and Ana Filipa Vrdoljak (eds), *The Oxford Handbook of International Cultural Heritage Law* (OUP 2020) 200, 219.

[38] Peters, 'New Perspectives' (n 25) 377.

found on or in the State's soil'.[39] As a result, although international conventions and agreements impose obligations on a State,[40] the international community lacks the ability to enforce directly such obligations through legal mechanisms, at least within the cultural heritage field. The International Court of Justice (ICJ) has rarely heard disputes concerning cultural heritage.[41] One exception was the border dispute between Cambodia and Thailand involving the Preah Vihear Temple.[42] More recently, the ICJ heard the claim of Armenia against Azerbaijan for violations of the Convention on the Eradication of Racial Discrimination through Azerbaijan's destruction, damage, and alteration of Armenian historical, cultural, and religious sites in the Nagorno-Karabakh region.[43] The International Criminal Court (ICC) has prosecuted individuals for destruction of cultural heritage.[44] The Rome Statute does not specifically prohibit the theft or removal of cultural objects, unless the thefts were interpreted to constitute directing an attack against one of the enumerated locations, such as a building dedicated to art, religion, or science.[45] International standard-setting instruments and other forms of established norms influence State practice, but international law recognizes States as the centre of authority and its enforcement is therefore largely dependent on the cooperation of States.

States choose which conventions to ratify and whether domestic legislation is needed for implementation, although some provisions of international conventions may become binding on States without ratification through customary international law.[46] The cultural heritage conventions do not always

[39] ibid, 367.

[40] The obligations of the 1972 UNESCO World Heritage Convention (n 18) (Arts 4 and 5) are explicitly limited by State sovereignty (Art 6). The 1954 Hague Convention imposes extensive obligations and restraints on States Parties but then bows to national sovereignty through the military necessity waiver that permits targeting of cultural property when imperatively required (Art 4(2)) and the omission of an enforcement mechanism for violations (Art 28). The Second Protocol tightens the definition of military necessity and requires States Parties to create specific criminal provisions in their national legislation. Second Protocol to the Hague Convention of 1954 for the Protection of Cultural Property in the Event of Armed Conflict (adopted 26 March 1999, entered into force 9 March 2004) 253 UNTS 172 arts 6 and 15.

[41] Francioni, 'Plurality and Interaction of Legal Orders' (n 28) 17.

[42] Case Concerning the Temple of Preah Vihear (*Cambodia v Thailand*) (Judgment of 15 June 1962) [1962] ICJ Rep 6; Request for Interpretation of the Judgment of 15 June 1962 in the Case concerning the Temple of Preah Vihear (*Cambodia v Thailand*) [2013] ICJ Rep 281.

[43] Application of the International Convention on the Elimination of All Forms of Racial Discrimination *(Armenia v Azerbaijan)* (Pending) General List No 180 <https://www.icj-cij.org/en/case/180> accessed 24 February 2022. The ICJ issued provisional measures that Azerbaijan needed, among other actions, to 'take all necessary measures to prevent and punish acts of vandalism and desecration affecting Armenian cultural heritage'. para 92.

[44] *Prosecutor v Al Mahdi* (Trial Judgment and Sentence) [2016] ICC-01/12-01/15-171; *Prosecutor v Al Hassan* ICC-01/12-01/18; *Prosecutor v Bosco Ntaganda* (Judgment on Appeal) [2020] ICC-01/04-02/06 (affirming the acquittal of the defendant on charges concerning damage to a church).

[45] See n 13. Cultural objects are protected from pillage as civilian objects under arts 8(2)(b)(xvi) and 8(2)(e)(v) of the Rome Statute.

[46] Jean-Marie Henckaerts, 'Study on Customary International Humanitarian Law: A Contribution to the Understanding and Respect for the Rule of Law in Armed Conflict' (2005) 87(857) IRRC 175, 180–81.

specify requirements, leaving individual States with considerable leeway as to how to implement their obligations.[47] The 1970 UNESCO Convention leaves it to States Parties to designate categories of movable cultural property that are to be protected.[48]

States are often recognized as the party in interest in international claims for restitution of cultural objects, particularly when such claims are dependent on treaty law or the disposition of movable objects is regulated by national law.[49] When cultural objects are returned, they are therefore returned to a State, rather than to a subset of the State, such as a local or regional governing body, a community, or an institution. To whom the State then gives the object depends on the domestic law and practice of the national government. This may result in a mismatch between the community or institution to which the object is culturally linked and the State that is recognized as the centre of authority under international law and by other States.

1.4.3 Local and Descendant Communities

Focus on a third category of interests has emerged—the interests of communities that live among the heritage or who use the heritage, or who may be the community descended from those who created the heritage, sometimes referred to as the 'community of origin'.[50] The Special Rapporteur in the Field of Cultural Rights noted the difficulty of defining community within the context of cultural rights:

> The term 'community' is too often assumed to suggest homogeneity, exclusivity, structure and formality. Such a construction is embraced not only by some outside observers not willing to recognize plurality and dynamism within groups,

[47] The 1970 UNESCO Convention establishes no discernible requirements for implementation. As a result, the method of implementation varies widely to the extent that some States may not even be recognized as implementing it at all. Patty Gerstenblith, 'The Disposition of Movable Cultural Heritage' in Anne-Marie Carstens and Elizabeth Varner (eds), *Intersections in International Cultural Heritage Law* (OUP 2020) 17, 29–35. The 1954 Hague Convention articulates no standards for criminal punishment for violations and leaves enforcement to States 'within the framework of their ordinary criminal jurisdiction'. 1954 Hague Convention (n 14) Article 28.

[48] 1970 UNESCO Convention (n 10) Article 1.

[49] This approach was reaffirmed in the decision of the Supreme Court in the Netherlands to return Scythian gold objects, which were on loan from museums in Crimea, to the State of Ukraine rather than to the museums that had loaned the objects. The court determined that the objects belong to the Ukrainian Museum Fund and are therefore subject to regulation by the Ukrainian government, even while conceding that the objects are also part of Crimea's cultural heritage. *Tavrida Central Museum and others v Ukraine* (High Council, Civil Chamber) 22/00270 (9 June 2023). Individuals or institutions may be able to litigate claims for return of stolen cultural objects outside of treaty law, as has happened in the extensive ongoing private litigation for return of artworks stolen during the Holocaust and in other cases where theft is alleged.

[50] Deutscher Museums Bund, Guidelines Care of Human Remains in Museums and Collections (2021) 15.

> but also by often self-proclaimed 'representatives' of the concerned groups—or presumed groups—themselves.[51]

She also acknowledged that the term 'community' can both empower individuals who wish to practise their culture with others and threaten the rights of 'dissenting or disempowered individuals'.[52] States may similarly view themselves as threatened by the recognition of the rights and interests of sub-State groups.

Lixinski suggests that allowing greater recognition of the role the market can play in heritage engages the community and thereby encourages the community to safeguard it.[53] The local community is undoubtedly the best protector of the heritage that surrounds it. Allowing for sustainable forms of economic development, while prohibiting unsustainable forms such as the looting of archaeological sites, is one way in which the local community can become invested in this heritage. The local community will also become more involved with heritage when its rights are recognized as distinct from those of the State and the international community.

The statements of the Prosecutor of the ICC during the trial of Al Mahdi for destruction of religious sites in Timbuktu[54] and the analysis of harms presented in the Reparations Report[55] for these destructions recognize the unique role that local communities play in cultural heritage and the distinctive harms that they suffer when heritage is destroyed or damaged.[56] Drumbl refers to the effect of the reparations order as 'localist' (neither internationalist nor nationalist) because the reparations funds were awarded to the local population in Timbuktu.[57] Vindicating and protecting these community or local rights are more challenging and perhaps are something that could only be made possible through the prosecution in the ICC. Therefore, this approach may not have broader applicability.

Focus on the local community raises the problem of disposition of cultural objects when there is no longer a descendant community living within the State that claims ownership.[58] This, however, risks judgements made by third parties, usually

[51] UNGA HRC 'Report of the Special Rapporteur in the field of cultural rights' (3 February 2016) 5 UN Doc A/HRC/31/59. The Rapporteur defined this third aspect of interests as '[I]ndigenous, tribal, minority, migrant, local or other communities formed in accordance with criteria such as language or ethnicity'. ibid.

[52] ibid, 6.

[53] Lixinski, 'A Third Way' (n 23) 586–89.

[54] Statement of the Prosecutor of the International Criminal Court, Fatou Bensouda, at the opening of the confirmation of charges hearing, *Prosecutor v Al Mahdi* [2016] ICC-01/12-01/15-171 https://www.icc-cpi.int/news/statement-prosecutor-international-criminal-court-fatou-bensouda-opening-confirmation-charges> accessed 28 June 2023.

[55] Karima Benoune, Reparations Phase, 27 April 2017, ICC-01/12-01.15, 18, 27–28, 38 <https://www.icc-cpi.int/RelatedRecords/CR2017_05022.pdf> accessed 3 May 2021.

[56] See also Lixinski, 'A Third Way' (n 23) 593–96.

[57] Mark A Drumbl, 'From Timbuktu to The Hague and Beyond: The War Crime of Intentionally Attacking Cultural Property' (2019) 17 JICJ 77, 82, 85–86. The international community (through UNESCO) and Mali each received a symbolic one euro in reparation.

[58] Drumbl, ibid, 89–90, based on Lostal, raises this question in connection with immovable heritage, such as the Bamiyan Buddhas and the classical sites of Palmyra and Dura-Europas. Drumbl comments, 'the anthropocentrism required by criminal law may limit the imaginary of which property is protected

those in Western institutions, as to whether a local community traces a connection to the cultural heritage in its midst. Such judgements are often based on an outsider's determination of the continuity of culture and sometimes on the requirement of a genetic connection to establish that cultural continuity.[59] Drumbl and Lostal assert that it is not possible to rely on the connection to local communities to preserve heritage or to appreciate its cultural significance when the community that produced the heritage is no longer extant. However, the history of the classical site of Palmyra in Syria presents an important contrast. In antiquity, it was a prominent site situated along ancient trade routes, flourishing during the Hellenistic and Roman periods. After a failed rebellion against Rome in the third century, it is typically characterized as deserted. In fact, it had an almost continuous history, with the Roman temple of Bel converted first into a church during the Byzantine period and then into a mosque. For 1,800 years the site was inhabited by a succession of religious and ethnic groups until the local population was removed in 1929 and resettled in a nearby town so that the site could be reconstructed to its ancient form.[60] An outside observer might conclude that the local population has little connection to the site, particularly when heritage value is conferred only on the ancient site, but those who lived within the site were connected to it and continued to be so even after their displacement.[61]

The role of the local community and the extent to which it is or can be recognized through international law varies. From a legal perspective, in most situations communities are effectively excluded, particularly from international law.[62] Allowing a community to operate at the international level outside of whatever role the State assigns or grants to the community may be seen as a challenge to State sovereignty.[63] This includes communities whose culture is either not represented by the dominant culture of the State within which they exist, or which span more than one modern State, or which are located entirely outside of the State where the

(or understood) as cultural. The fixation on the relational value of heritage to humans may further weaken claims, in a broad variety of venues, to the intrinsic value of heritage.' ibid, 90. See Marina Lostal, 'The Misplaced Emphasis on the Intangible Dimension of Cultural Heritage in the Al Mahdi Case at the ICC' (2017) 1 Inter Gentes 45–58, 56–57.

59 For example, *Bonnichsen v United States* 357 F 3d 962 (9th Cir 2004) (rejecting oral tradition evidence of cultural continuity between ancient human remains and current Native American tribes).

60 Stephennie Mulder, 'Imagining Localities of Antiquity in Islamic Societies' (2017) 6 International Journal of Islamic Architecture 229, 229.

61 Kanishk Tharoor, 'Life among the Ruins' (*New York Times*, 19 March 2016) <www.nytimes.com/2016/03/20/opinion/sunday/life-among-the-ruins.html> accessed 29 April 2021.

62 Lixinski, 'A Third Way' (n 23) 589–93, points out that communities are generally excluded from international courts. However, Francioni illustrates that courts intended for other purposes, particularly human rights, sometimes adjudicate cultural heritage rights. In *Moiwana Community v Suriname*, IACtHR Series C No 124 (28 November 2007) and *Yakye Axa Indigenous Community v Paraguay*, IACtHR Series C No 125 (17 June 2005), the Inter-American Court of Human Rights held that cultural communities and Indigenous groups could assert communal rights to Indigenous lands and cultural sites. Francioni, 'Plurality and Interaction of Legal Orders' (n 28) 18.

63 Lixinski, 'A Third Way' (n 23) 601–02.

community originated. Both in the past and in the present, cultures and cultural communities were not and are not coterminous with national boundaries.

Among cultural groups, Indigenous communities deserve special consideration. Indigenous groups often suffered the occupation of their land, frequently through military conquest by a non-Indigenous group. Indigenous groups attempt to maintain a distinct culture through religion, means of livelihood, lifestyle, language, and decentralized political institutions, typically organized at the community level. Conquest was generally followed by a process of colonization that often sought to eradicate the Indigenous population in an attempt to legitimate the claims of the colonizers to territorial acquisitions. Just as Indigenous peoples are distinguished by their 'connections to land ... [that] has often been intricate, subtle, and tremendously complex in ways that make the European criteria of ownership seem simplistic', so they were often forcibly displaced from these lands with the motive of acquisition of territory and the natural resources the land contained.[64] Indigenous communities today are often reduced to an enclave within a larger State and are subject to the legal system produced by the majority settler population.

Indigenous communities view themselves 'as descendants of the original inhabitants of lands with which they share a strong, often spiritual bond'.[65] Because claims to cultural heritage are often tied to territorial claims, and this is particularly true in the case of burials and the performance of certain rituals, forcible removals make it even more difficult to vindicate the cultural rights of Indigenous communities. This forced separation from their traditional lands is a fundamental reason why Indigenous groups struggle to reclaim rights in their cultural heritage, which is itself often tied to these lands.

> [T]he loss of real property is inextricably linked to the formation of cultural property claims.... [A] connection between land and identity is a defining element of [I]ndigenous peoplehood. In light of these ongoing collective attachments to land, it is impossible to protect [I]ndigenous peoplehood without also protecting [I]ndigenous relationships with tribal lands and the culture that grows out of those lands.[66]

Cultural communities exist within a State and may have recognition as independent or quasi-independent entities within that State, but their cultural heritage rights are ultimately determined by national law. A particular State's domestic law may recognize the rights of a cultural community located within it,[67] but these

[64] Richard J Perry, *From Time Immemorial: Indigenous Peoples and State Systems* (Univ Texas Press 1996) 8, 9.

[65] Siegfried Wiessner, 'Rights and Status of Indigenous Peoples: A Global Comparative and International Legal Analysis' (1999) 12 HHRJ 57, 115.

[66] Kristen A Carpenter, Sonia K Katyal, and Angela R Riley, 'In Defense of Property' (2009) 118 YLJ 1022, 1060–62.

[67] For example, the Native American Graves Protection and Repatriation Act, 25 USC §§ 3001–3013.

rights do not operate on the international level, thereby inhibiting claims for return of cultural objects. International law largely ignores the interests of the sub-State cultural community to the extent that its interests are distinct from those of the State. This is particularly problematic in the case of ethnic and religious minority groups, whose culture a State may not only fail to protect but that a State may at times intentionally choose to eradicate. While acknowledging the ubiquity of cultural and religious minorities within the modern State, Francioni also posits that international law is not 'indifferent' to the fate of such minorities and that the evolving role of universal human rights law provides protection and legitimacy to the claims of culturally distinct groups.[68] Nonetheless, the question of how international law can reconcile claims to rights and cultural heritage of minority groups poses perhaps one of the most difficult unresolved issues in addressing the question of to where and to whom should a movable cultural object be returned.

1.4.4 Contextualism

The three interests previously discussed—internationalism, nationalism, and communities—all play a valid role in the determinations of where cultural objects should be located and whether, having been removed, they should be returned. Traditionally, internationalism was given the greatest emphasis while we can recognize that, realistically, the State has the most legal authority today. It is suggested here that what is needed is a rebalancing of these interests, primarily by giving greater recognition to the roles of communities. An additional element that supports greater emphasis on the role of communities is contextualism. While both original and subsequent contexts have value for understanding cultural objects, original contexts should, in most cases, be given greater deference than has often been the case.

Morag Kersel presents a powerful critique of both the internationalist and nationalist perspectives. She aptly renames the older internationalist perspective the 'free-market approach' and argues instead for a contextual approach.

> The removal and retention of objects from ... formerly colonised nations in the name of preservation and for the greater good of humankind is viewed as a mere justification for trafficking objects. The free-market approach ... is a polite term for colonization and exploitation and is tantamount to a one-way street for artifacts leaving under-developed areas of the world towards the wealthiest nations.... The cultural nationalist and free-market positions are object-centered

[68] Francesco Francioni, 'Beyond State Sovereignty: The Protection of Cultural Heritage as a Shared Interest of Humanity' (2004) 25(4) MiJIL 1209, 1210–11.

> discourses of ownership, while the contextualist stance is part of the academic dialogue, which values knowledge over ownership.[69]

Kersel's call to move away from the dichotomies of the nationalist and internationalist perspectives, with their object-centred approach, and towards a context-oriented approach instead is appropriate and one of the underlying themes of this work. It also allows recognition of the critical contributions that creators, their descendants, and descendant communities made in creating these cultural objects and their essential role in enhancing understanding and appreciation for the cultural objects. It is from the relationship between the object and these communities that we can derive meaning and understanding. And it is these elements—the intangible values inherent in the tangible—that matter in the role that cultural objects play in forming identity, history, and knowledge.

1.5 Structure

In examining questions of the location of cultural objects through the lens of the law, questions of ownership and possession often arise. No one *owns* the past. The past is free to be claimed, reclaimed, explained, interpreted, and presented with only a few practical limitations. While no one owns the intangible past, questions of ownership, possession, and disposition of the tangible objects in which our cultural past is embodied are often the focus of contention and debate. This is a question to be determined in the first instance, but not exclusively, by reference to the law. While the legal framework is an obvious starting part, it is not sufficient. This study therefore also looks to history, cultural history, art history, anthropology, and archaeology to frame an answer.

Throughout the book, three interwoven strands are examined: first, the roles of armed conflict, imperialism, economic and political exploitation, and settler and extractive colonialism in the forcible removal of cultural objects from their original contexts; second, the role of museums, particularly the 'universal' or encyclopedic museum that aims to collect objects from throughout the world, often divorced from or regardless of their original contexts; and, third, the abstract values, including scientific and traditional knowledge and interpersonal ties that connect cultural objects to their original places and original communities and from which their meaning can be derived. The origins of these three strands may be traced to the end of the eighteenth and beginning of the nineteenth centuries. However, they persist with remarkable continuity in the contemporary discussions of where cultural objects should be located today.

[69] Morag Kersel, 'License to Sell: The Legal Trade of Antiquities in Israel' (Unpublished PhD dissertation, copy on file with author, 2006) 19–20.

A consistent theme is the role that armed conflict, imperialism, colonialism, and economic exploitation have played in the removal of cultural objects from their original contexts. These terms are often used interchangeably or, more properly, in conjunction; however, there are distinctions worth noting. An armed conflict occurs 'whenever there is a resort to armed force between States'[70] and exists even in the absence of open hostility, regardless of whether there is a formal declaration of war.[71] An increasingly relevant phenomenon in the theft and looting of cultural objects is the role of conflict among non-State actors or between States and non-State actors. These groups often receive monetary benefits from theft and looting.

Colonialism generally refers to territorial annexation and occupation of one State by another or the extension of political or military control by one State over territory that is not part of that State.[72] Colonialism is the practice of States, in most instances European States, dividing up other inhabited parts of the world for themselves[73] and typically involves the economic exploitation of the colonized region, often through extractive means. Closely related to colonialism, imperialism is understood to mean the 'domination and the imposition of one's own legal and economic systems onto another territory'.[74] Imperialism is usually carried out with 'a belief in the anthropological, cultural, and political superiority of the European powers and their people, which is sometimes masked as an educative mission'.[75] European powers assumed the governance of territories whose inhabitants were 'not deemed capable of sovereign rule', usually leading to the exploitation of natural and/or human resources, as well as the founding of European settlements.[76] Imperialism of the nineteenth century, also termed 'new imperialism', was shaped by industrial capitalism and led to significant expansion of the imperial powers beyond Europe.[77] All of these terms share the feature of political and military dominance used for the purpose of sometimes enlarging territory and always benefiting the colonial or imperial power economically, at the expense of the territory and its inhabitants. Because they share an exploitative and extractive character, these

[70] *Prosecutor v Dusko Tadic* (Decision on the Defense Motion for Interlocutory Appeal on Jurisdiction) ICT-94-1-A (2 October 1995) para 70.

[71] International Committee of the Red Cross, 'How is the Term "Armed Conflict" Defined in International Humanitarian Law?' (Opinion Paper) (March 2008) <www.icrc.org/en/doc/assets/files/other/opinion-paper-armed-conflict.pdf> accessed 28 February 2022.

[72] James T. Gathii, 'Imperialism, Colonialism, and International Law' (2007) 54 Buffalo Law Review 1013, 1013–14.

[73] Jörn Axel Kämmerer, 'Colonialism' in Anne Peters and Rüdiger Wolfrum (eds), *Max Planck Encyclopedia of Public International Law* (online edn, OUP 2018) para 1 (hereafter Kämmerer, 'Colonialism').

[74] Emmanuelle Jouannet, 'Universalism and Imperialism: The True-False Paradox of International Law?' (2007) 18 EJIL 379, 382.

[75] Kämmerer, 'Colonialism' (n 73) para 1.

[76] ibid, para 2.

[77] Margarita Díaz-Andreu, 'Archaeology and Imperialism: From Nineteenth-Century New Imperialism to Twentieth-Century Decolonization' in Bonnie Effros and Guolong Lai (eds), *Unmasking Ideologies: The Vocabulary and Symbols of Colonial Archaeology* (Cotsen Institute 2018) 3, 3.

terms describe the relationships that enabled the large-scale removal of cultural objects.

In the past, armed conflict, imperialism, and colonialism provided the primary opportunities for removal of cultural objects. Today, superior economic power, often built upon past exploitation of the colonized regions of the world, gives the former colonial powers and other Western States greater access to acquiring cultural objects on the market. While this market mechanism is superficially neutral, economic and market power built up over time and gives certain States, their institutions, and individuals superior ability to operate in the market for cultural objects. Reliance on the market as the means for achieving international movement of cultural objects and thus determining their location solidifies the continuing dominance of the former colonial powers. The past unidirectional flow of cultural objects is thereby perpetuated and often reinforced in the present.

The first three chapters of this work progress chronologically from the second half of the eighteenth century to the present day and focus on paradigmatic examples of removal of cultural artefacts. Chapter 2 explores the origins of the three strands that developed at the turn of the eighteenth to the nineteenth century. These strands became intertwined to provide the rationales and contexts for removal of cultural objects and continue to form the basis of the contemporary questions of where cultural objects should be located. The first strand is cultural looting during armed conflict and is exemplified by the looting carried out during the Napoleonic wars and the returns at the end of the conflict. The chapter then moves to the second strand—the origins of the universal or encyclopedic museum, with the founding of such museums as the British Museum and the Louvre. The chapter concludes with the third strand, which is the development of archaeology as a science and the beginnings of anthropology as a means of studying both the past and non-European cultures. Anthropology, in particular, included the development of pseudo-scientific theories that posited the superiority of Europeans and justified the appropriation of cultural objects.

Chapter 3 examines the long arc of the nineteenth century, often described as the great age of removals, during which colonialism and other forms of exploitation accounted for much of the movement of cultural objects. Three paradigmatic examples are chosen from among many that could be discussed: the taking of the Parthenon Sculptures by Lord Elgin at the turn of the century; the looting by British and French forces of the Yuanmingyuan in Beijing approximately mid-century (1860); and the British 'Punitive Expedition' in Benin at the end of the century (1897). Chapter 4 examines the particular issues of looting of archaeological sites, a phenomenon that became a significant factor in the middle of the twentieth century and continues today. The chapter examines the negative externalities and losses imposed on society through such looting, which increased as the application of scientific methodologies increased the knowledge that could be derived from proper excavation. These harms also include loss of cultural and intellectual capital to the communities and States of origin, damage to the artefacts, the acceptance of fakes and forgeries, and finally the funding of armed conflict and other illegal activities. The chapter then turns to the application of both *lex generalis* and *lex specialis* that developed on both the national and international levels. This discussion of the legal regime begins with the approaches of the Ottoman Empire during the nineteenth century and moves to contemporary laws that rely on State control and ownership of archaeological artefacts. The purpose of this legal regime is to discourage looting by imposing consequences on looters and all those involved in the market chain and to provide legal recourse for return of illegally taken artefacts.

The remaining three chapters then turn more specifically to the legal regime, ethical principles adopted by associations and institutions, and a rubric for return of cultural objects removed during the nineteenth and first part of the twentieth century, a time period to which neither contemporary legal nor ethical principles would apply. Chapter 5 presents an analysis of the legal structures that developed over the course of the twentieth century to limit the removal of cultural objects, primarily during armed conflict, and to determine when cultural objects should be returned if taken in violation of these legal provisions. The chapter first applies international humanitarian law to movable cultural objects. The chapter then examines the connection between cultural heritage and human rights, with an emphasis on disposition of human remains, burial objects, and sacred objects. and analyses the location of cultural objects through the lens of human rights law. The chapter concludes with consideration of the effectiveness of the two primary international conventions that regulate the movement of cultural objects today. Chapter 6 looks at attempts to deal with the problems of trade in, and acquisition of, cultural objects through ethical or voluntary approaches as well as scholarly engagement with possibly looted archaeological artefacts. While ethical policies and guidelines may fill gaps left by the legal regime, these policies are often inadequate, are poorly enforced, and do not reach back far enough in time with respect to many categories of cultural objects.

Chapter 7 begins with a discussion of the shortcomings of the law in confronting earlier appropriations that occurred during the late eighteenth, nineteenth and early twentieth centuries (ie, historical appropriations) and the justifications for the continued retention of these cultural objects. The chapter then turns to the question of how reparations might be achieved through the return of cultural objects removed as a result of colonialism, imperialism, and armed conflict. It argues that such objects should be returned to the places from which they were taken without free and informed consent. To the argument that the taking of such objects was 'legal' at the time, the response is posed that if the law itself at that time was unjust and discriminatory, then we today should not be bound by or even permitted to rely on that legal system. The chapter concludes by proposing a paradigm for return of cultural objects and resolving questions of use of associated intellectual productions in order to achieve reparatory justice.

Certain themes underscore the question of what is the proper disposition of movable cultural objects today. From the term 'cultural heritage', we derive the notions of obligation and responsibility, as well as the interconnectedness of the tangible with the intangible. From the term 'cultural property', we derive the limits that the law traditionally places on the ability to regain ownership or possession of cultural objects taken in the past. Reliance on the market to achieve contemporary international movement and to determine the disposition of movable cultural objects must be rejected because it fails to acknowledge the relationship among people with respect to a cultural object. Finally, a recognition of the importance of relationships raises the respective roles of the international community, the State, and the local or descendant community. Throughout these themes runs the roles that colonialism, physical and economic exploitation, and armed conflict played in the forcible removal of cultural objects from their places of origin and relocation to the centres of military and economic power. The question that ultimately confronts us is how to reverse some of the effects of conflict, imperialism, and colonialism through the return of cultural objects, thereby achieving a modicum of reparative justice.

2
Origins of the Debate Concerning Location of Cultural Objects

2.1 Introduction

The question as to the proper location of movable cultural objects today has its roots in three cultural developments of the second half of the eighteenth and first half of the nineteenth centuries: the disposition of cultural objects taken during the Napoleonic conflicts, the dawn of the Enlightenment as a way of understanding the world and the concomitant concept of the universal or encyclopedic museum, and the development of the science of archaeology as a means to recover and study the past, originally primarily focused on ancient European and Mediterranean cultures. Focus on these developments in the European context reflects the fact that most military and economic power was vested in Europe and so most of the cultural objects taken during this time became located in European, and later North American, museums and private collections. The endeavour to understand the question of where cultural objects should be located begins with an exploration of how these three strands emerged and became intertwined. The conflicts and contradictions among them continue to animate these questions. This chapter lays the foundations of the contemporary inquiry into the disposition of movable cultural objects.

2.2 Armed Conflict and Cultural Objects: Antiquity to the Beginning of the Modern Era

2.2.1 Antiquity to the French Revolution

The looting[1] of cultural and religious objects has accompanied armed conflict for millennia and, throughout much of history, was one of the primary means by

[1] The term 'looting' has several meanings. Most broadly, it is synonymous with theft in the sense of an unlawful taking of someone else's property. In addition to looting, several other terms, such as booty, plunder, and pillage, are used often interchangeably in common parlance, but incorrectly from a legal perspective. The distinctions between booty and plunder or pillage in the context of armed conflict are discussed in chapter 5. The term 'looting' has specific meaning when applied to archaeological artefacts, as discussed in chapter 4.

Cultural Objects and Reparative Justice. Patty Gerstenblith, Oxford University Press. © Patty Gerstenblith 2023.
DOI: 10.1093/oso/9780192872104.003.0002

which cultural objects moved. Victors often take artworks as a means to enrich themselves and as symbols of their conquests, thus destroying the historical, religious, and cultural memory of the conquered people and depriving them of the physical manifestations of their identity, their independence, and their distinct past. By usurping a society's cultural symbols, the victor both proves its victory and attempts to ensure its domination. In turn, these actions may lead to continuing cycles of cultural depredation as territories change hands and different cultural groups seek to exact revenge for earlier deprivations. Yet, from almost the earliest times, an evolving law of war has attempted to limit such destruction.

The history of the customs of armed conflict demonstrates ambivalence towards the practice of cultural plunder. According to Margaret Miles, the Eastern paradigm, as formulated particularly by the Persian Empire and relevant because of its military encounters with first the Greek city-states and later the Roman Empire, posited that looting during warfare was legitimate but that a magnanimous conqueror might restore looted property to the conquered people.[2] She contrasts this view with a uniquely Greek ethos that viewed looting of religious sites, especially temples, as a religious or moral violation that might bring adverse consequences to the looter.[3] In the Greek Archaic and Classical periods, most wealth was concentrated in temples, rather than in private collections, and sculptures, which often depicted deities as cult statues or were dedications to the gods, were considered sacred. Because looting was therefore carried out primarily in sacred precincts, religious overtones and fear of potential offence to the gods whose sanctuaries were desecrated shaped the ancient Greek attitude towards looting. These attitudes changed in the Hellenistic period as private wealth and therefore private ownership of artworks and other luxuries increased, decreasing the sacred aspects of art.[4]

The Romans routinely took artworks to display in their victory parades, adorn public buildings, and enrich the private coffers of military leaders. Because the military could keep or purchase property taken during conflict as their personal property, cultural looting became an impetus for the development of an art market in Greek art among the Romans.[5] The triumphal parade of Vespasian and Titus, after the destruction of the Second Temple in Jerusalem in 70 CE, is commemorated on the Arch of Titus, still extant in Rome (Figure 2.1). The depiction of the Menorah and other sacred implements from the Temple clearly demonstrates these goals of cultural looting, while booty taken from Judea funded construction

2 Margaret M Miles, *Art as Plunder: The Ancient Origins of Debate about Cultural Property* (CUP 2008) 16–19 (hereafter Miles, *Art as Plunder*).

3 ibid, 30–33.

4 ibid, 39.

5 While the dating of the inception of an art market is uncertain, Miles notes that a market existed by the mid-second century BCE following the sack of Corinth and included works from Sicily, Greece, and Asia Minor. ibid, 156. The looting of the Greek settlements in Italy and Sicily and later of the cities in Greece brought large quantities of Greek art to Rome and had a significant cultural impact on the Romans, stimulating both an art market in Greek originals and the production of Roman copies.

Figure 2.1 Arch of Titus, Rome, 81 CE Panel (copy), depicting the Triumphal March and Spoils of the Second Temple

of the Colosseum,[6] embodying the practice from earlier periods of putting booty to public use. Many of the sacred items taken from the Jerusalem Temple were displayed in the Temple of Peace, which was constructed by the Emperor Vespasian. It became a place of public display of artwork gathered by earlier emperors from throughout the Roman Empire. Based on the descriptions of the historian Josephus, Miles commented that 'everything worth traveling the world to visit was brought together in that one place. Implicitly, Rome now owned the whole world, in the form of its best art', thus forming the first example of a universal or encyclopedic museum 'with obvious dynastic and political overtones'.[7]

During the Roman Republic and Empire, principles evolved for the behaviour of a conquering army, including limits on how much booty could be taken and what should be done with it. Consistently, with some notable exceptions, the Romans tended to show respect for religious sanctuaries. Even when sanctuaries were looted, the plunder was often recycled for other religious or public purposes.[8] The legitimacy of such looting depended on whether the works were taken from religious or non-religious contexts, whether the works were taken for the victor's

[6] ibid, 260.
[7] ibid, 262.
[8] ibid, 66–82. Looting that fell outside of the rubric of authorized military conquest was disapproved of and often punished. ibid, 76–77.

personal benefit or for public benefit, and whether the works were taken as the result of legitimate warfare or were taken during civil administration or as a private action, which amounted to piracy. Nevertheless, Greek and Roman historians criticized the looting of artworks, sometimes even if the works were taken from non-religious contexts.

Even when looting might be permitted, the Romans believed that a sense of proportionality should limit the amount of plunder and leaders should not personally enrich themselves to an excessive degree. The Greek historian Polybius, writing in the second half of the second century BCE, questioned the excessive plundering of Siracusa, the most powerful of the Greek city-states in Sicily, after it fell to the Romans in 212 BCE:

> The Romans, then, decided ... to transfer all these objects to their own city and leave nothing behind. As to whether in doing so they acted rightly and in their own interest or the reverse, there is much to be said on both sides, but the more weighty arguments are in favor of their conduct having been wrong then and still being wrong .... At any rate these remarks will serve to teach all those who succeed to empire, that they should not strip cities under the idea that the misfortunes of others are an ornament to their own country.[9]

Polybius further made the point, which was echoed in later provisions intended to restrain cultural looting, that such plunder hinders future administration and rule over conquered territories.[10]

The Roman orator and lawyer, Cicero, elaborated on this theme in his prosecution in 70 BCE of Gaius Verres, the Roman civilian governor of Sicily, for corruption. Although not formally charged with these offences, Verres had committed wanton looting for personal enrichment of both privately owned and publicly dedicated religious artworks. Because Verres was not a conquering general, his depredations were even more problematic and outraged the Sicilian people.[11] Cicero distinguished between ordinary war booty (*spolia*), which a conqueror is free to take, and illegal removal of art (particularly religious art) and architectural decoration (*spoliatio*).[12] The later writings of the Roman historian Livy (59 BCE–17

[9] As translated and quoted in Margaret M Miles, 'Cicero's Prosecution of Gaius Verres: A Roman View of the Ethics of Acquisition of Art' (2002) 11 IJCP 28, 30–31 (hereafter Miles, 'Cicero's Prosecution of Gaius Verres').

[10] Margaret M Miles, 'Still in the Aftermath of Waterloo' in Peter G Stone (ed), *Cultural Heritage, Ethics, and the Military* (Boydell Press 2011) 29, 30–31 (hereafter Miles, 'Still in the Aftermath of Waterloo').

[11] Cicero prosecuted Verres at the request of the Sicilians. At the opening of the trial, he laid out his documentary evidence against Verres. At the conclusion of this opening, Verres chose to flee into exile, rather than continue the trial. The rest of Cicero's case against Verres was published as orations, as if they had been presented at trial. Miles, *Art as Plunder* (n 2) 119–43.

[12] Miles, 'Cicero's Prosecution of Gaius Verres' (n 9) 31. The terms 'booty', 'plunder', and 'pillage' were not clearly distinguished in antiquity, particularly in Rome. *Spolia* originally meant arms and armour taken from a defeated enemy but then came to mean booty in a more general sense. Artistic *spolia*

CE) and the Greek geographer and traveller Pausanias (second century CE) perpetuated the distinction between takings that were considered legitimate and those that were not.[13] Another theme found in Cicero's Verrine orations is the distinction between good uses of art (for public, commemorative, and religious purposes) and bad uses of art (for private, consumptive, and decadent purposes).

Cicero's writings and particularly the prosecution of Verres played a significant role in the future development of the law of warfare and more general attitudes with respect to cultural objects. The Verrine orations were well known to later Roman authors, such as Livy and Pliny, who wrote in the first century CE and who perpetuated Cicero's principles concerning looting.[14] Verres' actions were contrasted with those of the Roman General P Cornelius Scipio Aemilianus, who, after conquering Carthage, returned artworks to Sicily that the Carthaginians had earlier looted from there.[15] Authors and travellers in the late Renaissance and Enlightenment periods were also familiar with Cicero's writings.[16] The Verrine orations became a staple for European travellers, particularly those who went to Sicily, and Verres' depredations were often used as examples of bad administrative conduct during several phases of the British Empire. The British statesman and Member of Parliament, Edmund Burke, held up Cicero's prosecution of Verres as an example of the attempt to root out greed, and echoes of it may be found in Byron's criticisms of Elgin's taking of the Parthenon Sculptures.[17]

Despite these occasional expressions of limits, in practice, cultural heritage was not protected in times of war and conflict. The armies of the Fourth Crusade devastated the cultural heritage of the Eastern Mediterranean region, sacked Constantinople in 1204, and plundered palaces, churches, monasteries, and libraries.[18] Among the booty were the famed ancient horses which the Emperor Constantine had taken to Constantinople and which the Crusaders placed in the cathedral of San Marco in Venice.[19]

indicated works of art removed from one context and placed in another. Cicero used the term *spoliatio* to refer to art or architectural decoration taken out of its proper context. Miles, *Art as Plunder* (n 2) 15. Roman law prohibited architectural spoliation because it 'produced "disfigured" buildings that were an affront to urban decorum'. Dale Kinney, 'Introduction' in Richard Brilliant and Dale Kinney (eds), *Reuse Value: Spolia and Appropriation in Art and Architecture from Constantine to Sherrie Levine* (Routledge 2011) 1, 5 (hereafter Kinney, 'Introduction').

13 Miles, *Art as Plunder* (n 2) 91–94.

14 ibid, 91–92, 150–51.

15 ibid, 95–99. Many of these returned works were those stolen later by Verres. Scipio's example of restitution seems to be unique in antiquity and is matched in modern times only by the Duke of Wellington's actions and the large-scale restitutions that took place following the Second World War. ibid, 99, 329–30.

16 ibid, 286–97.

17 Miles, 'Still in the Aftermath of Waterloo' (n 10) 31–32.

18 Pietro Verri, 'The Condition of Cultural Property in Armed Conflicts: From Antiquity to World War II (Part I)' (1985) 25 (245) IRRC 67, 76 (hereafter Verri, 'The Condition of Cultural Property').

19 Miles, *Art as Plunder* (n 2) 280–81, 321; Charles Freeman, *The Horses of St. Mark's* (Overlook 2004).

The French plundered artworks and libraries during the Italian wars in the late 1400s and early 1500s.[20] German, Italian, and Spanish forces sacked Rome in 1527.[21] During the Thirty Years' War, the armies of the Holy Roman Empire captured Heidelberg in 1622 and seized the Elector Frederick V's famous library, the Palatina. Pope Gregory XV ordered that the library be brought to Rome, where it became part of the Vatican collections.[22] Upon capturing Munich in 1632, Gustavus Adolphus of Sweden seized the art collection of the Dukes of Bavaria.[23] Gustavus Adolphus' daughter, Christina, captured Prague in 1648 and seized the imperial collection there before the Peace of Westphalia could be concluded.[24] The Treaty of Westphalia (1648), which ended the Thirty Years' War, dictated that plundered property would not be restored, but it allowed for limited return of records, writings, documents, and other movables.[25]

Between the sixteenth and eighteenth centuries, legal commentators were divided as to whether cultural objects were legitimate war booty or whether they were a distinct form of protected property.[26] During this period, the concept of the 'just war' also developed. Any actions necessary to accomplish the purposes of a just war were legitimate, but most commentators agreed that appropriation of cultural objects did not contribute to accomplishing these purposes. In his work published in 1553, the international law commentator Jacob Przyluski stated that works of a religious, literary, and artistic nature should be protected.[27] On the other hand, Hugo Grotius, one of the earliest writers on international law in the early and mid-seventeenth century, departed from this developing view. In defence of the seizure of the Portuguese carrack *Santa Catarina* on behalf of the Dutch East India Company, he upheld the legal right to claim prizes.[28]

In 1758, the Swiss jurist, Emmerich de Vattel, drew a distinction between cultural property and those other types of property for which there was no obligation to protect. He wrote:

[20] Verri, 'The Condition of Cultural Property' (n 18) 79.

[21] ibid, 80.

[22] Jill Bepler, '*Vicissitudo Temporum*: Some Sidelights on Book Collecting in the Thirty Years' War' (2001) 32 (4) SCJ 953, 955.

[23] ibid, 956.

[24] Wayne Sandholtz, *Prohibiting Plunder: How Norms Change* (OUP 2007) 33–34.

[25] The Treaty of Westphalia required the restitution of archival records—'Rights, Documents, Writings, and Other Things Appertaining'. Treaty of Westphalia (entered into force 24 October 1648) Articles XV, XXXIV, CXIV <http://avalon.law.yale.edu/17th_century/westphal.asp> accessed 4 April 2021; Jirí Toman, *The Protection of Cultural Property in the Event of Armed Conflict* (Dartmouth Publishing Co 1996) 5 (hereafter Toman, *The Protection of Cultural Property in the Event of Armed Conflict*).

[26] Miles, *Art as Plunder* (n 2) 297–302; Roger O'Keefe, *The Protection of Cultural Property in Armed Conflict* (CUP 2006) 5–13.

[27] Toman, *The Protection of Cultural Property in the Event of Armed Conflict* (n 25) 5.

[28] ibid; Martine Julia van Ittersum, 'Hugo Grotius in Context: Van Heemskerck's Capture of the "Santa Caterina" and its Justification in "De Jure Praedae" (1604–1606)' (2003) 31 (3) Asian Journal of Social Science 511, 523–26, 541.

> ... for whatever cause a country be devastated, these buildings should be spared which are an honour to the human race and which do not add to the strength of the enemy, such as temples, tombs, public buildings and all edifices of remarkable beauty. What is gained by destroying them? It is the act of a declared enemy of the human race thus wantonly to deprive men of these monuments of art and models of architecture ...[29]

This passage may reflect a distinction in the degree of protection found first in Roman law between movable objects and historic structures and architecture, with a prohibition on the destruction of the latter.[30] De Vattel's principle that categories of property, including cultural property, that are not useful in a war effort should be protected became a consistent element in later international agreements concerning the law of armed conflict.[31] The lower degree of protection accorded to movable cultural objects seems also to have been perpetuated in contemporary legal instruments.

2.2.2 The French Revolution

The French Revolution, the Napoleonic Wars, and their aftermaths ushered in modern attitudes towards and treatment of cultural objects during armed conflict. The concept of cultural heritage or the *patrimoine culturel* as belonging to all peoples has its origins in the French Revolution. During the Revolution, artworks, Latin inscriptions, and other cultural monuments were intentionally destroyed, in large part because of their association with the Catholic Church and the aristocracy. In the earlier years of the Revolution, approximately 1789–1792, the revolutionary government attempted to protect the cultural remains, despite their association with the *ancien régime*. However, in 1792, the revolutionary government mandated the destruction of statues 'erected in honor of despotism', but it also urged conservation of items with 'a particular interest for the arts'.[32] The destruction culminated in the Terror of 1794. Nonetheless, a large quantity of artworks and other historical and literary properties, which had formerly been owned by the aristocracy and the Church, became owned by the collective, as the property of the people, thus arguably establishing the nation's duties and responsibilities to preserve that property.[33]

29 Quoted in Toman, *The Protection of Cultural Property in the Event of Armed Conflict* (n 25) 5.

30 Kinney, 'Introduction' (n 12) 5.

31 See n 1, above.

32 Joseph L Sax, 'Heritage Preservation as a Public Duty: The Abbé Grégoire and the Origins of an Idea' (1989–1990) 88 Michigan Law Review 1142, 1154 (hereafter Sax, 'Heritage Preservation as a Public Duty').

33 ibid, 1152–54. The collection of properties formerly belonging to the Church and the Crown provided the impetus for the formation of the Louvre as a public museum. Andrew McClellan, *Inventing*

To counter the destruction of cultural objects and properties during the Revolution, Abbé Grégoire, a member of the revolutionary government, prepared for the National Convention a defence against the proposal to destroy all Latin inscriptions on monuments. In his three reports, he argued that 'liberty is only realized where the talent and creative energies of the individual flourish', tolerance for difference and respect for creativity are prerequisites for the flourishing of liberty, and pursuit of knowledge and repudiation of ignorance are necessary for talent and creativity to develop.[34] Grégoire saw the preservation of France's artistic legacy as part of the freeing of its people from aristocratic oppression, and he cast past achievements as part of the capital of the citizens of the newly liberated nation. He did this, in part, by arguing that these artworks were the result of the individual artist's genius, rather than the products of the Church or the aristocrat who acted as patron.[35]

Thus, these cultural works belonged to all the people of France and '[t]he body of artifacts that embodied the best of the people was the quintessence of France, its heritage and patrimony'.[36] Another member of the Revolution, Joseph Lakanal, urged the protection of artworks, stating that 'they belong to all citizens in general; not to any one of them in particular; thus, it is with the rights of the entire city [of Paris] in hand, that I ask you to protect the arts against the new losses that threaten them'.[37] In Lakanal's 1793 report, Ginsburg also sees the link between protection of the author's domain and revolutionary ideals. 'Authors deserve exclusive rights not only because they bring forth the products of "genius", but particularly because that genius bears a strongly republican stamp.' Similarly, the public domain was viewed as a means of 'democratic access to a common cultural inheritance'.[38] This right of public access to the cultural inheritance may also be seen in the opening of the Louvre to the public.

the Louvre: Art, Politics, and the Origins of the Modern Museum in Eighteenth-Century Paris (University of California Press 1994) 91–93 (hereafter McClellan, *Inventing the Louvre*).

34 Sax, 'Heritage Preservation as a Public Duty' (n 32) 1155.

35 ibid, 1155–56. This shift from viewing the patron as the author to viewing the creator as the author is likely linked to the development of French copyright law during the Revolution and the French emphasis on the author's *droit moral*. For a discussion of the development of author's rights in literary property, see Susan P Liemer, 'On the Origins of le Droit Moral: How Non-Economic Rights Came to Be Protected in French IP Law' (2011) 19 JIPL 65, 105–11 (discussing the 1791 and 1793 intellectual property laws). Jane Ginsburg argues that protecting both the right of the public in literary creations and the individual author's rights in his or her own creations animated the Revolutionary intellectual property statutes. Jane C Ginsburg, 'A Tale of Two Copyrights: Literary Property in Revolutionary France and America' (1990) 64 Tulane Law Review 991, 1005–15.

36 Sax, 'Heritage Preservation as a Public Duty' (n 32) 1156.

37 Quoted in ibid, 1157. In the same vein, Grégoire wrote: 'The production of genius and the means of instruction are common property, national objects which, belonging to no one, are the property of all.' ibid, 1157–58.

38 Jane Ginsburg, '"Une Chose Publique"? The Author's Domain and the Public Domain in Early British, French and US Copyright Law' (2006) 65 Cambridge Law Journal 636, 656.

The idea that cultural objects belong to everyone and that this creates public obligations of protection and preservation is fundamental to our modern understanding of, and attitude towards, cultural heritage. It is a concept that appears in legal texts, such as the Preamble to the 1954 Hague Convention on the Protection of Cultural Property in the Event of Armed Conflict, as well as in the writings of cultural historians. Ironically, the idea that cultural objects belong to an amorphous everyone has been abused to justify the taking, theft, and pillage of cultural objects. It may also be the basis of the concept of State ownership and the public domain that is often applied today, particularly to archaeological artefacts.[39]

2.2.3 The Napoleonic Wars and Their Aftermath

When Napoleon undertook to conquer much of Europe, he envisioned recreating Paris as the 'new Rome'.[40] In pursuit of his dream, Napoleon first removed artworks from northern Europe. He later took Italian and Roman artworks *en masse* to Paris, including the Apollo Belvedere, the Laocoön (Figure 2.2), and the Discobolus from the Vatican and Capitoline museums. He also took Renaissance paintings, mineral and natural history collections, Vatican manuscripts, and even animals from zoos. Napoleon sought to legitimize many of these appropriations by inserting them into the peace treaties he negotiated. In contrast to earlier appropriations of artistic and cultural objects as the spoils of war and for enrichment, Napoleon's widespread usurpation of works of art took on a different justification, which he based on a belief in the superiority of the French nation and that artworks created in liberty belonged to, and needed to be situated in, the free French Republic.[41]

Napoleon's actions were very popular with the French populace, but they were not without criticism even within contemporary France. The French artist and architectural theorist Antoine Quatremère de Quincy severely criticized Napoleon's appropriations, comparing him to the Roman Verres. Relying on the ideas of Polybius and Cicero, Quatremère 'believed that the best art had a universal quality and therefore could not be possessed'; the 'best' art should be held in its original context, which was 'necessary for its full understanding and appreciation'.[42] While Quatremère de Quincy expressed these views in his *Lettres*

[39] State ownership of archaeological artefacts is discussed in chapter 4.

[40] For fuller discussion of the artworks removed from throughout Europe during the Napoleonic Wars, see McClellan, *Inventing the Louvre* (n 33) 114–23 and sources cited therein. At the time, archives and other manuscripts were considered particularly important to State sovereignty. Bénédicte Savoy, '1815: Musées d'Europe année?' in Patrick Boucheron (ed), *Histoire mondiale de la France* (Seuil 2017) 453, 455 (hereafter Savoy, '1815').

[41] David Gilks, 'Art and Politics during the "First" Directory: Artists' Petitions and the Quarrel over the Confiscation of Works of Art from Italy in 1796' (2012) 26 French History 53, 58–59 (hereafter Gilks, 'Art and Politics during the "First" Directory').

[42] Miles, *Art as Plunder* (n 2) 326.

Figure 2.2 Laocoön. Hellenistic style, date uncertain, possibly a Roman copy

au général Miranda sur le préjudice qu'occasionneraient aux arts et à la science le déplacement des monuments de l'art de l'Italie, they were also incorporated into a petition with fifty signatories, including many artists, such as Jacques-Louis David and Dominique-Vivant Denon, the future director of the Louvre Museum.[43]

In response to this petition, in 1796, other artists submitted a counter-petition to Napoleon in support of the confiscations:

> The Romans, once an uncultivated people, became civilized by transplanting to Rome the works of conquered Greece .... Thus ... the French people ... naturally endowed with exquisite sensitivity will ... by seeing the models from antiquity, train its feeling and its critical sense. The French Republic, by its strength and superiority of its enlightenment and its artists, is the only country in the world which can give a safe home to these masterpieces. All other Nations must come to borrow from our art, as they once imitated our frivolity.[44]

[43] ibid, 327.

[44] Quoted in Dorothy Mackay Quynn 'The Art Confiscations of the Napoleonic Wars' (1945) 50(3) AHR 437, 438–39. For more on this petition, see Gilks, 'Art and Politics during the "First" Directory' (n 41) 67–72.

Perhaps ironically, Grégoire joined in praising the looting of artworks as demonstrating both the superiority of French appreciation of culture and the French Republic's military success, arguing, 'More than the Romans, … we have the right to say that in combatting the tyrants we protect the arts. We gather their monuments even where our victorious armies penetrate.'[45] Gilks situates these petitions in terms of competing political views, opposition to military expansionism through foreign wars, and the goals of artists at the time. In so doing, he presents a different interpretation of these views on confiscation and repatriation of artworks from that traditionally presented in works on art and cultural heritage law.[46]

Nonetheless, we see in the counter-petition and the statements of Grégoire the enduring justification for the looting of cultural objects, which is now often referred to as the 'rescue narrative', in which the appropriator claims to be acting out of altruistic motives in saving the cultural objects. First, the justification focuses exclusively on the benefits that will accrue to the individual or nation by taking possession of the cultural objects. Second, it asserts a right to the object based on moral or intellectual superiority. The third element is an expression of altruism—namely, that because the possessor has a greater ability to care for and appreciate the object, the possessor is, in fact, not acting primarily for its own benefit but rather for the benefit of all humanity, including the original owner. Hence, we see the rescue narrative at work—the act of looting is done for the benefit of others, not the looter. This narrative demonstrates that the phrase 'common heritage' can be taken to mean different things and can be misinterpreted as granting license to theft and plunder. As Cherif Bassiouni commented: 'Napoleon reasoned that all Europeans shared a common heritage, but that France was the most appropriate center for the great works of art.'[47]

While Napoleon's approach harkened back to earlier views concerning the status of artworks during war, a nearly contemporary and little-known case from the War of 1812 illustrates the contrasting view. A ship, the *Marquis de Somerueles*, was carrying artworks from Italy to the newly founded Academy of Arts in Philadelphia (Figure 2.3 and Figure 2.4). The British seized the ship and took it to a court in Nova Scotia, where the judge held that the ship's cargo should be freed and permitted to proceed to Philadelphia. Among his reasons for releasing the artworks, Judge Croke saw that it was the role of Britain to help the young American nation,

[45] Sax, 'Heritage Preservation as a Public Duty' (n 32) 1156 n 73.

[46] Gilks, 'Art and Politics during the "First" Directory' (n 41) 53. For example, in contrast to the impression that Quatremère de Quincy was forward-thinking in emphasizing the original contexts of cultural objects, Gilks portrays him as a reactionary in the sense that he was a royalist and opposed to the Revolution; his letter criticizing the confiscation of artworks in Italy was more fundamentally an attack on the Directory and could be characterized as an attempt to defend and protect the papacy. ibid, 56–58, 61–62, 74.

[47] Cherif Bassiouni, 'Reflections on Criminal Jurisdiction in International Protection of Cultural Property' (1983) 10 Syracuse Journal of International Law and Commerce 281, 288 (hereafter Bassiouni, 'Reflections on Criminal Jurisdiction').

Figure 2.3 Salvator Rosa, *Rocky Landscape with Figures* (*c* 1650). Gift of the United States in Recognition of the historic 1813 decision respecting prizes of war. Presented by the United States Consul-General of Halifax, 1952

despite the war between them, because he believed that once the United States was educated in the arts, it would become a worthwhile ally and future partner with Britain. In his written opinion, Judge Croke denigrated Napoleon for his seizure of artworks and pointed out that the British should act in a superior manner. He described the artworks 'not as the *peculium* of this or of that nation, but as the property of mankind at large, and as belonging to the common interests of the whole species.'[48]

Judge Croke's expression of the universality of artworks seems to reflect the concept of the *société des belles lettres*—that is, that people of culture, knowledge, and sophistication had more in common with each other, regardless of their nationality, than with people of their own nation. Quatremère de Quincy expressed this concept when he wrote:

> It is as a member of this universal republic of the arts and sciences, and not as an inhabitant of this or that nation, that I shall discuss the concern of all parts in the

[48] *The Marquis de Somerueles*, Stewart's Vice-Admiralty Reports, 21 April 1813, 482 (Vice-Adm. Ct Halifax NS).

Figure 2.4 Salvator Rosa, *Landscape with Two Soldiers and Ruins* (*c* 1650) (right). Gift of the United States in Recognition of the historic 1813 decision respecting prizes of war. Presented by the United States Consul-General of Halifax, 1952

> preservation of the whole. What is this concern? It is a concern for civilization, for perfecting the means of attaining happiness and pleasure, for the advancement and progress of education and reason: in a word, for the improvement of the human race. Everything that can help toward this end belongs to all peoples; no one of them has the right to appropriate it for itself, or to dispose of it arbitrarily.[49]

While such individuals shared a common love of art, they also shared a responsibility to protect and preserve it. This view accords with the universalist or globalist view of cultural heritage, where it is the international community that should primarily take responsibility for, and reap the benefits from, preservation of cultural heritage. It is ironic that this notion of the universality and common ownership of

[49] Quoted in Ana Filipa Vrdoljak, *International Law, Museums and the Return of Cultural Objects* (CUP 2008) 24 (hereafter Vrdoljak, *International Law*). Quatremère de Quincy was criticized for having too few civic, rather than cosmopolitan, ties, while the signatories of the petition protesting Napoleon's confiscations were told to 'cease to be cosmopolitan … and try to love [their] *Patrie* a little more'. Gilks, 'Art and Politics during the "First" Directory' (n 41) 69. For a description of the *République des Lettres*, see Katherine Harloe, *Winckelmann and the Invention of Antiquity: History and Aesthetics in the Age of* Altertumswissenschaft (OUP 2013) 31–32 (hereafter Harloe, *Winckelmann and the Invention of Antiquity*).

cultural works could be used as a justification both for Napoleon's seizures and appropriations of artworks and for Dr Croke's idea that artworks should be immune from seizure during armed conflict. We find this same duality prevalent today, both as rationalization for reducing regulation of the market in artworks in order to facilitate their international movement to the world's economic centres and as justification for preservation of the original contexts of works of art.

At the end of the Napoleonic Wars in 1815, the British victors, the Duke of Wellington and Lord Castlereagh, forced the French to give up many of the artworks taken from other European nations and, more significantly, declined to take any artworks, either those that had been looted by Napoleon or those that were previously in France, as spoils of war. By refusing to do so, the Duke implicitly treated artworks as a category distinct from other types of property, echoing the outcome of the *Marquis de Somerueles* decision, in which Judge Croke recognized that artworks have a universal quality and were therefore not subject to seizure as ordinary war booty. This event marked the first time in modern history that a conqueror did not take advantage of an opportunity for self-enrichment or to enrich the nation.[50]

Competing factors played into the decision about what to do with the French collections. Under traditional rules of warfare, the objects could be claimed as booty. Wellington was concerned that the artworks might remain a focal point for French fervour, while the Prince Regent voiced an interest in the artworks and their removal so that they would not remind the French of their past victories.[51] On the one hand, the British would have been subject to accusations of hypocrisy that they wished to enrich themselves by taking the works that Napoleon had confiscated, thus engaging in the same conduct for which Napoleon had been condemned. On the other hand, the distribution of the artworks as 'spoils of war' among the allies that had opposed Napoleon would have resulted in an unequal distribution and would have laid the groundwork for possible future claims and counterclaims. This dilemma led the British to adopt the principle of restitution, by which cultural objects would be returned to their 'place of origin', defined as the place from which the French had taken them, rather than an earlier place of origin.[52] Four principles of restitution emerged from these decisions concerning the disposition of movable cultural objects and were later generalized to other conflicts: (1) restitution

[50] Miles, *Art as Plunder* (n 2) 96–99; 329–30. The earliest example of restitution was that of Scipio Aemilianus, see n 15 above.

[51] Miles, 'Still in the Aftermath of Waterloo' (n 10) 36.

[52] Vrdoljak, *International Law* (n 49) 25–27. Vrdolyak uses as an example the horses taken from the San Marco Basilica in Venice. The horses were returned to Venice, as their place of origin, rather than to Austria, which controlled Venice at the time the French took them, or to Constantinople (Istanbul) from which the Venetians had taken them in 1204 during the Fourth Crusade. ibid, 27; n 19 above. For a satirical piece written from the perspective of the horses, published in a London newspaper, see Miles, *Art as Plunder* (n 2) 339. The French refused to give to Austria Veronese's painting, *The Wedding at Cana*, which had been taken from Venice, but, in contrast to the horses of San Marco's Basilica, the painting remained at the Louvre. Savoy, '1815' (n 40) 456.

of artworks to Britain's allies from whom the French had taken them could be justified as a right of conquest in the same war; (2) however, the right of conquest did not give to the victors a right of 'new possession' to plunder works that had belonged to the French before the conflict; (3) unequal treaties exacted during war were not a basis for possession, and (4) artworks and scientific collections belong in a special, protected category that is to be treated differently than other goods.[53]

This decision to return artworks helped establish the fundamental link between cultural objects and a particular territory or people, a principle that gradually replaced the earlier principle of disposition of cultural objects based on either the nature of the object or the circumstances of its acquisition.[54] William R Hamilton wrote to Lord Elgin at the time of the Congress of Vienna stating '[t]hat these works are considered so sacred a property, that no direct or indirect means are to be allowed for their being conveyed elsewhere than where they came from'.[55] Acknowledging the connection of the artworks to the territory from which they had been removed led Hamilton to suggest the legitimacy of purchasing artworks. This allowed the British to reconcile what otherwise might be considered conflicting actions: restitution of the artworks taken by force by Napoleon to the territories from which they had been removed based on a territorial link, but retention of artworks purchased on the market because of their commercial value and their importance to the British nation through their placement in a national museum.[56]

Despite the restitutionary goals of the British, only a little more than half of the artworks taken by Napoleon were in fact returned to their original owners in Europe.[57] Further, there was no comparable concern for cultural objects taken from non-Europeans. After defeating the French in Egypt in 1801, the British had taken as spoils of war the antiquities collected by the French during Napoleon's expedition to Egypt, including the Rosetta Stone (Figure 2.5), although the British action arguably violated the terms of Article 16 of the Capitulation of Alexandria.[58] In an illustration of the double standard of how non-Europeans were treated under

[53] Miles, 'Still in the Aftermath of Waterloo' (n 10) 39–40.

[54] Vrdoljak, *International Law* (n 49) 23.

[55] Quoted by Arthur H. Smith, 'Lord Elgin and His Collection' (1916) 36 Journal of Hellenic Studies 163, 332; see also Vrdolyak, *International Law* (n 49) 23.

[56] Vrdolyak, *International Law* (n 49) 23, 29.

[57] Miles, *Art as Plunder* (n 2) 341.

[58] ibid, 328–29. This article stated that 'The members of the Institute may carry with them all the instruments of arts and science, which they have brought from France; but the Arabian manuscripts, the statues, and other collections which have been made for the French Republic, shall be considered as public property, and subject to the disposal of the general of the combined army.' Capitulation of Alexandria, History of the British expedition to Egypt (Egerton 1803). The disposition of the antiquities collected by the French should have been decided between the British and Ottoman armies, but this negotiation did not happen. The combined army was dissolved soon after the French defeat, so the status of the title to the seventeen antiquities at issue is unclear. Monica Hanna, 'The Rosetta Stone betrayal and the West's obsession with ancient Egypt' (*In Weekend* 2 September 2022) <www.thenationalnews.com/weekend/2022/09/02/the-rosetta-stone-betrayal-and-a-western-obsession-with-ancient-egypt/?fbclid=IwAR0j9JnzSAxvAr9LWKjYPqUKDqs7orGX4Zy1k6sKYqUNXAmmjsBMHQy85mE> accessed 15 September 2022.

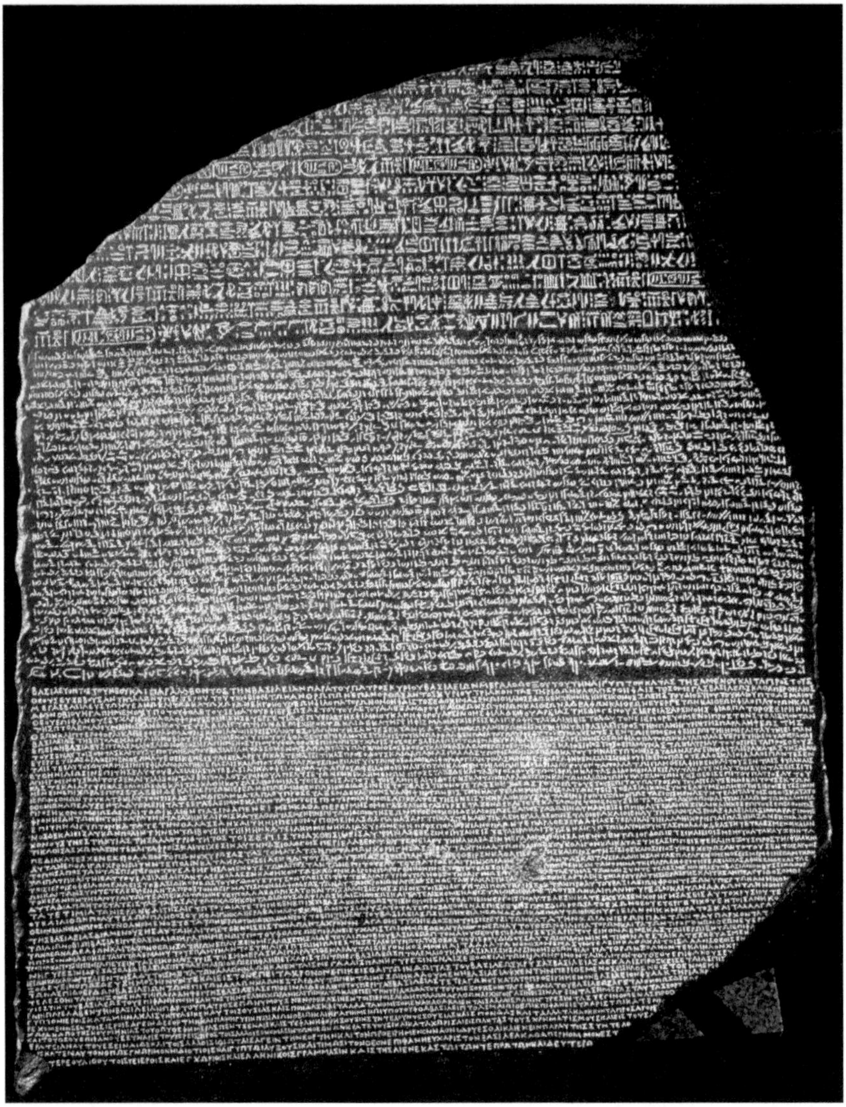

Figure 2.5 Rosetta Stone, Egypt, 196 BCE

the evolving international law of the nineteenth century, the British did not think they had any obligation to share these objects with the Ottomans or return any to Egypt, nor was there any general European sentiment to do so.[59]

[59] Vrdoljak, *International Law* (n 49) 27.

The denouement of the Napoleonic Wars thus gave both the first large-scale repatriation of artworks and the clearest statement of the modern principle that artworks do not belong to the victors.Bassiouni commented that with the restitution of artworks at the end of the Napoleonic Wars:

> [T]he concept of protecting cultural property had evolved from a theory developed by scholars to a practiced legal principle.... [T]he provisions contained in international agreements over the ensuing 150 years firmly established that the protection of cultural property is a basic and fundamental rule in the regulation of armed conflict. Its purpose is to preserve what can now be called the inalienable right of all peoples to their natural cultural heritage.[60]

The aftermath of the Napoleonic Wars thus had a significant influence on future responses to the question of the return of cultural objects at the end of armed conflict.[61]

2.3 The Encyclopedic or Universal Museum

With antecedents in the late sixteenth and seventeenth centuries, the Enlightenment unfolded during the eighteenth century, with changing approaches to human history and progress. These changes included growing confidence in the ability of individuals to improve and of human societies to develop in terms of political organization, economics, and cultural life. The Enlightenment encompassed developments not only in literature, arts, and sciences, but also in political philosophy, which emphasized reason, natural and individual rights, self-governance, and liberty. It represented a clear departure from the aristocratic and theocratic governments of the past, and its belief in human progress and equality among the social classes provided the philosophical underpinnings for both the American and French Revolutions.[62]

Key to the Enlightenment view was the belief in human progress towards an improved state rather than being caught in an inevitable decline from the time of antiquity. A second element was rationalism based on uniform principles, as expressed by the French philosopher René Descartes, to explain the natural world.[63] A belief in human progress applied to many aspects of life, including culture, technology, politics, commerce, and social organization.

[60] Bassiouni, 'Reflections on Criminal Jurisdiction' (n 47) 288–89.

[61] See Miles, *Art as Plunder* (n 2) 349–52.

[62] Bruce G Trigger, *A History of Archaeological Thought* (2nd edn, CUP 2006) 97, 99–100 (hereafter Trigger, *A History of Archaeological Thought*).

[63] ibid, 98.

> Through an empirical methodology, guided by the light of reason, one could arrive at knowledge and universal truths, providing liberation from ignorance and superstition that in turn would lead to the progress, freedom and happiness of mankind.... [The Enlightenment] was a period when the culture of the educated person was thought to take in the whole of human knowledge, a time of polymaths, when philosophy and science could not be divorced from theology, when men, and to an increasing extent women, did not specialize but instead could be artist, scientist, historian and philosopher all in one.[64]

Progress and change were thought to be part of a continuous sequence that was subject to consistent laws of nature and fostered by rational thought.[65] As a corollary, it was posited that human culture had evolved from the simple to the complex. The idea of progress was built on a notion of sequencing—that is, of linear movement rather than a static or repetitive cycle. Such sequencing implied, in turn, an order or classification of stages, whether of natural or of human cultural phenomena. 'Enlightenment philosophy [was] the most ambitious and influential systematization of a century characterized by system building.'[66] During the sixteenth and seventeenth centuries, the voyages of exploration led to significant strides in describing and classifying the plants and animals of the natural world, even setting the basis for taxonomies that are still in use today. These advances in observation, description, and classification culminated in the development during the nineteenth century of the three-age system utilized in the field of archaeology.[67]

Interest in describing, classifying, and eventually explaining the natural world was followed by an interest to do the same for the cultural world. This led, in turn, to the development of 'connoisseurship'—a 'method by which quality could be determined empirically'.[68] Specific criteria for evaluating objects were developed based on analysis of perceived quality and authenticity, and it was believed that this evaluation could indicate and judge the society to which the object belonged. By the middle of the eighteenth century, 'it was believed that connoisseurship, understood as a scientific, even philosophical system, might become an essential ingredient in arriving at a system for mapping the past'.[69] Consonant with

[64] Kim Sloan '"Aimed at universality and belonging to the nation": The Enlightenment and the British Museum' in Kim Sloan (ed), *Enlightenment: Discovering the World in the Eighteenth Century* (British Museum Press 2003) 12, 13 (hereafter Sloan, '"Aimed at universality and belonging to the nation"').

[65] Trigger, *A History of Archaeological Thought* (n 62) 101–02.

[66] ibid, 99.

[67] Robert Huxley, 'Challenging the Dogma: Classifying and Describing the Natural World' in Kim Sloan (ed), *Enlightenment: Discovering the World in the Eighteenth Century* (British Museum Press 2003) 70, 70–72, 79.

[68] Luke Syson, 'The Ordering of the Artificial World: Collecting, Classification and Progress' in Kim Sloan (ed), *Enlightenment: Discovering the World in the Eighteenth Century* (British Museum Press 2003) 108, 118.

[69] ibid, 120.

Enlightenment philosophy, the notion of human progress was engrained into this classification system and into a unifying theory that explained past civilizations.

The notion of ordering the past based on careful observation and analysis led to the development of a chronology based on the perceived evolution of artistic styles in Greek and Roman art. Antiquarians traditionally analysed classical remains through comparison to written evidence such as inscriptions, literary texts, and coins. Interest in collecting ancient remains was stimulated through the travels of wealthy Europeans, particularly from England and France, who toured the Mediterranean, first to Italy and later further afield to Greece and the Eastern Mediterranean. These travellers were interested in acquiring ancient objects to bring home to display and to demonstrate their knowledge of, and love for, antiquity. As with the Romans, who collected earlier Greek art for its aesthetic or monetary value, these collectors did not attempt a systematic collection of artefacts, and their interests were limited to the individual object.

In the eighteenth century, these collections stimulated the development of classical archaeology, influenced by the work of the German classicist and art historian Johann Joachim Winckelmann, as a branch of art historical studies.[70] Winckelmann, who published his book *Geschichte der Kunst des Alterthums* (*History of Ancient Art*) in 1764, applied systematic analysis of stylistic elements to ancient art in order to develop a taxonomic or classificatory system based on connoisseurship.[71] Consistent with Enlightenment philosophy, Winckelmann sought 'to uphold a naturalistic but universalistic explanation for the empirical variations observable when ancient monuments are compared, vindicating claims about ancient art's overall pattern of development by deriving it from the regular operation of uniform causes across different climactic and socio-political environments'.[72] This analytical methodology was based on 'the authority of the eye—the possibility of determining not only the quality of a painting but the identity of its master and whether it is an original or a copy on the basis of visual analysis'.[73] From this classification and by analysing both material culture and literary sources, Winckelmann built a chronology of ancient art based on what he characterized as a development

[70] Alain Schnapp, *The Discovery of the Past* (Harry N Abrams 1997) 258–66 (hereafter Schnapp, *The Discovery of the Past*). For the significant influence of Winckelmann on German philosophers of the nineteenth and early twentieth centuries and the development of *Altertumswissenschaft*, see Harloe, *Winckelmann and the Invention of Antiquity* (n 49) . In addition to his influence on German intellectuals, Winckelmann was also invoked by those who advocated for the movement of artworks to Paris as a means of placing them within a context of liberty, ibid 11, and he viewed himself as among the citizens of the Republic of Letters, ibid, 31–34; also see n 49.

[71] Harloe, *Winckelmann and the Invention of Antiquity* (n 49) 105–27. Winckelmann was influenced by the French and English Enlightenment writers, particularly Voltaire and Montesquieu, and perhaps Rousseau, to focus on history and the progress of the arts. ibid, 112–13.

[72] ibid, 114–15.

[73] ibid, 69. Winckelmann drew on earlier writers, such as the English essayist Jonathan Richardson the Elder (1665–1745), who had begun to use stylistic comparison as a means of attribution of artworks. ibid, 68–69, 71–77.

from the archaic phase of early Greek art of the sixth century BCE, to the high classical ideal of the Greek sculptor Phidias of the fifth century BCE, to the idealized naturalism of the Hellenistic sculptor Praxiteles of the fourth century BCE, and finally to the decadent and largely imitative phase of Roman art. In the process, however, his work moved beyond a history of art and became a history of the 'totality of the ways of living', and, in fact, a history of culture.[74]

The paradigm of cultural evolution applied to the Classical Mediterranean and European world differed markedly from the paradigm applied to areas that were colonized or otherwise subjugated by Europeans, particularly in Africa. Known as the degenerationist thesis and utilized to justify imposing colonialism, the European powers adopted the theory that the modern populations, who were viewed as inferior, could not have produced the ancient works that were often of high aesthetic and artistic skill and were greatly admired. Thus, this thesis posited that the modern populations were either not descended from the ancient cultural producers or they were debased and degenerate descendants.[75]

Enlightenment philosophy and attitudes towards the arts and sciences spurred the development of the modern museum. The ancestors of the modern museum were numerous, including the cabinet of curiosities that belonged to British aristocrats, royal collections of European monarchs and the Pope, and collections of art and antiquities taken during imperial conquests. The earliest art museums evolved in Europe from the royal collections of the French monarchy (the Louvre), the Medici in Florence, the Vatican museums, and the Dresden museum in Germany. But it was the taking of artworks from throughout Europe during the Napoleonic Wars for display in the Louvre that led to the concept of the encyclopedic museum—that is, a visual display of art taken from many locations that could be arranged chronologically, based on art historical principles, and understood as the pictorial illustration of an encyclopedia.[76]

The three aspects of a museum—public, national, and universal—are intertwined. There is some competition among museums to identify the first public museum. The Kunstmuseum Basel, which claims to be the world's first public art collection, was founded in 1661 with the purchase of the private collection of Basilius Amerbach, which consisted of works by the Holbein family and other Renaissance artists, such as Lucas Cranach the Elder.[77] Other early contenders

[74] ibid, 126–27.

[75] Annie Coombes, *Reinventing Africa: Museums, Material Culture and Popular Imagination in Late Victorian and Edwardian England* (Yale Univ Press 1994) 48–57.

[76] Karl E Meyer, *The Art Museum: Power, Money, Ethics* (William Morrow 1979) 20 (hereafter Meyer, *The Art Museum*). The word 'museum' derives from the ancient Greek word *mouseion*, meaning a sanctuary of the Muses. Ian Jenkins, 'Ideas of Antiquity: Classical and Other Ancient Civilizations in the Age of Enlightenment' in Kim Sloan (ed), *Enlightenment: Discovering the World in the Eighteenth Century* (British Museum Press 2003) 168, 168 (hereafter Jenkins, 'Ideas of Antiquity').

[77] See Kunstmuseum Basel <https://kunstmuseumbasel.ch/en/collection/history> accessed 15 February 2022.

include the Luxembourg Gallery in Paris, which was open to the public from 1750; the Uffizi in Florence, which was converted in 1743 into a public art museum; and the Museo Capitolino in Rome, which reportedly became a public art museum in 1471.[78] The British Museum was founded in 1753 as the first publicly accessible collection of manuscripts and natural history objects, which had been donated by or acquired from British aristocrats. However, for most of its first forty years, it was open only to visitors who applied in advance and received permission and thus would not qualify as a truly public museum.[79]

The 1793 opening of the Louvre to the public presented a radically different view of the role of art collections. In turn, this evolution engendered a new focus for European museums and served a democratizing function that aligned with the political reforms of the French Revolution.[80] The Louvre's encyclopedic nature came from the presence of the artworks Napoleon had taken from across Europe, but it was an encyclopedic museum limited to European art. Savoy questioned the Louvre's claim to being one of the first public museums, but she unites the characteristics of being a public and a universal museum—the Louvre's claim to being a universal museum was based on its being public and it needed to be public in order to be universal.[81]

The term 'universal' can therefore have two different meanings: universal in an 'ingathering' sense that the museum has collections from throughout the world and the term is then synonymous with encyclopedic; universal in an 'outgoing' sense that the museum reaches out and is universally available, that is, to the public. While today 'universal' is often used in the former sense, particularly by Western museum curators and directors, its roots as a public museum should be remembered. To this is added the aspect of a national museum, for which the Louvre also set the model that was copied during the nineteenth century throughout Europe, including Greece, which established its national museum in 1866.[82] While the concept of a national museum may seem to contradict the idea of an 'ingathering' universalism, many of the major universal museums are national museums, especially those outside of the United States.

Despite the roots of the museum concept in earlier time periods, the intellectual antecedent of the modern Western museum was Enlightenment philosophy based on scientific rationalism and the belief that classification systems could be devised that would explain the human past and its evolution into modern culture.

[78] McClellan, *Inventing the Louvre* (n 33) 13–16 (the Luxembourg Gallery); Sax, 'Heritage Preservation as a Public Duty' (n 32) 1152 and n 56 (citing Joseph Alsop, *The Rare Art Tradition* (Harper & Row Publishers 1982) 118, 164 (recounting the origins of the Uffizi and Museo Capitolino).

[79] Meyer, *The Art Museum* (n 76) 20.

[80] The transformation of the Louvre into a public collection, fulfilling the purposes of educating the public in both art and the principles of the Revolution, is well described in McClellan, *Inventing the Louvre* (n 33) 91–99.

[81] Savoy, '1815' (n 40) 456.

[82] Meyer, *The Art Museum* (n 76) 18–22.

The universal or encyclopedic museum has been described as 'a true product and even embodiment of the Enlightenment, and certainly one of its greatest achievements'.[83] It was intended to draw together all the arts and sciences towards a universalistic goal of bringing order to and advancing all branches of knowledge. The British Museum aspires to illustrate Enlightenment principles and presents itself as the pinnacle of 'a virtual encyclopedia of the state of knowledge of the world as it stood in the eighteenth century' with an obligation both to acquire knowledge and to share it, thus contributing to the 'progress, freedom and happiness of mankind and of course also to the glory and prosperity of the British nation'.[84] Although the universal museum was born of the Enlightenment and the desire to acquire, organize, and classify human knowledge for the benefit of all humankind, it was also something made possible only by a colonial empire that facilitated the acquisition of cultural objects collected from much of the world through the reach of that empire.

The British Museum put into practice the approach of arranging exhibits of artworks to demonstrate the chronological development of human progress and civilization from the archaic to artistic perfection and of dividing ancient artworks into different cultures. The organization of the artworks looted by Napoleon from Italy and displayed in the Louvre had a pedagogic purpose and owed something to these chronological and art historical principles, but the displays often sacrificed art historical coherence for decorative symmetry and internal visual harmony. Nonetheless, the first director of the Louvre, Dominique Vivant Denon, adopted a method of display that reflected a progressive-linear view of artistic development, rather than the cyclical one espoused by earlier theorists, such as the sixteenth century Italian artist and art historian, Giorgio Vasari.[85] Arrangement based on chronological development has since remained the primary organizational principle of the Western museum.

Despite its origins as a natural history museum, during the second half of the eighteenth century the British Museum shifted its focus from natural history to cultural history and to the collection, evaluation, and appreciation of the material remains of ancient cultures. By the early nineteenth century, the British Museum had become the foremost repository of sculpture and other artworks of the ancient classical Mediterranean and Mesopotamian world. The British Museum's collection of antiquities began with the acquisition in 1772 of Sir William Hamilton's collection of Greek vases found at Etruscan sites and other antiquities from Italy.[86]

[83] Sloan, '"Aimed at universality and belonging to the nation"' (n 64) 14.
[84] ibid.
[85] McClellan, *Inventing the Louvre* (n 33) 140–48.
[86] Hamilton, like many of his contemporary collectors and later Lord Elgin, was a diplomat and exploited his status as envoy to the Kingdom of Naples to facilitate his collecting and disregard for any legal restraints on excavating, exporting, and selling artefacts. Alice Procter, *The Whole Picture: The colonial story of the art in our museums & why we need to talk about it* (Cassell 2020) 27–35.

In 1802, the Museum acquired the Egyptian sculptures and inscriptions that had been collected by Napoleon during his Egyptian campaign but were captured by the British forces after they defeated the French in 1801. These include some of the most frequently visited objects in the British Museum, such as the Rosetta Stone. Between 1805 and 1814, the Museum purchased the collection of Roman sculptures and other antiquities of Charles Townley, and in 1815, the Museum acquired the sculptural frieze of the Temple of Apollo at Bassae, located in western Greece.

This set the stage for the Museum's acquisition of the most famously appropriated[87] and longest-contested ancient works, Lord Elgin's collection of fifth century BCE sculptures taken from the Parthenon and elsewhere on the Acropolis in Athens and purchased by Parliament in 1816. This addition to the Museum's collection was described as 'the single most important event in the history of the Museum's collections ... The sculptures of the Parthenon ... were presented as the highpoint of human achievement in antiquity. In the subsequent physical arrangement of the Museum's ever-increasing collections, all other works were seen to lead up to or away from the one supreme moment in ancient art.'[88] This acquisition allowed the Museum to fulfil the philosophy underlying its exhibitions to display the progress of human accomplishment towards the pinnacle of ancient classical art, while also educating the British public and artists.

The taking of the Parthenon Sculptures by Lord Elgin and their later acquisition by Parliament for the British Museum fit into the political reality of the military rivalry between France and Britain in the early nineteenth century. Just as Napoleon attempted to recreate Paris as the new Rome by appropriating artworks from Italy during his military campaigns, so the British saw London, with its classical Greek sculptures, as the reincarnation of democratic ancient Athens. As Napoleon and the French artists had done, Elgin invoked the rescue narrative, claiming that he was motivated by a desire to rescue and preserve the sculptures while also incidentally benefiting the English nation.[89] The presence of the Parthenon Sculptures in the British Museum has endured as the pre-eminent symbol of cultural heritage dispossession even to this day.

[87] The term 'appropriation' may be viewed as a form of taking of property, which is value-neutral, or an act that 'bears the ethical or moral value assigned to such acts in any given era or culture'. When a negative value is attributed, it may more properly be termed 'misappropriation' (as a taking without permission). Whether a positive or negative value is attributed to the act may be determined by circumstances, the political context, and 'in contemporary discourse it is frequently determined by the direction of the appropriation in relation to perceived distributions of power'. Kinney, 'Introduction' (n 12) 7–8.

[88] Jenkins, 'Ideas of Antiquity' (n 76) 174.

[89] The British justified Elgin's taking of the Parthenon Sculptures, in part, on the grounds that they would otherwise be taken by the French, just as the French had previously justified Napoleon's confiscations of artworks from Italy because otherwise they would be looted from Rome by other European powers. In this view, the French confiscations were necessary to ensure that the artworks remained publicly accessible. Gilks, 'Art and Politics during the "First" Directory' (n 41) 59. The role of the Parthenon Sculptures as expropriated artworks and symbols of the cultural heritage debate is considered in more detail in chapter 3.

Across the nineteenth and first half of the twentieth centuries, what has become known as the 'age of removal' saw the British Museum continue to acquire antiquities from around the world. These included Neo-Assyrian reliefs from ancient palace sites in northern Iraq, Pharaonic artefacts from Egypt, and cultural objects from India, China, and Africa, particularly the Benin bronzes and carved ivories taken by British forces during the Punitive Expedition of 1897 from the Kingdom of Benin, located in modern Nigeria. The Louvre and the British Museum were not alone in acquiring cultural objects from around the world. For example, the Berlin Museums acquired the Ishtar Gate from Babylon, the Pergamon Altar from northwest Turkey, and the sculptural head of the Egyptian queen Nefertiti of the fourteenth century BCE from Egypt.

The appropriation of ancient artworks and other cultural objects from around the world in the course of military conquest, colonialism, and empire building became an essential ingredient of the encyclopedic museum. It was only possible to present the art and cultural remains of the entire world if the museum was free to take, without need for the consent of the owners or creators and by whatever means were deemed acceptable at a particular moment in history, the artworks that the museum felt were necessary to complete its presentation of all the world's cultures.[90] Perhaps pre-eminently the British, but also the French, Germans, Italians, Belgians, Dutch, and other colonial powers, leveraged their military and economic power to reinforce the status of their national museums as encyclopedic or universal museums. This laid the groundwork for the essential question to be addressed later: where should the cultural objects taken by means of the exercise of this power be located today?

2.4 Development of the Study of the Past as a Science

While the concept of the universal or encyclopedic museum was developing as part of the Enlightenment, study of the past as a scientific endeavour was entering its early phases. The origin of scientific study of the past may be traced to a move away from reliance on revealed or authoritative knowledge and towards an understanding of the world based on 'observation, classification, comparison, and where possible experimentation to achieve this goal'.[91] Among the many disciplines that study the past, archaeology, which incorporates several scientific and humanistic disciplines, is primarily based on the study of material cultural remains. Archaeology 'tries to explain what has happened to specific groups of human beings in the past', but, since archaeologists cannot directly observe the behaviour of

[90] For example, Shahid Vawda, 'Museums and the Epistemology of Injustice: From Colonialism to Decoloniality' (2019) 71 Museum International 72, 74.

[91] Trigger, *A History of Archaeological Thought* (n 62) 26.

the people they study, they 'must conjure human behavior and ideas from the material remains of what human beings have made and used and the lasting physical impact of their activities on the environment'.[92]

2.4.1 Early Exploration of the Past

People have long sought to explain their surroundings, which include remains of earlier cultures. In some cases in ancient Egypt and Mesopotamia, rulers and religious leaders sought to study both physical and textual remains of the past. In the Roman period, in particular, the wealthy collected earlier Greek art voraciously, as with the example of Verres in his plunder of Sicily. This interest in collecting led to attempts by some ancient authors, such as Pliny and Pausanias, to describe ancient Greek art and artists in a systematic way, but the study of the past through material culture lagged behind study of the past through texts.

During the medieval period in Europe, Roman ruins and burials were robbed to supply building materials or precious objects, which were sometimes interpreted as holy relics. Christian theology's views of creation and of human history heavily influenced the understanding of the past.[93] The Crusaders and Christian pilgrims who travelled to the Eastern Mediterranean were perhaps the earliest collectors of ancient relics. The greatest prize was to find relics from the early Christian period. These relics were imbued with religious and often supernatural characteristics and were greatly valued by European rulers as a way of bringing prestige and pilgrims to their cities. However, the relics were sometimes the product of fabricated stories,[94] while forgeries with Bible-related content have been common both in the past and present.[95]

Interest in the identification and study of Roman architecture developed during the Renaissance. Cyriacus of Ancona, an Italian merchant, travelled frequently to Greece and the Eastern Mediterranean in the fifteenth century and is often

[92] ibid, 28–29.

[93] ibid, 48–52.

[94] Lowenthal describes the pillaging of Milan's relics of the Three Magi and their removal to Cologne in 1162. However, the Archbishop of Cologne created the story of the theft 'to promote the power of the emperor and the glory of Cologne.... This fabrication ... became an exemplar of other sacred translations - fragments of bone and dust that were easy to take, easy to steal, easy to move, easy to reassign to new saints as needed. It begot great value from wishful fantasy.' David Lowenthal, *The Heritage Crusade and the Spoils of History* (CUP 1998) xvi–xvii. See also David Lowenthal, 'The Tangible Past in a Commemorative Age' in Neil Asher Silberman and Ernest S Frerichs (eds), *Archaeology and Society in the 21st Century: The Dead Sea Scrolls and Other Case Studies* (Old City Press 2001) 177, 183.

[95] See Christopher A Rollston, 'Forging History: From Antiquity to the Modern Period' in Matthew T Rutz and Morag M Kersel (eds), *Archaeologies of Text: Archaeology, Technology and Ethics* (Oxbow Books 2014) 176. For the hold of Biblical or purported Biblical artefacts, see Neil Brodie and Morag M Kersel, 'The Social and Political Consequences of Devotion to Biblical Artifacts' in Paula K Lazarus and Alex W Barker (eds), *All The King's Horses: Essays on the Impact of Looting and the Antiquities Trade on Our Knowledge of the Past* (SAA Press 2012) 109.

identified as the first European in the post-antique world who collected information concerning ancient monuments, inscriptions, and smaller objects.[96] Works of art discovered in Rome (both accidentally and intentionally) inspired Renaissance artists, such as Michelangelo. Many of these earliest studies of past remains focused on associating the remains with specific rulers based on descriptions in ancient written texts. However, during the sixteenth century, studies of antiquity shifted from a primary focus on written texts to incorporate study of the material cultural remains themselves,[97] thus laying the groundwork for the beginnings of archaeological study.

What seems to be the first modern attempt to legislate the protection of ancient remains was a statute issued by Pope Pius II in 1462. The Pope expressed concern both for the churches and other ecclesiastical structures of Rome and for the ancient remains of the city:

> Since we desire that our Mother city remain in its dignity and splendour, we need to show all vigilant care ... that the antique and early buildings and their relics remain for future generations, for these buildings are an ornament to our city and give it its greatest dignity while they preserve in monumental form the ancient virtues that perpetuate its glory.... [W]e follow certain of our predecessors, Pontiffs of the Romans, of happy memory, who expressly forbad the demolition or destruction of these buildings ... and thus, under pain of excommunication and of financial penalties ... we formally forbid all and singular, ecclesiastical as well as secular, ... to dare to demolish, destroy, reduce, break down or use as if a quarry ... any ancient public building or the remains of any public building above ground in the said City or its district, even if on private property in the countryside or in a town.[98]

Raphael was among the Renaissance artists who attempted to record and protect ancient buildings. Unfortunately, as a letter written by Raphael in 1519 to Pope Leo X demonstrates, Pope Pius II's directive did little to secure the protection of many of Rome's ancient monuments and buildings. In this letter, Raphael catalogued Roman architectural monuments that had been dismantled so that their marble could be reused or ground into lime. He wrote, in part:

96 Schnapp, *The Discovery of the Past* (n 70) 110.

97 ibid, 125–30. This shift from sole reliance on ancient writers to observation of ancient architecture and other works that were still visible in Rome is demonstrated by Antonio Agostino, the Archbishop of Tarragona, when he said: 'I have more faith in medals, tablets and stones than in anything set down by writers.' ibid, 128.

98 ibid, 339–40. Among the penalties for violating the statute was the confiscation of the animals, tools, and other goods of those involved in the demolition or destruction of the ancient buildings. The Pope's directive was echoed in an ordinance issued in 1548 to protect the ancient Roman remains of the city of Nimes in southern France, following a visit to the city in the early sixteenth century by the French king François I, who greatly admired the Latin inscriptions and other remains. Sax, 'Heritage Preservation as a Public Duty' (n 32) 1149.

> [H]ow many of these Pontiffs have allowed the ruin and dismembering of ancient temples, statues, arches and other buildings, the pride of their ancestors.... With not a little emotion I am reminded how, in the short time I have been in Rome, not yet twelve years, many beautiful things have been destroyed, such as ... the Temple of Ceres on the Via Sacra, part of the Forum Transitorium, which a few days ago was burned and destroyed, its marbles made into lime, most of the basilica of the forum ruined ... in addition so many columns broken and split in two, so many architraves and fine friezes shattered, that it has been the shame of our age to have permitted it, and of which it could genuinely be said that even Hannibal and others like him could not have done worse.[99]

However, as Sax points out, such efforts to protect ancient remains were the exception, not the rule, and many ancient remains were destroyed, either intentionally or through neglect.[100]

Sax suggests that Raphael's letter, which was published in 1733, may have had an influence on Grégoire's thinking, although there is no evidence that Grégoire saw Raphael's letter. Sax notes a remarkable similarity between the sentiments expressed in the letter and the reports that Grégoire produced. Raphael wrote: '[W]hy should we bewail the Goths, the Vandals, and other perfidious enemies of the Latin name, when those who above all others should be fathers and guardians in the defense of the poor relics of Rome, have even given themselves over to the study - long study - of how these might be destroyed and disappear.'[101] Sax posits that Grégoire's use of the term 'vandalism' to describe the Revolutionaries' destruction of France's material heritage, a word that Grégoire coined, may be based on Raphael's reference to Vandals in this passage.[102]

Most European interest in the ancient world remained focused on Italy throughout the eighteenth century. One of the earliest systematic excavations began in 1783 at the site of Herculaneum, a city that had been buried in the eruption of Vesuvius in 79 CE.[103] Excavations at both Herculaneum and Pompeii allowed the large-scale clearing and recording of complete ancient structures and refocused interest on architecture and city plans, rather than solely on inscriptions and sculpture. Exploration expanded beyond the Italian Peninsula when the Society of Dilettanti, founded in England in 1734, sponsored surveys of monuments in Greece beginning in 1751, while Julien-David LeRoy was one of the first modern architects to study the Parthenon.[104]

[99] Letter of 1519 from Raphael to Pope Leo X, on the need to protect the antiquities of Rome and to create a plan for the city. Schnapp, *The Discovery of the Past* (n 70) 340–41.

[100] Sax, 'Heritage Preservation as a Public Duty' (n 32) 1150–51.

[101] ibid, 1149.

[102] ibid, 1149, 1160–61.

[103] Schnapp, *The Discovery of the Past* (n 70) 242–47.

[104] Trigger, *A History of Archaeological Thought* (n 62) 60.

Figure 2.6 The Colossi of Memnon. Baron Dominique Vivant Denon, study for *Voyage dans la Basse et la Haute Égypte, pendant les campagnes du Général Bonaparte*, Paris 1802

Interest in the study of the past gradually spread beyond a focus on the classical world to ancient Egypt and Assyria in northern modern Iraq. Napoleon brought academics, architects, engineers, artists, and scientists to Egypt during his military campaign of 1798–1799.[105] This group of savants recorded and described many aspects of contemporary Egyptian life, its natural landscape, fauna and flora, and ancient monuments. Central to this project was the surveying and documenting of the temples, monuments, tombs, and artefacts of ancient Egypt. One of the leaders of the savants, the artist Dominique-Vivant Denon, whom Napoleon later named as the director of the Louvre, returned to Paris in 1799 and soon after published his illustrated memoir, *Voyages dans la basse et la haute Égypte* (*Travels in Lower and Upper Egypt*) (Figure 2.6).[106] Between 1809 and 1828, the work of the savants was published in *Description de l'Égypte*. Consisting of twenty-three volumes, five of which were devoted to Egypt's antiquities, and with over three thousand illustrations, this publication was an inspiration to European artists and scholars throughout the nineteenth century. Upon Napoleon's defeat in Egypt, the treaty between the British and the French required the French to turn over all of their discoveries to the British, including the Rosetta Stone, which had been found in the town of Rosetta (el-Rashid). The Rosetta Stone, dating to 196 BCE, contained a trilingual inscription, in ancient hieroglyphs, in Demotic, a later Egyptian script, and in Greek.[107] The French linguist Jean-François Champollion deciphered the Egyptian hieroglyphic text in 1822, thus opening the door to the reading of ancient Egyptian texts. Earlier attempts to decipher hieroglyphs by Arab scholars, such as

[105] Lisa Small, *Napoleon on the Nile: Soldiers, Artists, and the Rediscovery of Egypt* (Dahesh Museum of Art 2006) 15.
[106] ibid, 17–19.
[107] ibid, 19.

ibn Wahshiyya in the late ninth century, are not typically credited in studies of the ancient world.[108]

Study of the Eastern Mediterranean and Mesopotamia was heavily influenced by the desire to find sites mentioned in the Bible and to prove the historicity of the Biblical narrative. Sporadic excavation had been carried out at the sites of Babylon and Ur, first in 1616 by Pietro della Valle and again at Babylon in the late eighteenth century.[109] In northern Iraq, between 1843 and 1846, Paul Émile Botta conducted the first systematic excavations in Mesopotamia at the palace of the Assyrian king Sargon (722–705 BCE) at the site of Khorsabad. In 1845, Austen Henry Layard began his excavations of the palace of Assurnasirpal II, the king of Assyria from 884 to 859 BCE, at the site of Nimrud. In 1847, he discovered at Nineveh the palace of Sennacherib (Assyrian king from 704 to 681 BCE) with a rich library of cuneiform texts. In the early nineteenth century, British teams carried out sporadic excavations at Babylon in southern Iraq. Hormuzd Rassam, a native of Mosul and the first Indigenous Mesopotamian archaeologist, carried on Layard's work at Nineveh and Nimrud and then conducted large-scale excavations on behalf of the British Museum at Babylon between 1879 and 1882, where he discovered a large quantity of cuneiform texts.[110] The German archaeologist, Robert Koldewey, carried out excavations there beginning in 1898. He discovered primarily remains of the Neo-Babylonian Empire of Nebuchadnezzar (ruled *c* 605–562 BCE).

Missionaries, whose primary motivation was conversion of the local inhabitants to Christianity, also explored the ancient remains around them. During the nineteenth century, American and British explorers, often under the heavy influence of Protestantism, began to study, record, and unearth remains, particularly in Jerusalem, Jericho, and the Dead Sea area. Sometimes called the father of Biblical archaeology and geography, the American geographer Edward Robinson travelled in Palestine in 1837 and identified Biblical sites by relying on the Biblical text as well as searching for Biblical names underlying the contemporary Arabic place names.[111] Robinson was followed by numerous American Protestant scholars, including William Foxwell Albright, during the twentieth century. Despite his goal of linking the Bible and archaeology, Albright established the scientific basis for

108 Heba Abd El Gawad, '(Re)claiming the Rosetta: The Rosetta Stone and the (Re)writing of Egypt's Modern History' <https://100histories100worlds.org/reclaiming-the-rosetta/> accessed 18 August 2022.

109 Trigger, *A History of Archaeological Thought* (n 62) 70.

110 See Julian Reade, 'Hormuzd Rassam and His Discoveries' (1993) 55 Iraq 39. Reade points out that as the first native-born Mesopotamian archaeologist, Rassam does not receive the recognition that he deserves.

111 John Davis, *The Landscape of Belief: Encountering the Holy Land in Nineteenth Century American Art and Culture* (Princeton Univ Press 1996) 34–37; Jay Williams, 'The Times and Life of Edward Robinson' (*The Bible and Interpretation*, May 2003) <https://bibleinterp.arizona.edu/articles/robinson> accessed 10 May 2021. Williams characterizes this naming of Biblical sites as a political act that later provided the basis for Western involvement, particularly of the United States, the United Kingdom, and Germany, in the political affairs of the Eastern Mediterranean region.

archaeology of the Levant through his formulation of ceramic typologies from his excavations at Tell Beit Mirsim.[112]

2.4.2 Towards the Science of Archaeology

One of the central problems for those who studied the ancient world, particularly before the decipherment of ancient scripts, was how to establish a timeline of human origins and chronology without contemporary texts. Until the nineteenth century, the prevailing view was that the world was only about six thousand years old based on literal interpretations of the Biblical creation story and Biblical history.[113] This belief truncated understanding of the human past and limited the time into which all human cultural evolution had to be compressed. But Enlightenment views of cultural evolution and understandings of stratigraphy set the stage for the transformation of antiquarian interest in the past into the science of archaeology during the nineteenth and twentieth centuries.

Early in the nineteenth century, the Danish scholar Christian Jürgensen Thomsen developed an understanding of 'closed finds'—that is, discrete groups of artefacts that had been found together—and typologies based on the form and technology of objects (known as seriation) that could be extended to other material remains found in the same context.[114] In 1819, Thomsen organized an exhibit at the Danish National Museum based on a relative chronological sequence divided into the Stone Age, Bronze Age, and Iron Age, a basic scheme known as the 'three-age system' that is still used today as the basis of European, Mediterranean, and Mesopotamian chronologies.[115] The Danish archaeologist Jens JA Warsaae later translated Thomsen's principles into a methodology for conducting field excavation, using stratigraphy (ie the study of different layers or strata) of sites to prove Thomsen's sequence based on the three-age system.[116]

[112] Thomas Levy and David Noel Freedman, 'William Foxwell Albright, 1891–1971: A Biographical Memoir' (*The Bible and Interpretation*, February 2009) <https://bibleinterp.arizona.edu/articles/albright5> accessed 10 May 2021. Silberman distinguishes American excavations as the product of colleges and universities, typically with a missionizing purpose, from the large-scale expeditions funded by the European imperial powers. Neil Asher Silberman, 'Whose Game Is It Anyway? The Political and Social Transformations of American Biblical Archaeology' in Lynn Meskell (ed), *Archaeology Under Fire: Nationalism, Politics and Heritage in the Eastern Mediterranean and Middle East* (Routledge 1998) 175, 178–85. See also Neil A Silberman, *Digging for God and Country: Exploration, Archeology, and the Secret Struggle for the Holy Land, 1799–1917* (Random House 1982).

[113] Brian M Fagan, *In the Beginning: An Introduction to Archaeology* (12th edn, Pearson 2009) 29–30 (hereafter Fagan, *In the Beginning*).

[114] Trigger, *A History of Archaeological Thought* (n 62) 121–29.

[115] Fagan, *In the Beginning* (n 113) 32. The three-age system had precursors in France, England, and Denmark in mid-eighteenth-century theories that stone tools had been used and shaped by humans before bronze tools and that bronze tools preceded those made of iron. Trigger, *A History of Archaeological Thought* (n 62) 105.

[116] ibid, 131–36.

In the first half of the nineteenth century, large engineering projects, which cut deeply through the earth, revealed fossils with distinctive features that were typical of particular strata. Different locations had similar sequences based on the types of fossils in each stratum. The early geologists, James Hutton in 1784 and Charles Lyell in 1833, independently proposed the theory of uniformitarianism—that the earth had been formed gradually over very long periods of time by natural processes that are still continuing, rather than through unique cataclysmic events. This gradual process contradicted the Biblical account of creation, extended by many millennia the length of human history, and laid the groundwork for Charles Darwin's theory of evolution.[117]

Scientific excavation techniques developed primarily at sites in southern England and France where archaeologists who excavated Paleolithic remains were heavily influenced by geologic and paleontological studies. The discovery of material cultural remains in association with bones of extinct animals and in geologically identified strata indicated the antiquity of human origins. This provided evidence of the longevity of human existence and contradicted the literal account of creation in the Bible. This further emphasized the central role of stratigraphic exploration, based on careful recording of finds in closed contexts so that the original placement of associated finds could be reconstructed, as key to understanding human cultural evolution. The work of the French geologist Jacques Boucher de Perthes, who found Paleolithic stone tools at the site of Abbeville in the Somme Valley of northern France during his excavations carried out between 1837 and 1860, furthered this methodology. A visit to Abbeville by two British scientists, John Evans and Joseph Prestwich, in 1859 convinced them of the antiquity of human origins—'an established antiquity that is one of the intellectual and practical foundations of all scientific archaeology'.[118]

However, many excavators of the nineteenth century failed to use this stratigraphic methodology and were no different from treasure hunters. The German archaeologist Heinrich Schliemann, who was as dedicated to identifying the locations mentioned in Homer's Iliad and Odyssey as the American and British missionaries were to identifying sites mentioned in the Bible, excavated at Troy and Mycenae in the 1870s and was known for using bulldozers on his sites. The scientific basis for archaeological field work was established in England, France, and Scandinavia concurrently with the more spectacular finds in the Mediterranean region, and it was these former, less spectacular developments that ultimately led to the adoption of more controlled methods of excavation based on the science of stratigraphy.

General Augustus Henry Lane Fox Pitt-Rivers excavated on his estates in England in the 1880s and 1890s and amassed a large collection of archaeological

[117] Fagan, *In the Beginning* (n 113) 30–31.
[118] ibid, 31.

and ethnographic artefacts from around the world. He arranged these finds, under the influence of the evolutionary principles of Charles Darwin, in an order to demonstrate human progress from the simple to the complex. The British archaeologist and Egyptologist William Flinders Petrie brought scientific methodology, based on careful measurements of ancient structures, to the excavations he carried out in Egypt over several decades beginning in 1880. In 1890, he conducted his first excavation in Palestine at the site of Tell el-Hesi in the Negev desert, which is considered to be the first scientific excavation based on stratigraphic methodology of a site in the 'Holy Land'.[119] He also developed a typology of Egyptian finds based on a system of seriation similar to that used by the Danish archaeologist Thomsen. This typology provided the basis for creating a relative chronology to date finds throughout the Eastern Mediterranean.

2.4.3 Archaeology and Imperialism

As archaeology developed, along with the related field of anthropology, several elements engaged in theories based on beliefs of racial or ethnic inferiority. These disciplines included a nearly consistent effort to divorce ancient remains from the contemporary people who were often descendants of the people who created the remains.[120] These beliefs and their influence on the study of the past underlie many attitudes, even contemporary ones, as to where cultural objects should be located and whether they should be returned to their place of origin. Silberman describes Petrie as attributing some of his conclusions concerning the material remains that he had excavated in the Negev and southern Levant to his belief in racial superiority based on eugenics.[121] Archaeologists of North America in the nineteenth century held to the belief in the fundamental inferiority of the contemporary Native Americans. Archaeologists therefore posited that the impressive earthworks and archaeological remains were those of a European-derived culture and divorced these ancient remains from the living Native American communities.[122] This artificial discontinuity between ancient remains and modern inhabitants has been ingrained in the legal treatment of Native American archaeological remains as divorced from the modern Native Americans in the Native American Graves Protection and Repatriation Act,[123] and, in particular, the interpretation given

[119] Neil Asher Silberman, 'Petrie's Head: Eugenics and Near Eastern Archaeology' in Alice B Kehoe and Mary Beth Emmerichs (eds), *Assembling the Past: Studies in the Professionalization of Archaeology* (University of New Mexico Press 1999) 69, 69 (hereafter Silberman, 'Petrie's Head').

[120] See n 75 above.

[121] Silberman, 'Petrie's Head' (n 119) 70–77.

[122] Trigger, *A History of Archaeological Thought* (n 62) 158–63; Margarita Díaz-Andreu, 'Archaeology and Imperialism: From Nineteenth-Century New Imperialism to Twentieth-Century Decolonization' in Bonnie Effros and Guolong Lai (eds), *Unmasking Ideologies: The Vocabulary and Symbols of Colonial Archaeology* (Cotsen Institute 2018) 3, 14 (hereafter Díaz-Andreu, 'Archaeology and Imperialism').

[123] 25 USC §§ 3001–3013.

to the statutory definition of 'Native American' in *Bonnichsen v United States*.[124] As Darwinian evolutionary theory, particularly natural selection, melded with archaeology to form nineteenth-century evolutionary archaeology, differences in cultural development were seen to justify imposing the European class system, gender and racial discrimination, and colonialism on the Indigenous population of North America.[125]

Craniometry—that is, the measurement of skulls to determine racial differences in brain size and intelligence—was a part of scientific racism, utilized in the nineteenth century to justify White superiority[126] and particularly the institution of slavery in the United States.[127] The use of skull size and shape to posit differences in intelligence began in the eighteenth century with the practice of phrenology but was not originally associated with distinctions based on race. However, with the rise of polygenism (the belief that not all human races shared a common ancestry), racial difference became viewed as static and immutable.[128] The American naturalist Samuel George Morton produced an extensive study of skulls and concluded that cranial sizes were attributable to racial differences and indicated immutable distinctions in intelligence and ability.[129] Morton posited that Native Americans were two distinct families and that the superior one, to which he attributed the construction of significant archaeological remains, had 'withdrawn' from North America.[130] In his study of skulls sent to him from Egypt, Morton concluded that ancient and modern Egyptians consisted of two races—a Caucasian race to which belonged the 'kings' of ancient Egypt, and 'Negroes' who held the social position of 'servants and slaves'.[131]

Although Morton's studies and the belief in polygenism have been discredited,[132] the work of Morton and other craniologists left a legacy of human

[124] 357 F3d 962 (9th Cir 2004).

[125] Trigger, *A History of Archaeological Thought* (n 62) 167–74.

[126] Policy on the Management of Human Remains in IZIKO Collections, 18 Jeremy Silvester, Museums Association of Namibia, Report on the Human Remains Management and Repatriation Workshop (13–14 February 2017) 3. In Namibia, it is often believed that 'collection of the mortal remains of the dead was linked to the decapitation of leaders' of resistance against German colonialism. ibid.

[127] Paul Wolff Mitchell and John S Michael, 'Bias, Brains, and Skulls: Tracing the Legacy of Scientific Racism in the Nineteenth-Century Works of Samuel George Morton and Friedrich Tiedemann' in Jamie A Thomas and Christina Jackson (eds), *Embodied Difference: Divergent Bodies in Public Discourse* (Rowman & Littlefield 2019) 77, 78–79 (hereafter Mitchell and Michael, 'Bias, Brains, and Skulls').

[128] ibid, 81.

[129] Jack F Trope, 'The Case for NAGPRA' in Sangita Chari and Jaime MN Lavallee (eds), *Accomplishing NAGPRA: Perspectives on the Intent, Impact, and Future of the Native Graves Protection and Repatriation Act* (Oregon State Univ Press 2013) 19, 21–22 (hereafter Trope, 'The Case for NAGPRA').

[130] Penn Museum, 'Biography' <www.penn.museum/sites/morton/life.php> accessed 10 May 2021.

[131] ibid (quoting Morton, *Crania Aegyptiaca or, Observations on Egyptian Ethnography, Derived from Anatomy, History and the Monuments* 65–66).

[132] Morton's work was attacked on grounds of poor methodology, even during the nineteenth century. ibid. The paleontologist Stephen J Gould attacked Morton's measurements as being the result of unconscious bias, but Mitchell and Michael attribute Morton's findings to conscious bias. Mitchell and Michael, 'Bias, Brains, and Skulls' (n 127) 80. In contrast to the work of Morton, and despite arguably similar resulting measurements, the German anatomist and physiologist Friedrich Tiedemann

remains, particularly crania, stored in museums in Europe and the United States. Morton collected skulls of Native Americans and enslaved Africans,[133] while approximately 200,000 Native American individuals were represented among the human remains held in US museums and federal agencies.[134] Their presence in US institutions is in part the result of the US Surgeon General's Order of 1867 adopting a policy directing army personnel to collect crania and other body parts of Native Americans for the Army Medical Museum for the purpose of aiding anthropological science. These remains, along with burial artefacts, were often stripped from burials located near the descendants' villages; other times, remains were taken directly from Native Americans who were killed in battle. The results of these studies were used to justify the settlement of North America by European colonists and the repeated removal of Native Americans from their homelands throughout the nineteenth century.[135] These activities constituted a massive violation of the basic human and civil rights of Native Americans, including the rights of respect for the dead and to practice religion.

As with the universal or encyclopedic museum, the practice of archaeology often depended on the extensive geographic reach of the umbrellas of imperialism and colonialism. During the course of the nineteenth century, archaeology evolved under the impetus of nationalism and imperialism and became intertwined with them. Whether the European country exercised its authority through direct colonialism, the new imperialism, or the broader reach of economic and political power, this authority facilitated the work of European (and later American) archaeologists who wished to excavate in other countries and bring home the results of their excavations. The development of archaeology as an accepted discipline resulted from the role that the study of the past, particularly the classical past of Greece and Rome, could play in bolstering the creation of a national history, proving the existence of the nation, and legitimizing the nation's character.[136] In regions such as North Africa, where Roman remains were located, archaeology of the Classical period was given priority and those areas were considered more advanced. Parts of the world that were not linked to the Classical past, particularly if textual material did not survive, were considered inferior.[137]

conducted studies of a relatively large sample of skulls and found that there was no significant difference in cranial size between Europeans and Africans. ibid, 82.

[133] Mitchell and Michael, 'Bias, Brains, and Skulls' (n 127) 87–89. The University of Pennsylvania Museum of Anthropology and Archaeology holds the Morton Cranial Collection which includes more than 1300 crania. The museum has expressed its intention to repatriate or rebury these human remains. Penn Museum, 'Morton Cranial Collection' <www.penn.museum/sites/morton/> accessed 10 May 2021.

[134] Michael F Brown and Margaret M Bruchac, 'NAGPRA from the Middle Distance' in John Henry Merryman (ed), *Imperialism, Art and Restitution* (CUP 2006) 193, 196

[135] Trope, 'The Case for NAGPRA' (n 129) 22–23.

[136] Díaz-Andreu, 'Archaeology and Imperialism' (n 122) 8.

[137] ibid, 13–14.

The imperial powers fostered the archaeological research of their nationals in the areas subject to their authority, so the research in a particular colonized area was often restricted to nationals of a particular European country.[138] The imperial powers also established institutions in their areas of research, initially in the Mediterranean rim countries and then further afield, particularly in Asia,[139] while the contributions of local populations to the study of archaeology were minimized or excluded. As previously mentioned, the Iraqi archaeologist Hormuzd Rassam does not receive adequate recognition commensurate with his accomplishments and comparable to that given to the European archaeologists who excavated Mesopotamian sites.[140] In Egypt, the French founder and director of the Department of Antiquities, Auguste Mariette (1821–1881), was so concerned that Indigenous Egyptians would wish to study hieroglyphic inscriptions in the museum that he forbade any Egyptians from working in the museum.[141] Even as countries of the Eastern Mediterranean developed departments of antiquities, these were often overseen by Europeans. The French Egyptologist Gaston Maspero (1846–1916) succeeded Mariette as the head of Egypt's Department of Antiquities and was therefore responsible for implementing the system of partage, whereby the discoveries made during an excavation were to be divided between the nation and the foreign excavation team, at the time of the discovery of the sculptural head of Nefertiti in 1912.[142] Similarly, following the First World War and creation of the French and British Mandates in Iraq, Palestine, and Syria, the Department of Antiquities for Palestine and Iraq was under the direction of British archaeologists, such as John Garstang who was the Director of Antiquities for the British Mandate of Palestine between 1920 and 1926.

2.5 Conclusion

From the mid-eighteenth century through the nineteenth century, three strands or dynamics emerged that form the historical bases for resolving the contemporary

[138] ibid, 11.

[139] ibid, 9–10. For discussion of the relationship between archaeology and US foreign policy and cultural diplomacy, particularly the role of the overseas research centres, beginning in the nineteenth century but continuing today, see Christina Luke and Morag M Kersel, *U.S. Cultural Diplomacy and Archaeology* (Routledge 2013).

[140] See n 110 above.

[141] Statement by the German scholar Heinrich Brugsch, quoted in Díaz-Andreu, 'Archaeology and Imperialism' (n 122) 11. Some Indigenous archaeologists took key roles and received recognition, such as the head of the Archaeological Museum in Constantinople, Osman Hamdi Bey (1842–1910), who drafted the Ottoman legislation and promoted scientific excavations and archaeological publications. ibid, 12.

[142] Kurt Siehr, 'The Beautiful One Has Come to Return' in John Henry Merryman (ed), *Imperialism, Art and Restitution* (CUP 2006) 114, 11–18. The system of partage is discussed in more detail in chapter 4.

question of where cultural objects should be located. The Napoleonic Wars, the thefts of artworks and other cultural objects from much of Europe, and the forced return of these objects set the basic legal principle that cultural objects should not be removed during armed conflict. If they were removed, they should be returned to the place from which they had been taken during the last conflict. However, this principle applied only among the recognized European States. The development at the same time of universal or encyclopedic museums served a democratizing function. The contradiction between a national museum with the goal of presenting the history of a particular State to its public and the encyclopedic museum whose mission was to collect from around the world became an accepted cultural element. The stated altruistic purpose of museums in displaying and studying cultural objects collected from around the world becomes an expression of universalism and a reason for not returning objects from where they were taken, regardless of the means by which they were taken. The third strand was the development of archaeology as a science, which eventually established the value of principled excavation methodology and techniques. However, archaeology, like the encyclopedic museum, reinforced concepts of nationalism and the perceived superiority of the European countries. Further, like the encyclopedic museum, the practice of archaeology was enabled by the ability of the imperial powers to authorize excavation and collecting from the regions over which they had authority, while the Indigenous people were largely excluded from that process of discovery and knowledge creation. These phenomena laid the groundwork for the large-scale expropriations of cultural objects from their places of origin and movement to Europe and North America over the course of the nineteenth century. This historical review of the three strands that continue to animate questions of where cultural objects should be located establishes a basic understanding of the origins of these questions and sets the stage for further consideration and possible resolution of these questions in subsequent chapters.

3
Historical Appropriations/ Historical Claims

3.1 Introduction

This chapter examines three episodes of cultural heritage expropriation over the course of the nineteenth century: the Parthenon Sculptures at the beginning of the century; the Yuanmingyuan objects from China in mid-century; and the Benin bronzes, ivories, and other artefacts taken at the end of the century. While many examples could be used to illustrate these points, these three are not only symbols of past expropriation but continue today at the vortex of the debate as to the proper location of cultural objects. The rationales for these expropriations tie into the themes discussed in the previous chapter, including the role of the universal museum, the presumed inferiority of the present inhabitants of non-European regions, and the right of conquerors to extract and retain looted cultural objects.

The end of the Napoleonic Wars established the precedent that cultural objects removed during conflict should be returned at the end of hostilities to the place from which they had been taken. However, according to the Western international legal system as it developed during the nineteenth century and coinciding with the new imperialism, only the European and settler States were included in the international community. As Vrodoljak quotes John Westlake, writing in 1894:

> [It is] the members of the international society which concern us, that of uncivilised natives international law takes no account. This is true, and it does not mean that all rights are denied to such natives, but that appreciation of their rights is left to the conscience of the state within whose recognized territorial sovereignty they are comprised.[1]

Colonized peoples lost any right to sovereignty, and, without sovereignty, they had no rights under international law but rather were subsumed within the territory of the colonial power.

[1] Ana Filipa Vrdoljak, *International Law, Museums and the Return of Cultural Objects* (CUP 2008) 49 (hereafter Vrdoljak, *International Law*).

Cultural Objects and Reparative Justice. Patty Gerstenblith, Oxford University Press. © Patty Gerstenblith 2023.
DOI: 10.1093/oso/9780192872104.003.0003

This approach drew on Darwinian evolution to posit that nations developed from uncivilized to civilized and only those nations that had been accepted into the society of nations had rights under international law.

> [T]he escalating economic and industrial might of European and settler States combined with their colonial ambitions meant that European international law was increasingly applied on a global scale to the gradual exclusion of any other systems of international law. Positivists rationalized this existing plurality not by applying a universal natural law, but with the explicit imposition of European international law over 'uncivilised' non-Europeans.[2]

International law thus evolved to protect the territorial aggrandizement and economic interests of the colonizing powers, while ignoring the needs and rights of the colonized people. The Berlin Conference of 1884–1885 aimed to reduce competition for natural resources and trading rights among the European colonial powers by dividing West Africa into spheres of influence.[3] It reiterated the principle of trusteeship that the European colonial powers owed some protections to the colonized people.[4] However, there would effectively be no regulation of these obligations as this would constitute an interference with sovereignty, and the obligations were viewed as moral, rather than legal. This discrepancy in international law laid the basis for the mass expropriation of cultural objects from outside of Europe and their movement to the centres of the colonizing States,[5] as this movement was viewed as internal within their own territories.[6] This double standard in international law is perpetuated today through non-retroactivity of present norms, and it still forms a fundamental obstacle to efforts at restitution of cultural objects removed during the nineteenth century.

While the European powers perpetrated colonialism and armed aggression in many parts of the world before and after the nineteenth century, the span of the nineteenth century provides paradigmatic examples of cultural heritage expropriation with which we still wrestle today. These expropriations were justified

[2] ibid, 50.

[3] ibid, 52–53.

[4] ibid. The obligations owed were to improve the 'moral and material conditions' of the Indigenous peoples and to guarantee free trade principles and equal access for the colonial powers to scientific expeditions within the territory. ibid, 53. For the influence of the colonial methods of acquiring cultural artefacts from colonized peoples on their display in European museums and on Western understanding of these objects, see ibid, 53–63.

[5] ibid, 46–67.

[6] While not a European State, the Ottoman Empire adopted similar legal principles. Artefacts were removed from throughout the Ottoman Empire and taken to Istanbul, including, for example, the Alexander Sarcophagus taken from the Sidon region, which today is part of Lebanon. A significant goal was the establishment of a museum in Istanbul to rival the Louvre. Michael Greenhalgh, *Plundered Empire: Acquiring Antiquities from Ottoman Lands* (Brill 2019) 331–32 (hereafter Greenhalgh, *Plundered Empire*). These objects were viewed as being moved from one part of Ottoman territory to another and thus constituted internal, rather than international, movement.

by the presumed superiority of European culture and civilization, promoted the rescue narrative that it was necessary for European powers to remove cultural objects to safeguard them, and promoted the formation of universal or encyclopedic museums in what were perceived to be the new centres of civilization in Western Europe.

3.2 The Parthenon Sculptures

The Parthenon and its Sculptures are central to the formation of Western ideas of philosophy, human progress, and artistic ideals, playing a critical role in the development of both Western identity and modern Greek national identity. These sculptures were executed in the mid-fifth century BCE at the pinnacle of the political and military power as well as artistic and cultural achievements of ancient Athens. The sculptures removed by Lord Elgin from the Acropolis have been in the British Museum for more than two hundred years, and Greece has demanded their restitution for almost as long. As such, the Sculptures are at the centre of the debate concerning cultural appropriation and historical restitution as symbols, depending on one's perspective, either of cultural heritage dispossession or of the rescue of cultural heritage. Even the name by which these Sculptures are known is a component of the debate, and one's position is often signalled by the name employed. As Timothy Webb has commented:

> Naming is rarely a neutral activity since it so often involves the imposition of identity or the staking of claims toward wider recognition and even fame by association. The history of these remains from the Acropolis is a frequent reminder that collectors sometimes achieved 'immortality' by enclosing their collections within the defining bounds of their own identities.[7]

The Sculptures have had three lives: their execution and original placement in ancient Athens; their removal to London and their impact on particularly British but also European and North American cultural development; and finally, their central place in the continuing debate of cultural heritage dispossession and restitution.

[7] Timothy Webb, 'Appropriating the Stones: The "Elgin Marbles" and English National Taste' in Elazar Barkan and Ronald Bush (eds), *Claiming the Stones, Naming the Bones: Cultural Property and the Negotiation of National and Ethnic Identity* (Getty Research Institute 2002) 51, 52–53 (hereafter Webb, 'Appropriating the Stones'). The lengthy treatment of the Parthenon Sculptures here is not intended to be an expression of 'Parthenon exceptionalism', an approach that is rightly criticised by Elizabeth Marlowe, 'From Exceptionalism to Solidarity: The Rhetoric of the Case for the Parthenon Sculptures' Return' (2022) 41 CAELJ 125, 129-50. Rather, this treatment is a reflection that more has been written about the manner of the Sculptures' acquisition and legality of their retention than possibly about any other removed work of art or cultural object.

3.2.1 The Sculptures in Antiquity

In the fifth century BCE, the victories of the Greek city-states, led by Athens, over the Persian rulers Darius and Xerxes were viewed as the triumph of a free, democratic West against what the Greeks viewed as a tyrannical and barbarian East.[8] In Athens, at this time, architecture, sculpture, vase painting, dramatic and historical literature, and the philosophy of Socrates flourished simultaneously. Balancing these cultural achievements in the modern Western mind is the view that fifth-century Athens is the source of Western-style democracy. That Athens did not in reality live up to its portrayal as a democracy, since only a small number of males had the rights of citizenship, has not detracted from Western reverence for this myth.

In the time of peace and prosperity for Athens after the victories over the Persians at Marathon (490 BCE), Salamis (480 BCE), and Plataea (479 BCE), Pericles ordered the rebuilding of the Acropolis, whose earlier structures the Persians had burned in 479 BCE.[9] Pericles planned an entire complex of new structures, including: the Parthenon; the Erechtheion temple, dedicated to the founder of Athens, Erechtheus; a smaller temple dedicated to Athena Nike, the goddess of victory; and a magnificent entrance, the Propylaea. The Parthenon temple was constructed between 447 and 432 BCE to honour Athens' patron deity, Athena, the warrior and goddess of wisdom. Placed near the summit of the Acropolis, the Parthenon temple was, and still is, the crown jewel of Athens. The Parthenon 'stands isolated against the Attic hills and sky, a transfixing point of reference ... Its order and power compel Athens to surround it: it takes dominion over citadel and city.'[10] The Parthenon was tightly tied not only to the setting of the Acropolis, but to the further landscape of mountains and valleys as well. Endlessly reproduced in modern times first in drawings, then photographs and posters, the Parthenon is the iconic Western representation of artistic excellence and classical purity.

The temple and its Sculptures were constructed entirely of marble. The temple was unique among ancient Greek structures. Its large size and the extensiveness of its sculptural programme guaranteed the Parthenon's preeminent place in architectural history. The greatest of the classical Greek sculptors, Pheidias, designed and directed the execution of the Parthenon's sculptural programme. Inside the

[8] In contrast to the Greek view, Hebrew sources depicted the Persians and particularly Cyrus the Great (*c* 600–530 BCE) positively, as the liberator of the Jews from Babylonian exile. Cyrus was even said to have permitted the Hebrew exiles to take many of the sacred vessels that the Babylonians had plundered from their conquest of the First Temple in 586 BCE back with them to Jerusalem. Margaret M Miles, *Art as Plunder: The Ancient Origins of Debate about Cultural Property* (CUP 2008) 18–19 (hereafter Miles, *Art as Plunder*); Amnon Netzer 'Some Notes on the Characterization of Cyrus the Great in Jewish and Judeo-Persian Writings' (1974) 2 Acta Iranica 35.

[9] Miles, *Art as Plunder* (n 8) 24–30.

[10] Jeffrey M Hurwit, 'Space and Theme: The Setting of the Parthenon' in Jenifer Neils (ed), *The Parthenon from Antiquity to the Present* (CUP 2005) 9, 9.

temple was the crowning achievement of the Parthenon's sculptures—a chryselephantine statue of the goddess, Athena Parthenos, likely executed by Pheidias himself. Nothing of the monumental statue remains today, although depictions on ancient coinage and miniature replicas give us an idea of its appearance. The base of the statue depicted the myth of the creation of the first woman, Pandora.

The outer colonnade was adorned with ninety-two metopes, placed in the spaces between the upper columns. The metopes, of which only about twenty survive today, depicted the sacking of Troy on the north side of the temple, the Amazonomachy on the west side, the battle between the gods and the giants in the east metopes, and the battle between Centaurs and Lapiths, as well as the tale of Erechthonios, on the south. The figures on the east metopes were hacked off the surface in the Christian period, leaving only the places where the figures were attached to the background,[11] while the central sections of the north and south metopes were destroyed in the explosion of 1687. Many of the mythic battle scenes were likely allegorical retellings of the Athenians' recent victory over the Persians, who were represented by the giants, the Amazons, and the Centaurs.

The pediments contained more than forty statues and depicted themes of the Olympian deities. The scenes depicted are difficult to interpret due to their fragmentary nature. The east pediment related the birth of Athena, fully armed, from the head of Zeus.[12] The west pediment related Athena's victory in her contest with Poseidon to become the patron goddess of Athens. Athena offered the city an olive tree, while Poseidon offered a well of salt water. Almost nothing remains of the west pediment sculptures, and reconstructions are based on the Carrey drawings done in 1674.

Around the upper outer walls of the *cella* (the inner temple) was a continuous Ionic frieze that depicts a procession that begins at the west end, divides to march down the north and south sides, and culminates at the east end with a ceremony. Although the frieze is almost entirely preserved today, the scene depicted is the least certain because the ancient writers who described the Parthenon seem to have ignored the frieze. The earliest Western traveller in the post-ancient world to describe the Parthenon and its sculptural programme, Cyriacus of Ancona, visited Athens in 1436 and 1444. He interpreted the frieze as a representation of 'the victories of Athens in the time of Pericles'.[13] Stuart and Revett in the mid-eighteenth century identified the scene as the Panathenaic procession, which is still accepted as the traditional interpretation.[14]

[11] Katherine A Schwab, 'The Parthenon East Metopes, the Gigantomachy, and Digital Technology' in Michael B Cosmopoulos (ed), *The Parthenon and its Sculptures* (CUP 2004) 150, 150–56.

[12] Georgios Mostratos, 'A Reconstruction of the Parthenon's East Pediment' in Michael B Cosmopoulos (ed), *The Parthenon and its Sculptures* (CUP 2004) 114, 114–20.

[13] Jenifer Neils, *The Parthenon Frieze* (CUP 2001) 2.

[14] Jenifer Neils, 'Classic Moments: Time in the Parthenon Frieze' in Michael B Cosmopoulos (ed), *The Parthenon and Its Sculptures* (CUP 2004) 43, 57–60. The Panathenaic procession was a quadrennial ceremony in which a new gown, called a *peplos*, which was woven by the girls and women of Athens,

The Parthenon building remained dedicated to Athena throughout the Hellenistic and Roman periods. Ancient writers, including the Roman author on architecture Vitruvius (*c* 80–70 BCE— *c* 15 BCE), the Greek biographer Plutarch (45–120 CE), and the Greek traveller and geographer Pausanias (*c* 110–180 CE), described it and its sculptures. Hellenistic rulers, including Alexander the Great and members of the Attalid and Seleucid dynasties, visited Athens, sent votive offerings to mark their victories, and provided funds for building and ornamentation projects.[15] The Roman commander Sulla plundered the city in 86 BCE.[16] In addition to buying Greek art, the Romans were responsible for executing myriad copies, which, in the early Renaissance, became the first sources of Western European knowledge of ancient Greek art.

The Parthenon was spared from intentional damage through the Gothic invasion of the late fourth century CE but suffered from a catastrophic fire in the third century CE, after which the interior was extensively repaired and remodelled.[17] With the coming of Christianity, the temple was rededicated as a church, perhaps as early as the fifth century. During this remodelling, the central sculptures of the east pediment were destroyed, the east metopes severely damaged, and some of the frieze figures disfigured..[18]

Athens was part of the Byzantine Empire until it came under the control of Venice in 1204 during the Fourth Crusade. The Parthenon was then converted into a Roman Catholic church and renamed Notre Dame. This is probably the point at which the central slabs of the east section of the frieze were removed and set on the ground nearby. Athens remained under the rule of various Italian city-states until the middle of the fifteenth century. Under Ottoman rule, which held sway over Greek territory from 1456 until the founding of the modern Greek nation in 1832, the Parthenon was changed into a mosque and a minaret was added.

The Parthenon was still largely intact when the French artist Jacques Carrey, at the behest of the French ambassador to the Ottoman Empire, sketched the sculptures in 1674. Several travellers, including the Turkish Evliya Chelebi (1667), the English Francis Vernon (1675), and the Frenchmen Jacob Spon (1675), Jean Baptiste Tavernier (1679), and Gravier d'Ortièr (1687), also drew or described

was presented to the statue of Athena Polias. Noel Robertson, 'Pandora and the Panathenaic Peplos' in Michael B Cosmopoulus (ed), *The Parthenon and its Sculptures* (CUP 2004) 86, 96.

15 Alexander the Great reportedly sent back to Athens the sculptures of the *Tyrannicides*, two Greeks who assassinated a member of the autocratic Peisistratid family, thereby paving the way for Athenian democracy. Xerxes took the sculptures from Athens to his capital, Susa, in Persia, and Alexander returned them after his conquest of Persia. Miles, *Art as Plunder* (n 8) 26–27.

16 ibid 24.

17 Williams St Clair and Robert Picken, 'The Parthenon in 1687: New Sources', in Michael Cosmopoulos (ed), *The Parthenon and its Sculptures* (CUP 2004) 166, 168 (hereafter St Clair and Picken, 'The Parthenon in 1687').

18 William St Clair, *Lord Elgin & The Marbles: The Controversial History of the Parthenon Sculptures* (3rd rev edn, OUP 1998) 59–60 (hereafter St Clair, *Lord Elgin & The Marbles*).

the Parthenon during the seventeenth century.[19] In various battles between the Venetians and Ottomans in Athens, first the Propylaea and later the Temple of Athena Nike were destroyed. In 1687 the Venetians, under the command of Francesco Morosini, lobbed shells at the Parthenon, one of which entered through the roof exploding the gunpowder stored there by the Ottomans. The explosion destroyed the entire central part of the building, and the nearby Erechtheion was badly damaged. The Ottomans stored explosives in the Parthenon, perhaps thinking that the Venetians would not attack the building. About three hundred local residents took shelter there, also thinking that they would be protected. The fact that these lives were lost in the attack is not often mentioned when the damage to the building is discussed.[20]

In addition to this catastrophe, the Venetians began the process of dismembering the remaining sculptures. When the central sculptures of the west pediment were being lowered, the cables broke, and the sculptures were destroyed. The Venetians, nonetheless, still managed to take home several sculptural heads as trophies.[21] In the fifty years following the explosion, the building seems to have been left largely as it was, as evidenced by a dearth of travellers' accounts and descriptions. However, a description written around 1699 may indicate that traces of the ancient polychromy that decorated the sculptures were still visible.[22] By 1739, when Lord Sandwich and Richard Pococke visited it, the building had been cleared of rubble, and the minaret removed, but the Turks did not damage the standing portions of the structure. The building remained largely in this condition until the late eighteenth century.

3.2.2 The Sculptures in the Eighteenth and Nineteenth Centuries

In the mid-eighteenth and nineteenth centuries, the Parthenon entered its second phase—that of artistic inspiration and the source of sculptural fragments for European aristocrats. Until this time, European knowledge and first-hand experience with antiquity had come from Roman architecture and sculptures, which

[19] St Clair and Picken, 'The Parthenon in 1687' (n 17) 166–68, 170–71.

[20] Daniel Mendelsohn, 'Deep Frieze: What does the Parthenon mean?' (*The New Yorker*, 7 April 2014) <https://newyorker.com/magazine/2014/04/14/deep-frieze> accessed 24 May 2021. Bouras commented that the people who, pressed by the needs of the Turkish-Venetian war, gave the Parthenon the additional use of a gunpowder magazine were clearly incapable of seeing in the monument anything beyond its value as a building which could withstand artillery fire. That brought about the disaster of 1687, after which everything changed. The Parthenon ceased to be a mosque and lost its sanctity as an entity, thus opening the way for looting and further depredation.

Charalambos Bouras, 'Restoration Work on the Parthenon and Changing Attitudes toward the Conservation of Monuments' in Panayotis Tournikiotis (ed), *The Parthenon and Its Impact in Modern Times* (Melissa Publishing House 1994) 310, 318 (hereafter Bouras, 'Restoration Work').

[21] St Clair, *Lord Elgin & The Marbles* (n 18) 60–62.

[22] St Clair and Picken, 'The Parthenon in 1687' (n 17) 174.

were often late Hellenistic works or copies of classical Greek sculptures. This reliance on Rome for classical inspiration began to change in the mid-eighteenth century. The publication of the studies of Julien-David Le Roy, *Les Ruines des plus beaux Monuments de la Grèce*, in 1758 and the second volume of *The Antiquities of Athens* with drawings of the Parthenon by James Stuart and Nicholas Revett in 1787 dramatically increased the knowledge and popularity of the Parthenon sculptures in Europe.[23] These publications provided the first detailed, scientific studies of the Parthenon and documented the state of the Parthenon Sculptures in the mid-eighteenth century along with their rapid deterioration by the end of the eighteenth century.

Exposure to original works of Greek art produced a significant shift in European understanding of the arts and their role in intellectual history, followed by debates as to whether Roman or Greek art was superior. Perhaps the most authoritative voice in this debate was the German art historian Johann Joachim Winkelmann, who advocated for ancient Greek superiority over notions of *romanità* espoused by the Italian engraver G B Piranesi and others. Winckelmann explained the superiority of Greek culture and particularly that of Athens 'because after the expulsion of the tyrants, a democratic form of government was adopted, in which the entire people had a share'.[24] Winckelmann believed that the best of Greek art was 'the embodiment of ideal beauty' and that contemporary artists should try to emulate it, a belief related to the growth of Neo-Classicism. While rationalist philosophy saw progress in human development and admired the perfection of classical art, a contrasting romanticism dwelled in nostalgia for the lost time and place of antiquity. The Romantic English poets, especially Keats, Byron, and Shelley, dwelled on the ancient glories of Greece and sympathized with the desire for Greek independence.

The custom of European aristocrats, particularly British, to take the grand tour of the continent, first to Italy and later to Greece and the Eastern Mediterranean, exposed them to ancient civilizations as part of their education and helped them to develop a taste for classical literature, architecture, and fine arts. However, the European practice of removing sculptural fragments both as mementos of their trips and to display their cultured taste at home posed a serious threat to the integrity of ancient monuments, while many fragments became dispersed throughout Europe or lost. The French nobleman, the Comte de Choiseul-Gouffier, who served as the French ambassador to the Ottoman Empire, worked with his agent, the painter Louis Fauvel, in Athens, to collect as many antiquities as possible. While never as successful as their British counterparts, Choiseul-Gouffier and Fauvel

[23] St Clair, *Lord Elgin & The Marbles* (n 18) 47.

[24] Savas Kondaratos, 'The Parthenon as Cultural Ideal: The Chronicle of its Emergence as a Supreme Monument of Eternal Glory' in Panayotis Tournikiotis (ed), *The Parthenon and Its Impact in Modern Times* (Melissa Publishing House 1994) 20, 38. For more on the influence of Winckelmann, see Katherine Harloe, *Winckelmann and the Invention of Antiquity: History and Aesthetics in the Age of* Altertumswissenschaft (OUP 2013).

established a systematic pattern for drawing, making casts, and removing sculptural pieces. The Ottomans did not give Choiseul-Gouffier permission to remove any of the Parthenon Sculptures, but he was able to obtain a few pieces that had previously fallen from the building.[25] However, the French Revolution cut short his larger ambitions. Choiseul-Gouffier's removals provided an excuse, based on British–French military and cultural rivalry, for the much larger-scale efforts of the British.

In 1799, Thomas Bruce, the seventh Earl of Elgin, arrived at the Sublime Porte as the British ambassador to the Ottoman Empire. Elgin saw his appointment as an opportunity to make drawings and plaster casts of sculptural and architectural fragments and brought with him artists and mold makers who would assist him in this enterprise. His original goal seems to have been only to bring back these drawings and three-dimensional casts from which British artists could learn, thereby improving British arts and society.[26] However, from the beginning, a core part of the narrative was that Elgin was saving the sculptures from 'neglect, disregard, and vandalism'.[27]

Grateful to the British for their victories over the French in Egypt and with the hope that Britain would return Egypt to Ottoman control, the Ottoman Sultan granted a series of permissions, known as a *firman*, to Lord Elgin.[28] None of these survives, although it has been asserted since 1816 that an official translation in Italian of the second *firman*, granted in July 1801, is extant. Reverend Philip Hunt, Elgin's private chaplain and secretary, gave an English version of this document to the Parliamentary Select Committee, and it was included in the Committee's Report during the hearings held in 1816 to determine whether the British nation should acquire the marbles.[29] Much of the Parliamentary debate concerning the acquisition turned on whether Elgin had acquired legitimate title, thus the contents of these documents are crucial to answering this question. In an exhaustive

[25] Webb, 'Appropriating the Stones' (n 7) 53–54.

[26] St Clair, *Lord Elgin & The Marbles* (n 18) 6–8. Much of the commonly accepted version of the saga of Lord Elgin and the Sculptures is based on A H Smith, 'Lord Elgin and His Collection' (1916) 36 Journal of Hellenic Studies 132–372, written on the hundredth anniversary of Parliament's acquisition of the Sculptures.

[27] David Rudenstine, 'Trophies for the Empire: The Epic Dispute between Greece and England over the Parthenon Sculptures in the British Museum' (2021) 39 CAELJ 377, 380 (hereafter Rudenstine, 'Trophies for the Empire').

[28] Dyfri Williams, 'Lord Elgin's firman' (2009) 21 Journal of the History of Collections 49, 56–57 (hereafter Williams, 'Lord Elgin's firman'). David Rudenstine, who has searched the Ottoman archives of this time period in Istanbul, was unable to find the original of the *firman* and agrees that it likely no longer exists. Rudenstine, 'Trophies for the Empire' (n 27) 428.

[29] St Clair, *Lord Elgin & The Marbles* (n 18) 337–41. St Clair found the Italian document in 1962 among the Hunt papers and published it in 1998. William St Clair, 'Imperial Appropriations of the Parthenon' in John Henry Merryman (ed), *Imperialism, Art and Restitution* (CUP 2006) 65, 78 (hereafter St Clair, 'Imperial Appropriations of the Parthenon'). The Italian version of the *firman* came into the possession of the British Museum in 2006. Williams, 'Lord Elgin's firman' (n 28) 49. Williams suggests that the original document would have been retained by the local Ottoman officials in Athens and then destroyed during the Greek War of Independence.

article, David Rudenstine concluded that the Italian document is not a translation of the firman but rather a draft created by Elgin, or one of his retainers, setting out Elgin's request for authorization and on which the firman was based.[30] John Henry Merryman, on the other hand, concluded that Parliament agreed to acquire the Sculptures 'in full knowledge of the facts',[31] while St Clair has vehemently disputed the doubts cast on the legitimacy and historical value of the Italian document.[32]

A perhaps more fundamental question exists as to exactly what Elgin had permission to do. As Rudenstine points out, it is unlikely that Elgin was given permission to do anything more than what he requested and so the extent of the permission would have been what was stated in the Italian document.[33] The document gives Elgin and his men permission to measure, draw, and make models or casts of the sculptures that still adorned the Parthenon temple and to excavate around the foundations to find ancient blocks. However, on the crucial question of removal of sculptures that were still attached to the building, the document is, at best, ambiguous. In St Clair's more literal translation, the Italian document states that the local officials in Athens should not 'make any opposition to the taking away of some pieces of stone with inscriptions, and figures ....'[34] St Clair interprets this as permission only to remove sculptures that had already fallen to the ground.[35] Rudenstine emphasizes that the permission to dig is limited to the area around the foundations of buildings, rather than permission to remove sculptures,[36] and that the permission given would cause 'no harm in the said figures and edifices being thus viewed, contemplated, and designed'.[37] If this is the correct interpretation, then Elgin's agents in Athens, led by the artist Lusieri, certainly exceeded the scope of this authority.

In the first ten months, Elgin's agents obtained at least seven of the metopes, twenty slabs of the frieze, and almost all the surviving figures of the pediments. They also collected examples of architectural elements and sculptures from other buildings on the Acropolis and from other sites throughout Greece. Elgin's agents

[30] Rudenstine, 'Trophies for the Empire' (n 27) 432–43. By this reasoning, the English document published by Parliament is a translation of the draft, although apparently with some alterations to make it appear to be a translation of the firman. Rudenstine attributes the deception as to the nature of the Italian document to Hunt and Elgin, and he further suggests that the Select Committee deceived Parliament so that the Sculptures would remain in England rather than being sold abroad. ibid, 443–45.

[31] John Henry Merryman, 'Thinking about the Elgin Marbles' (1985) 83 Mich L Rev 1881, 1896 (hereafter Merryman, 'Thinking about the Elgin Marbles').

[32] St Clair, 'Imperial Appropriations of the Parthenon' (n 29) 78.

[33] Rudenstine, 'Trophies for the Empire' (n 27) 445.

[34] St Clair, *Lord Elgin & The Marbles* (n 18) 341. The Italian reads: 'non si faccia opposizione al portar via qualche pezzi di pietra con inscrizioni, e figure ....' Merryman agrees that the firman is ambiguous on the question of whether Elgin could remove sculptures that were still attached to the structures and posits 'that the *firman* provides slender authority for the massive removals from the Parthenon'. Merryman, 'Thinking about the Elgin Marbles' (n 31) 1898–99.

[35] St Clair, 'Imperial Appropriations of the Parthenon' (n 29) 78–79.

[36] Rudenstine, 'Trophies for the Empire' (n 27) 448.

[37] ibid, 446.

had succeeded in convincing the *voivode* and *disdar* (the local Turkish officials) in Athens to allow these removals, probably through bribery. According to St Clair, these bribes amounted to significant sums and may be a basis for questioning the legitimacy of the officials' actions.[38] In the autumn of 1802, Elgin obtained a letter from Constantinople consenting to all the work performed by Elgin's agents in Athens, thus arguably giving retroactive approval.[39] Further permission given in 1810 to ship the remaining sculptures from Athens is also asserted to be a retroactive approval.[40]

Elgin's activities caused considerable damage to the ancient structure of the Parthenon, as the architectural elements surrounding the sculptures had to be thrown down in order to remove the desired pieces. Particularly the removal of the metopes weakened the integrity of the structure. The British traveller, Edward Dodwell, wrote:

> I had the inexpressible mortification of being present when the Parthenon was despoiled of its finest sculpture, and when some of its architectural members were thrown to the ground.... [I]t was necessary to throw to the ground the magnificent cornice by which the [metopes] were covered. The south east angle of the pediment shared the same fate; and instead of the picturesque beauty and high preservation in which I first saw it, it is now comparatively reduced to a state of shattered desolation.[41]

(Figure 3.1). Further threats to the Sculptures resulted from the dangers and vagaries of their trip to England. Many were kept at various European seaports, and one shipload sank off the island of Cythera; it took more than two years to raise all the Sculptures from the sunken ship, while other antiquities from the wreck of the *Mentor* continue to be discovered.[42]

[38] William St Clair, 'The Elgin Marbles: Questions of Stewardship and Accountability' (1999) 8 IJCP 397, 401–03. Merryman dismissed the bribery issue saying it was not illegal to induce an official through bribery to do an otherwise legal act. Merryman, 'Thinking about the Elgin Marbles' (n 31) 1902. Rudenstine disputes this, pointing out that bribery to initiate an act, not merely to speed the doing of an act, was not legally insignificant, especially where legitimacy depends on the unproven fact that the bribed officials had authority to do the act (ie permit Elgin to take the Sculptures). Rudenstine, 'Trophies for the Empire' (n 27) 453–56.

[39] Merryman relies on *post hoc* ratification by the Ottoman rulers to legitimate Elgin's actions, although they exceeded the original scope of Elgin's authority. Merryman, 'Thinking about the Elgin Marbles' (n 31) 1899. Rudenstine doubts the utility of such ratification, in part because it is not clear what the Ottoman officials in Constantinople knew of the source of the Sculptures. Rudenstine, 'Trophies for the Empire' (n 27) 452–53.

[40] Rudenstine, 'Trophies for the Empire' (n 27) 452–53.

[41] Quoted in St Clair, *Lord Elgin & The Marbles* (n 18) 102. Rudenstine, 'Trophies for the Empire' (n 27) 461.

[42] Caroline Goldstein, 'Marine Archaeologists Have Recovered Ancient Treasures from the Wreckage of Lord Elgin's Sunken Ship' (*ArtNet*, 18 October 2019) <https://news.artnet.com/art-world/shipwreck-discovery-lord-elgin-1680415> accessed 12 April 2021.

Figure 3.1 Edward Dodwell drawing of West front of the Parthenon (1821)

The competition between the British and the French to acquire classical sculptures reflected their military rivalry. Elgin's personal secretary, William Richard Hamilton, was in Egypt at the time of the final defeat of the French forces. Hamilton insisted that the peace terms between the French and the British require that the French surrender the Rosetta Stone and other antiquities to the British. Monica Hanna has suggested that the unilateral taking of antiquities by the British violated the terms of the Capitulation of Alexandria, whereby the disposition of antiquities was to be decided by the combined British and Ottoman forces.[43] Elgin's success in Athens, where the French had failed, became a symbol of national pride. The Parthenon Sculptures were thus adopted into British nationalism as a symbol of military victory, Britain's superior role as centre of the arts, and a new democratic spirit, inspired by Athenian democracy reborn in a British context. This shift in British perspective is celebrated in William Wordsworth's poem, *Ode Composed in January 1816*, at the time of Napoleon's defeat:

> Victorious England! Bid the silent Art
> Reflect, in glowing hues that shall not fade,
> Those high achievements; even as she arrayed
> With second life the deed of Marathon
> Upon Athenian walls;

[43] St Clair, *Lord Elgin & The Marbles* (n 18) 115; chapter 2, n 58.

So may she labour for thy civic halls:
And be the guardian spaces
Of consecrated places,
As nobly graced by Sculpture's patient toil;
And let imperishable Columns rise
Fixed in the depths of this courageous soil;
Expressive signals of a glorious strife . . .[44]

The Sculptures that were executed by Pheidias as part of Pericles' building programme to celebrate the defeats of Persia in the fifth century BCE, now served to celebrate the defeat of the French at the hands of the British. This casts the French in the role of the Persians and the British in the role of the Athenians, preserving democracy. This rationale also allowed the British claim to the Sculptures to transcend a right founded only on military conquest. Nonetheless, one member of Parliament, Hugh Hammersley, opposed acquisition of the Sculptures, in part, on the grounds that they should be held 'only in trust till they are demanded by the present, or any future, possessors of the city of Athens'.[45]

Elgin claimed that he was primarily motivated by the role that the Sculptures could play in advancing not only the arts in Britain but also its industries, manufactures, and cultural and intellectual life (Figure 3.2). The sculptures had an enormous impact on contemporary understanding of ancient art. The major artists of the day were allowed to view and sketch the sculptures, and, as they did so, the artists recognized their artistic superiority. The impact of the Sculptures also aligned with the Romantic ideal of the artistic creative genius that was becoming popular at the time; the Parthenon Sculptures were viewed as the product of just such a genius.

The Parthenon Sculptures were the first certainly authentic original Greek works, rather than Roman copies, available to contemporary artists and this British collection was therefore considered superior to collections in Rome and elsewhere on the European continent. However, the Parthenon Sculptures clashed with preconceived notions of how classical sculpture should look, particularly among the Dilettanti.[46] These views were based on Roman copies, which were often heavily restored, and focused on their completeness and their value as decoration for the

44 Quoted in Webb, 'Appropriating the Stones' (n 7) 76–77.

45 ibid, 81.

46 The Society of the Dilettanti was founded in 1734 in London by a group of scholars and aristocrats who had made the grand tour, many of whom collected Classical art. The Society was devoted to promoting the study of the Classical world, especially art and archaeology. Many of the Dilettanti, particularly Richard Payne Knight, criticized the artistic merits of the Parthenon Sculptures. J Paul Getty Museum (2008) 'Grecian Taste and Roman Spirit: The Society of Dilettanti' <www.getty.edu/art/exhibitions/dilettanti/> accessed 12 April 2021. The Society of the Dilettanti sponsored exploration expeditions to Greece and Asia Minor. Claire Lyons, 'Archives in Ruins: The Collections of the Getty Research Institute' in Michael S Roth (ed) *Irresistible Decay: Ruins Reclaimed* (Getty Research Institute 1997) 79, 88 (hereafter Lyons, 'Archives in Ruins').

Figure 3.2 Archibald Archer, The Temporary Elgin Room in 1819

country estates of the aristocracy. This approach is epitomized by the collection of Charles Townley, which was donated to the British Museum as the core of its classical collection, just as Elgin, perpetually short of funds, began the process of trying to sell his collection to the British nation. For some, the sculptures of the Elgin collection were jarring in their fragmentary state, and some found fault with their artistic quality, asserting that they were not the product of Pheidias, but rather of workmen and artisans.

Perhaps the best remembered today of Elgin's critics is the poet Lord Byron who first attacked Elgin's actions in his 1812 poem, *Childe Harold's Pilgrimage*, which recounted Byron's travels in the Eastern Mediterranean. One stanza gives the flavour of Byron's laments for the dismemberment of the Parthenon:

Cold is the heart, fair Greece! that looks on thee,
Nor feels as lovers o'er the dust they lov'd;
Dull is the eye that will not weep to see
Thy walls defac'd, thy mouldering shrines remov'd
By British hands, which it had best behov'd
To guard those relics ne'er to be restor'd.
Curst be the hour when from their isle they rov'd,
And once again thy hapless bosom gor'd,

And snatch'd thy shrinking Gods to northern climes abhorr'd![47]

In his contemporary but unpublished poem, *The Curse of Minerva*, Byron was even more acerbic in his condemnation of Elgin:

And last of all amidst the gaping crew
Some calm spectator, as he takes his view
In silent indignation mix'd with grief,
Admires the plunder, but abhors the thief.
***
Oh, loath'd in life, nor pardon'd in the dust,
May Hate pursue his sacrilegious lust![48]

Byron asserted that modern Greeks are descended from ancient Greeks, but that by remaining enslaved as part of the Ottoman Empire, they were failing to live up to their illustrious heritage. While philhellenism and Greek independence did not originate with Byron, his poems strengthened and spread these ideas. As St Clair commented, 'from the beginning the Parthenon became an integral part of the construction of the Modern Greek sense of national identity, a visible and tangible manifestation of the continuity which the myth required and asserted'.[49]

In 1816, Parliament acquired Elgin's collection for £35,000, and the Sculptures were transferred to the British Museum. One of the conditions of the sale was that the Sculptures were to be known as the 'Elgin Collection', thus engaging in a significant act of decontextualization and deracination through conferring the name that itself became subject to debate in future years.[50] The Sculptures proved immensely popular with both the public and the artists who learned from them. Casts were sent to many other museums so that their artistic value could be shared, and after 1834, the British Museum acquired casts of all new discoveries of Parthenon Sculptures from the Greek State.[51] The popularity and role of the Sculptures in the British Museum have fluctuated and the Sculptures' primary role as teachers

[47] St Clair, *Lord Elgin & The Marbles* (n 18) 184.

[48] Webb 'Appropriating the Stones' (n 7) 60, 62.

[49] St Clair, *Lord Elgin & The Marbles* (n 18) 189. Merryman denigrated Byron as perpetrating a 'romantic misrepresentation and distortion of values'. Merryman, 'Thinking about the Elgin Marbles' (n 31) 1905.

[50] In about 2015, the British Museum changed the nomenclature and now refers to them as 'The Parthenon Sculptures', apparently in violation of this stipulation. British Museum, 'The Parthenon Sculptures' <www.britishmuseum.org/about-us/british-museum-story/objects-news/parthenon-sculptures> accessed 31 May 2021.

[51] Casts made by Elgin and earlier by Fauvel of the sculptures while *in situ*, as well as casts made at the British Museum and later in 1872 for the then British consul provide important points of comparison with the original sculptures that remained in Athens and for assessment of the Sculptures' state of preservation. Emma M Payne, '3D Imaging of the Parthenon Sculptures: An Assessment of the Archaeological Value of Nineteenth-Century Plaster Castes' (2019) 93(372) Antiquity 1625 (hereafter Payne, '3D Imaging').

of modern artists has varied with their role as a source of artistic inspiration and as a tourist attraction. Their influence on the development of sculpture, painting, and architecture in nineteenth-century Europe and North America cannot be overstated.

3.2.3 The Parthenon Sculptures as Contemporary Symbol

The third and current phase of the Parthenon and its Sculptures began with the War of Greek Independence in the 1820s and the recognition of the new Hellenic Republic in 1832. By the 1830s, the Greek government had adopted a policy that prohibited the export of antiquities and the removal of artefacts from archaeological sites, although these restrictions were often difficult to enforce. Later a permit was required for the conduct of excavations.[52] The loss of artefacts from the Parthenon seems to have finally halted in 1874 when all of the objects on the Acropolis were collected and placed in a museum.[53] As soon as the Greek nation recovered possession of Athens, plans were initiated for the restoration of the Acropolis, and the decision was made to restore it, not surprisingly, to its Periclean peak of political, military, and artistic supremacy of the fifth century BCE. As with other sites of great historical significance, such as the Roman Forum and the Temple Mount area in Jerusalem, the selection of a particular time as the defining historical and cultural moment to which the site would be restored meant that later accretions, such as the churches, mosque, and other structures of the Roman, Byzantine, and Ottoman period, would be removed.[54] This also fostered and reinforced feelings of cultural continuity and nationalism, focusing on the Parthenon as the pre-eminent symbol of the new Greek State, without visible reminders of the centuries of foreign presence.

Since achieving independence, the Greek authorities have undertaken different reconstruction efforts of the ancient structures of the Acropolis. The most extensive programme of renovation of the main buildings on the Acropolis is the Acropolis Restoration Project. The project began with extensive studies and

[52] The earliest Greek legislation dates to 1834. Neil Brodie, 'Historical and Social Perspectives on the Regulation of the International Trade in Archaeological Objects: The Examples of Greece and India' (2005) 38 Vanderbilt Journal of Transnational Law 1051, 1056–57; Greenhalgh, *Plundered Empire* (n 6) 522–23, 545–46. Regulations were enacted to prevent removal of antiquities and to establish museums even before independence was achieved. ibid, 519.

[53] St Clair, *Lord Elgin & The Marbles* (n 18) 319–21. Payne concluded that most of the damage done to the Sculptures left on the Parthenon occurred between 1802 and 1872 and was probably attributed to intentional efforts to remove elements. This damage seems to have stopped once the Acropolis was adequately protected. Payne, '3D Imaging' (n 51) 1635–36.

[54] Bouras describes this as the 'doctrine of "purism"' and commented that the aesthetic and environmental ideals of the Parthenon were allowed to override historical and utilitarian values. Bouras, 'Restoration Work' (n 20) 320.

international meetings in the mid-1970s and early 1980s.[55] Each building has been taken apart, measured, conserved, and reconstructed. While the project aims to reuse as many original materials as possible, earlier reconstructions have sometimes made this impossible. The remaining sculptures on the Parthenon were removed and placed for safekeeping in the Acropolis Museum, while casts of some of the original sculptures have been placed on the Parthenon as part of the restoration programme.[56] The new Acropolis museum was opened to the public in 2009, and its design by the renowned architect Bernard Tschumi has been recognized as exceptional, particularly the interior.[57] A large room from which the Parthenon can be seen houses the Parthenon Sculptures that remain in Athens and awaits the return of the Sculptures from London.

Since the time of independence, the Greeks have been consistent in asserting their claim for restitution, and the British Museum and British government have been just as persistent in refusing it. Pittakis wrote, in the first guide to the classical antiquities of Athens produced after independence: 'I believe that in the state of independence we are entering we will have the right to reclaim from the English nation the masterpieces of our ancestors to put them back in the place which the divine Phidias chose for them.'[58] In 1890, the Greek Minister in London, Ioannes Gennadios, suggested that the architectural fragments should be returned, but this informal claim was rejected.[59] The Greek Minister of Culture and actress, Melina Mercouri, argued for their return in 1983.[60] In 2004, when Athens hosted the summer Olympics and sought to have the Sculptures returned for the event, eighteen Western museums issued the Declaration of the Importance and Value of the Universal Museum as a justification for retention of antiquities removed in the past.[61] As St Clair has pointed out, there were moments over the past two

[55] Bouras, 'Restoration Work' (n 20) 329–32. These current reconstruction efforts incorporate the following principles of modern conservation work, based on the Venice Charter: reversibility; retention of the self-contained nature of the architectural members; restriction of intervention to those areas that had previously been reconstructed; protection of the monument from atmospheric conditions (in particular, Athenian air pollution and humidity); and minimization of changes in the appearance of the structure.

[56] Jarrett A Lobell, 'The Acropolis of Athens' (*Archaeology*, 7 October 2015) <www.archaeology.org/issues/193-1511/features/3765-athens-acropolis-restoration-project>accessed 12 April 2021. The most recent plans for restoration work, intended to improve access and traffic management of visitors, have met with considerable criticism that the restoration of the west access and the reconstruction of the Propylaea gate to its condition during the Roman period rather than to its original appearance are historically inaccurate. William Summerfield, 'Acropolis renovation plans spark accusation that it's "just another way to fit in more tourists"' (*The Art Newspaper*, 28 April 2021) <www.theartnewspaper.com/news/acropolis-renovation-plans> accessed 24 May 2021.

[57] Suzanne Stephens, 'New Acropolis Museum' (*Architectural Record*, 19 October 2009) <www.architecturalrecord.com/articles/8193-new-acropolis-museum> accessed 24 May 2021.

[58] St Clair, *Lord Elgin & The Marbles* (n 18) 333 (quoting from K S Pittakys, L'Ancienne Athènes (Athens 1835) 379).

[59] St Clair, *Lord Elgin & The Marbles* (n 18) 333.

[60] Rudenstine, 'Trophies for the Empire (n 27) 379.

[61] Reproduced in James Cuno, 'View from the Universal Museum' in John Henry Merryman (ed), *Imperialism, Art and Restitution* (CUP 2006) 15, 34–36. The Declaration is discussed in chapter 7, section 7.3.2.

centuries in which the British considered returning the sculptures to Greece, generally at a point when a considerable political issue was at stake.[62] However, there never seemed to be a sufficiently important political concession that prompted the British to pay the price of restitution.

The question of where the Sculptures should be located today can be analysed from a legal perspective and from a broader historical and cultural perspective. The legal issues may be grouped into three categories. The first question is whether Elgin exceeded the scope of authority granted in the firman and, if so, whether his actions were ratified retroactively either in later firmans or through acquiescence. While it is unlikely that we will ever know exactly what Elgin was given explicit permission to do, defenders of the British Museum's position conclude that, at the least, Elgin's actions were ratified retroactively.[63] Others doubt the utility of such ratification, in part because it is not clear what the Ottoman officials in Constantinople knew of the contents when they approved the final shipments in 1810. Further, these subsequent ratifications may have been achieved through substantial bribery, which, according to Rudenstine, may have violated British law at the time, regardless of whether it violated Ottoman law.[64] Ultimately, the full facts of these issues seem unknowable, and they therefore have little value in assessing the proper location of the Sculptures.

A second legal argument is that Elgin acquired the Sculptures legitimately because the Ottoman Empire was recognized as having authority over the territory of what is today modern Greece. Under contemporary law, one might need to determine whether this was territory occupied by the Ottoman Empire or whether it was incorporated into the Empire. The successful revolt of the Greeks against the Ottoman Empire and establishment of independence three decades later indicate that the Greek people had a sense of nationhood as well as cultural continuity from ancient times and viewed themselves as subjugated and occupied by the Ottomans. This might suggest that the territory should be viewed as occupied, although this distinction was unlikely to be significant in the early nineteenth century.[65] The

[62] Probably the point at which the British most seriously considered returning the Sculptures was during the Second World War when the British wanted to encourage the Greeks to resist an Italian-German invasion. St Clair, *Lord Elgin & The Marbles* (n 18) 334.

[63] Merryman, 'Thinking about the Elgin Marbles' (n 31) 1899. Merryman reargued many of these points in a later article, 'Whither the Elgin Marbles?' in John Henry Merryman (ed), Imperialism, Art and Restitution (CUP 2006) 98.

[64] Rudenstine, 'Trophies for the Empire' (n 27) 452–56; St Clair, 'The Elgin Marbles' (n 37) 401–03. See also n 38 above. The question of whether Elgin was acting in his position as Ambassador to the Ottoman Empire or acting personally would be pertinent to whether he was entitled to compensation when he sold the Sculptures to the British nation, but this does not seem relevant to the question of whether the Sculptures should be returned.

[65] Merryman accepts the right of the Ottoman rulers to dispose of the Sculptures as presumptively valid under early nineteenth century international law. 'Even though their actions might seem regrettable, unsound, or unfeeling, one would not question their legality, except in the most unusual circumstances. In this instance the Ottomans had a solid claim to legal authority over the Parthenon because it was public property, which the successor nation acquires on a change of sovereignty.' Merryman, 'Thinking about the Elgin Marbles' (n 31) 1897. However, Merryman concedes in this quote that there

third issue is the problem of the passage of time. According to Merryman, even if Greece did have a claim to the Sculptures, Greece's failure to present a claim in British courts since the time of independence means that Greece would be barred from bringing such a claim.[66]

Nonetheless, Greece has submitted several requests for mediation before international tribunals and proposed various resolutions encouraging restitution or discussion of the question.[67] Following the United Kingdom's rejection of UNESCO's offer to mediate the dispute, Syllogos Ton Athinaion, a Greek association founded in 1895 to ensure the protection of the ancient monuments of Athens, filed a suit in the European Court of Human Rights, alleging violations of the European Convention on Human Rights.[68] The Court characterized the injury as occurring at the time of the Sculptures' removal in the early nineteenth century and dismissed the application as untimely. Furthermore, the Court held that the application failed to point to any provision of the Convention or its case law that 'gives rise to a general right to protection of cultural heritage of the nature contended for in the present case'.[69] Nonetheless, an analysis of the issue based on human rights supports the claim of Greece and its citizens that their rights have been violated.[70]

In late 2014, the British Museum took the unprecedented step of lending one of the Parthenon Sculptures, the river-god Ilissos from the west pediment, to the

may be 'most unusual circumstances' that would justify rejection of the law applicable at the time. This is discussed further in chapter 7.

66 Legal and equitable doctrines that bar an original owner's claim based on the passage of time and the non-retroactivity of later treaties and legal doctrines are discussed in chapter 7, section 7.1. Another practical obstacle is the provisions of the British Museum Act 1963 c. 24 s 4(4) that prohibit removal of objects from the Museum's collection except under specific circumstances, although acts of Parliament have modified the circumstances under which objects may be deaccessioned.

67 Greece presented a request for the restitution of the Parthenon Sculptures to UNESCO's Intergovernmental Committee for Promoting the Return of Cultural Property to its Countries of Origin or its Restitution in Case of Illicit Appropriation in 1984. The United Kingdom rejected the request in 2001. The UNESCO Committee has continued to suggest discussions to resolve the Sculptures' fate. Recommendation 5, Intergovernmental Committee (2012) ICPRCP/12/18.COM/6 <http://unesdoc.unesco.org/images/0022/002225/222590E.pdf> accessed 31 May 2021. In March 2015, the UK government rejected a 2013 UNESCO invitation to facilitate mediation. 'Elgin Marbles: UK declines mediation over Parthenon sculptures' (*BBC*, 8 April 2015) <www.bbc.com/news/uk-32204548> accessed 31 May 2021.

68 *Syllogos Ton Athinaion v United Kingdom* App no 48259/15 (ECtHR, 31 May 2016); European Court of Human Rights, 'Cultural Rights in the case-law of the European Court of Human Rights' (2017) 31 <https://www.fullegal.com/en/court-cases/european-court-of-human-rights-cases/syllogos-ton-athinaion-v-the-united-kingdom-1751585> accessed 27 July 2023.

69 ibid.

70 Based on Margaret Jane Radin's theory that some property is bound up with personal identity and is therefore inalienable, John Moustakas argued that some categories of cultural objects are so integrally related to group cultural identity that they are market inalienable. John Moustakas, 'Group Rights in Cultural Property: Justifying Strict Inalienability' (1989) 74 Cornell Law Review 1179; Margaret Jane Radin, 'Property and Personhood' (1982) 34 Stanford Law Review 957. Derek Fincham has argued that principles of justice should be applied, and that Athens should be recognized as the proper home of the Sculptures. Derek Fincham, 'The Parthenon Sculptures and Cultural Justice' (2013) 23 Fordham Intellectual Property, Media & Entertainment Law Journal 943.

Figure 3.3 Statue of the Greek river god Ilissos from the Parthenon on display at the Hermitage Museum in 2014

Hermitage Museum in St Petersburg on the 250th anniversary of the founding of the Hermitage (Figure 3.3). The announcement by the British Museum cited the legacy of the Enlightenment museums and the track record of loans between various Russian museums and British institutions.[71] Greece was outraged that the statue was allowed to travel to a third country, but not to Greece, and the Greek Prime Minister pointed out that the loan undercut any argument that the sculptures were too fragile to travel.[72] Display of the solitary sculpture set in a rotunda

[71] Neil MacGregor, 'Loan of a Parthenon sculpture to the Hermitage: a marble ambassador of a European ideal' (*British Museum Blog*, 5 December 2014) <https://blog.britishmuseum.org/loan-of-a-parthenon-sculpture-to-the-hermitage-a-marble-ambassador-of-a-european-ideal/accessed 12 April 2021>. The Hermitage was founded five years after the British Museum and the press release described the museums as 'sisters, almost twins, they are the first great museums of the European Enlightenment'. Quoting from Pericles' funerary oration, Neil MacGregor, the Director of the British Museum at the time, hypothesized that Pericles would have been pleased with the loan.

[72] Helena Smith, 'Parthenon marbles: Greece furious over British loan to Russia' (*The Guardian*, 5 December 2014) <www.theguardian.com/artanddesign/2014/dec/05/parthenon-marbles-greece-furi

suggests that another purpose of the loan was to demonstrate that the Parthenon Sculptures have meaning even in isolation and that therefore, their original context among the other sculptures and architecture of the Parthenon and the Acropolis was unnecessary for their full appreciation and understanding.

3.2.4 The Rescue Narrative and Contextualism

Two conflicting themes emerge from the debates concerning the legitimacy of Elgin's appropriation of the Parthenon Sculptures and their proper location. One theme is the rescue narrative employed as probably the most fundamental and long-lived justification for most removals of artworks from outside of Europe. The rescue narrative is responsible for universalizing the sculptures by incorporating the principle that specific location is not important to understanding the work. St Clair performs perhaps the ultimate act of deracination of the sculptures by stating:

> The sculptures of the Parthenon came from Greece, but it was the countries of modern Europe which gave them their fame, their iconic status, and their constantly changing meaning, as well as their new name. The Elgin Marbles were physically constructed in Athens, but, until the time of Greek independence, they were culturally constructed in Dresden, London, Paris, Rome, and Weimar.[73]

This universalism is used to argue that the Sculptures belong to the world, not to Greece. However, this does not determine where they should be located. As Rudenstine points out, this same argument equally delegitimizes the claim of the British Museum to own them. He concludes: 'The claim that the sculptures are of significance to all certainly is meritorious but fails to resolve the question of where they should be located.'[74] The other theme is contextualism and the role of the national and local communities from which the Sculptures were taken and the intent of the artists who created the work. Contextualism emphasizes the original location of works of art and the importance of the understanding that derives from that context.

ous-british-museum-loan-russia-elgin> accessed 12 April 2021. Another concern was that the loan came soon after Russia's annexation of the Crimean Peninsula and could have been seen as legitimizing Russia's action or creating the possibility that the Russians would retain the Sculpture for 'ransom', although the statue was returned on schedule.

[73] St Clair, *Lord Elgin & the Marbles* (n 18) 280.
[74] Rudenstine, 'Trophies for the Empire' (n 27) 464.

3.2.4.1 The Rescue Narrative

From the beginning, Elgin and some of his agents, particularly Hunt, justified their actions with the rescue narrative. The acquisition for Britain was deemed appropriate because the British claimed, like the French before them under Napoleon, that their superiority rendered them the only fit guardians for such superb artistic treasures. This resonated with the notion of rescue formulated from stories brought back by travellers over the previous half-century of Turkish failure to appreciate and protect the Sculptures. The British were granting the marbles 'an honourable asylum'.[75] However, this ignores the fact that the two most traumatic events inflicted upon the Parthenon were caused by Europeans—the attack by the Venetian Morosini[76] and the dismantling by Elgin, which significantly weakened the integrity of the structure.

The physical preservation aspect of the rescue narrative has been weakened or discredited, beginning almost immediately after the Sculptures' arrival in London. Ian Jenkins described the Sculptures as being damaged by dust generated from the stoves used to heat the galleries and the 'far greater menace, namely the deterioration of the London air by the increase of smoke emissions from coal-fires serving the city's ever growing population'.[77] In 1845, W R Hamilton, Elgin's former agent, wrote that the Sculptures 'are daily becoming more deteriorated by exposure to the London atmosphere, its smoke and dirt and the alterations of heated and damp air'.[78] A comparison of the Sculptures as they were at that time with artefacts brought more recently to London indicated to him that 'at the end of a century or less they may be irreparably injured'.[79] A comparative study of casts of five sections of the frieze made *in situ* by Elgin, casts made in 1872 of the frieze sections *in situ*, and the frieze sections today reveal that most of the damage to the Sculptures in Athens occurred during the nineteenth century, likely due to deliberate defacement, and that relatively little damage was done subsequently through air pollution or weathering.[80]

In the 1930s, the Sculptures were removed from display while the galleries in which they were housed were remodelled with funds provided by Joseph Duveen.[81]

[75] The Select Committee Report to Parliament, quoted in Webb, 'Appropriating the Stones' (n 7) 82; Rudenstine, 'Trophies for the Empire' (n 27) 425–26.

[76] Rudenstine points out that the British Museum website fails to mention that Morosini bombarded the Parthenon in 1687, an act that is often described using the passive voice. Rudenstine, 'Trophies for the Empire' (n 27) 462.

[77] Ian Jenkins, 'Cleaning and Controversy: The Parthenon Sculptures 1811–1939' (2001) 146 British Museum Occasional Paper 4 (hereafter Jenkins, 'Cleaning and Controversy').

[78] ibid, 4.

[79] ibid, 4.

[80] Payne, '3D Imagine' (n 51) 1632–36.

[81] St Clair, *Lord Elgin & the Marbles* (n 18) 293–313. St Clair claimed that the British Museum had covered up the incident. ibid, 306–08. In response, Ian Jenkins, former Senior Curator at the British Museum, refuted this. Jenkins, 'Cleaning and Controversy' (n 77) 1. See also John Boardman, 'The Elgin Marbles: Matters of Fact and Opinion' (2000) 9 IJCP 233; Ian Jenkins, 'The Elgin Marbles: Questions of Accuracy and Reliability' (2001) 10 IJCP 55.

Duveen was given access to the Sculptures. Much influenced by pure classicizing ideals in which Greek sculpture was admired for its purity and whiteness, Duveen instigated a process of cleaning or scraping the surfaces to remove the outer layer that had, with time, through erosion and leaching of the surface minerals, taken on a brownish colour. The Sculptures were frequently described as having a warm, honey, rich, or glowing surface. Depiction of such a surface on ancient ruins would have enhanced the melancholy and nostalgia that contemplation of the past was intended to evoke in the viewer.[82]

This outermost layer, which preserved the tool marks of the ancient sculptors, amounting to an estimated ten per cent of the original surface, was scraped away from several of the frieze panels and the remaining west pediment sculptures during the Duveen cleaning. Scholars study tool marks preserved on ancient sculptures to determine technological advances and their relationship to stylistic elements. Some scholars who had studied the tool marks in detail asserted that they had not known of the scraping incident.[83] The three-dimensional imaging study of frieze fragments in Athens revealed that an orange-brown patina is preserved on their surface. This patina is described as 'stable and uniform, preserving the original surface details'.[84] It is not clear whether Duveen's cleaning of the Sculptures in London removed this layer.

Also significant is the question of whether any remaining traces of the Sculptures' original polychromy were removed through the Duveen cleaning.[85] The presence of polychromy conflicts with our modern concept of how ancient sculptures and architecture would have looked. Winckelmann, writing in the eighteenth century, formulated his views that the essence of sculpture is form, not decoration, and the

Duveen was a prominent art dealer and market-maker in Old Master paintings, having captured the market of newly rich American industrialists, who wished to build art collections in competition with European aristocrats. Duveen's best clients included J Pierpont Morgan, Henry Clay Frick, Arabella Huntington, and Andrew Mellon, whose collection later formed the basis for the National Gallery of Art in Washington DC. See Meryle Secrest, *Duveen: A Life in Art* (Knopf 2004).

82 Lyons commented that: 'The transitory nature of human achievement and pleasure, the recognition of impending death (*memento mori*), and the reassurance of salvation are also evident in the illustrations of ruins.' Lyons, 'Archives in Ruins' (n 46) 85.

83 Statement of Olga Palagia at a conference held at the British Museum in 1999 to consider the extent of damage done to the Sculptures during the cleaning incident. Tool marks on the Parthenon Sculptures have been studied to determine when the running drill was introduced and whether its use related to the representation of drapery folds. However, it is now impossible to determine the relationship between the use of the running drill and that of the stationary drill. Olga Palagia, 'Marble Carving Techniques' in Olga Palagia (ed), *Greek Sculpture: Function, Materials, and Techniques in the Archaic and Classical Periods* (CUP 2006) 243, 258–59 (hereafter Palagia, 'Marble Carving Techniques').

84 Payne, '3D Imagine' (n 51) 1635. This patina is distinct from a crust caused by pollution that has been removed from these frieze fragments by laser cleaning.

85 While it is generally known that much of the Parthenon's Sculptures and architectural members, as with other ancient sculptures, were painted, little is known about the specifics of the colours. Palagia, 'Marble Carving Techniques' (n 83) 261 (stating that the draped parts of statues, as well as eyes, eyelashes, hair, lips, accessories, and the background of reliefs, were painted, according to both ancient sources and modern technical studies).

modern aesthetic of sculpture is based on the whiteness of marble.[86] St Clair takes this argument further and suggests that the 'cult of whiteness' is linked to fascist and Nazi ideology of racial purity. A fear of colour (or 'chromophobia') characterizes the Western art tradition and 'lies deep and unacknowledged in many attitudes, including of course those of European and American imperialism'.[87]

New technologies have enabled a better understanding of the use of colour in ancient statuary.[88] However, much of the public still sees the ancient world only in white, therefore assuming that everyone in the ancient world was white. Based on Winckelmann's establishment of the ideal aesthetic of ancient white males epitomized by the sculpture of the Apollo Belvedere, whiteness came to represent the classical ideal of beauty, while colour became linked to barbarism.[89] The idea that antiquity was white, buttressed through the common presentation of ancient sculpture, was used during the nineteenth and twentieth centuries and continues today to support the ideas of White supremacy.[90] Although memory of the Duveen incident has faded, it leaves unanswered questions about the role of racial purity in influencing Duveen; the inducement of financial contributions to permit a private individual this type of access to the Sculptures; the nature of the British Museum's care of the Sculptures; and the contribution of the scraping of the sculptures to undermining the rescue narrative and enhancing a narrative of White supremacy.[91]

[86] Scholars and architects of the mid-nineteenth century imagined the Parthenon and other Periclean structures as being coloured, in contrast to twentieth-century reconstructions, which tend to show these structures as all white. David van Zanten, 'The Parthenon Imagined Painted' in Panayotis Tournikiotis (ed), *The Parthenon and Its Impact in Modern Times* (Melissa Publishing House 1994) 259, 259.

[87] St Clair, 'Imperial Appropriations of the Parthenon' (n 29) 85; 82–90. Duveen was one conduit by which 'degenerate' artworks removed from German museums were sold onto the international market in the 1930s. St Clair, *Lord Elgin & the Marbles* (n 18) 294.

[88] Sarah E Bond, 'Why We Need to Start Seeing the Classical World in Color' (*Hyperallergic*, 7 June 2017) <https://hyperallergic.com/383776/why-we-need-to-start-seeing-the-classical-world-in-color/> accessed 30 May 2021 (hereafter Bond, 'Why We Need to Start Seeing the Classical World in Color'). Museums began to acknowledge the presence of polychromy with the exhibit *Gods in Color*, which originated at the Munich Glyptothek in 2003.

[89] Bond, 'Why We Need to Start Seeing the Classical World in Color' (n 88). The canon of whiteness in ancient art was reinforced by the white plaster casts of ancient sculptures that were used for teaching and 'as stand-ins for European enlightenment'. Lydia Pyne, 'Subverting the Whiteness of Antiquity' (*Hyperallergic*, 2 September 2019) <https://hyperallergic.com/513275/subverting-the-whiteness-of-antiquity/> accessed 31 May 2021.

[90] Bond, 'Why We Need to Start Seeing the Classical World in Color' (n 88). The idea that ancient sculptures were coloured has been used by White supremacists as a basis to attack scholars who are trying to present a more accurate understanding of antiquity. Colleen Flaherty, 'Threats for What She Didn't Say' (*Inside Higher Ed*, 19 June 2017) <www.insidehighered.com/news/2017/06/19/classicist-finds-herself-target-online-threats-after-article-ancient-statues> accessed 31 May 2021.

[91] St Clair wrote, 'Now that the British Museum's stewardship of the Elgin Marbles turns out to have been a cynical sham for more than half a century, the British claim to a trusteeship has been forfeited.' St Clair, *Lord Elgin & the Marbles* (n 18) 336.

3.2.4.2 Contextualism

In focusing on the Eurocentric perspective of the rescue narrative, other perspectives are sacrificed, particularly the value of the context in which the artists and architects had placed the Sculptures. Also lost is the perspective of the local people who valued the antiquities among which they lived and to which they attributed a broad range of meaning. Thomasson documents the history of the Sigeion inscription from an area on the northwest coast of Turkey, not far from the site identified today as ancient Troy. Over the course of the eighteenth century, the local inhabitants repeatedly thwarted attempts by British and French diplomats to remove the inscription, despite the permission granted by the Sultan and various other officials. However, Elgin succeeded in 1799, largely because of the British military force that assisted in the removal.[92]

European travellers and collectors dismissed the views and attachment of the local populations as being based on superstition and because the Europeans thought the local people did not appreciate the antiquity of the objects. The European attitude may have been a reaction to restrictions on the export of antiquities enacted by the Ottomans over the course of the nineteenth century. These restrictions were in response to Schliemann's taking of the Gold of Troy and other depredations. The European attitude may also reflect a jealousy that European travellers would choose to visit museums in Ottoman lands rather than European museums.[93] Even today, the attachment of the local inhabitants to these artefacts is questioned. Dyfri Williams, Keeper of Greek and Roman Antiquities at the British Museum, wrote in 2002: 'The reasons for this affection, as usual with antiquities, do not seem to have been engendered by any scientific sense of the sculptures' importance or even a sense of "national heritage" ... but rather by a mixture of superstition that their loss would bring bad luck and a belief that they were magical or contained gold.'[94] The local inhabitants' resistance persisted even in the face of offers of generous sums to purchase the antiquities.[95]

[92] Fredrik Thomasson, 'Justifying and Criticizing the Removals of Antiquities in Ottoman Lands: Tracking the Sigeion Inscription' (2010) 17 IJCP 493, 498–99 (quoting William Wittman, *Travels in Turkey, Asia Minor, Syria, and Across the Desert into Egypt During the Years 1799, 1800, and 1801, in Company with the Turkish Army and the British Military Mission* ... (London 1803) 65–66)) (hereafter Thomasson, 'Justifying and Criticizing'). As with the removal of the Parthenon Sculptures, this occurred when Britain was assisting the Ottomans in repelling the French invasion of Egypt and Syria. ibid, 498. The stele and an accompanying bas relief were the first objects to become part of Elgin's collection. Parliament purchased the inscription as part of the Elgin collection and it is still housed in the British Museum, where it is now placed in the basement.

[93] Greenhalgh, *Plundered Empire* (n 6) 538–45.

[94] Dyfri Williams, '"Of Publick Utility and Publick Property": Lord Elgin and the Parthenon Sculptures' in Athéna Tsingarida and Donna Kurtz (eds), *Appropriating Antiquity, Saisir l'Antique, Collections et collectionneurs d'antiques in Belgique et en Grande-Bretagne au XIXe siècle* (Le Livre Timperman 2002) 103, 139–40.

[95] Thomasson, 'Justifying and Criticizing' (n 92) 500. In another example of the resistance of local inhabitants, the French scholar Charles Clermont-Ganneau recognized the significance of the Mesha Stele, discovered at Dhiban in Jordan in 1868. After attempts to remove the stele, the local inhabitants became angered and broke the stele into fragments, most of which were recovered and bought in the Jerusalem antiquities market by Clermont-Ganneau on behalf of the Louvre; other fragments

The dislocation of cultural objects that had an original specific placement inevitably diminishes the beauty, meaning, and our understanding of the work. According to Webb, Byron's satirical description of the Sculptures 'amidst the gaping crew' in *The Curse of Minerva* demonstrates Byron's belief that the sculptures were out of place in London. This was echoed in the opinions of the contemporary French traveller, the Vicomte de Chateaubriand, who pointed out that the marbles themselves would not have the same aesthetic qualities in the London climate and light as they did in Athens: 'If the monuments of Athens are torn from the places for which they were made, they will not only lose part of their relative beauty but their actual beauty and will [also] be diminished.'[96] As Webb comments: 'A work of art was not merely a transportable object or a possession but something whose *very identity* was materially altered by surrounding circumstances and contexts.'[97]

The writings of the French critic of Napoleon, Antoine-Chrysostôme Quatremère de Quincy, focused on the loss of connection between the works of art that Napoleon had looted and their original location. He, like Byron, noted the deprivation imposed through the separation of artworks from their architectural and natural settings:

> The true museum of Rome . . . is, it is true, composed of statues, of colossi, of temples . . . but it is also composed fully as much of places, of sites, of mountains, of quarries, of ancient roads, of the placing of ruined towns, of geographical relationships, of the inner connections of all these objects to each other, of memories, of local traditions, of still prevailing customs, of parallels and comparisons which can only be made in the country itself.[98]

These concerns demonstrate a nascent sense of the importance of context, which is particularly apparent with sculptures removed from a specific architectural or natural site, what we today might call site-specific works of art, and the relationship between tangible and intangible heritage. Much of the meaning and aesthetic of such artworks are lost when they are separated from their original placement.

Quatremère de Quincy viewed the alternative placement of such works in a museum as a poor substitute. In 1815, he wrote: 'How many works have lost their real

were dispersed among British and German scholars. The stele's inscription dates to the ninth century BCE. Louvre, 'The Mesha Stele' <https://collections.louvre.fr/en/ark:/53355/cl010120339> accessed 12 April 2021.

[96] Quoted in Webb 'Appropriating the Stones' (n 7) 69.

[97] Webb, 'Appropriating the Stones' (n 7) 69 (italics in original). This led the French to coin the term '*elginisme*' to 'refer to the act of removing cultural property from its site.' '*Elginism*' may also be defined more specifically as 'an act of cultural vandalism.' See the blog, Elginism <www.elginism.com/definition/> accessed 12 April 2021

[98] Quoted in Webb, 'Appropriating the Stones' (n 7) 70.

value in losing their use! … Thus every day we see reduced to the tribute of barren admiration all the scattered mutilated fragments of antiquity—gods without altars, altars without worshippers.'[99] Webb notes that even if Quatremère de Quincy was motivated primarily by his opposition to Napoleon and his desire to defend the Catholic Church from Napoleon's depredations, 'his account of a deeper layer of relationship and of the delicate connective tissue between works of art and their originating contexts expresses a discomfort with the concept of a museum that is prophetically critical, and which can now be applied to the status of the Elgin Marbles with an appropriateness that he might never have imagined'.[100] Defenders of the universal museum argue that cultural objects are better understood when they can be compared in a museum with works from other cultures and locations.[101] However, works of art created for a specific cultural milieu and, in the case of the Parthenon sculptures, for a specific building that was placed in relation to a specific cultural and natural landscape lose the essence of their meaning, purpose, and cultural significance when they are removed and placed in isolation in a museum.

3.3 The Yuanmingyuan Palace Complex

Appropriation of cultural and artistic works accompanied the European colonial and imperial powers wherever they went. In the case of the Yuanmingyuan Palace of China, the British were allied with the French and their actions were inextricably intertwined with the goal of dominating foreign trade, which was very lucrative and perceived to be essential to the European nations. China's trade with European countries began with Portugal in the early sixteenth century. By the middle of the century, Portuguese traders served as middlemen between Japan and China in the cheap silver trade. This trade proved to be financially rewarding to the Portuguese who, among other activities, were able to fund the work of Jesuit missionaries in East Asia. The demand for silver in China and for Chinese products such as silks and porcelain in Europe fostered a developing trade between Europe and China. Portugal had the goals of establishing its control over the spice trade and expanding the influence of the Catholic Church, particularly after its decline in Europe following the Protestant Reformation. However, Portugal's attempted monopoly on

[99] Quoted in Thomasson, 'Justifying and Criticizing' (n 92) 508.

[100] Webb, 'Appropriating the Stones' (n 7) 71. Johan David Åkerblad, a Swedish diplomat, translator of the Demotic Greek inscription on the Rosetta Stone and friend of Edward Dodwell, also criticized these removals, particularly those of the French, for their lack of documentation of the finds and their original contexts. This may be a reflection of the greater interest among Scandinavians in archaeology based on scientific methodology. Thomasson, 'Justifying and Criticizing' (n 92) 505–07.

[101] James Cuno, 'Introduction' in James Cuno (ed), *Whose Culture? The Promise of Museums and the Debate over Antiquities* (Princeton University Press 2009) 1, 17–29.

trade in Asia was challenged by other Europeans, particularly the Dutch and the British.[102]

In the second half of the seventeenth century, the Qing Dynasty established control over all of China. During the decline of the preceding Ming Dynasty and the gradual establishment of the new dynasty, Catholic missionaries, particularly those of the Jesuit order, approached the Chinese with the goal of introducing Western scientific and technical knowledge, along with converting the Chinese to Christianity.[103] The missionaries had limited success, and their efforts were in decline by the late eighteenth century, but the exposure to Western learning and artistic endeavours had a significant impact on China during the Qing Dynasty. Jesuits imparted to the Imperial Court both technical knowledge, such as astronomy, mathematics, and cartography, and artistic skills, including painting, glassblowing, and architecture, along with the creation of gardens and fountains.[104]

While foreign traders often fell under suspicion, by the middle of the eighteenth century the British had come to dominate China's trade. In order to maintain tight control, the Chinese limited the conduct of foreign trade to the southeastern seaport of Canton and allowed trade to be carried out only under specific restrictions, although the system was ultimately unworkable. Nevertheless, trade flourished, given the European taste for Chinese silks and porcelains and, particularly among the British, tea, which became the most important commodity exported from China. By the 1780s, the East India Company needed to find a commodity that it could sell in China in exchange for tea and eventually promoted the sale of opium that grew in the British Indian colonies. Purchasing tea with opium was highly successful for the British, despite attempts by the Qing officials to prevent it due to the addiction that ensured continuing demand.[105]

In the early nineteenth century, China's economy weakened resulting in a shift in the balance of trade against China. Attempts by China to abolish the opium trade and resulting British resentment against restrictions on their ability to trade led to the First Opium War (1839–1842).[106] Following China's defeat, the Treaty of Nanjing, which granted trade concessions to the British, was concluded in 1842. These concessions included the opening of other port cities to British traders and the ceding of Hong Kong to Great Britain.[107] However, Britain and other foreign States were dissatisfied with implementation of the treaty provisions permitting foreign traders to trade in the interior of China and the establishment of permanent

[102] Joanna Waley-Cohen, *The Sextants of Beijing: Global Currents in Chinese History* (WW Norton 1999) 49–52; 55–56 (hereafter Waley-Cohen, *The Sextants of Beijing*).

[103] ibid, 70–71.

[104] ibid, 105–17.

[105] ibid, 98–102.

[106] ibid, 132–35; 140–48; Louise Tythacott, 'The Yuanmingyuan and its Objects' in Louise Tythacott (ed), *Collecting and Displaying China's "Summer Palace" in the West: The Yuanmingyuan in Britain and France* (Routledge 2018) 3, 9 (hereafter Tythacott, 'The Yuanmingyuan and its Objects').

[107] Waley-Cohen, *The Sextants of Beijing* (n 102) 148–51.

missions, while several rebellions within China weakened the Qing Dynasty. This situation led to the Second Opium War (1856–1860).[108]

When the Chinese captured and mistreated a negotiating team of thirty-nine diplomats and soldiers, the British and French forces marched for Beijing and arrived at Yuanmingyuan (the Garden of Perfect Brightness, now known as the Old Summer Palace) on the outskirts of Beijing on 6 October 1860. They spent two days looting the palace and then turned back to besiege Beijing. Nine days later the forces returned to burn down Yuanmingyuan and nearby imperial parks in Yihe Yuan (Garden of Clear Ripples, now restored and known as the Summer Palace) and further west. The British destroyed all of the wooden buildings and the Western-style palaces designed by the Jesuits.[109] Despite the protests of the French, the British did so, partly out of revenge for the harsh treatment of the kidnapped diplomatic team and partly as an implied threat to burn the Forbidden City in Beijing, to force the Chinese to ratify the Treaty of Tianjin, agreed to in 1858. The destruction of Yuanmingyuan 'was thus instrumental in the actual military conquest of China'.[110]

The palace complex was constructed by the Qing Dynasty between 1709 and 1772, mostly by the Qianlong Emperor. It was the principal residence of the emperor and became the official seat of the government (Figure 3.4).[111] The complex consisted of some 3,000 separate structures including palaces, pavilions, courts, temples, schools, museums, libraries, and other buildings built in classical Chinese style within a complex of artificial waterways, gardens, landscapes, and hills.[112] Gardens and landscapes formed complex relationships with both architecture and nature. 'Distinct garden units created beautiful quiet retreats, extraordinary vistas, enclosed and enchanted spaces. Each small area was conceived as an architectural and natural ensemble, deliberately designed to have a poetic atmosphere.'[113] In 1749, the Qianlong Emperor undertook a great expansion of the complex by constructing the Changchungyuan (Eternal Spring Garden) to the east of the original garden. The section known as the Western-Style Buildings (Xiyanglou) was constructed across the northern end of this new section.[114] Although earlier Chinese

[108] Tythacott, 'The Yuanmingyuan and its Objects' (n 106) 9.

[109] Greg M Thomas, 'The Looting of Yuanming and the Translation of Chinese Art in Europe' (2008) 7 Nineteenth-Century Art Worldwide <www.19thc-artworldwide.org/index.php/autumn08/93-the-looting-of-yuanming-and-the-translation-of-chinese-art-in-europe> accessed 17 May 2021 (hereafter Thomas, 'The Looting of Yuanming').

[110] Thomas, 'The Looting of Yuanming' (n 109).

[111] Tythacott, 'The Yuanmingyuan and its Objects' (n 106) 5.

[112] Zuozhen Liu, *The Case for Repatriating China's Cultural Objects* (Springer 2016) 8 (hereafter Liu, *The Case for Repatriating*); Thomas, 'The Looting of Yuanming' (n 109). For a detailed discussion of the history and architecture of Yuanmingyuan, see Young-tsu Wong, *A Paradise Lost: The Imperial Garden Yuanming Yuan* (University of Hawai'I Press 2001) (hereafter Wong, *A Paradise Lost*).

[113] Tythacott, 'The Yuanmingyuan and its Objects' (n 106) 6.

[114] Wong, *A Paradise Lost* (n 112) 59.

Figure 3.4 Hall of Audience, Yuanmingyuan palace (1845). Edward Paxman (engraver) and Thomas Allom (artist)

architecture exhibited foreign influences, this was the first large-scale incorporation of foreign architecture in an imperial garden.

Qianlong's interest in constructing a Western-style garden was influenced by his fascination with European fountains, which were very popular in France and Italy. Father Giuseppe Castiglioni, a Jesuit priest and artist who had lived in China, drew examples of Italian and French Baroque palaces to accompany the fountains.[115] The structures were constructed primarily by Europeans, who were not professional architects, with Chinese architects, engineers, and masons. The architectural layout of the largest palace, the Hall of the Calm Seas (Haiyantang), was reminiscent of the Court of Honor at Versailles. Outside the main façade were several fountains, one accompanied by a Chinese-style water clock. The clock was surrounded by twelve bronze animal heads representing the twelve-year cycle of birth and the two-hour periods into which the Chinese divided the day and night.[116] Every two hours, one of the animal heads spouted water, and at noon, they all spouted water together. Yuanmingyuan was also the home of the imperial collection of art and antiquities, which included paintings, calligraphy, bronzes, cloisonné, silks, textiles, and rare books. In sum, the Yuanmingyuan complex, which is described here

[115] ibid, 60–65. The Western-style palaces held extensive collections of European art, furniture, and *objets d'art*, although these at times had to accommodate Chinese taste. The 'Western plan' incorporating European architectural and decorative elements became a technical term in the 'Construction Proposal of the Yuanming Yuan.' ibid, 65.

[116] Wong, *A Paradise Lost* (n 112) 63–64.

only in brief detail, like the palace of Versailles to which it is sometimes compared, served as a repository of the country's greatest productions of royal culture, with particular emphasis on the decorative arts.[117]

During the 1860 attack, the French officers described being overwhelmed by the opulence and magnificence of the objects and palace furnishings. At the same time, the French exoticized the objects by comparing them to the stories of the Thousand and One Nights and decrying their state of decay and neglect, which was symbolic of how Europeans perceived the Chinese in the mid-nineteenth century.[118] Similar to the colonialist narrative used elsewhere by Europeans, particularly in Africa, the extant cultural objects were attributed to the past, which was viewed as of a high order of artistic accomplishment, while the contemporary society was considered to be degenerate and inferior and therefore no longer worthy of these past glories. The one element of the Yuanmingyuan complex particularly worthy of praise from the Europeans was the palace built in French style of the eighteenth century, which, with its furnishings of the same period, mirrored 'old France'.[119]

In a twist of fate, the leader of the expeditionary force was James Bruce, the eighth Earl of Elgin and son of the Lord Elgin who removed the Parthenon Sculptures, and it was he who ordered the destruction of the Palace in retaliation for the deaths of the British emissaries. Elgin acted brutally out of anger at the Chinese and despite the disapproval of his French allies. The French writer Victor Hugo compared the palace to the Parthenon and protested the fate of the palace in a manner similar to protests of the British poets against dismemberment of the Parthenon and of Quatremère de Quincy against Napoleon's plunder. Hugo wrote: 'This wonder has disappeared. One day two bandits entered the Old Summer Palace. One plundered, the other burned.... All the treasures of all our cathedrals put together could not equal this formidable and splendid museum of the Orient.'[120]

[117] Knowledge of the palace complex comes primarily from forty paintings executed in 1744, today located in the Bibliothèque Nationale in Paris. Tythacott, 'The Yuanmingyuan and its Objects' (n 106) 6; John Finlay, 'Henri Bertin (1920–1792) and Images of the Yuanmingyuan in Eighteenth-century France' in Louise Tythacott (ed), *Collecting and Displaying China's "Summer Palace" in the West: The Yuanmingyuan in Britain and France* (Routledge 2018) 123. Unfortunately, members of the inauspicious embassy of Lord Macartney in 1792 were not sufficiently impressed with the palace complex to record details of their surroundings. Wong, *A Paradise Lost* (n 112) 83–85.

[118] Thomas, 'The Looting of Yuanming' (n 109). Some of those reporting on displays of the Yuanmingyuan objects described them 'in typical Orientalist fashion as strange, irrational, and childlike'. In a few cases, commentators acknowledged that the objects reflected a high state of contemporary Chinese artistic skill and mastery. Greg M Thomas, 'Yuanmingyuan on Display: Ornamental Aesthetics at the Musée Chinois' in Louise Tythacott (ed), *Collecting and Displaying China's "Summer Palace" in the West: The Yuanmingyuan in Britain and France* (Routledge 2018) 149, 152–54 (discussing analysis of the French scholar of Chinese philosophy and history, Guillaume Pauthier) (hereafter Thomas, 'Yuanmingyuan on Display').

[119] Thomas, 'The Looting of Yuanming' (n 109).

[120] Victor Hugo, 'The sack of the Summer Palace', letter to Captain Butler, 25 November 1861, quoted in Liu, *The Case for Repatriating* (n 112) 8. Hugo explicitly compared the Parthenon, the epitome of European art and human idealism, with the Yuanmingyuan palace, as the epitome of Oriental art and human imagination. Thomas, 'The Looting of Yuanming' (n 109). Some French described the acts of the British as vandalism, while others acknowledged the military goal of bringing the conflict to a quicker

These actions are considered among the worst examples of imperialist aggression and perhaps even of cultural vandalism of all time.[121] They have remained an important element in the humiliation China felt it suffered at the hands of the European powers during the nineteenth century.

> [T]he burning of the summer palace passed into Chinese folklore as a benchmark of European imperialist atrocity, and it is still invoked to fuel nationalist fervor.... The age of European imperialism in China was well under way but its underside was the resurgence of determination among Chinese of many different backgrounds to restore China to a position of national strength.[122]

The utter destruction of the palace complex and the sparseness of its documentation 'magnified its symbolic reputation both in China and in Europe, where the destruction provoked complex new moral, museological, and artistic reactions related to Europe's own processes of empire formation'.[123] It was not until the 1980s that a research unit and museum were established at the site of the ruins, and in the 1990s, reconstruction and restoration of some of the buildings and gardens began. While the palace became a symbol of national identity, Hevia also suggested that 'the site of the gardens, almost an embarrassment for several generations, was being rediscovered and reworked by the Chinese government as a "site of memory"'.[124] However, he observed on a visit to Yuanmingyuan in 2013 that a display of the zodiac animal heads and their images then dominated the site of the ruins.[125]

Before Yuanmingyuan was destroyed, it was looted extensively.[126] The objects taken included jewels, silks, furs, gold, jades, enamels, porcelains, lacquer wares, furniture, and sculptures. The one aspect of high classical Chinese art that seemed unappreciated were paintings and calligraphy, few of which figured among the loot taken. British and French officers first selected the 'choicest spoils' to be sent to their respective sovereigns, Queen Victoria and Emperor Napoleon III. The grounds were then opened to the soldiers for random looting. Following 'trophy practices from colonial India', the British required the soldiers to turn in their objects to be auctioned, and the proceeds were then divided, with one-third going to officers

end through such cultural destruction. Another possible motive for Elgin in destroying the palace may have been to conceal the extent of the plunder. Wong, *A Paradise Lost* (n 112) 145–48.

121 Tythacott, 'The Yuanmingyuan and its Objects' (n 106) 12.

122 Waley-Cohen, *The Sextants of Beijing* (n 102) 164–65.

123 Thomas, 'The Looting of Yuanming' (n 109).

124 James L Hevia, 'The Afterlives of a Ruin: The Yuanmingyuan in China and the West' in Louise Tythacott (ed), *Collecting and Displaying China's "Summer Palace" in the West: The Yuanmingyuan in Britain and France* (Routledge 2018) 25, 26 (hereafter Hevia, 'The Afterlives of a Ruin').

125 ibid, 30.

126 Despite commercial as well as artistic value, many of the decorative objects were destroyed wantonly. A few of the European observers acknowledged the loss of cultural and financial wealth. Thomas, 'The Looting of Yuanming' (n 109).

Figure 3.5 Gold Cups of Eternal Stability (probably 1739–1740 and 1740–1741), made for the Quianlong Emperor (1711–1799) and acquired by Richard Wallace at auction in Paris in 1872

and two-thirds to soldiers.[127] French soldiers were allowed to keep the objects they took. The looted objects were thus transformed from 'emblems of imperial culture into military souvenirs and commodities before [being] pass[ed] off in Hong Kong or Europe as art or decorative art'.[128] Many objects subsequently appeared at auctions and in dealer galleries in London and elsewhere in Europe (Figure 3.5). Objects were labelled as being from the 'Summer Palace of the Emperor of China' as a way of conferring prestige, regardless of whether the origin of the objects sold could be verified. Objects identified as coming from the palace appeared soon after in museum exhibits and collections and in the collections of the regiments that had participated in its destruction.[129]

127 ibid. The Indian units received smaller shares than their British counterparts.

128 ibid. The objects looted in 1860 seem to have been appreciated on the market primarily as emblems of European military domination over China. In contrast, artefacts looted in the 1900 Boxer Uprising were by then appreciated as 'precious works of art'. ibid. Hevia attributes this transformation, in part, to studies and knowledge production carried out by Western diplomats working in China. Hevia, 'The Afterlives of a Ruin' (n 124) 31.

129 Tythacott, 'The Yuanmingyuan and its Objects' (n 106) 12; Hevia, 'The Afterlives of a Ruin' (n 124) 30–31.

The French and British commissions responsible for selecting objects for the sovereigns focused on 'transfer[ring] the political and cultural prestige attached to the emperor's belongings' through the high cultural value that these objects could confer.[130] The only objects selected for Queen Victoria were a gold and jade sceptre, symbolizing the 'heavenly sanctioned absolute authority of the monarch', and large cloisonné enamel vases. These became part of the British royal collection. The French officers presented a large group of objects, including jades, cloisonné, lacquers, textiles, and gold and bronze objects to Napoleon III and Empress Eugénie. These were displayed publicly first at the Tuileries Palace in Paris, and they were later moved to Fontainebleau Castle where they form their own museum, the Musée Chinois.[131] Thomas points out that the display is the result of the Chinese artists who made the objects, the French officers who selected them for the Empress, and the display choices made by the Empress, her designer, and his craftspeople.[132]

The museum originally housed about 400 Chinese objects and about sixty from Thailand. Objects from other parts of Asia, acquired from existing collections in France or as diplomatic gifts, were gradually added to the museum, which was therefore not composed entirely of Chinese objects. The museum was closed for extensive periods of time but, after a renovation between 1984 and 1991, it has now returned to its original appearance, as best as can be determined.[133] The objects were displayed in an order which, at best, reflected European understanding of museum aesthetics. Chinese notions of aesthetics, national history, cultural identity, and religious sensitivities, such as to Buddhism, played no part.[134] On the other hand, the placement of the objects in a museum located in a French palace built in the eighteenth century by the *ancien régime* provided a link to China of the eighteenth century when Yuanmingyuan, with its French palaces, was also constructed. This presented an 'essentially parallel pattern of imperial ideological framing', or, as the author of a contemporary news article explained, the objects 'have merely changed their address without compromising their dignity'.[135]

Thomas characterized the looting and subsequent movement of these objects as part of an intercultural transmission that 'radically transformed the meaning of the looted objects'.[136] The objects carried different levels of cultural, political, and

[130] Thomas, 'The Looting of Yuanming' (n 109).

[131] Vincent Droguet, 'Empress Eugénie's Chinese Museum at the Château of Fontainebleau: An Unusual Décor in the "House of the Ages"' in Louise Tythacott (ed), *Collecting and Displaying China's "Summer Palace" in the West: The Yuanmingyuan in Britain and France* (Routledge 2018) 138, 138–43; Thomas, 'Yuanmingyuan on Display' 151.

[132] Thomas, 'Yuanmingyuan on Display' (n 118) 149.

[133] Thomas, 'The Looting of Yuanming' (n 109).

[134] The descriptions, attributions of functions, and placements of Buddhist objects displayed a surprisingly high degree of ignorance of and distaste for Buddhism. Thomas, 'Yuanmingyuan on Display' (n 118) 152.

[135] Thomas, 'The Looting of Yuanming' (n 109) (quoting an Illustrated London News article).

[136] ibid.

economic meaning within the different value systems of China and Europe. These different meanings 'were variously appropriated, ignored, or destroyed based on competing systems of meaning and value'.[137] The appropriation of Chinese imperial culture through the looting reinforced France's own imperial ambitions during the reign of Napoleon III, and this process 'depended on an implicit, underlying recognition of similarity and even equivalence between' the imperial cultures of China and France.[138]

Napoleon in looting from Europe and Elgin in removing the Parthenon and other ancient sculptures had among their primary goals the inspiration and improvement of the arts among British and French artists and artisans. The destruction and looting of the Yuanmingyuan complex were motivated by revenge, military and political superiority, transfer of imperial power to the French and British monarchs, and financial gain through sale of artefacts on the European art market. However, the incorporation of these objects into the art market, public and regimental museums, and private collections also had the effect of inspiring and benefiting the development of the arts and artistic styles in Europe.[139]

This is seen primarily in Britain in the influence of Yuanmingyuan objects on the design reform movement[140] of the mid and later nineteenth century and the development of the so-called minor arts, particularly porcelains, enamels, and cloisonné. In some of the earliest displays of Yuanmingyuan objects, the two expedition leaders, Elgin and General Sir James Hope Grant, loaned pieces to the Bristol Exhibition of Industrial and Ornamental Art and the Exhibition of Industrial and Decorative Art in Edinburgh. Leaders of the design reform movement exhorted British industrial designers to adopt the flat patterns, linear elements, bright colours, and monochromatic ceramics of these Chinese objects.[141] The designer Owen Jones' publication, *Examples of Chinese Ornament Selected from Objects in the South Kensington Museum and Other Collections* (1867), was a study of patterns on Chinese vessels traceable to the Yuanmingyuan looting, although not explicitly identified as such.[142] The volume became a 'design reform sourcebook' and a '"valuable and instructive aid"' for artistic innovation inspired by these dislocated

[137] ibid. Thomas illustrates this with the fate of a set of jade beads that had little financial value in Europe but great political significance in China as a symbol of divine favour given by the sovereign.

[138] ibid.

[139] Katie Hill, 'The Yuanmingyuan and Design Reform in Britain', in Louise Tythacott (ed), *Collecting and Displaying China's "Summer Palace" in the West: The Yuanmingyuan in Britain and France* (Routledge 2018) 53 (hereafter Hill, 'The Yuanmingyuan and Design Reform').

[140] The design reform movement was stimulated by an 1836 report of the Parliamentary Select Committee on Art and Manufactures. The goal was to improve the quality of goods manufactured in Britain through advances in industrial design so British goods could compete more successfully with goods produced in France, Germany, and the United States. Sara J Oshinsky, 'Design Reform' in *Heilbrunn Timeline of Art History* (2006) <www.metmuseum.org/toah/hd/dsrf/hd_dsrf.htm> accessed 4 March 2022; Vrdoljak, *International Law* (n 1) 35–40.

[141] Hill, 'The Yuanmingyuan and Design Reform' (n 139) 57–59.

[142] ibid, 59.

works. Manufacturing, the use of underglaze blue and red designs for two-colour printing, and wallpaper production were among the industries that seem to have utilized Jones' volume as a design resource.[143] The looting of these works thus benefited British industry and stimulated development of new aesthetic tastes.

Objects from Yuanmingyuan continue to appear on the market, sometimes advertised as such, and often achieving very high sale prices.[144] There is no inventory of the looted objects, nor precise numbers, so it is difficult to determine which objects have a provenance traceable to the Yuanmingyuan looting. Perhaps the most securely attributed element from Yuanmingyuan is the Zodiac Fountain, the water-clock fountain at the Hall of Calm Seas (Haiyantang) Palace.[145] Twelve bronze animal heads flanked the fountain, representing the Chinese zodiac. The fate of seven of the zodiac heads illustrates the escalation in market prices for these objects. The horse head was sold for $367,000 in 1989 but was then resold for $8.9 million in 2007 to Stanley Ho, a wealthy Macau and Hong Kong-based casino developer. Ho subsequently donated the figure to China.[146] In 2000, the Poly Art Museum, which was founded by the Chinese government in 1998 and has links to the Chinese military, acquired three of the heads (the tiger, the monkey, and the ox) for a total of $1,000,000.[147] In 2003, Ho purchased the boar's head for $770,000 at auction in New York and donated it to the Poly Art Museum.[148]

In February 2009, Christie's auctioned two of the Zodiac figures, the rat and the rabbit, as part of the estate of the designer Yves Saint Laurent. The two figures were sold over strenuous objection from China, and a suit to prevent the sale brought by Chinese citizens living in France was rejected.[149] The winning bidder was a

[143] ibid, 62–64.

[144] An enamelled vase sold at a suburban London auction house for $69.5 million, although bidding started at $800,000. While dated to the time of Qianlong, it is not certain whether this vase was part of the Yuanmingyuan loot. John F Burns, 'Qing Dynasty Relic Yields Record Price at Auction' (*NY Times*, 12 November 2010) <www.nytimes.com/2010/11/13/world/europe/13vase.html?_r=0> accessed 17 May 2021. For discussion of other objects attributed to Yuanmingyuan sold at auction, see Hevia, 'The Afterlives of a Ruin' (n 124) 33.

[145] Hevia poses the question of how the zodiac heads and the redeveloped site of the European-style palaces, which 'are the least imperial of the imperial objects', have become 'an essential symbol of the Yuanmingyuan'. Hevia, 'The Afterlives of a Ruin' (n 124) 34. There is apparently no reference to the zodiac heads in any of the descriptions of the looting or of the objects taken. ibid, 33.

[146] Hugh Eakin, 'The Affair of the Chinese Bronze Heads' (*NY Rev Books*, 14 May 2009) <www.nybooks.com/articles/2009/05/14/the-affair-of-the-chinese-bronze-heads/> accessed 17 May 2021 (hereafter, Eakin, 'The Affair of the Chinese Bronze Heads').

[147] Yang Meng, 'China's long-lost national treasures put on display' (*CGTN.com*, 9 October 2018) https://news.cgtn.com/news/3d3d514d336b444d7a457a6333566d54/share_p.html accessed 4 March 2022.

[148] Andrea Wallace, Anne Laure Bandle, and Marc-André Renold, 'Two Bronze Animal Heads—China and Pierre Bergé' (*ArThemis*, August 2013) <https://plone.unige.ch/art-adr/cases-affaires/two-bronze-animal-heads-2013-china-and-pierre-berge> accessed 17 May 2021.

[149] Christie's stated that it had clear legal title for the works. James Hevia suggested that this was 'not simply preposterous, but Orwellian.' He called for a new way of thinking about events understood by the descendants of the victims 'as ongoing forms of humiliation.' James Hevia, 'Summer Palace Relics' (*The China Beat*, 24 February 2009) http://thechinabeat.blogspot.com/2009/02/james-hevia-on-summer-palace-relics.html accessed 24 May 2021

Chinese dealer, Cai Mingchao, who bid approximately $18 million for each figure, but he later refused to pay.[150] At first, Pierre Bergé, the beneficiary of the Saint Laurent estate, offered to return the sculptures to China if the Chinese government would grant human rights to Tibet.[151] Following the sale, the Chinese government tightened its customs rules against Christie's. Kering, the company that owned Christie's, subsequently acquired the heads, and on a trip to China, François-Henri Pinault, chief executive officer of Kering, offered to return the sculptures by donating them to the Poly Art Museum. The sculptures were returned soon after in a high-profile ceremony at the National Museum of China opposite Tiananmen Square. The Chinese government then granted Christie's a licence allowing it to be the first foreign auction house to operate independently in mainland China.

The fate of the remaining five sculptures is unknown and perhaps they were melted down over time. In 2010, the prominent Chinese contemporary artist, Ai Weiwei, executed a sculptural group in several versions (including in gold and bronze) of the twelve zodiac heads, entitled *Circle of Animals—Zodiac Heads*. The sculptural sets have been sent on exhibit at venues throughout the world.[152] Other reproductions have been placed at various sites in China.

China's art market is now ranked as either the second or third largest in the world.[153] The strength and lucrative nature of this market reflect China's economic growth and are why both Christie's and Sotheby's have competed to establish their market position in mainland China. This seems to have been a primary motivation for Christie's decision to return the two Zodiac figures as a donation, rather than persisting in its attempts to sell the sculptures. China is an example of a country whose past has been pillaged, but which seems to have sufficient contemporary economic power to compete on the world market to reacquire its cultural heritage, either directly through purchases or indirectly through pressure. However, many countries of origin are reluctant to purchase back their cultural objects on the international market, even if they are able to do so. Such a purchase may be construed as tacit recognition that the current possessor has valid title and may lead to escalation in market value of other objects, as seen in the increasing prices of the zodiac heads. Furthermore, repurchasing does not compensate for the historical humiliation and destruction caused by the expropriation and might give a veneer of legitimacy to the act of expropriation.

150 Nazanin Lankarani, 'Saint Laurent Auction Rich in Sentimental Value' (*NY Times*, 13 Nov 2009) <www.nytimes.com/2009/11/14/arts/14iht-raaysl.html> accessed 17 May 2021.

151 Eakin, 'The Affair of the Chinese Bronze Heads' (n 146). This offer presented a juxtaposition of human rights and cultural rights, a subject that will be considered in chapter 5.

152 'Circle of Animals/Zodiac Heads' <www.zodiacheads.com/index.html> accessed 17 May 2021.

153 Clare McAndrew, 'The Art Basel and UBS Global Art Market Report 2023' <https://www.ubs.com/global/en/our-firm/art/collecting/art-market-survey.html#artmarketreport2022> accessed 6 July 2023.

3.4 The Benin Cultural Objects

Particularly in the second half of the nineteenth century, several European States spread their influence, political power, and economic domination throughout much of Africa. In addition to access to natural resources and trade, motivation for this expansion was a mission of religious evangelism and cultural civilizing of the Indigenous populations. As seen elsewhere, the different European powers viewed the cultural remains of these territories as available to be taken back to Europe, and perhaps it was in Africa that the European powers were the most extractive of the cultural wealth of the Indigenous peoples. Vrdoljak described the nineteenth-century European expropriations from Africa as the 'collecting frenzy of European empires'.[154]

Major museum and private collections of African cultural objects were formed in Europe at this time. In 1861, the founder of the Musée Africain in Lyon exhorted missionaries in the Ivory Coast: 'We wish to have in our museum all your gods, first of all, and then weapons, tools, household utensils—in a word, nothing must be missing.'[155] While the artistic quality of these works was extolled, as they did elsewhere, the Europeans denigrated the contemporary populations and asserted that they were not worthy guardians or possessors of such objects.[156] According to Sarr and Savoy, the numerous European military raids and expeditions carried out in Africa and, to a lesser extent, Asia, were accompanied by experts responsible for advising on the targeting and collecting of cultural objects; these targets were sometimes chosen for their cultural, rather than their military value.[157] The plunder of cultural objects and their transport to Europe were 'at the heart of—and not at the margins—of the colonial enterprise',[158] thus echoing Napoleon's expedition to Egypt.

The British were perhaps responsible for the largest-scale looting of cultural objects from Africa during the late nineteenth and early twentieth centuries, including the looting of the treasure of Maqdala from Ethiopia while taking revenge on the Emperor Tewodros in 1868.[159] It reportedly required fifteen elephants

[154] Vrdoljak, *International Law* (n 1) 5.

[155] Silvie Memel-Kassi, 'The Illicit Circulation of Ivorian Collections: Challenges and Prospects' (2020) 4 Journal for Art Market Studies 1, 4. Objects typically circulated from the colonized territory to the colonizer. For example, cultural objects from the Ivory Coast, Gabon, and Mali primarily were taken to France. The art markets in the different European countries still reflect the cultural heritage of their respective former colonies. ibid, 5.

[156] Folarin Shyllon, 'Restitution of Antiquities to Sub-Saharan Africa: The Booty and Captivity' (2015) 20 AAL 369, 372–73 (hereafter Shyllon, 'Restitution of Antiquities to Sub-Saharan Africa').

[157] Felwine Sarr and Bénédicte Savoy, 'The Restitution of African Cultural Heritage. Toward a New Relational Ethic' (2018) 10–11 <http://restitutionreport2018.com/sarr_savoy_en.pdf> accessed 4 March 2022 (hereafter Sarr and Savoy, 'The Restitution of African Cultural Heritage').

[158] ibid, 13.

[159] Folarin Shyllon, 'Unraveling History: Return of African Cultural Objects Repatriated and Looted in Colonial Times' in James A R Nafziger and Ann M Nicgorski (eds), *Cultural Heritage Issues: The Legacy of Conquest, Colonization, and Commerce* (Martinis Nijhoff Publishers 2009) 159, 161–63 (hereafter Shyllon, 'Unraveling History'). Several of the royal objects taken were returned as gifts to Ethiopia

and 200 mules to carry away the objects, which included illuminated Bibles and manuscripts, gold crowns, chalices, vestments and icons from churches, arms, and shields dating from the fourteenth to the nineteenth centuries.[160] A British punitive expedition against the Asante in modern Ghana in 1874, waged in order to achieve domination over trade, resulted in the ransacking of the capital and the taking of gold artefacts produced through the cire perdue method of casting for which the Asante were well known.[161] Another British punitive expedition resulted in perhaps the best known and most contested of the objects removed by British military forces from Africa near the close of the nineteenth century.

Benin was a kingdom located in what is today Edo State in the modern nation of Nigeria, with its religious and political centre at Benin City.[162] Benin's wealth was based on its control of the land and river trade between the African interior and the Atlantic coast.[163] The kingdom reached the peak of its military power in the fifteenth and sixteenth centuries under the leadership of an Oba, a warrior king, who ruled in an unbroken succession from 1440.[164] This peak coincided with a period of artistic accomplishment. Among the best-known and most artistically respected works were the royally commissioned brass works, known as the Benin bronzes.[165] The plaques were a pictorial record of the history of the kingdom and could only be owned by the Oba. Hicks described Benin City in the nineteenth century as

but without any acknowledgement of fault. ibid, 160–61. In 1910, the most important private collector of Maqdala objects bequeathed her collection to the Ethiopian emperor. However, her will was overturned and the bequest invalidated. Shyllon, 'Restitution of Antiquities to Sub-Saharan Africa' (n 156) 376. A Tabot, a sacred stone object that was part of the Maqdala treasure, was held at Westminster Abbey and another in a church in Edinburgh. The latter has been returned but not the former. ibid, 377–78.

[160] ibid, 372–75. An archaeologist from the British Museum, whose presence had been specifically requested, accompanied the expedition against Ethiopia. Debbie Challs and Lucia Patrizio Gunning, 'Planned Plunder? The British Museum and the 1868 Maqdala Expedition' (Cambridge Core blog, 17 January 2023) <www.cambridge.org/core/blog/2023/01/17/planned-plunder-the-british-museum-and-the-1868-maqdala-expedition/> accessed 5 February 2023.

[161] Shyllon, 'Restitution of Antiquities to Sub-Saharan Africa' (n 156), 376. This method of gold casting requires a high degree of technical skill. Annie Coombes, *Reinventing Africa: Museums, Material Culture and Popular Imagination in Late Victorian and Edwardian England* (Yale Univ Press 1994) 17 (hereafter Coombes, *Reinventing Africa*). The British carried out many punitive and pacification expeditions in Africa during this time. Dan Hicks, *The Brutish Museums: The Benin Bronzes, Colonial Violence and Cultural Restitution* (Pluto Press 2020) 2 (hereafter Hicks, *The Brutish Museums*).

[162] Much of the following description of historical events is based on Hicks, *The Brutish Museums* (n 161); Neil Brodie, 'Problematizing the Encyclopedic Museum: The Benin Bronzes and Ivories in Historical Context' in Bonnie Effros and Guolong Lai (eds), *Unmasking Ideologies: The Vocabulary and Symbols of Colonial Archaeology* (Cotsen Institute 2018) 61 (hereafter Brodie, 'Problematizing the Encyclopedic Museum'); Salome Kiwara-Wilson, 'Restituting Colonial Plunder: The Case for the Benin Bronzes and Ivories' (2013) 23 DePaul Journal of Art, Technology & Intellectual Property Law 375 (hereafter Kiwara-Wilson, 'Restituting Colonial Plunder'); Coombes, *Reinventing Africa* (n 161) 7–28.

[163] Hicks, *The Brutish Museums* (n 161) 7.

[164] ibid, 7–8.

[165] The term 'bronzes' is a misnomer. The objects were not always composed of bronze but may have been made of zinc, brass, leaded bronze, or an alloy of copper, zinc, and lead in different proportions. Coombes, *Reinventing Africa* (n 161) 228 note 1.

a 'monumental landscape of courthouses, compounds, and mausoleums, the centre of royal and religious power encompassed in an ancient network of ditched and banked earthwork, enclosures, and with central repositories of thousands of unique artefacts that bore witness to the kingdom's past'.[166]

Beginning in the sixteenth century, Benin traded extensively with Portugal and later with other European powers. By the late nineteenth century, Great Britain was the dominant foreign power in the region. After the decline in the slave trade in the early nineteenth century and of palm oil in the late nineteenth century, British traders were seeking new commodities and access to raw materials, which necessitated expansion of British military and political authority into the interior beyond the coast.[167] In 1885, the British declared the Oil Rivers Protectorate over the eastern Niger delta, which was confirmed by the Berlin Conference, and then sought to expand into the Benin River area.

The Oba at first resisted treaty terms that the British tried to enforce on Benin. Nonetheless, in 1892, the British vice consul, Captain Henry Galway, negotiated a treaty with Oba Ovonramwen, which gave the British authority over Benin's foreign relations, greatly reduced the Oba's sovereign power, and required the Oba to allow free trade to all nations within his kingdom.[168] In 1893, the British extended the borders of the Oil Rivers Protectorate to incorporate the Kingdom of Benin within the new Niger Coast Protectorate. However, when the Oba continued to control the trade, especially in oil palm kernels, and the anticipated trade expansion did not occur, the new vice consul, Ralph Moor, and then his deputy, James Phillips, initiated plans to remove the Oba from power and replace him with a native council.

Phillips planned a visit to the Oba in January 1897, which unfortunately coincided with a sacred festival during which foreigners were forbidden to enter the city. The Oba tried to prevent Phillips from coming, as did the British Foreign Office, whose instructions did not reach Phillips. Phillips ignored the Oba's message, and his party was attacked, an action the Oba also opposed, killing all but two of the British officials and many of the African porters who accompanied him. In retaliation, although also in furtherance of the British goal of attaining control over the Benin Kingdom, the British mounted a punitive expedition, which 'was billed as just war, morally justifiable … to avenge the massacre … .'[169] Despite resistance,

166 Hicks, *The Brutish Museums* (n 161) 8.

167 Brodie, 'Problematizing the Encyclopedic Museum' (n 162) 62–64.

168 Coombes, *Reinventing Africa* (n 161) 9. Whether the Oba accepted the treaty terms is uncertain, given the difficulties of multiple translations and the Oba's refusal to directly sign the treaty. Brodie, 'Problematizing the Encyclopedic Museum' (n 162) 64.

169 Kiwara-Wilson, 'Restituting Colonial Plunder' (n 162) 384 n 68 (quoting Robert Home, *City of Blood Revisited: A New Look at the Benin Expedition of 1897* (1982) 102–03). Hicks collects the various justifications the British employed for the destruction of Benin City and their denials of the extent of the attack and resulting destruction, which he describes as 'untruthful framing'. Hicks, *The Brutish Museums* (n 161) 40. Other justifications for British aggression in Africa over the course of the nineteenth century included conversion to Christianity, rescuing the inhabitants from human sacrifice, cannibalism, slaughter rituals, and fetish worship, and bringing civilization. British goals are presented as altruistic,

Benin City fell and the Oba was later captured. However, unlike many other leaders, the Oba was not executed but rather exiled, while the monarchy was abolished, and Benin was incorporated into the British Protectorate of Nigeria. When the Oba died in 1914, the British permitted his oldest son, Oba Eweka II, to succeed to the throne, and the Benin royal family continues to this day. The kingdom was first subject to British authority and is now subject to the authority of the Nigerian government. However, the distinct artistic traditions of earlier centuries continue in Benin City.

When Benin City fell, the British looted and burned the city for two days, recovering 'spoils of war'.[170] The estimated number of total objects taken of bronze, wood, coral, and ivory range in the many thousands and the number will never be known accurately.[171] In the palace, the British found brass plaques, ivory carvings, ceremonial objects, altars, staffs of office, body ornaments, and the famous ivory Queen Mother masks.[172] (Figure 3.6. The carved ivory tusks and bronze heads were removed without any record of their placement, which would have assisted in understanding their relationship to the various Obas and in reconstructing the history of Benin. The bronze heads are the equivalent of historical records, as at the death of an Oba, a bronze head was cast, thus embodying the history of the Kingdom of Benin back to the twelfth century.[173] The commemorative plaques, heads, and carved ivory tusks recording the Obas' achievements presented a 'unique historical record of sovereignty, of politics, and of culture'.[174] However, when the objects were looted, their original locations and associations were not recorded. The loss of this contextual association means that the dating of the objects and other historical information have been lost.[175]

The response of the British to the quality of the artworks was contradictory. At the time of the expedition, the British 'thought that the treasures they had recovered were created by the Portuguese, because "their artistic quality and advanced technology were apparent to even the most prejudiced eye"'.[176] Or they thought, at the least, that Europeans had taught the Edo how to apply their skills in clay modelling to the technique of metal casting.[177] This fit with a narrative that the contemporary population of Benin represented a degenerate society that was not

with the desire to establish trade monopolies rarely mentioned. ibid, 43; Coombes, *Reinventing Africa* (n 161) 10, 17.

170 Hicks, *The Brutish Museums* (n 161) 110–13.

171 Brodie, 'Problematizing the Encyclopedic Museum' (n 162) 66 (more than 3,000 objects); Hicks, *The Brutish Museums* (n 161) 8, 136–37 (more than 10,000 royal and sacred objects).

172 Hicks, *The Brutish Museums* (n 161) 140–41.

173 Shyllon, 'Unraveling History' (n 159) 163.

174 Hicks, *The Brutish Museums* (n 161) 139.

175 Barbara Plankensteiner, 'Introduction' in Barbara Plankensteiner (ed) *Benin Kings and Rituals: Court Arts from Nigeria* (Snoeck Publ 2007) 21, 28 (hereafter Plankensteiner, 'Introduction').

176 Kiwara-Wilson, 'Restituting Colonial Plunder' (n 162) 385. See also Coombes, *Reinventing Africa* (n 161) 45–46.

177 Coombes, *Reinventing Africa* (n 161) 26; Elazar Barkan, 'Aesthetics and Evolution: Benin Art in Europe' (1997) 30 African Arts Special Issue: The Benin Centenary 36, 38 (hereafter Barkan, 'Aesthetics

Figure 3.6 Queen Mother Pendant Mask. Benin City, Edo State, Nigeria. Early sixteenth century. Metropolitan Museum of Art

capable of producing this quality of work. For their conduct to fit within the colonialist justification, it was necessary for the British to ascribe the objects of high-quality workmanship to the ever more distant past, while claiming that there was no evidence of contemporary craft.[178] Nonetheless, the reception of these objects

and Evolution'). Some also attributed the high level of skill to Egyptian influence. Coombes, *Reinventing Africa* (n 161) 27.

[178] Coombes, *Reinventing Africa* (n 161) 22–23. This disassociation of contemporary people from past societies as a way of denigrating and delegitimizing the claims of contemporary people to their cultural heritage is a consistent feature, seen in the context of Indigenous groups, as discussed earlier. The

in Europe and North America fundamentally changed the perception of the artistic and technological skills of the Benin artists and bronze casters.

The understanding and later reception of the Benin objects in Europe illustrate several themes common to the treatment of cultural objects created outside of Europe and then transported, as a part of colonialism and armed conflict, to Europe. When the Benin objects were brought to the United Kingdom, they became central to the professionalization and institutionalization of the emerging field of anthropology. What came to be known as ethnographic museums were often constructed specifically for housing objects taken as colonial plunder, while the field of anthropology became useful for assisting in colonial mastery and administration.[179] The rejection of an Egyptian origin for the Benin bronzes placed them outside of the traditional realms of archaeology and antiquity, which focused on the Mediterranean and Mesopotamia, and became a source of validation for the departments of ethnology or anthropology, particularly at the British Museum.[180] These objects were not initially treated as 'art' or placed in art museums, but rather as ethnographic objects that were the product of a tribal or 'primitive' society.[181] However, the Benin objects were later transformed and became treated as 'high art' in an art historical and aesthetic sense. In the process of that transformation, we can see the changes in meaning and significance given to the objects.

A plaque located in the British Museum, and one of the subjects of Neil MacGregor's history based on one hundred objects in the British Museum, illustrates the competing perspectives that can be brought to bear on the Benin objects.[182] The plaque depicts the Oba flanked by two of his chiefs and two smaller Europeans (Figure 3.6). Sani Yakubu Adam points out that three narratives have evolved surrounding the plaque.[183] The plaque likely depicts a ceremony created by Oba Ewuare (1440–1473) that commemorates the Oba's extension of power over the chiefs. The plaque also seems to indicate the Oba's superiority over the

barbarity and savagery ascribed to the Benin City residents, in particular the emphasis on human sacrifice recorded by members of the expeditionary forces, reinforced the attempt to delegitimize claims of the contemporary society to the artistic production.

[179] Sarr and Savoy, 'The Restitution of African Cultural Heritage' (n 157) 11, 14.

[180] Coombes, *Reinventing Africa* (n 161) 62.

[181] Rosemary J Coombe, 'The Properties of Culture and the Politics of Possessing Identity: Native Claims in the Cultural Appropriation Controversy' (1993) 6 Canadian JL & Juris 249, 257–58.

[182] Neil MacGregor, A History of the World in 100 Objects (Penguin Books 2010). The plaque is object number 77 in MacGregor's publication and its museum number is AF1898,0115.23 <www.britishmuseum.org/collection/object/E_Af1898-0115-23> accessed 17 May 2021. As part of the international exhibit 'A History of the World in 100 Objects', the plaque has been on display in many parts of the world beginning in 2010, but, before that, it seems to have been displayed only between 1970 and 1973.

[183] Sani Yakubu Adam, 'The Benin Plaque and Competing Narratives of the African Art' (*100 Histories of 100 Worlds in 1 Object*, 2020) https://100histories100worlds.org/the-benin-plaque/ accessed 17 May 2021 (hereafter Adam, 'The Benin Plaque'). For discussion of the three levels on which cultural objects should be understood, see also chapter 1.

Europeans, who are represented in miniature. The plaques gain local meaning from their depiction of historical events, perhaps serving as mnemonic devices. Adam describes that the word in Edo that means 'to commemorate' literally means 'to cast a pattern in brass', indicating the connection between the artistic production and historical record.[184] Once removed from their historical context, the plaques lost this aspect of their meaning, even as they became subject to universalism.

The national or regional level on which the Benin works are understood is based on their role in a narrative that shows connections among the different parts of Nigeria, including the Nok and Igbo Ukwu cultures. This raises the question of whether the Benin objects belong to the Kingdom of Benin, located within Nigeria, or to Nigeria, represented by the national government, and the important corollary of to whom they should be returned.[185] The third narrative or understanding of the Benin objects derives from their transformation from ethnographic examples of material culture to 'art'. Their desirability by museums, collectors, and the art market indicates this transformation.[186] Universal value has been conferred, and the Benin objects are viewed as part of the world's shared heritage.[187] The inclusion of a Benin plaque in the British Museum's exhibits and in Macgregor's publication of *A History of the World in 100 Objects* indicates the placement of these objects as part of universal culture.

Hicks disputes the frequently stated point that the proceeds from the sales of the objects were used to pay the costs of the Punitive Expedition.[188] Approximately 300 of the brass plaques were sent to London, of which about 200 were retained by the British Museum, and the other hundred were sold off by the Foreign Office to various museums, collectors, and dealers.[189] The remaining approximately 700 looted plaques were sold to dealers and were in Berlin's Ethnological Museum and in the United States at, among others, the Metropolitan Museum of Art, the

[184] Adam, 'The Benin Plaque' (n 183).

[185] ibid; Barkan, 'Aesthetics and Evolution' (n 176) 41.

[186] Initially there was a strong market in Benin artefacts when they were first sold between 1897 and 1900, but the market then seemed to decline. Barkan, 'Aesthetics and Evolution' (n 177) 38–39. One of the largest private collections was formed by General Pitt Rivers whose grandson sold off many of the objects in the 1960s and 1970s and many of these were purchased by US museums. Plankensteiner, 'Introduction' (n 175) 33. Following the restoration of the Oba, a contemporary school of Benin crafts was initiated responding both to the restoration and patronage of the palace and to external market demand. Barkan, 'Aesthetics and Evolution' (n 177) 40; Paula Girshick Ben-Amos, *The Art of Benin* (rev edn, British Museum Press 1995) 60–63.

[187] As part of a catalogue publication accompanying an exhibit of Benin artefacts in Vienna, Berlin, Paris, and Chicago, Barbara Plankensteiner described the place of the Benin objects in museums throughout the world 'where they now bear witness and spread the knowledge of a major West African empire and its long history and fascinating culture and are considered as indispensable contribution to world cultural heritage.' Plankensteiner, 'Introduction' (n 175) 25. While the National Commission for Museums and Monuments of Nigeria is credited as a cooperating institution, the exhibit did not go to Nigeria.

[188] Hicks, *The Brutish Museums* (n 161) 142. While Hicks disputes that the objects were sold to pay for the expedition as an apparent whitewashing, the notion that the victims of aggression need to pay for the costs of the aggression seems as reprehensible as any other justification for looting.

[189] Hicks, *The Brutish Museums* (n 161) 143–45.

Museum of Fine Arts, Boston, and the Art Institute of Chicago.[190] Uncarved ivory tusks were sold and the proceeds went to the Protectorate.[191] The third category of looted artefacts is everything else, taken with 'sheer chaos and haphazard contempt shown for royal and sacred objects in the dispersal of the loot'.[192] These objects, while undocumented and uncounted, have come to light over the decades, to a large extent through the estate sales of those who participated in the Punitive Expedition and their descendants. While the exact numbers and locations of the Benin artefacts are not known, Dan Hicks has created an inventory and a list of institutions holding many of the Benin objects.[193]

From the time of independence in 1960, Nigeria has made several requests for return of the objects. When a museum was being planned for Benin City in 1968, Nigeria requested return of Benin objects through the International Council of Museums; however, the appeal did not result in any returns.[194] Nigeria purchased, at auction, several Benin bronzes that had previously been on display in the Benin gallery in the National Museum in Lagos and later, in 1980, purchased other works of art, including three Benin bronzes, at Sotheby's in London for £800,000.[195] Nigeria also requested the loan of an ivory pendant mask from the British Museum for a pan-African cultural festival in 1977 but was refused.[196] In the lead-up to the centenary of the Benin Punitive Expedition, several efforts at voluntary repatriation were undertaken, again without any success. Suggestions of pursuing legal action in either the International Court of Justice or courts in the United Kingdom were rejected in favour of continued diplomatic efforts.[197]

In 2010, Sotheby's announced the sale of a sixteenth-century ivory mask and five other Benin objects, which were in the possession of the descendants of Henry Galway, who took part in the Punitive Expedition and would have received the mask as a spoil of war (Figure 3.7).[198] Extensive protests through social networking

190 Hicks, based on Kathryn Wysocki Gunsch, *The Benin Plaques: A 16th-Century Imperial Monument* (Routledge 2018), lists the locations of the 868 plaques as Germany (330), the UK (223), the US (120), Nigeria (78), and the remainder in Austria, Russia, Sweden, the Netherlands, Belgium, Switzerland, and Canada. Hicks, *The Brutish Museums* (n 161) 145, 243–44.

191 ibid, 143.

192 ibid, 146.

193 ibid, 243–52. The Sarr-Savoy Report gives detailed statistics on artefacts of African origin held in French institutions and inventories of the Quai Branly-Jacques Chirac Museum, but Benin objects do not seem to be present. Sarr-Savoy, 'The Restitution of African Cultural Heritage' (n 157) 137–234.

194 Shyllon, 'Unraveling History' (n 159) 162.

195 ibid.

196 ibid; see also Folarin Shyllon, 'Cultural Heritage Legislation and Management in Nigeria' (1996) 5 IJCP 235; Folarin Shyllon, 'One Hundred Years of Looting of Nigerian Art Treasures 1897–1996' (1998) 3 AAL 253.

197 Shyllon, 'Unraveling History' (n 159) 163.

198 The mask depicts the head of the queen mother. It had previously been displayed publicly in London in 1947 and 1951 but had not been seen since then. The mask was estimated to sell at between £2.5 million and £4.5 million. Cristina Ruiz, 'Qatari sheikh's rare ivory mask, stolen from Benin City by the British, is one of five on public display—none in Nigeria' (*The Art Newspaper*, 4 November 2022) <www.theartnewspaper.com/2022/11/04/qatari-sheikhs-rare-ivory-mask-stolen-from-benin-city-by-the-british-is-one-of-five-on-public-displaynone-in-nigeria> accessed 10 November 2022.

Figure 3.7 Brass Triad Plaque depicting the Oba flanked by two attendants and two Europeans shown on either side of his head. Benin City, Edo State, Nigeria. sixteenth–seventeenth century

and an online petition resulted in sufficient public pressure that the consignors decided to withdraw the objects from sale. The mask is now in the Al-Thani Collection on display in Paris.[199] In contrast, Dr Mark Walker, the descendant

[199] ibid. There are only five known ivory masks like this. The other four are located in Western museums.

of another individual, Captain Philips Walker, who participated in the Punitive Expedition, voluntarily returned two bronze objects, one an ibis bird and the other a royal bell, to the Oba in July 2014.[200]

Despite their earlier difficulty selling the mask, Sotheby's subsequently succeeded in selling other Benin objects. It sold an Edo terracotta head, dated to the sixteenth century, in May 2015. The heads used for royal altars were made of brass. The terracotta heads were non-royal and were placed on altars used for the ancestors of members of the brass-casting guild; these altars or shrines are known to still be in use today. The head sold by Sotheby's was dated, based on its style and execution, to the first half of the sixteenth century or possibly a little earlier. Its listed provenance history goes back to the early 1950s when it was acquired by New York collectors in Benin City, and the head's acquisition was thereby separated in time from the booty taken during the Punitive Expedition. The presale estimate ranged from $400,000 to $600,000, but the head sold for more than three times the high estimate at $1,930,000.[201] In 2017, Sotheby's sold a bronze head from the Edo kingdom of the seventeenth–eighteenth centuries for €1,869,000, with a presale estimate of €600,000–900,000. The provenance information dates only to 1932 when it was with a French gallery, and it was then purchased in 1936 by the French collector, Louis Carré.[202] In 2018, Sotheby's offered two Benin plaques, dating to the sixteenth–seventeenth centuries, that were in the collection of James Awadagin Thomas, the owner of a rubber plantation in Nigeria; apparently only one of the plaques sold.[203]

Folarin Shyllon's comments about the role that the Benin bronzes play in Benin history are particularly apt for the question of restitution:

> [T]he Benin bronzes are not merely cultural objects but part of the history of Nigeria. The 160 bronze heads taken away by the Benin punitive expedition among other items are the Benin equivalent to chronological records. Since each

[200] Samuel Reilly, 'Private enterprise—the individuals who are taking restitution into their own hands' (*Apollo*, 1 August 2020) <www.apollo-magazine.com/private-restitution-colonial-art-africa/> accessed 17 May 2021.

[201] Sotheby's, 'Edo Terracotta Head, Benin Kingdom, Nigeria, ca 16th century' African, Oceanic & Pre-Columbian Art Catalogue, Lot 188 (May 2015) <www.sothebys.com/en/auctions/ecatalogue/2015/african-oceanic-n09347/lot.188.html> accessed 12 April 2021. The sale price includes the buyer's premium.

[202] Sotheby's, 'Tête, Edo, Royaume de Benin, Nigeria' Arts d'Afrique et d'Océanie, Lot 67 (12 December 2017) <www.sothebys.com/en/auctions/ecatalogue/2016/arts-afrique-oceanie-pf1718/lot.67.html?locale=en accessed 17 May 2021.

[203] Sotheby's 'Plaque en bronze, Edo, Royaume du Benin, Nigeria' Arts d'Afrique et d'Océanie Lot 199 (12 December 2018) <www.sothebys.com/en/auctions/ecatalogue/2018/arts-dafrique-et-docanie-pf1818/lot.199.html?locale=en> accessed 17 May 2021; Fragment de plaque en bronze, Edo, Royaume du Benin' Arts d'Afrique et d'Océanie Lot 198 (12 December 2018) <www.sothebys.com/en/auctions/ecatalogue/2018/arts-dafrique-et-docanie-pf1818/lot.198.html?locale=en> accessed 17 May 2021. The plaque that sold, Lot 198, had a presale estimate of €10,000–15,000 and sold for €37,500. Lot 199 had a considerably higher presale estimate of €120,000–180,000.

> head represented an Oba, they recorded dynasties back to the 12th century. When an Oba died, a formal head was cast in bronze to furnish an altar erected to his memory. The refusal to return such cultural objects is tantamount to keeping a people's history and heritage in captivity. And there is no doubt that the colonial powers knew the import and the devastating effect of the removal of irreplaceable cultural heritage.[204]

In attempting to recover its history as part of its intangible cultural heritage, and in light of the considerable ongoing market in Benin artefacts, Nigeria and the Benin royal family cannot buy back their artefacts to any significant extent through the market, as the prices that these objects can command are considerable. Nor should they be expected or required to buy back what is theirs.[205] However, the taking of these objects in the late nineteenth century preceded the adoption of international legal and voluntary rules that would apply to their return. While the prospect of large-scale restitution to African nations seemed unlikely until a few years ago, and the public pressure that was sufficient to cause the withdrawal of the Galway objects from public sale at Sotheby's and the voluntary gesture of Dr Walker indicate greater public awareness of the fate of the Benin objects, it has been considered unlikely, until recent years, that these efforts would result in further restitution on any significant scale.[206]

The looting of the Benin palace and similar looting episodes that accompanied violence in Africa over the course of the nineteenth century bear similarities to Napoleon's thefts, the taking of the Parthenon Sculptures, and the looting of Yuanmingyuan. European justification for the looting of cultural artefacts from Africa were part of an effort to impose European cultural and religious mores on their often misperceived ideas of what African culture and civilization were. African societies were depicted as murderous and blood-soaked in an effort to justify what were military and political gains fuelled by economic motives. Contemporary African societies were labelled degenerate, despite recognition that their artistic production was of high quality and became admired by European institutions and individuals. Similar to the justifications offered by Napoleon and contemporary French artists, as well as the British leaders and artists, the taking of artefacts from Africa served to promote the newly developing academic study

204 Shyllon, 'Unraveling History' (n 159) 163.

205 Sarr and Savoy list the extent of movable cultural objects held in European museums: British Museum (69,000), Weltmuseum of Vienna (37,000), Musée Royal de l'Afrique Centrale in Belgium (180,000), Humboldt Forum in Berlin (75,000), and Musée du Quai Branly-Jacques Chirac (70,000). Sarr and Savoy, 'The Restitution of African Cultural Heritage' (n 157) 15.

206 The status of restitution of Benin objects has changed, with smaller museums and educational institutions agreeing or promising to return objects. For example, Peggy McGlone, 'Smithsonian to give back its collection of Benin bronzes' (*Washington Post*, 8 March 2022) <www.washingtonpost.com/arts-entertainment/2022/03/08/smithsonian-benin-bronzes-nigeria-return/> accessed 8 March 2022. This is discussed further in chapter 7, section 7.3.

of anthropology and the founding of ethnographic museums to display these artefacts. At the same time, recognition of the artistic and aesthetic value of the Benin artefacts did not, in an ultimately contradictory fashion, alter the European perception of Africans as uncivilized and inferior.[207]

3.5 Conclusion

Over the course of the nineteenth century, the rescue narrative remained the primary justification for the removal and expropriation of cultural objects from regions outside of Europe, providing a veneer of legitimacy and making these removals acceptable to European societies at the time. The rescue narrative, at its core, is based on the European view that non-Europeans are not worthy of retaining the cultural objects that they or their ancestors created. Their cultural objects therefore needed to be 'rescued' from their contemporary communities through removal. The legal system codified the rescue narrative into the formulation of international law at that time. Although the end of the Napoleonic Wars established the precedent applicable within Europe that, at the conclusion of hostilities, cultural objects should be returned to the places from which they had been taken, the Berlin Conference established the principle that these rules did not apply to non-Europeans. The Benin Punitive Expedition was perhaps the starkest illustration of this principle with respect to the disposition of cultural objects.[208] These three episodes involving the Parthenon Sculptures, the Yuanmingyuan Palace, and the Benin objects, establish not only a financial and historical debt owed by the European States but also a deep cultural debt based on these expropriations that substantially reduced the cultural capital and inheritance of regions outside of Europe. European museums, private collectors, dealers, artists, anthropologists, and archaeologists benefited from this cultural deprivation enabled by nineteenth-century colonialism, imperialism, and armed conflict. It is a debt that has so far been insufficiently acknowledged and is still far from being repaid. This constitutes a moral and cultural basis, although not a direct legal one, for the return of these cultural objects to their places of origin. Chapter 5 will turn to the legal restraints that were put into place over the course of the twentieth century to reduce these deprivations. But recognition of the cultural and moral debt incurred during the removals of the nineteenth century is a necessary first step towards resolving the question based on both legal claims and ethical-moral claims of the location of cultural objects today.

[207] Coombes, *Reinventing Africa* (n 161) 7–9.

[208] Even in 1914, the British Manual of Military Law maintained that the evolving rules of warfare applied only to conflict among 'civilised' nations and not between the European nations and 'uncivilised states and tribes'. Vrdoljak, *International Law* (n 1) 65.

4
Appropriation of Archaeological Heritage: Market Demand and Legal Responses

4.1 Introduction

This chapter turns to the period from the mid-twentieth century to the present and addresses the status of a particular category of movable cultural objects: archaeological artefacts that have been removed directly from the ground without documentation or knowledge of their existence. In addition to armed conflict, colonialism, and imperialism, which enabled the removal of cultural objects and that were described in the previous chapters, the significant growth of the international market after the Second World War became an additional impetus for removal of cultural objects. Unsatisfied market demand can be met by the 'production' of new objects through the looting of archaeological sites and dismemberment of historic structures; the undocumented nature of these cultural objects makes it particularly difficult for law enforcement and owners to track and recover them.[1] The predominant pattern of this contemporary movement replicates the earlier paths from the formerly colonized areas of the world to the wealthier market States in Western Europe and North America.[2] In many parts of the world, the looting of archaeological sites has become an organized business motivated primarily by profit.

Two types of harm result from the looting of archaeological sites. First, in a universalistic sense, looting imposes harms on global society through the detriment to our knowledge and understanding of the past and through losses of cultural and scientific values.[3] The second type of harm is to the State of origin or discovery

[1] The term 'looting' in reference to antiquities or archaeological artefacts has a more specific definition. Looted antiquities are those taken from the ground or 'from their place as an integral part of, or attachment to, a temple or other ancient structure'. Simon RM Mackenzie, 'Dig A Bit Deeper: Law, Regulation and the Illicit Antiquities Market' (2005) 45 British Journal of Criminology 249, 251 (hereafter Mackenzie, 'Dig A Bit Deeper'). A looted antiquity is one removed from the ground, underwater, or an historic structure in an unscientific manner and without appropriate recording of the excavation context and preservation of associated physical remains, regardless of its legal status, which may vary depending on the laws of the place where the object was discovered or where it is presently located.

[2] Morag M Kersel, 'License to Sell: The Legal Trade of Antiquities in Israel' (Unpublished PhD dissertation, copy on file with author, 2006) 19–20. Other areas of the world, including the Gulf States, China, and Australia, also now participate in this market.

[3] Value, as used here, indicates the intangible worth and significance of original contexts and cultural associations; it is not the same as market or monetary value. The translation of this abstract value into

Cultural Objects and Reparative Justice. Patty Gerstenblith, Oxford University Press.
DOI: 10.1093/oso/9780192872104.003.0004

and the local community. This is a particular harm suffered through deprivation of cultural assets. Both of these types of losses result from the destruction of context and constitute negative externalities as the looters, smugglers, sellers, buyers, and others who 'consume' these objects impose these harms on others and do not themselves suffer a loss or pay the cost of these harms;[4] in fact, they often benefit financially and in academic and social prestige from these activities. The purpose of a legal regime is to reduce societal harm by forcing the actors to internalize the costs, thereby discouraging the harmful activity. Because of its link to the looting of sites, the trade in undocumented antiquities raises legal, ethical, and societal concerns distinguishing it from the trade in other forms of cultural objects.

Artefacts looted from the ground are unknown and undocumented until they appear on the market or in a public or private collection or are intercepted by law enforcement.[5] The undocumented nature of looted artefacts makes tracking them and establishing their legal status difficult, thereby posing challenges to the formulation of legal doctrine and to effective law enforcement efforts. Specialized legal doctrine has therefore developed to supplement the general legal approaches to the recovery of stolen cultural objects. This chapter turns, first, to focus on these harms and, second, to explain the particularized legal responses devised to disrupt the market in undocumented archaeological artefacts, thereby discouraging the looting of archaeological sites and helping to preserve their intangible contextual values.

4.2 The Role of the International Market in Antiquities

Dr Clemency Coggins chronicled the relationship between the looting of cultural objects and the market when she wrote in 1969 of the dismemberment of monumental sculptures in Central America and their subsequent smuggling into the United States for sale.[6] A few years later, Karl Meyer documented the looting of sites in Central America and the Mediterranean region.[7] Ethnographic studies of

economic terms is difficult. The term 'cost' indicates any harmful effect imposed on an individual or on society as a whole.

[4] Demsetz presents the classic statement of the effects of negative externalities, but he focuses on costs only in the monetary sense. Howard Demsetz, 'Toward a Theory of Property Rights' (1967) 57 American Economic Review 347.

[5] Other types of cultural objects may be undocumented before their removal. For Indigenous communities, documentation of cultural objects may violate religious or traditional notions of secrecy. Sarah K Harding, 'Value, Obligation and Cultural Heritage' (1999) 31 Arizona State Law Journal 291, 313–15. Other cultural objects in a private or public collection may be undocumented for practical reasons such as lack of financial resources, or documentation may be destroyed during armed conflict or intentionally removed during colonialism.

[6] Clemency C Coggins, 'Illicit Traffic of Pre-Columbian Antiquities' (1969) 29 Art J 94.

[7] Karl E Meyer, *The Plundered Past: The Story of the Illegal International Traffic in Works of Art* (MacMillan Publishing Company 1977).

site looting in different parts of the world demonstrate that looting activities respond to market demand for particular types of artefacts, and looting has moved in many countries from an occasional, opportunistic activity to a sophisticated, organized business.[8] While it is important that looting at sites be interdicted, the law in market countries should also impose detrimental consequences on intermediate and end-market participants in order to disrupt the market by reducing the economic incentive to loot archaeological sites.

Justifications for the market posit, first, that by placing a high monetary value on cultural objects, the market finds those collectors, both public and private, that are best able to care for cultural objects. Second, the market serves to move objects throughout the world, thereby making them accessible to larger numbers of people, although that movement is primarily a one-way flow from areas of the world that are rich in cultural heritage to collectors and institutions in a few large cities located mostly in the West. Third, the market serves an educational function through appreciation of the object. Yet, the market's appreciation for decontextualized objects and its emphasis on private ownership remain mired in a one-dimensional view of the value of objects as primarily aesthetic and sometimes monetary. While scientific excavation does not impede this aesthetic value, although it slows down the rate at which new objects are unearthed, the unregulated market impedes scientific study. In response to the arguments in favour of encouraging the international market in antiquities, the following critique will focus on five detrimental aspects: the loss of what may be termed cultural and educational capital for the communities from whom the antiquities were taken; the detriment to knowledge caused by the loss of archaeological context; the damage done to individual artefacts in response to market taste and demand; the acceptance of unprovenanced or poorly provenanced[9] artefacts, which may be forgeries and may therefore corrupt the historical and cultural record, and the funding of armed conflict and other criminal activity through the sale proceeds of looted artefacts.

[8] For example Simon Mackenzie and Tess Davis, 'Temple Looting in Cambodia: Anatomy of a Statue Trafficking Network' (2014) 54 Brit Journal of Criminology 722 (hereafter Mackenzie and Davis, 'Temple Looting') (discussing historic patterns of looting of temple sites in Cambodia); Elizabeth C Stone, 'An Update on the Looting of Archaeological Sites in Iraq' (2015) 78 NEA 178 (hereafter Stone, 'An Update'); Monica Hanna, What Has Happened to Egyptian Heritage after the 2011 Unfinished Revolution? (2013) 1(4) JEMAHS 371; Morag M Kersel and Meredith S Chesson, 'Looting Matters: Early Bronze Age Cemeteries of Jordan's Southeast Dead Sea Plain in the Past and Present' in Sarah Tarlow and Liv Nilsson Stutz (eds), *The Oxford Handbook of the Archaeology of Death and Burial* (OUP 2013) 677, 680.

[9] The term 'provenance' refers to the ownership history of a cultural object. In the case of archaeological artefacts, 'provenience' refers to the archaeological find spot. 'Country of origin' or 'country of discovery' indicates the country within whose modern boundaries an archaeological object was discovered. Patty Gerstenblith, 'Provenience and Provenance Intersecting with International Law in the Market for Antiquities' (2020) 45 North Carolina Journal of International Law 457 (hereafter Gerstenblith 'Provenience and Provenance').

4.2.1 Loss of Cultural and Intellectual Capital

In 2021, large numbers of antiquities were returned to their countries of origin, including 180 returned to eleven countries from the Michael Steinhardt collection[10] and approximately 17,000 returned to Iraq from the Hobby Lobby Corporation, the Museum of the Bible, and Cornell University.[11] While these restitutions vindicate the interest of the country as owner of the antiquities, opportunities for development of the country's educational and cultural capital have been lost. The Western scholars who study and publish the artefacts take these values and thereby reap academic recognition and advancement, and their students take funding and educational opportunities. This has particularly been the case with the large number of cuneiform tablets looted from Iraq during the 1990s, such as the Gilgamesh 'Dream' Tablet (Figure 4.1), and following the 2003 Gulf War. Thousands of cuneiform tablets appeared on the market beginning as early as 2008.[12] Elizabeth Stone identified the pattern of looting of archaeological sites in Iraq as responsive to the portability and market popularity of particular types of artefacts, including cuneiform tablets, cylinder seals, and coins of later periods. She described this pattern as 'almost certainly the result of the strong market in cuneiform texts, reflected in the publication of many new collections of tablets dating to precisely this time frame'.[13] ortability has also been a factor in the looting of coins and small objects from sites in Syria.[14]

[10] New York County District Attorney, 'Statement of Facts in the Matter of a Grand Jury Investigation into a Private New York Antiquities Collector' (6 December 2021).

[11] *United States v Approximately Four Hundred Fifty (450) Cuneiform Tablets and Approximately Three Thousand (3,000) Ancient Clay Bullae*, CV 17-3980 Verified Complaint in Rem (EDNY 2017); *United States v One Cuneiform Tablet known as the 'Gilgamesh Dream Tablet'*, CV 20-2222 Amended Verified Complaint in Rem (EDNY 2021); *United States v One Cuneiform Tablet known as the 'Gilgamesh Dream Tablet'*, CV 20-2222 Decree of Forfeiture (EDNY 2021); Patty Gerstenblith, 'Hobby Lobby, the Museum of the Bible and the Law: A Case Study of the Looting of Archaeological Artifacts from Iraq' in Layla Hashemi and Louise Shelley (eds), *Antiquities Smuggling in the Real and Virtual World* (Routledge 2022) 59.

[12] Manuel Molina, 'The Looting of Ur III Tablets after the Gulf Wars' in W Sommerfeld (ed), *Dealing with Antiquity: Past, Present & Future. Proceedings of the 63rd Rencontre Assyriologique Internationale, 460 Alter Orient und Altes Testament* (Ugarit-Verlag 2019) 233. It is likely that these tablets were looted during the 2003 Gulf War, as the first corpus of tablets identified as coming from the unlocated site of Iri-Saĝrig was intercepted by Jordanian law enforcement at the border with Iraq in July 2003. ibid, 241. Other tablets, such as the Gilgamesh 'Dream' Tablet were clearly looted earlier, apparently during the 1990s.

[13] Stone, 'An Update' (n 8) 185. For examples of publications of unprovenanced cuneiform tablets following the 2003 Gulf War, although some of these corpora were likely looted during the 1990s following the first Gulf War, see David L Owen and Rudolf H Mayr, *The Garšana Archives. 3 Cornell University Studies in Assyriology and Sumerology* (Pennsylvania State University 2007); David Owen, *Cuneiform Texts Primarily from Iri-Saĝrig/Āl-Šarrākī and the History of the Ur III Period* (Pennsylvania State University Press 2013). Many of the Hobby Lobby cuneiform tablets were published in Marcel Sigrist and Tohru Ozaki, *Tablets from the Iri-Saĝrig Archive, 40 Cornell University Studies in Assyriology and Sumerology* (Pennsylvania State University Press 2019). The Gilgamesh 'Dream' Tablet was published in Andrew George, 'The Civilizing of Ea-Enkidu: An Unusual Tablet of the Babylonian Gilgameš Epic' (2007) 101(1) Revue d'assyriologie et d'archéologie orientale 59.

[14] Neil Brodie and Isber Sabrine, 'The Illegal Excavation and Trade in Syrian Cultural Objects: A View from the Ground' (2018) 43(1) Journal of Field Archaeology 74 (hereafter Brodie and Sabrine, 'The Illegal Excavation').

Figure 4.1 Gilgamesh 'Dream' Tablet, *c* 1600 BCE. Returned to Iraq in 2021, now in the Iraq Museum

As Neil Brodie has pointed out, despite recognition of Iraq's national interest in the restituted objects, the Iraqi polity has suffered 'socio-cultural harms' that are not necessarily repaired through restitution.[15] The return of these artefacts means that the costs of curation and storage are shifted to Iraq. Their intellectual value, which in the case of textual materials is primarily in the transliteration, translation, and publication of the texts, has been 'sucked dry' by the scholars who published them. The Western scholars who ignore legal and ethical constraints in publishing these artefacts bear the responsibility to remedy this situation.

4.2.2 Loss to Knowledge

Loss of knowledge results from the looting of archaeological sites. As discussed in chapter 2, section 2.3, the science of archaeology developed during the nineteenth century. Following the Second World War, the rapid development of

[15] Neil J Brodie, 'Restorative Justice? Questions Arising out of the Hobby Lobby Return of Cuneiform Tablets to Iraq' (2020) 12(23) Revista memória em Rede 87, 101.

interdisciplinary methodologies for the study of the past coincided with the post-war growth of the international art market. The melding of sophisticated scientific techniques with linguistic, philological, art historical, and anthropological analyses formed an interdisciplinary means to gain a holistic understanding of the past. This reduced the relative importance of art historical analyses and connoisseurship to but one among many disciplines that are used to understand the past, and the study of the decontextualized object became less important.

The expanding application of scientific methodologies, including stratigraphic retrieval, surface survey, remote sensing, dating methods, and technical analyses,[16] meant that greater quantities of information could be recovered from the controlled excavation of sites. The looting of sites therefore causes increasingly greater losses to our knowledge and understanding of the past. The controlled excavation of archaeological sites, which is an inherently slow and methodical process, inevitably conflicts with the desire of the market to have the maximum numbers of objects available with minimal regulation. Therefore, with a finite number of objects available for the market, looting of archaeological sites and dismemberment of historic structures increased to satisfy the growing market demand. That demand and the looting to satisfy it constitute a significant detriment to the study of the past.

Decontextualized artefacts can tell us little about the past other than what is intrinsic within the object itself, rather than what could have been learned from the object's full associated context.[17] Maximum understanding of the past through controlled, scientific excavation of archaeological sites permits the archaeologist to determine the spatial and chronological relationship of the remains and to reconstruct aspects of past life including economics, trade, health, diet, religious ritual and function, burial methods, family structure, political and social organization, technology, and literature. Artistic and utilitarian objects, faunal and floral remains, architectural features, human remains, and their original contextual relationship to each other are all equally essential. This full body of contextualized, intangible information is a non-renewable cultural resource. Once it is destroyed, it cannot be regained. An example of the tension between acquisition of objects and

[16] See Robert J Muckle and Stacey L Camp, *Introducing Archaeology* (3rd edn, University of Toronto Press 2020). See also Joe Watkins, 'The Politics of Archaeology: Heritage, Ownership, and Repatriation' in Laetitia La Follette (ed), *Negotiating Culture: Heritage, Ownership, and Intellectual Property* (University of Massachusetts Press 2013) 15, 16–18 (hereafter Watkins, 'The Politics of Archaeology').

[17] Laetitia La Follette, 'The Trial of Marion True and Changing Policies for Classical Antiquities in American Museums' in Laetitia La Follette (ed), *Negotiating Culture: Heritage, Ownership, and Intellectual Property* (University of Massachusetts Press 2013) 38, 42–44, 51–54; Alex W Barker, 'Provenience, Provenance and Context(s)' in Michael A Adler and Susan Benton Bruning (eds), *The Futures of Our Pasts: Ethical Implications of Collecting Antiquities in the Twenty-first Century* (University of New Mexico Press 2012) 19, 20 ('[C]ontext … refers to the association of an object that allows its importance or significance to be assessed.').

Figure 4.2 Sarpedon Krater. Euphronios (painter) and Euxitheos (potter). Attic red-figure calyx-krater, *c* 515 BCE. Returned to Italy, now in the Museo Nazionale Cerite (Cerveteri)

the loss to knowledge is illustrated by the Euphronios or Sarpedon krater acquired by the Metropolitan Museum in New York in 1972[18] and subsequently returned to Italy (Figure 4.2). Much information was lost, including the exact location where the krater was discovered, the individual's age, sex, health, social status, occupation, and likely cause of death, and the death rituals that accompanied the burial.

Another type of knowledge loss through the antiquities trade is the suppression of provenance and provenience information concerning particular objects.[19]

[18] Thomas Hoving, *Making the Mummies Dance: Inside the Metropolitan Museum of Art* (Touchstone 1993) 307–40.

[19] Abdul Salam Taha, 'The Role of Academia in Enabling the Illicit Antiquities Market: The Damage to Iraq's Cultural Heritage' in Lorenzo Kamel (ed), *Collapse and Rebirth of Cultural Heritage: The Case of Syria and Iraq* (Peter Lang AG 2020) 129, 135, 148.

This is done in part to elude law enforcement efforts to recover objects without a legitimate background. The suppression of this information means that it is more difficult to determine where objects were found and therefore both their legal and cultural histories are obfuscated. This phenomenon is compounded by the use of false information on import documents, which require a statement of country of origin, which, in the case of archaeological objects, is the country within whose modern boundaries the object was discovered. To evade import restrictions, importers of antiquities may use a false declaration of country of origin.[20]

4.2.3 Physical Integrity

A third detrimental effect is that the market often fails to do what it purports to do best—that is, preserve the physical integrity of objects by placing a market value on them. Artefacts may be distorted or reshaped in order to appeal to market taste. Objects may also be destroyed, either intentionally or through negligence, if they are not viewed as saleable on the market or if the looters do not have the means of properly conserving fragile objects, such as unbaked cuneiform tablets.[21]

Severe damage was done to the pre-Iconoclastic period Byzantine mosaics of the sixth century from the Kanakaria church located in northern Cyprus. Following the Turkish invasion of the island in 1974, its partition into a northern Turkish sector and a southern Greek sector, and the transfers of populations between the two sectors, the Greek Orthodox churches in the northern sector fell into disuse and were vandalized. In one case, mosaics of the pre-Iconoclastic Byzantine period, from which few artistic works survive, were removed from the Kanakaria church, sold to a Turkish dealer in Germany, and four of them ultimately resold to an Indianapolis art dealer, Peg Goldberg.[22] In her marketing efforts, Goldberg had these rare mosaics reset and flattened as she felt that would make them more saleable. Under the lure of the market, irreparable damage was done to these artworks.[23]

[20] For example, *United States v An Antique Platter of Gold* 991 F Supp 222 (SDNY 1997), aff'd on other grounds 184 F3d 131 (2nd Cir 1999); *United States v Approximately Four Hundred Fifty (450) Cuneiform Tablets and Approximately Three Thousand (3,000) Ancient Clay Bullae*, CV 17-3980 Verified Complaint in Rem (EDNY 2017); Gerstenblith 'Provenience and Provenance' (n 9) 490–95.

[21] Broken or fragmentary cuneiform tablets are often discarded as not saleable, despite the fact that many of the most important preserved ancient texts were pieced together from fragments. It was estimated that during the 2003 Gulf War in Iraq, for every saleable object, 2,000 sherds and 1,000 small finds were discarded. Benjamin A Foster, Karen Polinger Foster, and Patty Gerstenblith, *Iraq Beyond the Headlines: History, Archaeology, and War* (World Scientific 2005) 222.

[22] *Autocephalous Greek-Orthodox Church of Cyprus and the Republic of Cyprus v Goldberg & Feldman Fine Arts, Inc* 917 F2d 278 (7th Cir 1990). The Church and its mosaics were documented before the theft by AHS Megaw and EW Hawkins, *The Church of the Panagia Kanakaria at Lythrankomi in Cyprus: Its Mosaics and Frescoes* (1st edn, Dumbarton Oaks 1977).

[23] Catherine Sease and Danaë Thimme, 'The Kanakaria Mosaics: The Conservators' View' in Kathryn W Tubb (ed) *Antiquities Trade or Betrayed: Legal, Ethical, &. Conservation Issues* (Archetype Publs 1995) 122.

4.2.4 Forgeries

The acceptance of undocumented artefacts on the market may lead to the proliferation of forgeries with resulting corruption of the historical record. Categories of ancient artefacts, such as Cycladic figurines of the third millennium BCE, are represented almost completely by looted examples. The function of these figurines, their age, and the islands in the Aegean from which they originate are difficult to determine.[24] It is also difficult to be certain which are authentic, and which are not.

Numerous epigraphic examples with purported Biblical connections have been shown to be forgeries often after initial acceptance as authentic.[25] Forgeries include the so-called 'Gospel of Jesus's Wife'[26] and the numerous 'Dead Sea Scroll' fragments acquired by Evangelical-related institutions such as the Museum of the Bible.[27] Scientific analyses may be able to determine conclusively that an object is fake, but it rarely, if ever, can conclusively determine that an object or inscription is authentic. The inability to determine which objects are authentic and which are not leads to a paradox. On the one hand, an inauthentic work that is accepted corrupts the historical record. On the other hand, an authentic work, if it does not sufficiently resemble other known works of that artist or time period, may be rejected.

Many scholars and market participants rely on connoisseurship, the study of objects based on form, decoration, and other aesthetic criteria, to determine authenticity. Because connoisseurship determines authenticity by comparing newly discovered objects with previously known exemplars, looted artefacts do not expand our knowledge. When a new type of archaeological artefact is excavated, it adds to our corpus of knowledge, but when a new type is known only from the market, it may be rejected as fake. Such a reaction has produced a conservatizing trend in scholarship, as explained by Chippindale and Gill:

[24] Christopher Chippindale and David Gill, 'Cycladic Figures: Art versus Archaeology?' in Kathryn W Tubb (ed) *Antiquities Trade or Betrayed: Legal, Ethical & Conservation Issues* (Archetype Publications 1995) 131, 133–35; Colin Renfrew and others (eds), *The Settlement at Dhaskalio: The Sanctuary on Keros and the Origins of Aegean Ritual Practice: The Excavations of 2006–2008* (McDonald Institute for Archaeological Research 2013).

[25] Christopher A Rollston, 'Forging History: from Antiquity to the Modern Period' in Matthew T Rutz and Morag M Kersel (eds), *Archaeologies of Text: Archaeology, Technology, and Ethics* (Oxbow Books 2014) 176; Christopher A Rollston, 2004. 'Non-Provenanced Epigraphs II: The Status of Non-Provenanced Epigraphs within the Broader Corpus of Northwest Semitic' (2004) 11 Maarav 57; Christopher A Rollston, 'Non-Provenanced Epigraphs I: Pillaged Antiquities, Northwest Semitic Forgeries, and Protocols for Laboratory Tests' (2003) 10 Maarav 135. For discussion of the influence of Biblical artefacts, see Neil Brodie and Morag M Kersel, 'The Social and Political Consequences of Devotion to Biblical Artifacts' in Paula K Lazarus and Alex W Barker (eds), *All the King's Horses: Essays on the Impact of Looting and the Antiquities Trade on Our Knowledge of the Past* (SAA Press 2012) 109.

[26] Ariel Sabar, 'The Unbelievable Tale of Jesus's Wife' (*The Atlantic*, July/August 2016) <www.theatlantic.com/magazine/archive/2016/07/the-unbelievable-tale-of-jesus-wife/485573/> accessed 4 March 2020.

[27] Museum of the Bible, 'A Journey for the Truth: Investigating the Recent Dead Sea Scrolls Fragments' <https://museumofthebible.org/dead-sea-scroll-fragments> accessed 11 May 2021.

> [N]ew objects and the way they are treated contribute to our consolidated knowledge insofar as they confirm, reinforce, and strengthen the existing patterns of knowledge. Surfacing without secure information beyond what is immanent in themselves, the objects are unable to broaden our basis of knowledge. Interpreted and restored in light of prior expectations, they are reconciled with what we presently know, but they cannot amend and improve our present knowledge much, if at all. ... [T]he truly unusual items that surface remain incomprehensible until their oddity is matched by a find for which there is a real security of knowledge. At that point, they can take up their accustomed role of confirming the correctness of that knowledge.[28]

4.2.5 Funding of Armed Conflict and Other Criminal Activity

A final identified detrimental consequence of the acceptance of undocumented antiquities in the international market is that the marketing and sale of looted artefacts exist at times in a symbiotic relationship with the funding of armed conflict and other forms of violence or criminal activity. The sale of looted and stolen artworks funded armed conflict in the past through awarding objects to soldiers as a form of payment, as in the looting of the Yuanmingyuan, discussed in chapter, 3, section 3.3. Sales of cultural objects by Nazi Germany occurred during the Second World War.[29] The relationship between funding and looting has become clearer during the armed conflict in the Eastern Mediterranean and Iraq in the first part of the twenty-first century.

During the 2003 Gulf War, the first indications of a link between the looting of antiquities and the funding of terrorism and armed conflict were noted.[30] The civil war in Syria with its spill-over into Iraq demonstrated more clearly that looting and sale of cultural artefacts could help to fund armed conflict and terrorism. Multiple parties to the conflict engaged in theft and looting.[31] The various State and non-State actors reaped economic reward through taxation of sales, licensing of sites

[28] Christopher Chippindale and David WJ Gill, 'Material Consequences of Contemporary Classical Collecting' (2000) 104 American Journal of Archaeology 463, 504–05; see also Neil Brodie and Christina Luke, 'Conclusion: The Social and Cultural Contexts of Collecting' in Neil Brodie and others (eds), *Archaeology, Cultural Heritage, and the Antiquities Trade* (University Press of Florida 2006) 303, 309–10.

[29] Germany sold 'degenerate' artworks onto the international market for the purpose of raising hard currency, thereby helping to perpetuate armed conflict and genocide. Uwe Fleckner, 'Marketing the Defamed: On the Contradictory Use of Provenances in the Third Reich' in Gail Feigenbaum and Inge Reist (eds), *Provenance: An Alternate History of Art* (Getty Publications 2012) 137, 145.

[30] Matthew Bogdanos, 'The Terrorist in the Art Gallery' (*New York Times*, 10 December 2005) <www.nytimes.com/2005/12/10/opinion/the-terrorist-in-the-art-gallery.html> accessed 4 March 2020. For the looting of archaeological sites in Iraq, see Elizabeth C Stone, 'Patterns of Looting in Southern Iraq' (2008) 82(315) Antiquity 125; Stone, 'An Update' (n 8) 179–80.

[31] UNITAR, 'Ebla (Tell Mardikh)' 2014 <http://unosat.web.cern.ch/unosat/unitar/downloads/chs/ebla.pdf> accessed 11 May 2021; Brian I Daniels and Katharyn Hanson, 'Archaeological Site Looting in Syria and Iraq: A Review of the Evidence' in France Desmarais (ed), *Countering Illicit Traffic in Cultural Goods: The Global Challenge of Protecting the World's Heritage* (ICOM 2015) 83.

for looting, control of smuggling routes, and direct sale of artefacts. Anecdotal reports,[32] confirmed through satellite imagery,[33] and documents recovered from a raid on an Islamic State in Iraq and the Levant (ISIL) compound in May 2015[34] indicated that ISIL had orchestrated large-scale looting of sites and thefts from institutions to provide a stream of income to fund its terrorist activities and conflict. While some artefacts were found in the compound, images of other artefacts were found in computer files. However, the artefacts themselves were not found, and it is presumed that they had been smuggled out of Syria and sold onto the market.[35]

One multi-disciplinary study attempted to estimate the quantity and value of looted artefacts based on data for excavated artefacts from two sites in Syria: Dura Europos and Tell Bi'a.[36] Similar to Elizabeth Stone's results for looting in Iraq, this study found that small artefacts are particularly desirable on the market.

> Small, commonplace, and mundane artifacts ... are massively present at auction, and their modest prices add up to a sizeable market. ... [N]early every item, no matter how small, can find a buyer and ... market participants may be dividing up significant numbers of marketable objects from just a single site.[37]

Based on their interviews of those involved in the looting and trade in Syria, Brodie and Sabrine concluded that the objects most in demand are those that are small,

[32] Amr al-Azm, Salam al-Kuntar, and Brian I Daniels, 'ISIS' Antiquities Sideline' Op-Ed (*New York Times*, 2 September 2014) <www.nytimes.com/2014/09/03/opinion/isis-antiquities-sideline.html?_r=0> accessed 2 June 2021.

[33] Susan Wolfinbarger and others, 'Ancient History, Modern Destruction: Assessing the Status of Syria's World Heritage Sites Using High-Resolution Satellite Imagery' (*American Association for the Advancement of Science* 2014) <www.aaas.org/page/ancient-history-modern-destruction-assessing-current-status-syria-s-world-heritage-sites-using> accessed 2 June 2021.

[34] Remarks of Andrew Keller, Deputy Assistant Secretary Bureau of Economic Affairs, US Department of State (16 October 2015) <http://eca.state.gov/video/conflict-antiquities-panel-1-video/transcript> accessed 2 June 2021. The extent of funding ISIL realized from looted cultural objects is unknown. Based on information obtained from the raid on the ISIL compound, US government officials estimated that ISIL earned several million dollars during an approximate year from mid-2014 to mid-2015.

[35] Department of Justice, 'United States Files Complaint Seeking Forfeiture of Antiquities Associated with the Islamic State of Iraq and the Levant (ISIL)' 15 December 2016 <www.justice.gov/usao-dc/pr/united-states-files-complaint-seeking-forfeiture-antiquities-associated-islamic-state> accessed 2 June 2021 (seeking forfeiture of four archaeological objects—two Roman gold coins, a gold ring, and a carved stele—depicted in photographs during the Abu Sayyef raid).

[36] Fiona Greenland and others, 'A Site-Level Market Model of the Antiquities Trade' (2019) 26 IJCP 21.

[37] ibid, 40. In 2003 and 2004, the journalist Joanne Farchakh interviewed looters at archaeological sites in southern Iraq. She reported that looters were paid $4 for a cuneiform tablet and $20–$50 for a decorated vase. A sculpture could be worth about a hundred dollars. Joanne Farchakh, 'Témoignages d'une Archéologie Héroïque' (*Archaeologia*, May 2004) 14, 25. The value of these objects on the international market is considerably higher, with, for example, a cuneiform tablet being worth an average of $1,000–$,2000 in London or New York. However, Brodie and Sabrine reported sales of antiquities in Syria for considerably higher prices, which may be equal to, or even higher than, what is obtained on the international market, such as gold and silver coins selling for up to $1,500. Brodie and Sabrine, 'The Illegal Excavation' (n 14) 81.

portable, and easy to conceal, such as coins, other small metal objects, and glass vessels.[38]

A study of looting and trafficking of artefacts in Cambodia and Thailand similarly demonstrated the networks that linked the looting of sites with the military and organized criminal gangs during the Cambodian civil war between 1970 and 1998.[39] The individual at the centre of this network in Bangkok was later identified as Douglas Latchford. The Pandora Papers verified Latchford's notorious dealing in artefacts whose looting and sale helped to fund the Cambodian civil war and his use of offshore havens for hiding his funds and collection.[40] He was indicted in 2019[41] but passed away before he was brought to trial.

In an attempt to prevent looted antiquities from serving as a possible funding stream for terrorism and armed conflict, the UN Security Council adopted Resolution 2347 in 2017.[42] The Security Council noted the connections between looting, theft, and smuggling of antiquities and other artworks and the funding of terrorism, stating its concern about 'the links between the activities of terrorists and organized criminal groups that, in some cases, facilitate criminal activities, including trafficking in cultural property, illegal revenues and financial flows as well as money-laundering, bribery and corruption'.[43] The links to funding of terrorism and armed conflict prompted the European Union to include dealing in works of art, including antiquities, above €10,000 in its anti-money laundering regulations.[44] In 2021, Congress directed the Financial Crimes Enforcement Network of the US Treasury Department to adopt regulations to implement the application of the Bank Secrecy Act to dealing in antiquities.[45]

4.3 Legal Responses

Looted archaeological artefacts typically pass through several countries en route from the ground to their ultimate buyer. Three stages in the trafficking process

38 Brodie and Sabrine, 'The Illegal Excavation' (n 14) 82.

39 Mackenzie and Davis, 'Temple Looting' (n 8) 727, 734–35, 737.

40 Peter Whoriskey and others, 'Global Hunt for Looted Treasures Leads to Offshore Trusts (*Washington Post*, 5 October 2021) <www.washingtonpost.com/world/interactive/2021/met-museum-cambodian-antiquities-latchford/> accessed 25 October 2021.

41 *United States v Latchford* 19 Crim 748 (SDNY 2019). Latchford was charged with several counts of conspiring to commit and commission of overt acts to engage in wire fraud, violation of US customs laws on importation of merchandise by use of fraudulent and false statements, and import of stolen property.

42 S/RES/2347 (2017).

43 ibid. Preamble.

44 EU 5th Anti-Money Laundering Directive 2018/843 (30 May 2018) Art 1 (c).

45 Anti-Money Laundering Act of 2020, § 6110; 'FinCEN Launches Regulatory Process for New Antiquities Regulations' <www.fincen.gov/news/news-releases/fincen-launches-regulatory-process-new-antiquities-regulations> accessed 25 October 2021.

may be identified: the archaeologically rich country or country of modern discovery, the transit markets, and the destination markets.[46] As objects move across borders and through the market, their legal status may also change. An object that was illegally excavated or one that was legally obtained but illegally exported may be legal in a transit or destination country whose laws have not been violated by such conduct. Even a stolen object may be considered legally obtained in a country that recognizes the good faith purchaser doctrine.[47] A legal object may become illegal if it is improperly imported into the country where it is currently located. Conversely, while there is some disagreement on this point,[48] an object that is illegally exported from one country may not be illegal in an importing country, unless the importing country has agreed to make it a violation of its law to import an illegally exported cultural object. This variation in applicable laws allows title to objects, particularly to antiquities, to be laundered if they are passed through or are ultimately located in countries whose laws do not regard them as illegal.

While physical protection of archaeological sites and keeping objects in their original contexts are a priority, it is in the transit and destination countries that the law may best impose costs on the traffickers and ultimate purchasers. Because looting is primarily motivated by profit, the rate of looting should respond to the economic law of supply and demand. If through concern to avoid legal consequences, collectors in the market States refuse to buy artefacts of uncertain background, then incentives for the contemporary looting of artefacts should decrease.

[46] Morag M Kersel, 'From the Ground to the Buyer: A Market Analysis of the Trade in Illegal Antiquities' in Neil Brodie and others (eds), *Archaeology, Cultural Heritage, and the Antiquities Trade* (University Press of Florida 2006) 188, 189–94. On transit States, see Lyndel V Prott and Patrick J O'Keefe, *Law and the Cultural Heritage Vol. 3 Movement* (Butterworths 1989) 531–74 (hereafter Prott and O'Keefe, *Law and the Cultural Heritage*). In their study of the looting of Cambodian antiquities during the Khmer Rouge period, Simon Mackenzie and Tess Davis identified the role of the 'Janus' figure as the interface between the legal and illegal trades. Mackenzie and Davis, 'Temple Looting' (n 8) 723, 729. See also Peter B Campbell, 'The Illicit Antiquities Trade as a Transnational Criminal Network: Characterizing and Anticipating Trafficking of Cultural Heritage' (2013) 20 IJCP 113.

[47] The continental European countries follow the good faith purchaser doctrine, under which a good faith purchaser may be able to acquire title to stolen property, in contrast to the rule of common law countries where a thief can never convey title. Transferring stolen property to a good faith purchaser in a country that follows the good faith purchaser doctrine allows title to be laundered. Although a thief cannot transfer title to stolen property in a common law jurisdiction, an original owner may be barred from recovery due to various legal doctrines, including those based on the passage of time. See chapter 7, section 7.1. For change in the legal status of cultural objects as they move through the market, see Gerstenblith, 'Provenience and Provenance' (n 9).

[48] The question of the enforceability of an export control is often characterized as whether the export control falls into the category of public laws that are not enforced by another State. Prott and O'Keefe, *Law and the Cultural Heritage* (n 46) 652–60; Kurt Siehr, 'Private International Law and the Difficult Problem to Return Illegally Exported Cultural Property' (2015) 20(4) Uniform Law Review 20(4) 503; James Gordley, 'The Enforcement of Foreign Law: Reclaiming One Nation's Cultural Heritage in Another Nation's Courts' in Francesco Francioni and James Gordley (eds), *Enforcing International Cultural Heritage Law* (OUP 2013) 110, 110–19; Robert K Paterson, 'The Legal Dynamics of Cultural Property Export Controls: *Ortiz* Revisited' (1995) Special Issue UBC Law Review 241, 247–50; Paul Bator, 'An Essay on the International Trade in Art' (1982) 34 Stanford Law Review 275, 287.

The law should therefore impose a cost on those who contribute directly or indirectly to the looting of sites by punishing the handling, selling, and buying of looted antiquities. *Lex generalis* addresses the criminal and civil aspects of theft and recovery of stolen cultural objects. However, *lex specialis* has developed to address the particularized harms imposed on society by trafficking in undocumented archaeological objects.

As Mackenzie pointed out, London and New York are the two largest destination markets for antiquities in the world.[49] In order to reduce market demand, some market States have adopted legal responses that impose costs and consequences on intermediaries and, sometimes, the ultimate private and public collectors of looted antiquities. One international legal response was ratification and implementation of the 1970 UNESCO Convention on the Means of Prohibiting and Preventing the Illicit Import, Export and Transfer of Ownership of Cultural Property (hereafter 1970 UNESCO Convention).[50] This provides a basis for States Parties to recognize the export controls of other States Parties on cultural property, making an illegally exported cultural object an illegal import.[51] Recognition of foreign State ownership laws, which vest ownership of undiscovered antiquities in the State, is another legal response. Pursuant to such vesting laws, export of an artefact without permission constitutes theft, and the object is characterized as stolen property. These specialized legal responses work with general law, particularly law regarding import and export and law dealing with stolen property.

4.3.1 Development of Laws Protecting Archaeological Heritage

Laws protecting archaeological heritage have a long history, have taken different forms, and have aimed to curtail different types of conduct.[52] Some of the earliest such laws were adopted in Greece[53] and by the Ottoman Empire during the

[49] Mackenzie, 'Dig A Bit Deeper' (n 1) 252.

[50] Convention on the Means of Prohibiting and Preventing the Illicit Import, Export and Transfer of Ownership of Cultural Property (adopted 14 November 1970, entered into force 24 April 1972) 823 UNTS 231 (hereafter 1970 UNESCO Convention).

[51] Robert Peters, 'New Perspectives Beyond State Sovereignty and Territoriality in the Protection of Cultural Heritage' in Anne-Marie Carstens and Elizabeth Varner (eds), *Intersections in International Cultural Heritage Law* (OUP 2020) 364, 377.

[52] Laws to protect cultural remains date back to a statute of Pope Pius II in 1462 intended to protect the secular and ecclesiastical ancient remains of Rome. Alain Schnapp, *The Discovery of the Past* (Harry N Abrams 1997) 339–40.

[53] Greece enacted its first laws protecting its archaeological heritage in 1834, but national ownership was embodied in its Law 5351/32 'On Antiquities' of 1932. Neil J Brodie, 'Historical and Social Perspectives on the Regulation of the International Trade in Archaeological Objects: The Examples of Greece and India' (2005) 38 Vanderbilt Journal of Transnational Law 1051, 1057 (hereafter Brodie, 'Historical and Social Perspectives').

nineteenth century. The Ottoman government enacted its first regulation of antiquities in 1869, followed by the Antiquities Law of 1874.[54] This law ensured that the Imperial Museum (now the Archaeological Museum of Istanbul) would receive one-third of all artefacts recovered through excavations, thereby limiting the number of artefacts that could be removed from the Empire. The remaining share was divided between the excavator or finder and landowner. However, antiquities that were discovered fortuitously belonged to the State. The 1884 Antiquities Law (or Decree) established imperial ownership of all artefacts excavated in the Ottoman Empire and protected archaeological sites by requiring excavation permits.[55] A third Ottoman Decree adopted in 1906 reaffirmed State ownership, which has continued since that time until today.[56]

At the conclusion of the First World War, the region of the Ottoman Empire was divided, with the United Kingdom holding the League of Nations Mandate over what would later become Jordan, Israel, and Palestine, and France holding the Mandate over what later became Syria and Lebanon.[57] Archaeology played a surprisingly significant role in this reorganization of the Ottoman Empire. Article 421 of the 1920 Treaty of Sèvres established principles for the regulation of archaeological excavation and finds, including a definition of archaeological artefacts as predating 1700; the reporting of chance finds in exchange for a reward; a requirement of licences for excavation, survey work, and export; equality in the treatment of all foreign nationals; and a requirement that finds from excavations should be divided between the host country and the excavators in a system known as *partage*, thereby reversing the provisions of the 1884 Ottoman law.[58]

Laws developed under British colonial or Mandate rule had an impact on the laws of formerly colonized nations even after they attained independence. In the region of the Palestine Mandate, the British archaeologist John Garstang, the first

[54] Morag M Kersel and Mounir Bouchenaki, 'Middle East and North Africa' in Francesco Francioni and Ana Filipa Vrdoljak, *The Oxford Handbook of International Cultural Heritage Law* (OUP 2020) 931, 936 (hereafter Kersel and Bouchenaki, 'Middle East and North Africa').

[55] Kersel points out that the 1884 law can be viewed either as a national ownership law, in that all antiquities were owned by the National Museum in Constantinople, or as a legalization of cultural imperialism by appropriating artefacts from the regions of the Empire. Morag M Kersel, 'The Trade in Palestinian Antiquities' (2008) 33 Jerusalem Quarterly 21, 24 (hereafter Kersel, 'The Trade in Palestinian Antiquities').

[56] Ece Velioglu Yildizci, 'State Ownership of Archaeological Heritage: International, Swiss and Turkish Law Perspectives' (unpublished PhD dissertation, 2019) 61, 73–74 (hereafter Yildizci, State Ownership). For analysis of the 1906 decree by US courts, see *Republic of Turkey v Christie's Inc* 425 F Supp 3d 204, 214-17 (SDNY 2019); 2021 US Dist LEXIS 169215, *16-18 (SDNY 2021); *Republic of Turkey v OKS Partners* 1994 US Dist LEXIS 17032, *3 (D Mass 1994).

[57] Kersel and Bouchenaki, 'Middle East and North Africa' (n 54) 935. Iraq was supposed to be part of a British Mandate but revolted before the mandatory government could be established. ibid.

[58] Yildizci, State Ownership (n 56) 60–61; James F Goode, *Negotiating for the Past: Archaeology, Nationalism, and Diplomacy in the Middle East, 1919–1941* (University of Texas Press 2007) 33–34 (hereafter Goode, *Negotiating for the Past*). The close connection between diplomats and archaeologists facilitated this sort of pressure in government negotiations. ibid, 33–39. For a summary of laws pertaining to archaeological heritage among the countries of the Middle East and North Africa, see Kersel and Bouchenaki, 'Middle East and North Africa' (n 54) 931.

Director of the Department of Antiquities, promulgated the Antiquities Ordinance for Palestine of 1920. This law followed the Ottoman pattern of vesting ownership of antiquities in the civil government, but it also established a regulated legal trade in those antiquities that were not deemed appropriate for the national repository.[59]

The system of partage, described as a *sine qua non* for Western archaeologists,[60] was imposed on countries of the Eastern Mediterranean, either through the influence of the European powers over the course of the nineteenth century or following the First World War. The purpose of the system was to ensure a continued supply of archaeological remains for European museums, even after the Ottoman authorities began to assert their right to control the archaeological heritage of their domains. Turkey refused to ratify the Treaty of Sèvres and therefore did not adopt partage, but the countries that were subject to the Mandates were required to adopt the system.[61]

One of the most contentious examples of the use of partage occurred in Egypt. Under partage, foreign excavation teams were required to have a permit to dig, but they were entitled to half of the excavation finds.[62] The bust of the Queen Nefertiti was discovered in late 1912 at Tell el-Amarna, the capital of the Eighteenth Dynasty Pharaoh Akhenaten in the fourteenth century BCE (Figure 4.3). The bust was found during the excavations of the German Archaeological Institute in Cairo under the direction of Ludwig Borchardt and funded by a German merchant, James Simon. At the time, the head of the Egyptian Antiquities Service was a French Egyptologist, Gaston Maspero, and the partage of the Amarna finds was managed by Gustave Lefébvre. Why the Antiquities Service did not take the bust for Egypt is not clear.[63] It is possible that during the process of dividing the finds, the Nefertiti bust was either hidden or disguised, so that informed consent was never given by

[59] Kersel, 'The Trade in Palestinian Antiquities' (n 55) 25–26. This combination of national ownership with a legal trade persists in Israel. Even after the end of colonialism, the cultural heritage laws of India relate to the British model and adopt the concept of treasure trove in which finds must be reported to the government, which has the right to acquire the find. If the government does not acquire it, the finds are divided between the finder and the landowner. Other statutes require a licence for the export of antiquities and protect designated archaeological sites and monuments. Brodie, 'Historical and Social Perspectives' (n 53) 1059–60.

[60] Goode, *Negotiating for the Past* (n 58). Donors who funded excavations often did so out of a desire to obtain antiquities to display in prominent Western museums.

[61] Yildizci, State Ownership (n 56) 61.

[62] Egypt enacted a series of laws protecting its cultural heritage, beginning with the ordinance of 1835, Ordonnance du 15 août 1835 portant mesures de protection des antiquités. Its earliest vesting law dates to 1883. An 1891 decree reiterated vesting of antiquities in the State but also stated the excavator's right of partage. These basic provisions were continued in Law No 14 of 1912. The later Law No 215 of 1951 and Law No 117 of 1983, which will be discussed later, eliminated the right of partage.

[63] Kelly Culbertson, 'Contemporary Customary International Law in the Case of Nefertiti' (2012) 17 AAL 27, 30–31, 49–50; Claudia Breger, 'The "Berlin" Nefertiti Bust: Imperial Fantasies in Twentieth Century German Archaeological Discourse' in Regina Schulte (ed), *The Body of the Queen: Gender and Rule in the Courtly World, 1500–2000* (Berghahn Books 2006) 281, 285–86 (hereafter Breger, 'The "Berlin" Nefertiti Bust'). It is possible that the bust did not appear important as it is unfinished, or that, being brightly painted, it conflicted with perceived ideas of how ancient art should look. ibid, 288.

Figure 4.3 Nefertiti Bust. Thutmose (sculptor). Amarna Period, New Kingdom, 18th Dynasty. Egypt, *c* 1340 BCE. Neues Museum, Staatliche Museen zu Berlin

the authorities, who were not themselves Egyptian but French.[64] The Egyptian authorities may have only discovered the bust's existence when it went on display in

[64] As Siehr wrote, '[t]he Egyptians were often not masters in their house' and until 1922 were effectively under British occupation. In addition to Maspero and Lefébvre, Borchardt was a member of the Comité d'Egyptologie, which advised the Egyptian authorities. Kurt G Siehr, 'The Beautiful One Has

Berlin in 1923, having not been displayed earlier due to a policy of Borchardt to keep the bust secret.

For several decades after the Second World War, the bust was displayed in the Egyptian Museum in Berlin-Charlottenburg. It was displayed in its own room, separated from the other archaeological artefacts from the site, and was set off from the viewer. It was thus distinguished from archaeological remains and treated as universalistic 'high' art.[65] This display as a singular work of art continues in the current installation of the bust in the Neues Museum. The bust became incorporated into the German national identity, even in an imperial sense.[66] The question of whether Germany should return the Nefertiti bust is the subject of continuing contention.[67] Most countries abrogated partage as they gained their independence, but some in the Western museum system argue that partage should be reinstated as a way of encouraging both excavation and the building of more universal museums.[68]

Today, most States control terrestrial and underwater exploration and excavation of archaeological remains. Italy's Code of the Cultural and Landscape Heritage is a typical example.[69] The regulation applies to cultural property defined as 'immovable and movable things ... which possess artistic, historical, archaeological or ethno-anthropological interest'.[70] The Ministry has the exclusive right to conduct 'archaeological searches and, in general, activities for finding [cultural property] in any part of the national territory'.[71] It also has the authority to grant concessions to public or private entities to carry out these activities and searches.[72] Anyone who accidentally discovers cultural property must 'report the discovery ... within twenty-four hours and shall provide for the temporary conservation of the things, leaving them in the condition and place in which they were found'.[73] Many countries follow a similar pattern of vesting

Come—To Return: The Return of the Bust of Nefertiti from Berlin to Cairo' in John H Merryman (ed), *Imperialism, Art and Restitution* (CUP 2006) 114, 132 (hereafter Siehr, 'The Beautiful One Has Come').

[65] Breger, 'The "Berlin" Nefertiti Bust' (n 63) 286–87.

[66] ibid, 291.

[67] Siehr, 'The Beautiful One Has Come' (n 64) (arguing that the bust should be returned to Egypt); Stephen K Urice, 'The Beautiful One Has Come—To Stay' in John H Merryman (ed), *Imperialism, Art and Restitution* (CUP 2006) 135 (arguing that the bust should remain in Berlin).

[68] James Cuno, *Who Owns Antiquity? Museums and the Battle over our Ancient Heritage* (Princeton University Press 2008) xxxiii.

[69] D Lgs No 42, 22 January 2004, GU Supp No 45, 24 February 2004 (hereafter Italy Code of the Cultural and Landscape Heritage).

[70] ibid, Article 10. Italy regulates exploration for archaeological and historical objects found in the seabed extending for twelve marine miles from its national waters under the 2001 UNESCO Convention on the Protection of the Underwater Cultural Heritage (opened for signature 2 November 2002, entered into force 2 January 2009) 2562 UNTS 3, Article 94.

[71] Italy Code of the Cultural and Landscape Heritage (n 69) Article 88(1).

[72] ibid, Article 89 (1).

[73] ibid, Article 90(1).

exclusive control over the conduct of archaeological exploration and excavation in the relevant government ministry.[74]

4.3.2 State Ownership of Antiquities

4.3.2.1 Vesting Laws

Many States with a rich archaeological heritage vest ownership of antiquities in the State. Vesting of ownership in the State allows objects to be characterized as stolen property in market States. Such laws deny title to looted antiquities to the looter, the smuggler, and subsequent purchasers; impose a risk of loss of the object and its market value; and impose a risk of criminal prosecution on the traffickers and ultimate purchasers. Vesting laws also allow the country of origin to realize the current economic value, through tourism, scholarship, and education, that derives from its cultural past.

An example of a vesting law is Article 91 of Italy's Code of the Cultural and Landscape Heritage, which states: 'The things [defined as cultural property under Article 10], found underground or in sea beds by whomsoever and howsoever, shall belong to the State and, depending on whether they be immovable or movable, shall become part of government property or of its inalienable assets.'[75] An accidental finder who has permission from the landowner to search the land on which the object is found and the holder of a concession from the Ministry are entitled to a reward not to exceed one-quarter of the value of the object.[76] Despite the entitlement of the finder to a reward, the important element for analysis of State ownership is that the State is the owner *ab initio*, without the need for a subsequent transfer of title to the State or any judicial or administrative process and regardless of the payment of the reward.

State ownership of archaeological artefacts raises two questions concerning the status of such objects as they move through the international market to other countries. On the one hand, are such laws distinguishable from export controls, which are often not enforced by other countries in the absence of a specific agreement to do so?[77] On the other hand, are objects subject to State ownership characterized as stolen property, even though they had never been in the physical possession of

[74] For example, Egypt: Law No 117 of the Year 1983 concerning the Issuance of Antiquities' Protection Law as amended by Law No 3 of 2010 promulgating the Antiquities' Protection Law Article 5 (hereafter Law No 117); Jordan: Law of Antiquities, Law No 21 for the year 1988, amended by Law No 23 for the year 2004, Arts 2(11), 14–20; Regulations for Archaeological Projects in Jordan based on the provisions of the Jordanian Antiquities Law Number 21 for the year 1988 and its amendments. See also Kersel and Bouchenaki, 'Middle East and North Africa' (n 54) 936–55.

[75] Italy Code of the Cultural and Landscape Heritage (n 69) Article 91(1).

[76] ibid (n 69) Article 92(1). Under some circumstances the finder may be entitled to a reward of up to half of the value of the objects found: Article 92(2).

[77] See above n 48.

the foreign State that asserts ownership? While the courts in market States could simply accept the characterization given by the States of origin to the ownership status of antiquities, the courts in two of the largest art market countries, the United States and the United Kingdom, have insisted on conducting their own analyses to determine the ownership status of undocumented archaeological artefacts.

4.3.2.2 Foreign State Ownership in Courts of Market States

In *United States v McClain*, a US court gave the first extended analysis of the concept of foreign State ownership in a market State.[78] This case involved the prosecution and conviction of a group of dealers for conspiring to transport, in interstate commerce, in violation of the National Stolen Property Act (NSPA),[79] pre-Columbian artefacts taken in violation of Mexico's ownership of antiquities.[80] The *McClain* court distinguished between illegal export, which would not constitute a violation of US law, and the handling of stolen property, which would. The characterization of the artefacts as stolen is decided under US law, but the law of the country of origin determines the prior issue of who owns the property.[81] Because an object retains the characterization of ownership given under local law, an object that is stolen in one country is still considered to be stolen property in a second country, thus implicating the second country's laws concerning stolen property. While ownership is a product of private law, export controls are often characterized as public laws, which a foreign State typically will not enforce in the absence of an agreement to do so.[82] It is therefore necessary to distinguish between an ownership law, which vests title to the artefacts in the State, and an export control, which limits the export of objects, even those that may be legitimately owned by an individual.

This distinction was significant in the outcome of *Attorney-General of New Zealand v Ortiz*.[83] This case involved the illegal export from New Zealand of five antique Maori carved panels. New Zealand's Historic Articles Act of 1962 provided for forfeiture of protected categories of ethnographic objects to the national

[78] 545 F2d 988 (5th Cir 1977); 593 F2d 658 (5th Cir 1979). *United States v Hollinshead* was the first US case to consider foreign State ownership of an archaeological artefact and involved stele fragments, which were smuggled out of Guatemala through Belize. 495 F2d 1154 (9th Cir 1974). The court characterized the fragments as stolen property, and the defendants were convicted of conspiracy to transport stolen property in international commerce.

[79] 18 USC §§ 2314–2315 (prohibiting the transport or transfer 'in interstate or foreign commerce [of] any goods ... with the value of $5,000 or more' as well as receiving, possessing, storing, selling, or disposing of such goods with knowledge that they were stolen).

[80] 545 F2d 988, 991–92. The Fifth Circuit reversed the defendants' convictions on substantive counts twice, finally allowing only their conviction on a conspiracy charge to stand, as the court held that only Mexico's 1972 statute was clearly an ownership law.

[81] *United States v Portrait of Wally* 105 F Supp 2d 288, 292 (SDNY 2000) ('federal law determines whether property has been stolen, local law controls the analytically prior issues of (a) whether any person or entity has a property interest in the item such that it can be stolen, and (b) whether the receiver of the item has a property interest in it'.).

[82] See above n 48.

[83] [1982] 1 QB 347, [1982] 3 WLR 571 (CA), [1983] 3 WLR 809 (HL). The decisions of the different judges are discussed in Prott and O'Keefe, *Law and the Cultural Heritage* (n 46) 653–55.

government upon illegal export. When New Zealand attempted to recover the panels, the UK courts held that the provision was an export control and, as a public law, was not enforceable in a foreign State, although the reasoning among the different judges was not uniform.

In 2002, a prominent New York antiquities dealer, Frederick Schultz, was convicted on one count of conspiring to deal in antiquities stolen from Egypt in violation of Egypt's ownership law, Law No 117, enacted in 1983.[84] Egypt's Law No 117 states unambiguously that: '[a]ll antiquities are considered public property—except for charitable and religious endowments ... It is impermissible to own, possess or dispose of antiquities except pursuant to the conditions set forth in this law and its implementing regulations.'[85] The law also prohibits private possession except of those antiquities privately owned before Law No 117 was enacted. Both the trial and appellate courts concluded that Law No 117 created an ownership interest in antiquities in the State and that the law is vigorously enforced within Egypt, not just upon illegal export.[86] The courts thus reiterated that property owned by a foreign sovereign under a vesting law and removed without permission is to be treated no differently than any other type of stolen property, even if the State has not previously taken physical possession of the object. Foreign State ownership of archaeological artefacts has been used as the basis for criminal prosecutions[87] and restitution through private replevin actions brought by the foreign State,[88] civil forfeiture actions,[89] and negotiated returns from private collectors and US museums, including the Metropolitan Museum of Art in New York, the Boston Museum of Fine Arts, the Princeton Art Museum, the J Paul Getty Trust, the Cleveland Art

[84] *United States v Schultz* 178 F Supp 2d 445 (SDNY 2002), aff'd 333 F3d 393 (2nd Cir 2003). Schultz and his British co-conspirator, Jonathan Tokeley-Parry, fabricated a fake 'old' collection to which these artefacts allegedly belonged and manufactured fake provenance documentation. Peter Watson, 'The Investigation of Frederick Schultz' (2002) 10 Culture Without Context 21. See also *Schultz* 333 F3d, 396–98. Tokeley-Parry was convicted for his role in the conspiracy. *R v Tokeley-Parry* [1999] Crim LR 578 (CA 1999).

[85] Law No 117 (n 74) Article 6.

[86] *United States v Schultz* 178 F Supp 2d 445, 447, 448 (SDNY 2002). The courts looked, in particular, at whether discoverers of artefacts were required to turn them over to the authorities and whether those who failed to do so were prosecuted.

[87] *United States v Latchford* (n 41); *New York v Wiener*, Criminal Complaint (21 December 2016) (dealer charged with possession of and conspiracy with intent to possess, buy, smuggle, launder, and sell antiquities stolen from Afghanistan, Cambodia, China, India, Pakistan, and Thailand, based on their respective vesting laws).

[88] For example, *Republic of Turkey v Metropolitan Museum of Art* 762 F Supp 44 (SDNY 1990) (recovery of the Lydian hoard by Turkey); *Republic of Turkey v OKS Partners* 1994 US Dist LEXIS 17032 *6 (D Mass 1994) (recovery by Turkey of the Elmali hoard of 1,750 rare ancient coins).

[89] For example, *United States v An Antique Platter of Gold* 184 F3d 131 (2nd Cir 1999). Forfeiture actions are *in rem* proceedings in which the plaintiff is the government, the defendant is the property, and the claimant is anyone who asserts an interest in the property, such as an importer or purchaser. Stefan D Cassella, 'Using the Forfeiture Laws to Protect Archaeological Resources' (2004) 41 Idaho Law Review 129, 132–36 (hereafter Cassella, 'Using the Forfeiture Laws').

Museum, and the Museum of the Bible to Italy, Greece, Turkey, Cambodia, Egypt, and Iraq.[90]

The *McClain* and *Schultz* decisions set out four elements required to recognize that an undocumented archaeological object is owned by a foreign State: (1) the vesting law must be clearly an ownership law on its face so as to give notice to one who might be adversely affected by these laws, particularly in a criminal prosecution; (2) the State's ownership rights must be enforced domestically and not only upon illegal export;[91] (3) the object must have been discovered within the territorial boundaries of the country claiming ownership so that the law does not have extraterritorial effect; and (4) the object must have been located within the country at the time the law was enacted so that the law does not have retroactive effect.

The third and fourth elements require a fact-intensive investigation into both the provenience and the provenance of the object. The provenience is important for establishing the modern country within whose boundaries the object was discovered and therefore the applicable law for determining ownership. Provenance, which is the ownership history of the object from its time of discovery, establishes the timeline location of the object and of applicable laws.[92] While the German courts look to prior foreign private law to determine ownership, similar to the US and UK courts, they do not seem to enforce foreign public law, such as export controls.[93] The importance of establishing provenance is illustrated in a case in which the Berlin High Regional Court found that Egypt had failed to demonstrate that the antiquities at issue were exported from Egypt after the date of enactment of Egypt's 1983 vesting law. Egypt therefore could not recover the artefacts.[94]

The UK decisions in *Government of the Islamic Republic of Iran v The Barakat Galleries Ltd*[95] involved application of Iran's State ownership law to determine the disposition of a collection of antiquities imported into England by a dealer, Barakat Galleries. These artefacts consisted of eighteen chlorite jars, bowls, and cups and were allegedly looted from burials in the Jiroft region of Iran. Asserting that the

[90] For returns by US museums and private collectors, see above nn 10–11; Patty Gerstenblith, 'Theft and Illegal Excavation' in Francesco Francioni and Ana Filipa Vrdoljak, *The Oxford Handbook of International Cultural Heritage Law* (OUP 2020) 200, 210.

[91] In subsequent litigation, this element has received less emphasis and has arguably been collapsed into the first element. In *Republic of Turkey v Christie's Inc and Steinhardt*, the court stated that the claimant 'may also—but is not required to—offer evidence, for example of the state's "active enforcement of its ownership rights," to "confirm the intent of the law"'. 425 F Supp 3d 204, 215 (SDNY 2019) (quoting *Schultz*, 333 F3d, 402).

[92] See Gerstenblith, 'Provenience and Provenance' (n 9) 468–69.

[93] Matthias Weller, 'Iran v. Barakat: Some Observations on the Application of Foreign Public Law by Domestic Courts from a Comparative Perspective' (2007) 12(3) Art Antiquity and Law 279, 283–88 (hereafter Weller, 'Iran v. Barakat').

[94] Application for export ban on archaeological objects by means of injunction: proof of ownership or possession by the applicant foreign state. Higher Regional Court of Berlin, judgment of 16 October 2006–10 U 286/05, Neue Juristische Wochenschrift (NJW) 2007, 705. The court also held that Egypt's Law No 66/1963 was an export control and not an ownership law. Weller, 'Iran v. Barakat' (n 93) 284.

[95] [2007] EWHC 705 (QB), revd [2007] EWCA Civ 1374; [2008] 1 All ER 1177.

antiquities found in London were taken in violation of its ownership law, Iran sued Barakat in conversion to recover the objects. The trial court held that none of Iran's statutory enactments made a sufficiently clear statement of State ownership. Because acquisition by means of a State ownership law was a means available only to sovereigns, the trial court further held that the law was public in nature and therefore Iran's claim was not justiciable in a foreign court.

In an extensive decision, the appellate court reversed, holding first that a claimant could bring a cause of action in conversion based on an immediate right to possession, as well as based on a proprietary right.[96] In determining the nature of Iran's interest in the antiquities, the appellate court utilized a more functional approach and articulated the standard as

> not the label which foreign law gives to the legal relationship, but its substance ... The issue with which we are concerned is whether the rights enjoyed by Iran in relation to the antiquities equate to those that give standing to sue in conversion under English law.[97]

Thus, rather than looking exclusively to the literal terms of the Iranian law, the court considered the fundamental nature of property ownership and its associated rights, including the right of possession.[98] The court concluded that Iran's 1979 Legal Bill confers on the State both ownership and an immediate right to possession of newly discovered antiquities with all the rights that are incidents of ownership.[99]

The appellate court concluded that the vesting of State ownership in the 1979 Legal Bill was not penal as it was not retroactive and it did not deprive an owner of an existing interest in the artefacts. The Iranian law only determined the ownership of previously unowned antiquities. Because Iran had not acquired title by confiscation or compulsory process, but rather did so through legislative enactment, it did not need to have physical possession of the antiquities before their illegal removal in order to assert its rights in a foreign court.[100] The court further recognized that if actual possession were required before a State could recover looted antiquities, as a practical matter such antiquities could never be recovered since such artefacts, by being looted directly from archaeological sites, are not in the State's actual possession.[101] Following the pattern of judicial decisions discussed earlier that the law of the State of origin determining ownership is private law, the court held that 'when

96 [2007] EWCA Civ 1374; [2008] 1 All ER 1177 paras 19–31.
97 ibid, para 49.
98 ibid, para 73.
99 ibid, paras 84, 86. Because the parties agreed that the Jiroft antiquities at issue in the case left Iran between 2000 and 2004, the 1979 Legal Bill was the applicable statute.
100 ibid, paras 143–50.
101 ibid, para 163.

a state owns property in the same way as a private citizen there is no impediment to recovery'.[102]

The court further held that, even if Iran's ownership law were a public law, British courts are not barred from enforcing a public law unless it is against public policy to do so.[103] In evaluating public policy, the court cited international instruments to which the United Kingdom is a party, including the 1970 UNESCO Convention, the European Union's Council Directive 93/7 on the return of cultural objects unlawfully removed from the territory of a Member State,[104] and the Commonwealth scheme for the protection of the material cultural heritage.[105] While acknowledging that none of these legal instruments was directly applicable to this case, the court interpreted them as indicating that the international community recognized the desirability of protecting cultural heritage and the need for mutual assistance among States to protect that heritage.[106] The court thus concluded that it is British public policy to recognize the ownership claim of a foreign State to antiquities that are part of its cultural heritage.

4.3.2.3 UNESCO–UNIDROIT Model State Ownership Law

The scrutiny that courts in market States give to the State of origin's legal characterization of undocumented antiquities may be viewed as a continuation of a colonialist mindset. Nonetheless, for the mechanism of foreign State ownership to be effective, it is necessary for States of origin to adapt their domestic laws so that the courts of market States will recognize them as ownership laws. Egypt's Law No 117 of 1983 and Iraq's Antiquities Law No 59 of 1936 and Antiquities and Heritage Law No 55 of 2002 are good examples of statutes that clearly define the types of artefacts to which they apply and clearly state that all such artefacts are public property—that is, owned by the State. This characterization includes those antiquities that are not yet in the physical possession of the State and those that are discovered on private land. To promote the goal of encouraging States to adopt similarly clear vesting statutes, in 2012 UNESCO and UNIDROIT developed the Model Provisions on State Ownership of Undiscovered Cultural Objects.[107] States can use

[102] ibid, para 136 (citing *Kuwait Airways Corp v Iraq Airways Co* (no 3) [2002] UKHL 19 at 13, [2002] All ER 209 at 13, [2002] 2 AC 883, where the court stated: 'governmental acts affecting proprietary rights will be recognised by an English court as valid if they would be recognised as valid by the law of the country where the property was situated when the law takes effect').

[103] [2007] EWCA Civ 1374, [2008] 1 All ER 1177, paras 151–163.

[104] Council Directive 93/7/EEC of 15 March 1993 on the Return of Cultural Objects Unlawfully Removed from the Territory of a Member State. The Directive was recast as Directive 2014/60/EU with some modifications.

[105] Patrick J O'Keefe, 'Protection of the Material Cultural Heritage: The Commonwealth Scheme' (1995) 44 ICLQ 147. The scheme was promulgated in response to the decision in *Attorney-General of New Zealand v Ortiz* (n 83), but it was left to each member of the Commonwealth to adopt it into domestic law.

[106] [2007] EWCA Civ 1374, [2008] 1 All ER 1177, paras 154–55.

[107] UNESCO–UNIDROIT Model Provisions on State Ownership of Undiscovered Cultural Objects (2012) < https://www.unidroit.org/instruments/cultural-property/2012-model-provisions/> accessed

the model statute as a basis for drafting their domestic laws vesting ownership of undiscovered archaeological artefacts. Such laws would be more easily understood by courts in market States and would facilitate the return of looted and smuggled archaeological artefacts. The Model Provisions could be of great benefit, but it does not seem that any State has used them as the basis for enacting new vesting statutes.

The Model Provisions consist of six provisions. The first reiterates that States have responsibility for protecting their undiscovered cultural objects and for preserving them for the future. The second offers a definition of the types of objects to which the provisions apply. However, it is unclear whether State ownership would apply to all cultural objects or only to archaeological artefacts.[108] The third provision states the status of ownership, which should clarify that State ownership applies to relevant objects *ab initio* and not only after their registration or the payment of an award to a finder. The fourth provision states the definition of stolen objects, while the fifth defines limits on the alienability of such objects. The sixth reiterates the character of these objects and the obligation of other States to return them.

4.3.2.4 Influence of the UNIDROIT Convention

The 1995 UNIDROIT Convention on Stolen or Illegally Exported Cultural Objects (1995 UNIDROIT Convention)[109] arguably incorporates State ownership in stating, in Article 3(2), that 'a cultural object which has been unlawfully excavated or lawfully excavated but unlawfully retained shall be considered stolen, when consistent with the law of the State where the excavation took place'. This provision eliminates any question of the legal status of looted undocumented archaeological objects and accomplishes the purpose of characterizing such objects as stolen property. Similar to vesting statutes, this characterization means that generic legal provisions dealing with stolen property apply to such artefacts.

However, the UNIDROIT Convention provision goes further than most vesting statutes in that it applies not only to objects that were illegally excavated but also to ones that may have been legally excavated or discovered fortuitously but then unlawfully kept from relevant government authorities. Exactly how broadly this applies is as yet untested. For example, some countries may not vest ownership of undiscovered artefacts in the State but may require that an individual who

27 July 2023. The most in-depth analysis of the Model Provisions is Yildizci, State Ownership (n 56) 193–219.

[108] Yildizci, State Ownership (n 56) 205–05. The Model Provisions should borrow elements commonly found among current vesting statutes, such as by requiring an age or a date threshold. Kersel and Bouchenaki, 'Middle East and North Africa' (n 54) 936–40, 942–46. The provisions should also clarify whether objects privately owned before enactment of the vesting statute would remain in private ownership, and, if so, whether such objects are saleable or otherwise transferable.

[109] UNIDROIT Convention on Stolen or Illegally Exported Cultural Property (opened for signature 24 June 1995, entered into force 1 July 1998) 34 ILM 1322.

accidentally discovers an artefact give notice to government authorities of the discovery within a limited time period. The failure to give notice and turn the object over to proper authorities would constitute unlawful retention of the object and it would be characterized as stolen property in another State Party, if consistent with the law of the State of origin. Some market States that have not ratified this Convention have adopted statutory provisions that accomplish the same purpose as this section of the UNIDROIT Convention.[110]

4.3.2.5 Analysis of State Ownership

Despite the evolution of legal doctrine in market States to characterize archaeological artefacts removed from a State of origin in violation of a vesting statute as stolen property, some legal scholars and market proponents, particularly in the United States, have criticized this recognition of foreign State ownership. These critics do not view the modern State as the legitimate representative of the ancient culture that produced the archaeological remains.[111] The narrative among the European colonial powers that some areas outside of Europe were uninhabited until their 'discovery' and settlement by Europeans facilitates the imposed cultural discontinuity between the past and current inhabitants. To the extent that Europeans acknowledged the present inhabitants, the Indigenous people were viewed as either non-descendants or not worthy descendants of those who produced these cultural artefacts, as discussed in chapter 3.[112] The denial of a claim to ownership by the current inhabitants meant that the cultural objects were unowned, and the archaeological remains, due to their universalistic quality, were perceived as available to become owned by whoever first reduced them to possession and removed them. Thus, according to this logic, the archaeological remains, particularly those that were still buried in the ground, became owned by the Western expropriators, and the Indigenous people were denied any right or title to this type of cultural object.

[110] The Netherlands ratified only the 1970 UNESCO Convention. However, its implementing legislation, citing Article 3(2) of the UNIDROIT Convention, prohibits the import of unlawfully appropriated cultural materials, defined to include illegally excavated materials from archaeological sites. Act of 9 December 2015 Relating to the Combining and Amendment of Rules Regarding Cultural Heritage. The United Kingdom's 2003 Dealing in Cultural Objects (Offences) Act, Chapter 27, criminalizes dealing in 'tainted cultural objects'. <www.legislation.gov.uk/ukpga/2003/27/contents> accessed 2 June 2021. Tainted cultural objects are those whose excavation or removal from a structure of historical or archaeological interest, including an archaeological site or excavation, constitutes an offence under local law (Arts 2(2) and (2)(4)). This provision therefore applies to previously undocumented, looted archaeological artefacts.

[111] For example, Cuno, *Who Owns Antiquity?* (n 68) 64–65 (discussing Iraq), 75, 81–87 (discussing Turkey), 92–96 (discussing China).

[112] These views allowed the Europeans to impose a cultural discontinuity between the ancient remains and the present inhabitants and thereby deny the rights of the Indigenous peoples in these remains. See Dane Morrison, 'In Whose Hands Is the Telling of the Tale?' in Dane Morrison (ed), *American Indian Studies: An Interdisciplinary Approach to Contemporary Issues* (Peter Lang Inc 1997) 5, 10–13. In contrast, Watkins emphasized that the 'descendants of those cultures whom the archaeologist studies exist in the present'. Watkins, 'The Politics of Archaeology' (n 16) 16.

Based on the idea that archaeological artefacts are unowned until they are reduced to physical possession, market proponents argue that courts in market States should not recognize ownership unless the claimant State first had physical possession. If this approach were adopted, whereby whoever first reduces an ancient object to possession becomes the owner, a race to remove artefacts from the ground as quickly as possible would ensue. This would lead to over-exploitation of cultural heritage resources through the law of capture,[113] in this circumstance by incentivizing a rush by looters to remove artefacts in order to be the first to reduce them to physical possession. Courts in market States[114] have rejected a requirement of physical possession before States of origin could assert their ownership rights, for the very reason that the latter States had done all they could to establish their ownership rights and that recognition of these rights would encourage the preservation of archaeological heritage.

The main difference in the analyses of the State ownership doctrine in the *Schultz* and *Barakat* cases seems to rest on the different degree of clarity required for the vesting law. The *Schultz* court focused on two aspects of Egypt's national ownership law: what Egypt said *prima facie* and the intent behind the law, which was established through domestic enforcement.[115] The court in *Barakat* took a functional approach in analysing the Iranian law, looking to the fundamental nature of property ownership and possession and then determining whether Iran could maintain its claim based on an identification of inherent property rights. As such, the *Barakat* decision displayed a more nuanced understanding of fundamental property law principles.

The analysis of Turkey's ownership law in an earlier US decision, *Republic of Turkey v OKS Partners*, which involved a hoard of rare ancient coins looted from Turkey, more closely resembles that of the *Barakat* decision, as is perhaps appropriate since these are both private replevin actions and not criminal prosecutions. After analysing the respective rights of a finder and the State, the court concluded:

[113] The law of capture requires physical possession before something unowned becomes owned. While physical possession is one method of acquiring ownership, it has been rejected as the exclusive method, based on both law and policy, as wasteful and inefficient. Judge Richard Posner asserted that a system in which ownership is based only on physical possession 'entails heavy investments in the maintenance of such control. It also makes no provision for rights to future, as distinct from present, use .... This system encourages wasteful present use as a method of staking a claim to the future use of the [resource].' Richard A Posner, 'Savigny, Holmes, and the Law of Economics of Possession' (2000) 86 Virginia Law Review 535, 552. Constructive possession, premised on a clear communication of intent to exercise dominion, is a more economically efficient alternative that is less wasteful of natural resources.

[114] For example, *Barakat* [2007] EWCA Civ 1374, paras 143, 148–49.

[115] The emphasis in *McClain* and *Schultz* on the *prima facie* clarity of the ownership law may have been necessitated by the due process requirement of giving fair warning to a potential criminal defendant of what conduct is prohibited. In *Republic of Turkey v Christie's Inc*, the court characterized the second prong of the *Schultz* criteria as requiring that the foreign State must establish the intent behind its vesting law to distinguish it from an export control, but that it does not need to prove active enforcement of the law. 425 F Supp 3d 204, 214–16 (SDNY 2019) (citing *United States v One Tyrannosaurus Bataar Skeleton*, 2021 US Dist LEXIS 165153 *29–*31 (SDNY 2012)).

> If 'title' is envisioned as a bundle of severable rights, the state has the biggest part of the bundle, and whatever attenuated rights remain in the finder depend upon strict compliance with [Turkey's] 1983 law. What is critical for the purpose of this case is that the Republic [of Turkey] has an immediate and unconditional right of possession which accrues immediately upon the discovery of the antiquities.[116]

The court then held that this interest was sufficient for Turkey to maintain its replevin action against the current possessors.

This leads to the point that States can establish ownership of undiscovered archaeological artefacts through statutory enactment and, as an attribute of sovereignty, can alter through statute the boundary between private and public ownership.[117] Within the framework of both international and domestic law, the line dividing public and private property and the ability of a State to adjust the exact boundaries between them are recognized by other States, as a result of comity and respect for the inherent authority of sovereign States.[118] The public interest in the preservation of cultural objects imposes a public duty that can, at times, limit or even negate private ownership.

In an effort to protect cultural objects associated with the aristocracy and the Church from destruction during the French Revolution, the Abbé Grégoire and Joseph Lakanal propounded that artistic works were the product of the people of France and were therefore part of its patrimony or inheritance.[119] Lakanal argued that this imposed obligations of preservation on the French people and that they should 'protect the arts against the new losses that threaten them'.[120] The purpose of this form of common ownership was to provide protection and not to assign private ownership rights to the first taker, which might, in fact, cause their destruction. Further, as Joseph Sax described, the goal of preserving cultural objects and in particular of moving beyond an emphasis on private ownership involves

[116] 1994 US Dist LEXIS 17032 *6 (D Mass 1994).

[117] This recognition of sovereign rights is echoed in Judge Wisdom's statement in *McClain* that '[t]he state comes to own property … *when it declares itself the owner; the declaration is an attribute of sovereignty*'. *McClain* 545 F2d 1002–03 (emphasis added).

[118] To provide greater protection to archaeological artefacts, the definition of what qualifies in the United Kingdom as treasure trove under the 1996 Treasure Act has evolved, expanding the categories of artefacts that belong to the Crown and diminishing those that belong to private individuals. 'Summary of the Treasure Act'<http://finds.org.uk/treasure/advice/summary> accessed 2 June 2021. See also Joseph W Singer, 'Sovereignty and Property' (1991) 86 Northwestern University Law Review 1, 41–42 (describing how the State makes choices as to what property will be considered private and what will be considered public).

[119] Joseph L Sax, 'Heritage Preservation as a Public Duty: The Abbé Grégoire and the Origins of an Idea' (1989–90) 88 Michigan Law Review 1142, 1156. The impact of the French Revolution on the development of the concept of national ownership of cultural heritage is discussed further in chapter 2, section 2.2.

[120] ibid, 1157, fn 76.

> the endeavor to build a perspective of time into public policy, to institutionalize the long view, and to employ preservation not as a glorification of the past but as a promise to the future that the present will not impoverish it. In selecting the artifacts it wishes to pass on, preservation policy goes beyond simply saving certain objects and becomes a symbolic shaping of the national agenda. It serves as a banner announcing what the nation represents, or at least what it aspires to represent.[121]

In the United Kingdom and the United States, where there is greater legal protection of private property rights, the law has evolved to expand the types of cultural resources that are subject to public control or ownership. The earliest legislation enacted in the United Kingdom to limit what a landowner could do with archaeological or historical remains was the 1873 Bill to Provide for the Preservation of Ancient Monuments. This legislation had the goal of protecting from development particularly Roman and prehistoric remains, which were largely privately owned, including Stonehenge.[122] By restricting the landowner's right to develop property, the legislation recognized that privately owned cultural resources could be subject to State control because the owner acted as a trustee or guardian on behalf of the public. 'The Ancient Monuments bill shifted the line between public and private authority a considerable distance for that time.'[123]

Many States and communities draw upon the ancient past as a source of identity and inspiration and view themselves as the legitimate representative of an ancient community, regardless of how outsiders evaluate questions of ethnic, religious, or cultural continuity. By reinforcing the idea that the modern community is the descendant and inheritor of the ancient culture, ownership laws allow the modern community to formulate its cultural identity and to become invested in the preservation of the remains of past cultures. Such remains can become a source of sustainable development through cultural tourism, development of intellectual resources, and continuation of ancient historic and artistic traditions as embodied in modern cultural productions. The investment of the local community in the preservation of the past enables such remains to be studied so that all, encompassing both the local and global communities, can benefit from this preservation.

[121] Joseph L Sax, 'Is Anyone Minding Stonehenge? The Origin of Cultural Property Protection in England' (1990) 78 California Law Review 1543, 1544.
[122] ibid, 1545–46.
[123] ibid, 1549.

4.3.3 Cultural Property Agreements and International Conventions

Another method of preventing international trade in undocumented and likely looted archaeological artefacts is through agreements that make it illegal to import an illegally exported cultural object. The core international convention that aims to regulate the international market in cultural objects is the 1970 UNESCO Convention. Article 1 of the Convention includes the products of archaeological excavations (both regular and clandestine) and elements of dismembered historical monuments and archaeological sites in the definition of cultural property. Article 1 also requires that the cultural property be specifically designated by each State Party, and this requirement may pose an impediment to including undocumented archaeological artefacts in the Convention's provisions.[124] Archaeological artefacts are included in both Article 3, which applies to all cultural property, and Article 9, which applies only to archaeological and ethnological objects.

In enacting domestic implementing legislation for the 1970 UNESCO Convention, most market States have adopted reciprocal import restrictions. These States implement Article 3 of the Convention by making it illegal to import cultural objects that were exported from their country of origin (or discovery) in violation of an export control adopted under the Convention.[125] This approach utilizes designation by category or type rather than documentation in an inventory or on a list, and it is therefore effective for dealing with the problem of archaeological objects that are looted from the ground and are therefore undocumented. This is a proactive approach that negates the need to enact new import restrictions in response to a specific emergency.

Only Switzerland and the United States require that other States Parties to the 1970 Convention enter into a bilateral agreement that prohibits the import of illegally exported cultural materials. Switzerland implements Article 3 and so its

[124] The only court decision to analyse the requirement of specific designation deemed it satisfied if the object fits into a category that has been designated as subject to export control by another State Party. *R v Yorke* [1998] 166 NSR (2d). Some countries' implementing legislation does not require specific designation. Convention on Cultural Property Implementation Act, 19 USC § 2601(6) (not requiring specific designation).

[125] For example, Canada, Cultural Property Export and Import Act, RSC 1985, c C-51, sec 37(2); Germany, Act on the Protection of Cultural Property (Cultural Property Protection Act—KGSG) 31 July 2016, BGBl I, 2016, 1914; Federal Government Commissioner for Culture and the Media, 'Key Aspects of the new Act on the Protection of Cultural Property in Germany' (September 2016), 7. <www.bundesregierung.de/Content/DE/_Anlagen/BKM/2016/2016-09-23-kulturgutschutz-informationen-englisch.pdf?__blob=publicationFile&v=2> accessed 10 May 2021. See also Robert Peters, 'The Protection of Cultural Property: Recent Developments in Germany in the Context of New EU Law and the 1970 UNESCO Convention' (2016) 2 SAACLR 85, 96–97; Patty Gerstenblith, 'Implementation of the 1970 UNESCO Convention by the United States and Other Market Nations' in Jane Anderson and Haidy Geismar (eds), *The Routledge Companion to Cultural Property* (Routledge 2017) 70. Those States that have ratified the 1995 UNIDROIT Convention also recognize the export controls on cultural materials of other States Parties.

import restrictions apply to a broad range of cultural materials.[126] However, the Swiss legislation allows the Federal Council to respond to crisis situations without need to negotiate an agreement with the affected State by imposing import restrictions on an emergency basis under Article 9 of the 1970 UNESCO Convention. The United States, on the other hand, implements Article 9, and not Article 3, and so its import restrictions for undocumented cultural objects apply only to archaeological and ethnological materials.[127] This reactive approach is not well suited to respond to crisis situations. In the case of the two emergency situations in Iraq and Syria, the UN Security Council felt it necessary to adopt Resolutions specifically mandating prohibition of trade in cultural materials illegally removed from Iraq after 1990[128] and from Syria after 2011.[129]

4.3.4 Customs Laws

Foreign State ownership and agreements to impose import restrictions work together with generic customs laws to provide several bases for seizing and forfeiting archaeological artefacts. An importer may be inclined to falsely declare the country of origin (or discovery) of an archaeological object if the country of origin is known to have a vesting law or if the importing country restricts the import of illegally exported artefacts. However, the false declaration itself becomes a basis for forfeiture. In contrast to a private replevin action brought by a foreign government, since 1997 the US government has become the primary litigant in the recovery of archaeological artefacts through the mechanism of civil forfeiture.[130] The use of civil forfeiture based on violation of the customs statute, because the object is characterized as stolen property, because of a misdeclaration of value or country of origin, or because the goods are otherwise imported contrary to law,[131] alters the burdens of proof and spares the country of origin the expense and difficulties of litigation in a foreign country.

[126] Federal Act on the International Transfer of Cultural Property (Cultural Property Transfer Act) (20 June 2003), Article 7; Federal Office of Culture, 'Bilateral agreements' <www.bak.admin.ch/bak/en/home/cultural-heritage/transfer-of-cultural-property/bilateral-agreements.html> accessed 10 May 2021.

[127] Convention on Cultural Property Implementation Act, 19 USC §§ 2602–2603. Although the US legislation allows for the imposition of import restrictions in emergency situations, this is a misnomer, as the requesting State must first bring a request to the United States for a bilateral agreement and that request must be reviewed under State Department procedures. 19 USC § 2603.

[128] UNSC Res 1483 (22 May 2003) UN Doc S/RES/1483.

[129] UNSC Res 2199 (12 February 2015) UN Doc S/RES/2199, paras 15–17. Both Security Council Resolutions are discussed further in chapter 5, section 5.4.3.

[130] *United States v An Antique Platter of Gold* 991 F Supp 222 (SDNY 1997), aff'd on other grounds, 184 F3d 131 (2nd Cir 1999); see n 11 above; Cassella, 'Using the Forfeiture Laws' (n 89) 135–36.

[131] 'Merchandise which is introduced or attempted to be introduced into the United States contrary to law shall be treated as follows: (1) The merchandise shall be seized and forfeited if it – (A) is stolen, smuggled, or clandestinely imported or introduced.' 19 USC § 1595a(c).

UK government authorities have become more active in seeking to return illegally taken antiquities through forfeiture and other means. UK customs forfeited a group of cuneiform tablets, which were misdeclared, originating from sites in southern Iraq and likely associated with the artefacts acquired by Hobby Lobby.[132] A *kudurru* stone, an official document recording a grant of land or other gift from the king and clearly originating from Iraq, was declared upon attempted import as a 'carved stone for home decoration' from Turkey with its value also misstated.[133] UK customs authorities seized and returned an ancient Greek sculpture that was from the site of Cyrene in Libya. Upon import into the United Kingdom, its country of origin was declared to be Turkey and its value to be £72,000, rather than its actual worth, which was later estimated to be £1.5 million.[134] Civil forfeiture is increasingly becoming the primary method of intercepting and returning archaeological artefacts to their country of origin. While this accomplishes the purpose of restitution and recognizes the rights of the country of origin, civil forfeiture may have relatively little impact on deterring the trade in looted archaeological artefacts as civil forfeiture typically does not carry with it the potential of criminal punishment.

4.4 Conclusion

Archaeological artefacts that are looted from the ground and are therefore undocumented pose particular threats to the public interest and cultural heritage on the universalist, national, and local levels. Laws vesting title to antiquities in the State afford a unique legal solution to this unique problem—that, by definition, such objects are undocumented and unknown before they appear on the international art market or in a collection in a destination market country. Rather than having to reduce all such objects to physical possession so that they can be inventoried and documented, an impossible task and one that is contrary to best archaeological and scientific practice, States may vest ownership in themselves, rendering such artefacts stolen property when removed from their territory without permission. The alternative basis for interdicting archaeological artefacts is through enforcement of a foreign State's export controls based on multilateral and bilateral agreements. Many market countries accept these legal solutions. These legal doctrines thus

132 Jonathan Taylor (Twitter, 30 August 2019) <https://twitter.com/JonTaylor_BM/status/1167405875168010240> accessed 2 June 2021.

133 Dalya Alberge, 'Babylonian treasure seized at Heathrow to be returned to Iraq' (*The Guardian*, 10 March 2020) <www.theguardian.com/culture/2019/mar/10/babylonian-treasure-seized-at-heathrow-to-be-returned-to-iraq> accessed 2 June 2021. The stone is likely to be from the region of Nippur in southern Iraq and dates between 1126 and 1103 BCE.

134 *HM Revenue & Customs v Al Qassas*, unpublished, Westminster Magistrates Court (1 September 2015); Neil Brodie, 'The Role of Conservators in Facilitating the Theft and Trafficking of Cultural Objects: The Case of a Seized Libyan Statue' (2017) 48 Libyan Studies 117.

bring the major market States into alignment, allowing them to be more effective in reducing the financial incentives for looting archaeological sites.

The looting of archaeological sites to supply antiquities for the international market became a more significant phenomenon in the second half of the twentieth century, just as the development of scientific techniques enabled greater recovery from sites of information about the past. The argument for returning such artefacts to their countries and communities of origin or discovery is based not only on a return principle but also the goal of disincentivizing further looting and loss of knowledge. As will be discussed further in chapter 7, the reach of the law to require the return of looted or stolen artefacts does not, for the most part, extend earlier than the twentieth century, and this reach is often considerably shorter depending on the date of a State vesting law or implementation of the 1970 UNESCO Convention by both market States and States of origin. Ethical policies, as will be discussed in chapter 6, often do not extend before 1970. Therefore, further developments in law and policy need to be adopted to effectuate returns, as will be discussed in chapter 7.

5
The Right to Objects of Cultural Heritage

5.1 Introduction

The historical background to the removals of cultural objects during imperialism, colonialism, and armed conflict and the role of market demand, particularly in providing an incentive to loot archaeological sites, was set out in previous chapters. This chapter turns to the international legal framework that developed over the course of the twentieth and early twenty-first centuries to prevent the removal, without the consent of States and communities, of their movable and sometimes dismembered cultural objects and, at times, to require the return of such objects. The disposition of cultural objects may be viewed from the perspective of three pillars: international humanitarian law with respect to cultural objects, primarily as embodied in the Hague Convention regime; human rights law, which articulates the right to culture and cultural heritage with a particular focus on Indigenous community rights; and the international framework that attempts to regulate the movement of cultural objects. While the previous chapter considered aspects of the market and legal regulation that pertain specifically to archaeological artefacts, the last section of this chapter looks at broader market regulation applicable to all cultural objects. In analysing these legal principles, this chapter again focuses exclusively on the movement, removal, and return of cultural objects, while minimizing discussion of the impact of these legal principles on other forms of cultural heritage. These analyses provide the primary legal framework for attempting to answer the question of where cultural objects should be located.

5.2 The Law of Armed Conflict: The Hague Conventions

5.2.1 The 1899 and 1907 Hague Conventions and the Two World Wars

Francis Lieber, a Prussian soldier and classicist, who was present at the Battle of Waterloo at the end of the Napoleonic Wars, later became a professor of history in the United States and drafted the first codification of the law of armed conflict for the Union army during the US Civil War, known as the Lieber Code.[1] The Lieber

[1] Instructions for the Government of Armies of the United States in the Field, General Orders No 100 (24 April 1863). The Lieber Code required protection of works of art and other movable objects

Cultural Objects and Reparative Justice. Patty Gerstenblith, Oxford University Press. © Patty Gerstenblith 2023.
DOI: 10.1093/oso/9780192872104.003.0005

Code influenced the Brussels Conference of 1874, which proposed a declaration for, among other aspects, prohibiting seizure of movable objects, and the Oxford Manual of the Institute of International Law in 1880.[2] In 1899, Czar Nicholas II of Russia sponsored a conference of twenty-four countries at the Hague in the Netherlands, which resulted in the 1899 and 1907 Hague Conventions.[3]

The 1907 Convention contained the two core provisions that were introduced in the Lieber Code and have remained part of subsequent legal instruments: prohibition on intentional targeting of cultural sites and repositories and prohibition on seizure and appropriation of cultural objects during armed conflict and military occupation.[4] Nonetheless, the early Hague Conventions failed to protect cultural objects from looting and destruction during the two world wars and served only as the basis for restitution and punishment of the perpetrators at the conclusion of the respective conflicts. At the end of the First World War, the Treaty of Versailles directed Germany to give to the victorious Allies both objects that Germany had taken during the war and objects that had no connection to the war. As reparations, Germany was required to transfer to the University of Louvain manuscripts, maps, books, and other archival materials comparable to those Germany had destroyed in the burning of the Library of Louvain and was required to return movable cultural objects to France, including objects taken during the war of 1870–1871. Among the objects that had no connection to the First World War, but that Germany had to relinquish, were two panels from the Ghent Adoration of the Lamb Altarpiece, which had been sold by the church in the nineteenth century; the skull of Chief Mkwawa, who led resistance to German colonial rule in East Africa in the 1890s; and the Quran of the Caliph Othman.[5]

from injury (Art 35) and prohibited the seizure of the property of charitable institutions (Art 34) and the sale, private appropriation, and wanton injury or destruction of such objects (Art 36).

[2] Jiří Toman, *The Protection of Cultural Property in the Event of Armed Conflict: Commentary on the Convention for the Protection of Cultural Property in the Event of Armed Conflict and its Protocol* (UNESCO/Dartmouth 1996) 9–10 (hereafter Toman, *The Protection of Cultural Property*).

[3] Convention (IV) Respecting the Laws and Customs of War on Land and its Annex: Regulations concerning the Laws and Customs of War on Land (open for signature 18 October 1907, entered into force 26 January 1910) 187 CTS 227 (hereafter 1907 Hague Convention (IV)); Hague Convention (II) with Respect to the Laws and Customs of War on Land and its Annex: Regulations concerning the Laws and Customs of War on Land (adopted 29 July 1899, entered into force 4 September 1900) 187 CTS 429 (hereafter 1899 Hague Convention (II)) (collectively, the 1899 and 1907 Hague Conventions). The provisions governing cultural heritage in the two treaties are substantially the same, with the 1907 Hague Convention (IV) supplanting the earlier 1899 Hague Convention (II) for Parties to both treaties.

[4] 1907 Hague Convention (IV), Articles 27 and 56. Both the 1899 and 1907 Hague Conventions prohibit pillage in general during armed conflict (Arts 23(g) and 28) and during occupation (Art 47).

[5] Toman, *The Protection of Cultural Property* (n 2) 337. The skull of Chief Mkawawa was brought to Germany after his defeat. British leaders wanted to return the skull to Africa to curry favour as Britain was the colonial power in East Africa (later Tanzania) pursuant to a League of Nations mandate. The skull was not returned until after the Second World War. The Quran mentioned in the Treaty of Versailles was reputed to be one of the original authoritative Qurans prepared by the Caliph Uthman. The Ottomans removed it from Medina, took it to Istanbul, and later gave it to the German Kaiser. Treaty of Peace between the Allied and Associated Powers and Germany, Versailles, 28 June 1919, in force 10 January 1920, Cmd 516 (1920) Art 246.

Between the two world wars, there was interest in a new international convention to protect cultural heritage. In 1935, the Washington Pact for the Protection of Artistic and Scientific Institutions and of Historic Monuments, also known as the Roerich Pact, was signed by twenty-one countries and ratified by eleven.[6] However, it had little impact during the Second World War, as only nations in the Americas are parties to it. In response to the Spanish Civil War, the League of Nations asked the International Museums Office to draft yet another international convention.[7] However, the Second World War intervened before any formal action could be taken.

The Second World War saw the largest destruction and displacement of cultural sites and objects known to human history.[8] The German leaders systematically plundered and looted artworks throughout Europe. Even to the extent that the illusion of a sale from a private owner was created, such transactions were often illegal, and many transactions were forced sales and sales under duress. The 1943 London Declaration allowed the Allies and governments-in-exile to nullify sales and transfers of property to the occupying Germans, regardless of 'whether such transfers or dealings have taken the form of open looting or plunder, or of transactions apparently legal in form, even when they purport to be voluntarily effected'.[9] The question of which of these transactions should be considered theft or the equivalent of theft so that the transaction would be nullified plays a continuing role in the litigation brought by Holocaust victims and their successors in the attempt to recover

[6] Treaty on the Protection of Artistic and Scientific Institutions and Historic Monuments (adopted 15 April 1935, entered into force 26 August 1935) 167 UNTS 289 (hereafter Roerich Pact); Toman, *The Protection of Cultural Property* (n 2) 16–17. Nicholas Roerich (1874–1947) was a Russian visionary, engaged in archaeology, the arts (painter and set designer), and music. He travelled widely throughout Europe, the United States, and Asia, particularly India. In 1929, Roerich proposed establishing a treaty and an organization, modelled on the Red Cross, for the protection of cultural property during both war and peace. He designed the 'Banner of Peace' that would be flown over all places under its protection. Nicholas Roerich Museum, 'Biography', <www.roerich.org/roerich-biography.php> accessed 7 July 2021.

[7] Preliminary Draft International Convention for the Protection of Historic Buildings and Works of Art in Time of War, proposed by the International Museums Office (October 1936). See Toman, *The Protection of Cultural Property* (n 2) 10–11; Kevin Chamberlain, *War and Cultural Heritage: A Commentary on the Hague Convention 1954 and its Two Protocols* (2nd edn, Institute of Art and Law 2013) 9, 209–13 (hereafter Chamberlain, *War and Cultural Heritage*).

[8] Lynn Nicholas, *The Rape of Europa: The Fate of Europe's Treasures in the Third Reich and the Second World War* (Alfred A Knopf 1994). Other sources include Konstantin Akinsha and Gregorii Kozlov, *Beautiful Loot: The Soviet Plunder of Europe's Art Treasures* (Random House 1995) (hereafter Akinsha and Kozlov, *Beautiful Loot*); Hector Feliciano, *The Lost Museum: The Nazi Conspiracy to Steal the World's Greatest Works of Art* (Basic Books 1997). For a comprehensive list of laws, ethical statements, national commissions, and other actions by country, see The Central Registry of Information on Looted Cultural Property 1933–1945 <www.lootedart.com/> accessed 28 August 2022.

[9] Inter-Allied Declaration against Acts of Dispossession Committed in Territories under Enemy Occupation or Control. United States Diplomatic Papers Vol 1 (1943) <https://history.state.gov/historicaldocuments/frus1943v01/d456> accessed 7 July 2021. See Ana Filipa Vrdoljak, 'Gross Violations of Human Rights and Restitution: Learning from Holocaust Claims' in Lyndel V Prott, Ruth Redmond-Cooper, and Stephen Urice (eds), *Realising Cultural Heritage Law: Festschrift for Patrick O'Keefe* (Institute of Art and Law 2013) 163, 164–69.

their works.[10] At the same time, the Germans intentionally and indiscriminately destroyed art collections, libraries, and historic structures in Eastern Europe and the Soviet Union. This led the Soviet Union to adopt a policy of retention of cultural objects taken from Germany as unilateral reparations.[11]

The official policy of the Western Allied forces was to preserve as much of the cultural heritage of Europe as possible and to prohibit theft and expropriation.[12] One of the most effective efforts of the Allied military was the creation of the Monuments, Fine Arts and Archives team (MFA&A). This group, consisting of art historians, archaeologists, museum curators, conservators, and other arts professionals, was responsible for assisting in the restitution of looted art works to their original owners at the end of the war. While readily identifiable works were returned, the United States soon adopted a policy of external restitution, according to which cultural objects were turned over to the countries where the objects were located at the end of the war, rather than to their individual owners.[13] The Nazis sold other works onto the international art market, and these are still found in private collections and museums. The efforts of the descendants of victims to achieve full restitution continue, primarily through private litigation and through government art spoliation commissions and dispute resolution mechanisms.[14]

[10] For example, *Zuckerman v Metropolitan Museum of Art* 928 F3d 186 (2nd Cir 2019); *Vineberg v Bissonette*, 548 F3d 50 (1st Cir 2008). See also *Heirs Simon Bauer v Toll*, Court of Cassation—First civil chamber, judgment No 810, 11 September 2019 (18–25.695).

[11] Akinsha and Kozlov, *Beautiful Loot* (n 8). The legal status of such objects is still unclear. In 1998, Russia enacted a law committing it to return artworks and other valuables taken from the victims of the Nazis but also providing that Russia would keep any artworks that belonged to Germany. Despite this commitment, Russia has returned very little, even to victims of the Nazis. Patricia Kennedy Grimsted, 'Legalizing 'Compensation' and the Spoils of War: The Russian Law on Displaced Cultural Valuables and the Manipulation of Historical Memory' (2010) 17 IJCP 217. This contrasts with significant restitutions to Germany made by several of the former Soviet Socialist Republics, including Georgia and Ukraine. Kurt Siehr, 'Return of Cultural Treasures to Germany' (1997) 6 IJCP 134.

[12] One of Eisenhower's orders directed that 'souvenir hunting' was a military offence. Quoted in Robert M Edsel, *Rescuing Da Vinci* (Laurel Publishing, LLC 2006) 130. An order issued by Lt General Omar N Bradley stated: 'We are a conquering army, but we are not a pillaging army.' ibid, 136. Despite this policy, Allied troops engaged individually in illegal theft. For example *Kunstsammlungen zu Weimar v Elicofon*, 678 F2d 1150 (2nd Cir 1982) (theft of two Dürer works from the storage of the Kunstsammlungen zu Weimar); William H Honan, Treasure Hunt (Fromm International 1997) (theft of Medieval manuscripts and other cultural objects from the Quedlinburg Church by a US serviceman; objects were eventually returned after Germany paid a 'finder's fee' to the serviceman's family).

[13] *von Saher v Norton Simon Museum of Art at Pasadena* 578 F3d 1016, 1019, 1023–24 (9th Cir 2009).

[14] Private litigants face many obstacles to recovery. See *Kunstsammlungen zu Weimar v Elicofon* (n 12) (statute of limitations); *Zuckerman v Metro Museum of Art* 928 F3d 186 (2nd Cir 2019), *cert denied*, 140 S Ct 1269 (2020) (laches); *Heirs Simon Bauer v Toll* (n 10) (acquisitive prescription); Cassirer v Thyssen-Bornemisza Collection Foundation 142 S Ct 1502 (2022) (acquisitive prescription); *Republic of Austria v Altmann* 541 US 677 (2004) (sovereign immunity); *FRG v Philipp*, 141 S Ct 703 (2021) (sovereign immunity); *von Saher v Norton Simon Museum of Art* 897 F3d 1141, 1148–56 (9th Cir 2018), *cert denied* 139 S Ct 2616 (2019) (act of state doctrine). The Holocaust Expropriated Art Recovery Act (HEAR Act), Pub L 114–308, 130 Stat 1524, enacted in 2016, abrogated the statute of limitations for Holocaust recovery claims but left the laches defence in place. This is discussed further in chapter 7, section 7.2.

The plunder of public and private property was included in the Nuremberg Charter and Control Council Law No 10 as a war crime, and when accompanied by discrimination based on religion and when the impact on the victim was sufficiently severe, such plunder could constitute a crime against humanity.[15] The Nuremberg International Military Tribunal convicted Alfred Rosenberg for war crimes and crimes against humanity under the 1899 and 1907 Hague Conventions, as well as principles of customary international law. Rosenberg had been the head of the Einsatzstab Reichsleiter Rosenberg (ERR), which was the primary organization responsible for carrying out the confiscations of artworks and cultural objects. The indictment listed the extensive quantities of cultural objects looted from throughout occupied territory in both Western and Eastern Europe.[16]

5.2.2 The Framework of the 1954 Hague Convention

Following the horrific experiences of the Second World War, the international community established the United Nations and the United Nations Economic, Scientific and Cultural Organization (UNESCO) and adopted several legal instruments focused on humanitarian issues. The first broadly adopted convention to address exclusively the fate of cultural property during armed conflict was the 1954 Hague Convention on the Protection of Cultural Property in the Event of Armed Conflict (1954 Hague Convention)[17] and its First Protocol,[18] followed by the Second Protocol in 1999.[19] The Hague Convention should be understood in

[15] Trial of the Major War Criminals before the International Military Tribunal (Nuremberg 14 November 1945–1 October 1946) 27, *United States and others v Göring and others*, Indictment International Military Tribunal (E) Plunder of Public and Private Property 55–60. Booty is property of the State taken during war that is necessary for the conduct of war, such as food, munitions, and other supplies; the taking of booty is permissible. 1907 Hague Convention (IV) (n 3) Art 53. Plunder and pillage are the taking of property not needed for the war effort and are prohibited. ibid, Arts 28 and 47.

[16] *United States and others v Göring* (n 15) 56, stating that 'works of art, artistic objects, pictures, plastics, furniture, textiles, antique pieces, and similar articles of enormous value to the number of 21,903' were plundered from Western countries between 1940 and 1944; museums in Nantes, Nancy, and Old Marseilles were looted, as were private collections of artworks by Raphael, Vermeer, Van Dyck, Rubens, Holbein, Rembrandt, Watteau, and Boucher; France was forced to give the Van Eyck altarpiece, The Mystic Lamb 'which Belgium had entrusted to her'. ibid, 58. The indictment further stated that the Germans destroyed 427 museums in Russian cities and stole or destroyed 4,000,000 books, magazines, manuscripts, and other artistic productions from Kyiv. ibid, 59.

[17] Convention for the Protection of Cultural Property in the Event of Armed Conflict (adopted 14 May 1954, entered into force 7 August 1956) 249 UNTS 240 (hereafter 1954 Hague Convention).

[18] Protocol for the Protection of Cultural Property in the Event of Armed Conflict (adopted 14 May 1954, entered into force 7 August 1956) 249 UNTS 358 (hereafter 1954 First Protocol).

[19] Second Protocol to the Hague Convention of 1954 for the Protection of Cultural Property in the Event of Armed Conflict (adopted 26 March 1999, entered into force 9 March 2004) 253 UNTS 172 (hereafter 1999 Second Protocol). Although review of the 1954 Hague Convention began with an attempt to resolve some of the defects perceived in the Convention, the 1999 Second Protocol also updated the Convention following the experiences of the Balkan Wars. Patrick J Boylan, 'Review of the Convention for the Protection of Cultural Property in the Event of Armed Conflict (The Hague Convention of 1954)' (1993) UNESCO Doc CLT-93/WS/12 101. For the Second Protocol, see Jiří Toman, *Cultural Property in War: Improvement in Protection: Commentary on the 1999 Second Protocol*

light of the massive destruction and looting of cultural property during the Second World War. Like the other humanitarian law conventions written in the immediate post-war period, it was a reaction to these events, and this historical context explains both its strengths and some of its current weaknesses.

The Convention's Preamble expresses the universality of cultural heritage through the phrase 'cultural heritage of all mankind' and the obligation to protect cultural heritage because of its 'great importance for all peoples of the world'. This aspect of universality derives from a tradition of imposing obligations on States to observe minimal standards of care for cultural property and is not a justification for granting States or individuals 'rights of appropriation or ownership'.[20] At the same time, the Preamble also recognizes the State or community values of heritage in stating that 'each people makes its contribution to the culture of the world'. Article 1 includes within the definition of 'cultural property' movable cultural objects such as 'works of art; manuscripts, books and other objects of artistic, historical or archaeological interest; as well as scientific collections' and the repositories for such movables. Cultural property is further defined as having 'great importance to the cultural heritage of every people'.[21]

5.2.2.1 Prohibitions on Theft, Pillage, and Misappropriation

While Article 4(1) of the Convention prohibits targeting of all cultural property, including movable objects, it is subject to the military necessity waiver in Article 4(2). The only provision that specifically addresses movable objects is Article 4(3), which states the obligation 'to prohibit, prevent and, if necessary, put a stop to any form of theft, pillage or misappropriation of, and any acts of vandalism directed against, cultural property . . .'. This provision is not subject to the military necessity waiver found in Article 4(2). Because Article 4(3) falls under the obligation of respect, according to Article 19, it applies to armed conflicts not of an international character and therefore to non-State, as well as State, actors.[22]

Until the looting of the Iraq Museum in Baghdad during the 2003 Gulf War, this provision and its interpretation attracted little attention. At the time of the war, the United States took the position that it had no obligation to prevent looting by

to the Hague Convention of 1954 for the Protection of Cultural Property in the Event of Armed Conflict (UNESCO 2009).

[20] Robert K Paterson and Dennis S Karjala, 'Looking Beyond Intellectual Property in Resolving Protection of the Intangible Cultural Heritage of Indigenous Peoples' (2003) 11 Cardozo Journal of International and Comparative Law 633, 653. Cultural property is further defined as having 'great importance to the cultural heritage of every people'.

[21] O'Keefe states that the reference to the 'cultural heritage of every people' means the cultural heritage of each State Party as it determines with respect to the cultural property in its own territory, thus giving a State-oriented or heterogeneous significance to what otherwise appears to be universalistic. Roger O'Keefe, *The Protection of Cultural Property in Armed Conflict* (CUP 2006) 210 (hereafter O'Keefe, *The Protection of Cultural Property*).

[22] Chamberlain, *War and Cultural Heritage* (n 7) 52–55.

those who were not part of its own military. Following the extensive criticism of its failure to prevent this looting, the United States modified its position but more as a reflection of policy than of law. The US Department of Defense Law of War Manual, issued in June 2015, states that '[m]ilitary commanders have an obligation to take reasonable measures to prevent or stop any form of theft, pillage ....' It describes this obligation as 'part of the obligation to take feasible precautions to reduce the risk of harm to cultural property'.[23]

It is unclear whether Article 4(3) imposes an obligation to prevent third parties from engaging in theft and vandalism or whether it applies only to preventing one's own military from doing so. If read literally, the provision seems to impose an absolute obligation to prevent the acts in question, regardless of who the actors are.[24] On the other hand, one may interpret this provision in the context of the Second World War, where the Nazi forces engaged in massive theft and misappropriation, but the local civilian population, for the most part, did not. However, this issue is clarified under customary international law. Incorporating Article 4(3) of the 1954 Hague Convention, customary international law also prohibits theft, pillage, misappropriation, and vandalism of cultural objects carried out by one's own military forces.[25] In addition, a party to the conflict that is in effective control of territory must prohibit similar actions taken by others and prevent and put a stop to such acts, subject to an obligation 'of due diligence'.[26] This provision of customary

[23] Department of Defense, Law of War Manual (2016) para 5.18.6.1, at 301 <www.hsdl.org/?abstract&did=797480> accessed 10 May 2021. The Manual further comments that 'efforts to identify cultural property ... and secure it from theft or pillage are a prudent part of the planning process of military operations. For example, such efforts may deny opposing forces the opportunity to exploit harm to cultural property for propaganda purposes.' ibid. See Elizabeth Varner, 'Comparing Interpretations of States' and Non-State Actors' Obligations Toward Cultural Heritage in Armed Conflict and Occupation: Military Manuals and the Law of War' in Anne-Marie Carstens and Elizabeth Varner (eds), *Intersections in International Cultural Heritage Law* (OUP 2020) 56, 75. The limitation of feasibility derives from the Second Protocol and other aspects of international humanitarian law.

[24] O'Keefe, *The Protection of Cultural Property* (n 21) 133; Roger O'Keefe, 'Protection of Cultural Property Under International Criminal Law' (2010) 11 MJIL 339, 363 note 123 (hereafter, O'Keefe, 'Protection of Cultural Property'). O'Keefe infers that the obligation is subject to a feasibility standard derived from Article 43 of the 1907 Hague Convention Regulations. However, this Article applies to occupation and only requires an Occupying Power 'to restore and ensure, as far as possible, public order and safety'. This article applies only to restrain the conduct of the local population once occupation has been established.

[25] ICRC, *Customary International Humanitarian Law*, rule 40 <https://ihl-databases.icrc.org/customary-ihl/eng/docs/v1_rul_rule40> accessed 7 July 2021. Reflecting customary law, Article 3(d) of the Statute of the International Criminal Tribunal for the former Yugoslavia stated that 'seizure of, destruction or willful damage done to institutions dedicated to religion, charity and education, the arts and sciences, historic monuments and works of art and science' are violations of the laws or customs of war. Updated Statute of the ICTY, Article 3(d) <www.icty.org/en/documents/statute-tribunal> accessed 10 May 2021. While it is likely that looting of cultural sites occurred, the cultural property aspects of the Balkan conflict centred on intentional destruction of immovable heritage and the prosecutions did not involve theft and displacement of movable objects.

[26] Roger O'Keefe, 'Cultural Heritage and International Humanitarian Law' in Francesco Francioni and Ana Filipa Vrdoljak (eds). *The Oxford Handbook of International Cultural Heritage Law* (OUP 2020) 43, 58–59.

international law incorporates the principle of feasibility,[27] which is also present in the Hague Convention's Second Protocol.

The Second Protocol defines serious violations for which States Parties must enact corresponding domestic criminal provisions with appropriate penalties and extend 'criminal responsibility to persons other than those who directly commit the act', thus creating command responsibility. Among those offences are 'extensive destruction or appropriation' of protected cultural property (Article 15(1)(c)) and 'theft, pillage or misappropriation of, or acts of vandalism directed against' protected cultural property (Article 15(e)). Article 16 requires States Parties to extend jurisdiction to non-nationals for certain offences, including the offence of 'extensive destruction or appropriation' of protected cultural property (Article 16 (1)(c)).[28]

The primary legal instruments addressing international humanitarian law immediately following the Second World War included the four Geneva Conventions of 1949,[29] which were supplemented in 1977 with the Additional Protocols. The 1949 Geneva Conventions omit specific protections for cultural heritage, perhaps because this was not viewed as a sufficiently significant issue.[30] General provisions applying to civilian objects in Article 33 of the Fourth Geneva Convention forbidding pillage and Article 53 prohibiting the destruction during occupation of real or personal property, whether publicly or privately owned, include cultural property without specifically mentioning it.

The 1977 Additional Protocols to the 1949 Geneva Conventions prohibit acts of hostility directed against historic monuments, works of art, and places of worship 'which constitute the cultural or spiritual heritage of peoples'[31] in both international (Article 53, Protocol I)[32] and non-international armed conflict (Article 16,

[27] The principles of feasibility, distinction, and proportionality are generally accepted as a part of customary international law. Roger O'Keefe, Camille Péron, Tofig Musayev, Gianluca Ferrari, *Protection of Cultural Property Military Manual* (UNESCO 2016) ¶¶ 95–99 (distinction); ¶¶ 113–114 (proportionality); ¶¶116–120 (feasibility).

[28] However, Article 16 does not impose individual criminal responsibility or jurisdiction over the members of the armed forces of a State that is not a Party to the Protocol. Article 16(2)(b). This provision therefore does not apply in conflicts such as that in Ukraine where one or more of the States involved is not a party to the Second Protocol.

[29] Geneva Conventions of 1949 (adopted 12 August 1949, entered into force 21 October 1950) 75 UNTS 287 (hereafter Geneva Conventions).

[30] Marina Lostal, 'Syria's World Cultural Heritage and Individual Criminal Responsibility' (2015) 3 International Review of Law and Economics 7–8 <http://dx.doi.org/10.5339/irl.2015.3> accessed 20 March 2022. The omission arguably led to secondary status of cultural heritage protection and decreased emphasis on cultural heritage protection during training of military forces.

[31] This phrase is considered equivalent to the phrase 'of great importance to the cultural heritage of every people' found in the definition of cultural property in Article 1 of the 1954 Hague Convention.

[32] Protocol Additional to the Geneva Conventions of 12 August 1949, and Relating to the Protections of Victims of International Armed Conflicts, Geneva (adopted 8 June 1977, opened for signature 12 December 1977, entered into force 7 December 1978) 1125 UNTS 3; O'Keefe, *The Protection of Cultural Property* (n 21) 207–18. Additional Protocol I applies also to 'armed conflicts in which peoples are fighting against colonial domination and alien occupation and against racist regimes' (Art 1(4)).

Protocol II).[33] These provisions are not subject to a military necessity waiver but are subordinate to the 1954 Hague Convention. If a State has ratified both instruments, the provisions of the 1954 Hague Convention would control, including the availability of the military necessity waiver. Except to the extent that the looting or theft of cultural objects ('works of art') may be considered an act of hostility directed against them, the Geneva Conventions and Additional Protocols do not prohibit the theft or looting of cultural objects, nor do they address the subsequent disposition of such objects.

The Rome Statute of the International Criminal Court makes the intentional directing of attacks against 'buildings dedicated to religion, education, art, science or charitable purposes [and] historic monuments' a war crime but does not specifically address theft or looting of cultural objects.[34] However, when theft and appropriation are done in such a way as to destroy a cultural, religious, or historic monument, such an action should be interpreted as constituting an 'attack' under these articles. Large-scale looting of archaeological sites, such as that carried out by the Islamic State of Iraq and the Levant and other actors during the Syrian conflict, as well as thefts from religious shrines, mosques, and monasteries, should constitute an attack on historic monuments and buildings dedicated to religion, regardless of whether the physical structure was destroyed.

Cultural objects receive protection under both treaty law and customary international law[35] in the general provisions that prohibit pillage. Cultural property is not considered useful for the conduct of war and its appropriation or pillage is therefore never excused as military necessity.[36] Article 52(2) of Additional Protocol I prohibits attacks on civilian objects, defined as an object whose destruction

[33] Protocol Additional to the Geneva Conventions of 12 August 1949, and Relating to the Protections of Victims of Non-International Armed Conflicts, Geneva (8 June 1977, opened for signature 12 December 1977, entered into force 7 December 1978)1125 UNTS 609; O'Keefe, *The Protection of Cultural Property* (n 21) 230–32.

[34] Rome Statute, Article 8(2)(b)(ix) (applying to international armed conflict), Article 8(2)(e)(iv) (applying to non-international armed conflict). Rome Statute of the International Criminal Court (adopted 17 July 1998, entered into force 1 July 2002) 2187 UNTS 3. The cases heard by the International Criminal Court concern intentional destruction of religious structures in Mali, but not the question of movable objects. *Prosecutor v Al Mahdi* (Trial Judgment and Sentence) [2016] ICC-01/12-01/15-171 (27 September 2016); *Prosecutor v Al Hassan* ICC-01/12-01/18 (4 February 2020) <www.icc-cpi.int/mali/al-hassan>. In *Prosecutor v Bosco Ntaganda*, the Trial Chamber suggested that the 'special status' of a protected object may be relevant in assessing whether Articles 8(2)(b)(ix) and 8(2)(e)(iv) apply to protect the cultural property. ICC-01/04-02/06-2359 (8 July 2019), para 1136, note 3147. To the extent this suggests that cultural property must have a specific status or universal significance before it is protected, the State and local community interests in cultural property may be sacrificed in favour of the universalistic interest.

[35] ICRC, *Customary International Humanitarian Law*, rule 52 <https://ihl-databases.icrc.org/customary-ihl/eng/docs/v1_rul_rule40> accessed 7 July 2021.

[36] O'Keefe, *The Protection of Cultural Property* (n 21) 336 (stating that '[s]ince there can be no legitimate military reason for seizing cultural property, the rule [prohibiting plunder] amounts, in practice, to an absolute prohibition' on seizure or theft of cultural objects). In contrast, the destruction of cultural property may be excused on the grounds of military necessity or that the cultural property constituted a military objective, as decided with respect to the Old Bridge at Mostar. *Prosecutor v Prlić et al*, Appeal Judgment, Vol I, IT-04-74-A (29 November 2017) para 411.

would not 'make an effective contribution to military action ... or offer a definite military advantage'. Cultural objects qualify as civilian objects and thus fall under these broader protections.[37] The Rome Statute includes pillage, defined as appropriation for private or personal use, as a war crime under Articles 8(2)(b)(xvi) and 8(2)(e)(v). Article 8(2)(a)(iv) characterizes as a war crime the extensive appropriation of property, not justified by military necessity and 'carried out unlawfully and wantonly'. Article 8(2)(b)(xiii) also prohibits the seizing of enemy property, subject to military necessity but without a requirement that the appropriation be wanton.[38] This would apply to archaeological artefacts that are subject to State ownership and if the State is the enemy, but it would not apply broadly to other types of cultural objects that may be owned by religious or secular cultural institutions and that are not State property.

5.2.2.2 Removal from Occupied Territory

The status of cultural objects removed from occupied territory is addressed primarily in the First Protocol to the 1954 Hague Convention.[39] Fewer States have ratified the First Protocol than the main Convention, and even fewer have enacted implementing legislation. The provisions dealing with movable cultural objects were put into a separate instrument at the insistence of the Western market nations, particularly the United States and the United Kingdom, which did not wish to take on the responsibility of the return of movable objects found in their territory.[40] The Protocol imposes obligations on an occupying power to prevent the export of cultural objects from occupied territory and to compensate a good faith purchaser of any cultural objects that are returned under the Protocol.[41] It also

[37] O'Keefe, *The Protection of Cultural Property* (n 21) 204.

[38] Article 8(2)(e)(xii) is the analogous provision in non-international armed conflict but uses the term 'adversary' rather than 'enemy'.

[39] Toman, *The Protection of Cultural Property* (n 2) 344; Chamberlain, *War and Cultural Heritage* (n 7) 99–100. The UNESCO draft of the Protocol was based on the Allied Declaration of 1943 (n 9). Provisions of the 1970 UNESCO Convention apply to the theft or illegal removal of cultural objects from occupied territory, most particularly Article 11. Convention on the Means of Prohibiting and Preventing the Illicit Import, Export and Transfer of Ownership of Cultural Property, (adopted 14 November 1970, entered into force 24 April 1972) 823 UNTS 231 (hereafter 1970 UNESCO Convention).

[40] Toman, *The Protection of Cultural Property* (n 2) 343. The transmittal of the Convention to the US Senate in 1999 included a recommendation to utilize the opt-out provision of the First Protocol to ratify only the second part, which would have relieved the United States of the responsibility to return cultural property illegally removed from occupied territory. Transmittal of the Hague Convention for the Protection of Cultural Property in the Event of Armed Conflict and, for Accession, the Hague Protocol to the Senate Foreign Relations Committee, S Treaty Doc No 106-1, III–IV, IX (1999). After ratifying the Convention in 2009, the United States has taken no further step to ratify the First Protocol.

[41] While subject to Articles 4 and 5 of the main Convention but without mentioning the First Protocol, the Second Protocol reiterates the obligation of an occupying power to prohibit and prevent 'any illicit removal or transfer of ownership' of cultural objects from occupied territory. Article 9(a). The Second Protocol adds the word 'illicit' whereas the First Protocol only prohibits export from occupied territory without the requirement that the export be 'illicit' or 'illegal'. The Second Protocol defines 'illicit' as 'under compulsion or otherwise in violation of the applicable rules of the domestic law of the

imposes obligations on any State Party to take into custody cultural objects imported either directly or indirectly from occupied territory and to return at the end of hostilities any cultural objects illegally removed from occupied territory.

The Protocols raise issues of possible interference with private property rights, the need to enact implementing legislation, and the requirement to compensate good faith purchasers.[42] For example, the Antiphonitis Church located in the northern part of Cyprus was unable to recover four icons in the Netherlands that had been stolen from the Church after it fell under Turkish occupation in 1974. The court held that the Protocol did not grant a private right of action and the rights of the defendant, particularly as a good faith purchaser, were protected under Dutch civil law.[43] However, several European market States subsequently ratified the First Protocol and some have adopted implementing legislation.[44] Germany and the Netherlands applied their implementing legislation to cultural objects removed from occupied territory after each State initially ratified the First Protocol (1967 and 1959, respectively). The United Kingdom applied its implementing legislation to cultural property removed from occupied territory after 1956 (the date when the First Protocol went into effect) but imported into the United Kingdom after 2017 (the date when the implementing legislation went into effect).[45]

The efficacy of the First Protocol and provisions of the Second Protocol related to treatment of cultural property during occupation[46] may be limited if

occupied territory or of international law'. Article 1. The addition of transfer of ownership as a prohibited activity demonstrates the relationship to the 1970 UNESCO Convention (n 38).

[42] Stephan Matyk, 'The Restitution of Cultural Objects and the Question of Giving Direct Effect to the Protocol to the Hague Convention for the Protection of Cultural Property in the Event of Armed Conflict' (2000) 9 IJCP 341 (hereafter Matyk, 'The Restitution of Cultural Objects'); Patrick J O'Keefe, 'The First Protocol to the Hague Convention Fifty Years On' (2004) 9 Art Antiquity and Law 99, 110; Liesbeth Lijnzaad, 'Sleeping Beauty, the untold story of the (first) Protocol to the 1954 Hague Convention' in Nout van Woudenberg and Liesbeth Lijnzaad (eds), *Protecting Cultural Property in Armed Conflict: An Insight into the 1999 Second Protocol to the Hague Convention of 1954 for the Protection of Cultural Property in the Event of Armed Conflict* (Martinus Nijhoff Publishers 2010) 147, 153–54.

[43] *Autocephalous Greek Orthodox Church in Cyprus v Lans*, Rb (First Instance Ct) Rotterdam 4 February 1999, NJ 1999, 37; Autocephalous Greek Orthodox Church in Cyprus v Lans, Hof (Appeals Ct). The Hague 7 March 2002, NIPR 2002, No 248. See Evelien Campfens, 'Whose Cultural Heritage? Crimean Treasures at the Crossroads of Politics, Law and Ethics' (2017) 22 AAL 193, 204–05; Matyk, 'The Restitution of Cultural Objects' (n 42).

[44] For example, The Netherlands: Cultural Property Originating from Occupied Territory (Return) Act in March 2007 implementing the First Protocol. Stb 2007, 123, currently codified as ss 6.9–6.15 of the Act of 9 December 2015, Relating to the Combining and Amendment of Rules Regarding Cultural Heritage (Heritage Act 2016) <www.eui.eu/projects/internationalartheritagelaw/netherlands> accessed 7 July 2021; Germany: Transformation Act of 25 April 2007; Implementation Act of 18 April 2007; BGBl I, Nr 21 (23 May 2007) Article 4.

[45] Cultural Property (Armed Conflicts) Act 2017 (United Kingdom) , ss 16(2) and 17(2). The UK legislation defines unlawful removal as 'in contravention of the laws of the territory from which the property is exported' or 'in contravention of any rule of international law'. ibid, s 16(3).

[46] In addition to a prohibition on illicit export of cultural objects from occupied territory, Article 9 of the Second Protocol also forbids the carrying out of archaeological excavation in occupied territory except 'where this is strictly required to safeguard, record or preserve cultural property' and 'any alteration

'occupation' is interpreted to require that the occupation be by a State.[47] According to the traditional view, only a State can be an occupying power and therefore the First Protocol applies only where occupation is carried out by a State.[48] In the UK's implementing legislation, 'occupied territory' is interpreted to refer only to occupation by a State and not to occupation by non-State actors.[49] According to the explanatory notes that accompanied the UK legislation, this limitation to States is based on the definition of belligerent occupation given in Article 42 of the 1907 Hague Regulations, which states that: 'Territory is considered occupied when it is actually placed under the authority of the hostile army. The occupation extends only to the territory where such authority has been established and can be exercised.'[50] Although this provision requires the occupier to have effective authority over the relevant territory, Article 42 does not explicitly require that the occupier be a State.

This limitation is the product of a time when conflict with non-State actors was less common and when non-State actors were not considered subject to or beneficiaries of international law.[51] It may be based on the reluctance of States to grant any degree of legitimacy to non-State actors, particularly within the context of nineteenth and early twentieth century colonialism. This view may be further criticized as all three of the Hague Convention instruments specifically apply to non-international armed conflict and, by implication, to non-State actors.[52] Benvenisti argued, in the context of the status of protected persons, that the qualifying factor, following the text of Article 42, should be whether the occupier has control over

to, or change of use of, cultural property which is intended to conceal or destroy cultural, historical or scientific evidence'.

[47] Roger O'Keefe posits that there can be no belligerent occupation in a non-international armed conflict so that the First Protocol does not apply unless the occupation is by a State. O'Keefe, *The Protection of Cultural Property* (n 21) 97–99, 192. Chamberlain takes the plain text of para 2 of the First Protocol as referring to *any* occupation but is not clear whether he limits 'Occupying Power' to States. Chamberlain, *War and Cultural Heritage* (n 7) 103–04. However, Chamberlain states clearly, citing para 10(c), that the Protocol applies to both international and non-international armed conflict, like the Convention itself. ibid, 100.

[48] For discussion of the generally accepted requirement that occupation must be carried out by a State and does not exist in non-international armed conflict, see O'Keefe, *The Protection of Cultural Property* (n 21) 98–99; Anne-Marie Carstens, 'The Hostilities-Occupation Dichotomy and Cultural Property in Non-International Armed Conflicts' (2016) 52 Stanford Journal of International Law 1, 9.

[49] The UK legislation limits unlawful export to export 'from a territory which at the time was occupied by a state that was a party to the First or Second Protocol' or 'from a territory which at the time was territory of a state that was a party to the First or Second Protocol, and was occupied by another state'. Cultural Property (Armed Conflicts) Act 2017 (n 28) s 16(1)(a)(b).

[50] Hague Convention Respecting the Laws and Customs of War on Land (hereafter Hague IV), 36 Stat 2277, Treaty Series 539.

[51] See M Cherif Bassiouni, 'The New Wars and the Crisis of Compliance with the Law of Armed Conflict by Non-State Actors' (2008) 98 Journal of Criminal Law and Criminology 711, 715–20.

[52] Article 19 of the main Convention provides that 'In the event of an armed conflict not of an international character occurring within the territory of one of the High Contracting Parties, each party to the conflict shall be bound to apply, as a minimum, the provisions of the Convention which relate to respect for cultural property'.

the occupied territory, not whether the occupier is a State.[53] He suggested that the law of occupation should apply to situations of non-international armed conflict extending the definition of occupation to 'the case when an organized secessionist government which has established its authority within a state is engaged in armed conflict with the metropolitan state during which it seizes territory . . .'.[54]

The wording of the first and fourth paragraphs of the First Protocol explicitly impose obligations on the occupying State Party, which is obliged to prevent export from the occupied territory and pay compensation to a good faith possessor. However, paragraphs 2 and 3 refer to the obligations of a State Party that is not the occupying power but, rather, is a 'third party' into which the exported cultural objects have been imported. These obligations are to take such objects into custody and to return them at the end of hostilities. It would seem in accordance with the text that the imposition of these obligations on a 'third party' does not depend on the status of the occupier, whether as a State or a non-State actor. In the case of the First Protocol, the question is not whether the non-State actor is subject to the obligations of an occupier but whether a State Party that is not the occupier has an obligation of restitution. The character of the occupier should not absolve a non-occupying State Party from the obligation of restitution.

While Article 4(3) of the main Convention prohibits looting and appropriation of cultural objects, the initial illegality of a violation of Article 4(3) pertains only to the perpetrator. Illegality does not attach to the object, following it onto the international art market and into destination countries, even if they are parties to these instruments. In contrast, under the First Protocol, which is limited to cultural objects removed during occupation, illegality attaches to the object and therefore includes an obligation of restitution. The unfortunate result of these limited interpretations is that removal of cultural objects in violation of Article 4(3) and of cultural objects from territory occupied by non-State actors, such as the Islamic State of Iraq and the Levant, do not trigger an obligation to return these cultural objects under the 1954 Hague Convention regime. The inapplicability of the Hague Convention provisions or other legal mechanisms to the market in cultural objects looted during armed conflict from Iraq and Syria necessitated adoption of Security Council Resolutions and enactment of implementing legislation to prevent this trade.[55] However, this is an inefficient, unreliable, and under-productive approach, not likely to be adopted in all cases of looting and theft of cultural objects from territories involved in armed conflict and occupation, such as occurred in Yemen,

[53] With respect to the status of protected persons, Benvenisti wrote: 'The protections of the law should not be cast into doubt because the belligerents dispute the status of territory. The better test would focus not on the occupant's characterization as an enemy of the population, but on the relationships between the administrations and the individuals and communities subject to its rule.' Eyal Benvenisti, *The International Law of Occupation* (2nd edn, OUP 2012) 59.

[54] ibid, 61.

[55] For example UNSC Res 1483 (22 May 2003) UN Doc S/RES/1483 (Iraq); UNSC Res 2199 (12 February 2015) UN Doc S/RES/2199, paras 15–17 (Syria).

Libya, Ukraine and elsewhere. Both a broader interpretation of 'occupied territory' and other broader legal mechanisms are required if cultural objects taken during armed conflict and occupation are to be returned.

5.2.2.3 Safeguarding

The First Protocol in paragraph 5 provides that one State Party may deposit cultural objects with another State for the purpose of protection against the 'dangers of an armed conflict'. At the end of hostilities, the latter State must return the cultural objects to 'the competent authorities of the territory from which it came'.[56] This provision has rarely been invoked and is of relatively little significance as States can enter into an agreement assuring return of the objects.[57]

The concept of providing safe haven for cultural objects during armed conflict is problematic. It recalls the 'rescue narrative', which was used to justify both Napoleon's looting of artworks from throughout Europe and the British appropriation of the Parthenon Sculptures. Iraq invoked the rescue narrative and the First Protocol when it removed artworks and cultural objects from museums and private collections in Kuwait during the 1990 Gulf War.[58] Market proponents have invoked the rescue narrative following the destruction of the Bamiyan Buddhas in Afghanistan and some of the collection in the National Museum by the Taliban in 2001.[59] It was used again during the 2003 Gulf War and the Arab Spring conflicts, while Russia has used the idea of safeguarding to justify removal of artworks from

[56] The main Convention also has provisions for transport of cultural property under special protection both internally and externally and such objects are to be immune from seizure and capture. Articles 12–14. Article 18 of the Regulations elaborates the obligations of the State in whose territory the cultural property is deposited.

[57] Chamberlain, *War and Cultural Heritage* (n 7) 107. Israel returned to Egypt archaeological artefacts excavated in the Sinai while under Israeli occupation following the 1967 war. Although both Israel and Egypt are parties to the 1954 Convention and the First Protocol, the Convention was not cited in the restitution agreement. Talia Einhorn, 'Restitution of Archaeological Artifacts: The Arab-Israeli Aspect' (1996) 5 IJCP 133, 142.

[58] Harvey E Oyer III, 'The 1954 Hague Convention for the Protection of Cultural Property in the Event of Armed Conflict – Is It Working? A Case Study: The Persian Gulf War Experience' (1999) 23 Columbia Journal of Law and the Arts 49, 58–62; Toman, *The Protection of Cultural Property* (n 2) 349; Iraq ultimately returned most of these objects to Kuwait under pressure from the United Nations and sanctions, but some objects were never returned. Etienne Clément, 'Some Recent Practical Experience in the Implementation of the 1954 Hague Convention' (1994) 3 IJCP 11, 17. In late 2016, Iraqi authorities seized from a former Iraqi soldier a valuable manuscript that was stolen from the Kuwait Museum and was reportedly being offered for sale for $45 million. Alaa Al-Huwaijel, 'Iraq seizes manuscript worth millions stolen in Kuwait' (*Kuwait News Agency*, 23 December 2016) <www.kuna.net,kw/ArticleDetails.aspx?id=2583045&language=en> accessed 7 July 2021.

[59] A project was initiated in Switzerland to acquire Afghan artefacts and protect them in a 'museum in exile'. These were later returned. UNESCO, *Museum-in-Exile: Swiss Foundation safeguards over 1,400 Afghan artefacts* <www.unesco.org/new/en/culture/themes/museums/museum-projects/archive/museum-in-exile-swiss-foundation-safeguards-over-1400-afghan-artefacts/> accessed 11 July 2021. The Oriental Institute of the University of Chicago carried out a long-term cooperative project with the National Museum to record and preserve its collection. Preservation of Cultural Heritage in Afghanistan <https://oi.uchicago.edu/research/projects/oi-nma-partnership> accessed 7 July 2021. Since the Taliban take-over in August 2021, the status of cultural objects in Afghanistan is uncertain.

Ukraine.[60] The notion of safe havens triggers connotations of the 'universal' museum that benefited from plunder enabled by colonialism and armed conflict over past centuries. As Weiss and Connelly noted, 'the use of safe havens will depend on trust',[61] a sentiment that may be in short supply based on past history, rhetoric, and conduct by many Western museums. Nonetheless, a more robust international system would, at times, benefit the people and the countries to whom the heritage belongs. In addition to the practical difficulties of funding for safe movement of heritage possibly through conflict zones, the domestic laws of countries that might be the recipients and guardians of such heritage are, for the most part, not adequate, posing obstacles of bureaucracy and concerns with immunity from seizure or legal process.

In 2008, the International Law Association proposed Guidelines for the Establishment and Conduct of Safe Havens for Cultural Materials, which established standards for legislation to be adopted by individual States.[62] France,[63] the United Kingdom, Italy, Germany, and China have all considered or enacted legislation to effectuate the idea of refuges, but enacted legislation seems not to be comprehensive or sufficiently responsive to practical impediments.[64] Switzerland enacted legislation in 2014, and, while helpful, it requires a treaty between Switzerland and the depositor country, something that could likely not be done in a period of crisis.[65] Alessandro Chechi points out that the Swiss legislation departs from the ILA Guidelines, in particular by not requiring storage and display in accordance with the laws and traditions of the State of origin.[66] In other countries,

[60] James Cuno, 'Saving Antiquities from Islamic State' (*Wall Street Journal*, 21 September 2015) <www.wsj.com/articles/saving-antiquities-from-islamic-state-1442875759>> accessed 7 July 2021. When Russian forces withdrew from Kherson, it evacuated several museum collections to museums in occupied Crimea. Taylor Dafoe, 'Before Retreating from Kherson, Russian Troops Emptied One of Ukraine's Top Museums of Nearly 15,000 Objects' (*Artnet News*, 14 November 2022) <https://news.artnet.com/art-world/russian-troops-loot-kherson-museum-2209777> accessed 9 July 2023.

[61] Thomas G Weiss and Nina Connelly, 'Cultural Cleansing and Mass Atrocities: Protecting Cultural Heritage in Armed Conflict Zones' (2017) 1 J Paul Getty Trust Occasional Papers in Cultural Heritage Policy 36–37.

[62] International Law Association, Resolution No 2/2008, Article 4(b) and (e); Nikolaus Thaddäus Paumgartner, 'The Rise of Safe Havens for Threatened Cultural Heritage' (2018) 25 IJCP 323, 326–27 (hereafter Paumgartner, 'The Rise of Safe Havens'). Safe havens can also be internal to the affected country, as encouraged in Article 16 of UN Security Council Resolution 2347. UNSC Res 2347 (24 March 2017) UN Doc S/RES/2347.

[63] Code du Patrimoine article L111-11, 7 juillet 2016, <www.legifrance.gouv.fr/affichCodeArticle.do?idArticle=LEGIARTI000032857167&cidTexte=LEGITEXT000006074236&dateTexte=20160709> accessed 7 July 2021. This provision allows the temporary deposit of cultural goods in France in a situation of urgency and severe danger due to an armed conflict or catastrophe. Immunity from seizure is given to those objects. Objects may also be loaned to another country so long as it can guarantee immunity from seizure.

[64] Paumgartner, 'The Rise of Safe Havens' (n 62) 327–29.

[65] Loi fédérale sur la protection des biens culturels en cas de conflit armé, de castastrophe ou de situation d'urgence (LPBC) RS 520.3 (20 juin 2014), art 12 <www.admin.ch/opc/fr/official-compilation/2014/3545.pdf> accessed 10 May 2021. Paumgartner, 'The Rise of Safe Havens' (n 62) 323; Alessandro Chechi, 'Rescuing Cultural Heritage from War and Terrorism: A View from Switzerland' (2015) 2 SAACLR 83, 86–93 (hereafter Chechi, 'Rescuing Cultural Heritage from War and Terrorism').

[66] Chechi, 'Rescuing Cultural Heritage from War and Terrorism' (n 65) 92–93.

complying with existing immunity from seizure legislation and return guarantees often poses significant obstacles by limiting the amount of time that an object can be in the country or by requiring that the object be on display.

In 2016, the United States enacted legislation to provide refuge with an automatic grant of immunity from seizure for objects entering the United States, but this legislation is limited to cultural property from Syria.[67] Use of the refuge mechanism depends on several conditions being satisfied including that the owner or lawful custodian requests that the cultural materials be temporarily located in the United States for protection purposes and that the materials are to be returned to the owner or lawful custodian upon request.[68] This legislation gives museums with whom objects are deposited for safeguarding considerable latitude as to what they can do with the objects. The ability of an institution to study, conserve, exhibit, and restore these objects, without consulting the country of origin, is a deprivation of the country of origin's rights in the cultural materials; actions that an institution may take without the consent of the country of origin or depositor should be limited to necessary conservation measures.

A provision of the 2021 National Defense Authorization Act creates automatic immunity from seizure for cultural objects legally exported from Afghanistan and imported into the United States pursuant to a loan agreement with an educational or other charitable institution. This provision also expands the purposes for which immunity from seizure may be granted.[69] Despite the failure of the United States to ratify the First Protocol, these legislative provisions represent an incremental approach to codifying elements of the Protocol.

Efforts to provide effective safeguarding mechanisms in ways that do not implicate the nineteenth-century mantra of the rescue narrative leave other questions unanswered. These include: who may request safe haven; to whom and when should objects be returned, particularly if the identity of the original owner or government has changed; what event or threat triggers the safe haven provisions; is a formal agreement or treaty required; may the cultural objects be studied, displayed, or conserved or must there first be consent and consultation with the depositor; do the objects receive immunity from seizure; and must UNESCO or some other international or intergovernmental agency approve the granting of safe haven or

[67] Protect and Preserve International Cultural Property Act, Pub L 114-151, 130 Stat 369 (2016) § 3(c)(4) (hereafter 'PPICPA').

[68] If no owner or lawful custodian can be reasonably identified, the materials may be imported if the President determines that such materials should be temporarily located in the United States for purposes of protecting and preserving the materials. ibid, § 3(c)(2)(A). The term 'lawful custodian' is not defined in the legislation and is vague as to how the lawful custodian should be determined. The requirement that a request for deposit in the US must come from the owner or lawful custodian should mean that objects removed or retrieved under unclear circumstances are not eligible for this safe haven procedure. Finally, the materials may be imported only if there is no credible evidence that granting a waiver would contribute to illegal trafficking or financing of criminal or terrorist activities. ibid, § 3(c)(2)(B), (C).

[69] National Defense Authorization Act for 2021, Pub L 116–283 § 1216.

be otherwise involved. Economic sanctions and travel restrictions may pose other obstacles to effective assistance. The export and corresponding import of cultural objects may also be hampered by the very provisions of conventions, such as the 1970 UNESCO Convention, that require legal export before a cultural object may be legally imported.

Although the Hague Convention regime and other international humanitarian law instruments represent an advance with respect to the protection of cultural property during armed conflict and occupation, their effectiveness with respect to movable cultural property is limited. Limiting factors include a low rate of ratification and implementation of the First and Second Protocols, a definition of occupation limited to that carried out by a State, the failure of any initial illegality in removal or appropriation of cultural objects in violation of Article 4(3) of the Convention and Article 9 of the Second Protocol to attach to the objects once they are on the international art market, and the failure to impose an obligation of restitution. The Rome Statute fails to make the theft and appropriation of cultural objects a war crime, leaving them to the general provisions that prohibit plunder and pillage. These failures are striking in light of the knowledge of the drafters of the Hague Convention that artworks looted during the Holocaust were sold onto the international art market in order to raise funds to assist the German war effort where they have continued to circulate illegitimately for decades after the end of the war. One must conclude that some States involved in the drafting of the Hague instruments intentionally chose to limit applicability so that their art markets could continue to function regardless of the source of these artworks.

The Hague Convention framework remains hampered by these limitations, even as so much else in our understanding of cultural heritage has evolved. New forms of asymmetric warfare, the funding of terrorism and armed conflict through theft and looting of cultural objects, and growing numbers of internal conflicts and non-State actors require a continuing evolution of the legal regime for cultural heritage. The unique nature of cultural objects and the historical, aesthetic, religious, and cultural understandings that they embody have led to a new role for cultural heritage in the current conflicts. During armed conflict, both immovable and movable cultural heritage has come to represent something to be protected but equally, at times, a symbol to be destroyed when there is propaganda value to be realized or when, as in earlier conflicts, one group seeks to wipe out the cultural memory of another group.

5.3 A Human Rights Approach to the Disposition of Cultural Objects

In the immediate post-Second World War period, the international community adopted a series of humanitarian conventions and instruments. In addition to the

Geneva Conventions, these included the 1948 Universal Declaration of Human Rights[70] and the 1948 Convention on the Prevention and Punishment of the Crime of Genocide.[71] However, cultural rights are often considered secondary to or given less attention within the broad range of human rights.[72] The right to cultural heritage, whether immovable or movable, often takes a subsidiary place within the spectrum of cultural rights and exists within the realm of human rights, at least until recently, only to the extent that it is linked to one of the recognized aspects of the right to culture.

5.3.1 The Role of Cultural Genocide

The blueprint for the Convention on Genocide was developed during the inter-war period by the Polish lawyer, Raphael Lemkin. Lemkin described two acts, acts of barbarism and acts of vandalism, that should be considered among the acts against the law of nations. In his work, *Acts of Vandalism*, he characterized culture as both universalistic and the product of a collective or community:

> An attack targeting a collectivity can also take the form of systematic and organized destruction of the art and cultural heritage in which the unique genius and achievement of a collectivity are revealed ... The contribution of any particular collectivity to world culture as a whole forms the wealth of all of humanity, even while exhibiting unique characteristics.
>
> Thus, the destruction of a work of art of any nation must be regarded as acts of vandalism directed against world culture. The author causes not only the immediate irrevocable losses of the destroyed work as property and as the culture of the collectivity directly concerned (whose unique genius contributed to the creation of this work); it is also all humanity which experiences a loss by this act of vandalism.
>
> In the acts of barbarity, as well as in those of vandalism, the asocial and destructive spirit of the author is made evident. This spirit, by definition, is the opposite of the culture and progress of humanity....[73]

[70] Universal Declaration of Human Rights, UN General Assembly Resolution 217A (10 December 1948).

[71] Convention on the Prevention and Punishment of the Crime of Genocide (adopted 9 December 1948, entered into force 12 January 1951) 78 UNTS 277 (hereafter Genocide Convention).

[72] Valentina Vadi, 'The Cultural Wealth of Nations in International Law' (2012) 21 Tulane Journal of International and Comparative Law 87, 112–14 (hereafter Vadi, 'The Cultural Wealth of Nations').

[73] Raphael Lemkin, 'Acts Constituting a General (Transnational) Danger Considered as Offences Against the Law of Nations' (1933) <www.preventgenocide.org/lemkin/madrid1933-english.htm> accessed 10 May 2021.

Cultural genocide may include 'the abolition of a group's language, restrictions upon its traditional practices and ways, [and] the destruction of religious institutions and objects . . .'[74] Cultural genocide may also occur 'when artistic, literary, and cultural activities are restricted or outlawed and when national treasures, libraries, archives, museums, artifacts, and art galleries are destroyed or confiscated'.[75] Lemkin's term 'vandalism' recalls the usage coined by the Abbé Grégoire to describe the destruction of cultural property perpetrated during the French Revolution. Grégoire wrote that 'I created the word to destroy the thing'. As Sax commented, 'Grégoire made cultural policy a litmus test of civilized values, and located it in the ideological geography of the French Revolution. The nation decides what it will be as it stands before its artistic, historical, and scientific monuments, hammer in hand.'[76] As discussed in chapters 2 and 4, it may be possible to trace to the French Revolution the origin of the idea of preserving cultural heritage by vesting its ownership in the State or its people, an idea that is now embodied in the concept of State ownership. Similarly, the idea that destruction of cultural heritage is an infringement on the cultural rights of a community may also be traced to the French Revolution or even further back to the words of Raphael, who compared destructive activities to those of the Vandals.

Lemkin included cultural genocide in the draft Genocide Convention as one of the eight dimensions of genocide: political, social, cultural, economic, biological, physical, religious, and moral, 'each targeting a different aspect of a group's existence'.[77] The elements of cultural genocide included: prohibition on the use of the national language; systematic destruction of books printed in the national language or of religious works; systematic destruction of historical or religious monuments or their change to different uses; and destruction or dispersal of documents and objects of historical, artistic, or religious value, and of objects used in religious worship.[78] The Armenian genocide conducted in Anatolia and neighbouring regions at the end of the First World War[79] and the genocide conducted during the European

[74] David Nersessian, 'Rethinking Cultural Genocide Under International Law, Human Rights Dialogue: "Cultural Rights"' (2005) Carnegie Council for Ethics in International Affairs, <www.carnegiecouncil.org/publications/archive/dialogue/2_12/section_1/5139.html> accessed 10 May 2021 (hereafter Nersessian, 'Rethinking Cultural Genocide').

[75] ibid.

[76] Joseph L Sax, 'Heritage Preservation as a Public Duty: The Abbé Grégoire and the Origins of an Idea' (1989–1990) 88 Michigan Law Review 1142, 1160-61.

[77] Nersessian, 'Rethinking Cultural Genocide' (n 74).

[78] Hirad Abtahi and Philippa Webb, *The Genocide Convention: The Travaux Préparatoires* (Brill 2008) 234–36 (hereafter, Abtahi and Webb, *The Genocide Convention*); O'Keefe, 'Protection of Cultural Property' (n 24) 386. Lemkin pointed out that cultural genocide is 'a policy which by drastic methods, aimed at the rapid and complete disappearance of the cultural, moral and religious life of a group of human beings'. Abtahi and Webb, *The Genocide Convention*, 235. Dr Bramson, the representative of Poland, referred to the destruction of 50 million books in Poland during the Second World War as an example of cultural genocide, an act committed against a group as a whole. ibid, 193.

[79] Heghnar Zeitlian Watenpaugh, *The Missing Pages: The Modern Life of a Medieval Manuscript from Genocide to Justice* (Stanford University Press 2019) 27–35; 39–47.

Holocaust were both characterized by large-scale destruction and looting of cultural heritage in an attempt to erase the memory of cultural groups. Nonetheless, cultural genocide was ultimately excluded from the Convention due to objections from former colonial powers and settler States, which were concerned that the recognition of cultural rights of ethnic and religious minorities would undermine State sovereignty.[80]

Despite its exclusion from the Convention, the concept of cultural genocide has returned in different contexts, particularly as a useful tool for courts to set out principles for the greater protection of cultural heritage and to link cultural heritage destruction with the crime of genocide and crimes against humanity.[81] In the ICTY case of *Prosecutor v Krstić*, the Trial Chamber and Appeals Chamber used cultural heritage destruction during the Balkan Wars as a method of establishing the genocidal intent of the Serbs against the Bosnian Muslims.[82] The Trial Chamber stated that 'where there is physical or biological destruction there are often simultaneous attacks on the cultural and religious property and symbols of the targeted group as well, attacks which may legitimately be considered as evidence of an intent to physically destroy the group'.[83] It therefore considered 'the deliberate destruction of mosques and houses belonging to members of the group' as evidence of intent to destroy the group.[84]

In some cases, the ICTY found that the discriminatory plunder of property could constitute the crime against humanity of persecution. In the *Krajišnik Trial*, the Trial Chamber, referring to the Nuremberg judgment, concluded that 'an act of appropriation or plunder that has a severe impact on the victim, carried out on discriminatory grounds, and for which the general elements of crimes against humanity are fulfilled, constitutes the crime of persecution'.[85] However, as with the

[80] Abtahi and Webb, *The Genocide Convention* (n 78) 163–67, 726–31. For example, the French government believed that cultural genocide should be excluded as it is a question that should be addressed to the protection of minorities and therefore invited the risk of political interference in the domestic affairs of States. ibid, 383. See also Lawrence Davidson, *Cultural Genocide* (Rutgers University Press 2012) 127–30.

[81] Federico Lenzerini, 'Terrorism, Conflicts and the Responsibility to Protect Cultural Heritage' (2016) 51(2) International Spectator 70, 78 (destruction carried out with discriminatory intent may constitute a crime against humanity or evidence of genocidal intent). See also UNESCO, Declaration concerning the Intentional Destruction of Cultural Heritage (17 October 2003) (characterizing in the Preamble the intentional destruction of cultural heritage as having 'adverse consequences on human dignity and human rights'); Francesco Francioni and Federico Lenzerini, 'The Destruction of the Buddhas of Bamiyan and International Law' (2003) 14 EJIL 619, 630–38.

[82] Nersessian, 'Rethinking Cultural Genocide' (n 74); O'Keefe, 'Protection of Cultural Property' (n 24) 388–89.

[83] *Prosecutor v Krstić* (Trial Judgment) ICTY-98-33-T (2 August 2001) para 580.

[84] ibid. This view was cited approvingly in Application of the Convention on the Preventing and Punishment of the Crime of Genocide (*Bosnia and Herzegovina v Serbia and Montenegro*) (Judgement) [2007] ICJ Rep 43, para 344. The ICJ reiterated this point in Application de la Convention pour la Prévention et la Répression du Crime du Génocide (*Croatie v Serbie*) [2015] ICJ Rep 3, para 390, stating that the court 'may take account of attacks on cultural and religious property in order to establish an intent to destroy the group physically'.

[85] *Prosecutor v Krajišnik* (Trial Judgment) ICTY-00-39-T (27 September 2006) 281 para 771; O'Keefe, 'Protection of Cultural Property' (n 24) 383; Elisa Novic, *The Concept of Cultural Genocide* (OUP 2016)

Nuremberg trials, the plunder and appropriation of cultural objects were used as evidence, but the crime charged was based on plunder and appropriation of civilian objects and not specifically cultural objects. The Rome Statute does not specify the destruction of cultural heritage as an independent crime against humanity or as a form of genocide. The Policy of the Office of the Prosecutor treats attacks on or destruction of cultural heritage instrumentally as a means of establishing the required elements of discriminatory intent and targeting of a group in the commission of crimes against humanity or genocide.[86]

Recent decisions of the United States courts indicate an evolving definition of genocide to include acts that might be termed cultural genocide in determining what constitutes a violation of international law. In a series of cases, descendants of Jewish victims of Nazi Germany sued foreign sovereign instrumentalities in US federal courts to recover expropriated works of art or compensation. The plaintiffs needed to establish jurisdiction over the foreign sovereign under the 'expropriation exception' of the Foreign Sovereign Immunities Act.[87] One of the provisions of this exception is that the expropriated property was taken in violation of international law.[88] Courts of Appeals have held that because commission of genocide is universally recognized as a violation of customary international law, predating adoption of the Genocide Convention, expropriation of property from Jews during the Holocaust was a violation of international law.[89] The Circuit Court for the District of Columbia extended this analysis in *DeCsepel v Republic of Hungary*[90] and *Philipp v Republic of Germany*[91] to include the expropriation of works of art

130. Lenzerini noted that 'in most instances of deliberate destruction of cultural heritage the target of perpetrators is not the heritage in itself but, rather, the communities and persons for whom the heritage is of special significance'. This supports the characterization of such destruction as based on 'discriminatory and persecutory intent against the targeted cultural groups'. Federico Lenzerini, 'Intentional Destruction of Cultural Heritage' in Francesco Francioni and Ana Filipa Vrdoljak (eds), *The Oxford Handbook of International Cultural Heritage Law* (OUP 2020) 75, 82.

[86] Office of the Prosecutor, 'Policy on Cultural Heritage' (n 21) paras 67–76 (pertaining to crimes against humanity); paras 79–84 (pertaining to the crime of genocide).

[87] Foreign Sovereign Immunities Act of 1976, 28 USC §§ 1602–1611 (hereafter 'FSIA').

[88] 28 USC § 1605(a)(3).

[89] In *Simon v Republic of Hungary* 812 F3d 127, 142–43 (DC Cir 2016), the court stated: 'the alleged takings did more than effectuate genocide or serve as a means of carrying out genocide. Rather, we see the expropriations *as themselves genocide*.... Expropriations undertaken for the purpose of bringing about a protected group's physical destruction qualify as genocide.' ibid, 142 (internal citation omitted) (emphasis in original). See also *Abelesz v Magyar Nemzeti Bank* 692 F3d 661, 675 (7th Cir 2012) (emphasizing that the genocidal components included theft of property to fund the genocide and deprivation of the means of support for those who survived). The Genocide Convention defines genocide, in part, as an act 'committed with intent to destroy, in whole or in part, a national, ethnic, racial or religious group' including '[d]eliberately inflicting on the group conditions of life calculated to bring about its physical destruction in whole or in part'. Genocide Convention, Article 2(c).

[90] *de Csepel v Republic of Hungary* 859 F3d 1094, 1101–02 (DC Cir 2017). *DeCsepel* involved the extensive art collection of the Herzog family from pre-war Hungary. The artworks were not a means of support for the victims, and thus the artworks' expropriation did not have a direct effect on the victims' condition of life.

[91] 894 F3d 406 (DC Cir. 2018), *rev'd sub nom, Federal Republic of Germany v Philipp* 141 S Ct 703 (2021).

and other cultural objects. In some cases, Germans sold expropriated artworks onto the international market to raise funding for the war effort. Thus the expropriations helped to perpetuate the genocide itself. The fact that the expropriations were carried out within the broader context of genocide rendered the takings of the artworks acts of genocide and therefore a violation of customary international law.

However, in *Federal Republic of Germany v Philipp*, the Supreme Court interpreted narrowly what constitutes a taking in violation of international law under the FSIA as implicating the international law of expropriation and not broader international law, including human rights law. In the case, three Jewish art dealers in Germany in the early 1930s had acquired the *Welfenschatz*, a unique collection of medieval relics and devotional art dating from the eleventh to fifteenth centuries, but they were pressured or forced into selling the treasure to Göring. The Court of Appeal held that because the treasure was allegedly expropriated from dealers, this was a deprivation of the victims' means of support. However, the Supreme Court held that the relevant law is the 'domestic takings rule' under which a foreign sovereign's taking of its own citizens' property is 'a domestic affair' and 'that what a country does to property belonging to its own citizens within its own borders is not the subject of international law'.[92] International law prohibiting genocide was therefore not considered relevant to the expropriation exception of the FSIA. While the Supreme Court thus narrowed significantly the meaning of a taking 'in violation of international law' for the purpose of obtaining jurisdiction over a foreign sovereign under the FSIA, the underlying point remains that the expropriation of property and, in particular, of cultural objects can constitute a part of the commission of genocide.

5.3.2 Human Rights and Cultural Objects

As human rights protections developed after the Second World War, the legal instruments embodying these rights focused first on the rights of individuals. Many States resisted international recognition of human rights as group or collective rights belonging to either minority groups or Indigenous groups. These States considered recognition of collective rights as undermining the integrity of the State.[93] Conversely, collective cultural rights could be viewed as infringing on the rights of the individual,[94] as they are based 'on the perceived uniqueness of the legacy that

[92] ibid, 141 S Ct 600.

[93] Matthias Åhrén, 'Protecting Peoples' Cultural Rights: A Question of Properly Understanding the Notion of States and Nations?' in Francesco Francioni and Martin Scheinin (eds), *Cultural Human Rights* (Martinus Nijhoff Publishers 2008) 91, 98–101. Part of the debate centred on whether the right of self-determination applied only in the colonial context.

[94] Francesco Francioni, 'Culture, Heritage and Human Rights: An Introduction' in Francesco Francioni and Martin Scheinin (eds), *Cultural Human Rights* (Martinus Nijhoff Publishers 2008) 1, 4–6 (hereafter Francioni, 'Culture, Heritage and Human Rights').

binds a group or community to a shared memory' that is the source of the feeling of identity and belonging that distinguish the cultural group.[95] Therefore, in the post-war era, cultural rights were considered to be rights held by the individual. However, it is necessary to protect the rights of individuals acting separately and in communities, as individuals and communities are dependent on each other to develop their respective identities and well-being.[96]

The right to culture and to cultural self-determination was recognized only gradually as part of human rights with the promulgation of several human rights legal instruments.[97] The Universal Declaration of Human Rights focuses on the right 'freely to participate in the cultural life of a community, to enjoy the arts and to share in scientific advancement and its benefits' and the right 'to the protection of the moral and material interests resulting from any scientific, literary or artistic production of which he [or she] is the author'.[98] While the second provision protects the rights of creators as individuals to engage in the act of creation, the first provision protects the right of individuals to participate in culture both individually and in a communal setting as well as to enjoy the arts. Other than the author's right to create and derive benefit, these cultural rights focus primarily on intangible activities rather than on a right to tangible heritage. However, to the extent that the removal of cultural works from a community impinges on the right of authors to continue to create, such removal would constitute the deprivation of a human right. In addition to the right of access, the most common right is the protection of religious liberty, as in the International Covenant on Civil and Political Rights, which protects the rights of members of ethnic, religious, and linguistic minorities 'in community with the other members of their group, to enjoy their own culture, to profess and practice their own religion, or to use their own language'.[99]

[95] ibid, 3.

[96] Siegfried Wiessner, 'The Cultural Rights of Indigenous Peoples: Achievements and Continuing Challenges' (2011) 22 EJIL 121, 125 (hereafter Wiessner, 'The Cultural Rights of Indigenous Peoples'). Lenzerini notes that the definition of culture given in the 1982 Mexico City Declaration on Cultural Policies as 'the whole complex of distinctive spiritual, material, intellectual and emotional features that characterize a society or social group' means that the existence of culture presupposes a group or collective. Federico Lenzerini, 'Indigenous Peoples' Cultural Rights and the Controversy over Commercial Use of Their Traditional Knowledge' in Francesco Francioni and Martin Scheinin (eds), *Cultural Human Rights* (Martinus Nijhoff Publishers 2008) 119, 122.

[97] Universal Declaration of Human Rights (1948) (hereafter UDHR); International Covenant on Economic, Social and Cultural Rights (adopted 16 December 1966, entered into force 3 January 1976) 999 UNTS 3 (hereafter ICESCR); International Covenant on Civil and Political Rights (adopted 16 December 1966, entered into force 23 March 1976) 999 UNTS 171 (hereafter ICCPR); UNESCO Convention for the Safeguarding of the Intangible Cultural Heritage (adopted 17 October 2003, entered into force 20 April 2006) 2368 UNTS 3; UNESCO Convention on the Protection and Promotion of the Diversity of Cultural Expressions (adopted 20 October 2005, entered into force 18 March 2007) 2440 UNTS 311; and United Nations Declaration on the Rights of Indigenous Peoples, UNGA A/RES/61/295 (13 September 2007) (hereafter UNDRIP).

[98] UDHR, Article 27.

[99] ICCPR, Article 27.

The International Covenant on Economic, Social and Cultural Rights also guarantees the right 'to take part in cultural life' (Art 15(1)(a)) and recognizes that States Parties have an obligation of conservation as a means for achieving the 'full realization' of cultural rights (Art 15(2)). General Comment No 21 to Article 15 mentions cultural heritage sparingly.[100] It defines 'access' to include the right 'to benefit from the cultural heritage and the creation of other individuals and communities' (para 15 (b)). The Comment also includes the right to develop cultural heritage, traditional knowledge, and traditional expressions among the rights of particular concern to Indigenous peoples (para 37). It defines the obligations of respect and protection to include a requirement that States ensure access to cultural and linguistic heritage (para 49 (d)) and includes types of tangible cultural heritage, such as libraries and museums, among the cultural goods and services that should be available to all (para 16 (a)). States must also provide what is necessary to foster programmes aimed at preserving and restoring cultural heritage (para 54(b)). Perhaps the broadest statement in the Comment is that States must '[r]espect and protect heritage in all its forms, in times of war and peace, and natural disasters':

> Cultural heritage must be preserved, developed, enriched and transmitted to future generations as a record of human experience and aspirations, in order to encourage creativity in all its diversity and to inspire a genuine dialogue between cultures. Such obligations include the care, preservation and restoration of historical sites, monuments, works of art and literary works, among others. (para 50(a))

While these earlier instruments focused on the rights of the individual, they incorporated a right to participate in and have access to culture either individually or in community. As a result, these instruments were gradually reinterpreted to recognize community-based rights, along with those exercised by individuals.[101] As the Office of the High Commissioner for Human Rights has written:

> Cultural rights protect the rights for each person, individually and in community with others, as well as groups of people, to develop and express their humanity, their world view and the meanings they give to their existence and their

[100] UN Committee on Economic, Social and Cultural Rights, General comment No 21, Right of everyone to take part in cultural life, E/C.12/GC/21 (21 December 2009). The Comment represents an expansion on the understanding of what constitutes culture 'as a way of life of a society and, consequently, as a dynamic process apart from its material side and products'. Yvonne Donders, 'Cultural Heritage and Human Rights' in Francesco Francioni and Ana Filipa Vrdoljak (eds), *The Oxford Handbook of International Cultural Heritage Law* (OUP 2020) 378, 391 (hereafter Donders, 'Cultural Heritage and Human Rights').

[101] Ana Filipa Vrdoljak, 'Self-Determination and Cultural Rights' in Francesco Francioni and Martin Scheinin (eds), *Cultural Human Rights* (Martinus Nijhoff Publishers 2008) 41, 56–61 (hereafter Vrdoljak, 'Self-Determination').

> development through, inter alia, values, beliefs, convictions, languages, knowledge and the arts, institutions and ways of life. They may also be considered as protecting access to cultural heritage and resources that allow such identification and development processes to take place.[102]

The recognition of collective rights advanced significantly with the adoption in 2007 of the United Nations Declaration on the Rights of Indigenous Peoples, which states that 'Indigenous peoples have the right to the full enjoyment, as a collective or as individuals, of all human rights and fundamental freedoms' including a right to cultural institutions; the right to maintain, control, protect, and develop their cultural heritage, traditional knowledge, and traditional cultural expressions; and the right to be free from destruction of their culture.[103]

Since adoption of the 2003 and 2005 UNESCO Conventions,[104] the intersection between cultural heritage and human rights has shifted to emphasize intangible heritage, such as language, music, crafts, dance, traditional and religious practices, folklore, and traditional knowledge. In this context, tangible cultural heritage often plays an instrumental role in providing a means for the realization of these cultural rights, rather than as rights worth fulfilling on their own. Movable tangible heritage encompasses the physical objects that embody both diverse cultural expression and intangible heritage. The ability to engage in these traditional practices is inextricably connected to tangible cultural heritage and often requires access to historic structures, sacred and traditional landscapes, written documents, and cultural artefacts, which are the physical embodiments of intangible culture.

Tangible and intangible heritage thus exist in a symbiotic relationship. While tangible cultural heritage provides the setting within which and the means by which the right to culture may be actualized, intangible heritage gives meaning and expression to tangible heritage.[105] The two must be understood as inextricably connected and, from this flows the human right to both tangible and intangible heritage. As Karime Bennoune, the Special Rapporteur to the UN Human Rights Council in the Field of Cultural Rights, noted:

> Cultural heritage includes not only tangible heritage composed of sites, structures and remains of archaeological, historical, religious, cultural or aesthetic value, but also intangible heritage made up of traditions, customs and practices, aesthetic

[102] United Nations Human Rights Office of the High Commissioner, International Standards <www.ohchr.org/EN/Issues/CulturalRights/Pages/InternationalStandards.aspx> accessed 7 July 2021.

[103] UN Doc A/RES/61/295 (13 September 2007) Articles 1, 5, 8, and 31. For detailed discussion of the Declaration, see Dalee Sambo Dorough and Siegfried Wiessner, 'Indigenous Peoples and Cultural Heritage' in Francesco Francioni and Ana Filipa Vrdoljak (eds), *The Oxford Handbook of International Cultural Heritage Law* (OUP 2020) 407 (hereafter Dorough and Wiessner, 'Indigenous Peoples and Cultural Heritage').

[104] See n 97 above.

[105] Donders, 'Cultural Heritage and Human Rights' (n 100) 385.

> and spiritual beliefs, vernacular or other languages, artistic expressions and folklore. Both of these categories should be understood in broad and holistic terms.[106]

The recognition given to the right to manifest one's culture, both individually and collectively, and to maintain and to develop one's cultural identity inevitably means the right to control the disposition of one's tangible cultural heritage. In fact, rights with respect to tangible cultural heritage should be treated as freestanding rights within the array of cultural rights and they deserve equal recognition to the other human rights.[107]

The shift from the State-centric and universalistic approach of the 1972 UNESCO Convention on the World Cultural and Natural Heritage to a focus on communities and individuals is 'a key means through which heritage practice can be democratized'[108] and reflects a more participatory and human-rights approach to cultural heritage. Viewing cultural heritage through the lens of human rights enables a more integrated understanding of the role that cultural heritage plays in the lives of human beings, whether as individuals or in community. Human rights now encompass tangible heritage that comes from sacred and traditional contexts, as well as human remains and burial items. The Operational Guidelines for the 1972 UNESCO World Heritage Convention recognize the integrated nature of the tangible heritage of sites and landscapes with traditional knowledge and practices that are often crucial for understanding tangible heritage.[109]

In the case of *Cambodia v Thailand, concerning the Temple of Preah Vihear*, the International Court of Justice (ICJ) elucidated the relationship between cultural heritage and human rights.[110] The case involved a boundary dispute between Cambodia and Thailand as to which country had sovereignty over the Temple of Preah Vihear (Figure 5.1) and was sparked in its later iteration by Cambodia's effort to have the site inscribed on the World Heritage List. The border dispute had erupted into fighting between the two countries, which resulted in the loss of human life and also endangered the historic structure. The Court viewed the site as one of religious and cultural significance for all the people in the region and, as a site of continuing religious significance, the local people had a right of free access to the Temple. In referring to both the Temple's status as a World Heritage Site and

[106] Report of the Special Rapporteur in the field of cultural rights, A/HRC/31/59 (3 February 2016) para 49, at 12.

[107] For example, Vadi, 'The Cultural Wealth of Nations' (n 72) 118.

[108] Janet Blake, 'Safeguarding Intangible Cultural Heritage' in Francesco Francioni and Ana Filipa Vrdoljak (eds), *The Oxford Handbook of International Cultural Heritage Law* (OUP 2020) 347, 362; Donders, 'Cultural Heritage and Human Rights' (n 100) 384.

[109] UNESCO, World Heritage and Indigenous Peoples <https://whc.unesco.org/en/activities/496/> accessed 10 May 2021.

[110] *Request for Interpretation of the Judgment of 15 June 1962 in the case concerning the Temple of Preah Vihear (Cambodia v Thailand)* (Judgment) [2013] ICJ Rep 281.

Figure 5.1 Temple of Preah Vihear. Khmer Empire, *c* eleventh–twelfth century. Cambodia

as a religious and spiritual centre for the local people, the Court acknowledged both the local and universal significance of the Temple site.[111]

In his separate opinion in the Court's Provisional Measures—Order, Judge Cançado Trindade suggested that the Court had not sufficiently emphasized the link among territoriality, preservation of human life, and the cultural and spiritual heritage of humankind in the interest of preventing spiritual damage. As he described, in establishing a demilitarized zone around the Temple, the Court 'encompassed the human rights to life and to personal integrity, as well as cultural and spiritual world heritage. In sum, the Court's order went "well beyond State territorial sovereignty, *bringing territory, people and human values together*," well in keeping with the *jus gentium* of our times.'[112] His opinion that the preservation

[111] *Request for Interpretation of the Judgment of 15 June 1962 in the Case concerning the Temple of Preah Vihear (Cambodia v. Thailand)* (n 110) para 106. The Court also emphasized the obligation of Cambodia and Thailand, as States Parties to the World Heritage Convention and under the UN Charter, to cooperate in finding a peaceful resolution. ibid.

[112] *Request for Interpretation of the Judgment of 15 June 1962 in the Case concerning the Temple of Preah Vihear (Cambodia v. Thailand)* (n 110) [2013] Separate Opinion of Judge Cançado Trindade [2013], para 33 (omitting internal citations) (emphasis in original). Alessandro Chechi, 'The 2013 Judgment of the ICJ in the Temple of Preah Vihear Case and the Protection of World Cultural Heritage Sites in Wartime' (2016) 6 Asian Journal of International Law 353, 358–59. In the 1962 case, Cambodia requested that Thailand return statues, stelai, monument fragments, and pottery that it had removed from the Temple illegally during the time that it controlled the Temple. The Court ordered the restitution but also noted that there was no evidence that Thailand had removed such objects. *Case concerning the Temple of Preah Vihear (Cambodia v Thailand)* (Merits, Judgment) [1962] ICJ Rep 6, 10–11, 37.

of cultural heritage plays an important role in the spiritual and cultural lives of the local community who live among the heritage leads to a melding of human values and cultural heritage as a part of customary international law.

The International Court of Justice addressed the role of cultural heritage a second time within the framework of human rights in *Armenia v Azerbaijan*.[113] Following the return of the Nagorno-Karabakh region from Armenia to Azerbaijan, Armenia alleged that Azerbaijan was violating the International Convention on the Elimination of All Forms of Racial Discrimination[114] through the destruction, damage, and alteration of Armenian historical, cultural, and religious sites. The ICJ linked cultural heritage and human rights in issuing provisional measures that Azerbaijan needed to 'take all necessary measures to prevent and punish acts of vandalism and desecration affecting Armenian cultural heritage'.[115]

A significant step towards integration of cultural heritage and human rights occurred when the Special Rapporteur in the Field of Cultural Rights, Farida Shaheed, in 2011 presented recommendations on the mainstreaming of cultural heritage protection within human rights, emphasizing the right to access and enjoy cultural heritage as a part of international human rights.[116] This path was followed by the successor Rapporteur, Karima Bennoune. Both Special Rapporteurs noted that the significance of cultural heritage at the individual and community levels is what imbues cultural heritage with the human dimension and is the source of its interconnection with human rights.[117] Bennoune noted:

> Cultural heritage is significant in the present, both as a message from the past and as a pathway to the future. Viewed from a human rights perspective, it is important not only in itself, but also in relation to its human dimension, in particular its significance for individuals and groups and their identity and development processes. Cultural heritage is to be understood as the resources enabling the cultural identification and development processes of individuals and groups which they, implicitly or explicitly, wish to transmit to future generations.[118]

[113] Application of the International Convention on the Elimination of All Forms of Racial Discrimination *(Armenia v Azerbaijan)* (Pending) General List No 180 <www.icj-cij.org/en/case/180> accessed 24 February 2022.

[114] International Convention on the Elimination of All Forms of Racial Discrimination (adopted 21 December 1965, entered into force 4 January 1969) UNGA Res 2106 (XX) annex, 660 UNTS 195.

[115] *Armenia v Azerbaijan* (n 113) para 92.

[116] Office of the High Commissioner for Human Rights (hereafter OHCHR), 'Report of the independent expert in the field of cultural rights, Farida Shaheed' (2011) A/HRC/17/38 (21 March 2011) paras 9–17 (hereafter, OHCHR, 'Report of the independent expert in the field of cultural rights').

[117] ibid, para 7.

[118] OHCHR, 'Report of the Special Rapporteur in the field of cultural rights' (2016) A/HRC/31/59 (3 February 2016) para 47 (internal citations omitted) (hereafter UNHCR, 'Report of the Special Rapporteur in the field of cultural rights').

Figure 5.2 Religious Site, Timbuktu, Mali

Both Special Rapporteurs labelled the intentional destruction of cultural heritage as a human rights violation.[119] During Bennoune's mandate, the Human Rights Council unanimously adopted Resolution 33/20, which brought the ability to access and enjoy cultural heritage within the right to take part in cultural life, condemned the intentional destruction of cultural heritage and the looting and trafficking of movable heritage, and called for 'recognition of the protection of cultural heritage as an important component of humanitarian assistance'.[120]

In *Prosecutor v Al Mahdi*, involving the destruction of shrines and a mosque in Timbuktu in Mali (Figure 5.2), the Prosecutor noted the significance of the cultural sites to the three perspectives discussed previously: the local community, the State, and, as a World Heritage Site, the world community.[121] She referred to the importance of the sites for the ongoing religious practices of the local community and stated that it 'became impossible for the inhabitants of Timbuktu to devote

[119] OHCHR, 'Report of the independent expert in the field of cultural rights' (n 116) para 15; UNHCR, 'Report of the Special Rapporteur in the field of cultural rights' (n 118) paras 45, 69–72.

[120] OHCHR, Res 33/20 on Cultural Rights and the Protection of Cultural Heritage (30 September 2016) UN Doc A/HRC/RES/33/20 (6 October 2016).

[121] Statement of the Prosecutor of the International Criminal Court, Fatou Bensouda, at the opening of the confirmation of charges hearing in the case against Mr Ahmad Al-Faqi Al Mahdi (1 March 2016) <www.icc-cpi.int/Pages/item.aspx?name=otp-stat-01-03-16> accessed 11 July 2021.

themselves to their religious practices. These practices were deeply rooted in their lives. These practices signified the deepest and most intimate part of a human being: Faith. These practices were part of their shared life together.'[122] She also cited the close link of these structures to the cultural heritage and history of Timbuktu, as the mausolea are the identifying symbol of the city. The Prosecutor described their cultural value: 'To destroy Timbuktu's mausoleums is to erase this element of collective identity that the people of Timbuktu built throughout the ages.'[123]

Bennoune, the expert appointed by the International Criminal Court (ICC), in her Reparations Report again analysed the importance of the cultural heritage of Timbuktu from a human rights perspective, incorporating its significance to the local community, State, and international community, while recognizing that the local community had the greatest interest. She noted the particular gravity of attacks on cultural heritage that were, in fact, attacks on cultural diversity and cultural rights with the purpose of 'erasing memory of current and past events, civilizations and peoples; erasing evidence of the presence of minorities, other peoples, philosophies, religions and beliefs; or deliberately targeting or terrorizing individuals and groups on the basis of their cultural, ethnic or religious affiliation, or their ways of life and beliefs'.[124]

Despite this multi-layered approach to identification of the victims and their harm, the Expert recognized that the local population suffered the greatest harm and therefore should be the primary beneficiary of any reparations awarded.[125] The associated intangible values mean that the destruction of the mausolea and mosque transcended monetary value. The value of a human rights approach to the preservation of cultural heritage is that:

> [B]eyond preserving and safeguarding an object or a manifestation in itself, the human rights approach to cultural heritage obliges one to take into account the rights of individuals and communities in relation to such object or manifestation and, in particular, to connect cultural heritage with its source of production .... [T]he obligations to respect and to protect freedoms, cultural heritage and cultural diversity are interconnected. It is impossible to separate a people's cultural heritage from the people itself and their rights.[126]

[122] ibid.

[123] ibid. In assessing the seriousness of the crimes, the Trial Court emphasized the significance of the structures to the world community and to the local community as religious buildings and their 'psychological role to the extent of being perceived as protecting the people of Timbuktu'. *Prosecutor v Ahmadi Al Faqi Al Madhi* (Judgment and Sentence) ICC-01/12-01/15 (27 September 2016) paras 78–80.

[124] Karima Bennoune, Report Reparations Phase, ICC-01/12-01/15 (27 April 2017) 14–15, 18–22 <https://icc-cpi.int/RelatedRecords/CR2017_05022.pdf> accessed 7 July 2021.

[125] ibid, 18, 27–28, 38.

[126] ibid, 16, paras 70–71.

This demonstrates the connection between the tangible and the intangible, with the intangible giving meaning to the tangible and the tangible enabling actualisation of the intangible.[127]

In contrast to the destruction of intangible cultural heritage, the intentional destruction of tangible cultural heritage has been accepted as a violation of international humanitarian law for over a century, and such destruction is now accepted as a violation of human rights.[128] The appropriation of movable cultural heritage and the dismemberment of immovable heritage, causing damage and at times destruction, also constitute a recognized violation of international humanitarian law when carried out during armed conflict and would today constitute a comparable violation of human rights. Many of the appropriations discussed in chapters 2 and 3 occurred at a time either when the appropriation did not constitute a violation of contemporary law, as a product of colonialism and armed conflict, or when international law was beginning its evolution over the course of the nineteenth century. Yet the deprivation of movable cultural heritage from communities is not just a wrong that occurred in the past. These are ongoing deprivations, divorcing communities from their heritage and causing harm in the present. The Special Rapporteur in the Field of Cultural Rights stated, '[t]he disconnection which may occur between cultural heritage and the people concerned is an important human rights issue'.[129] The contemporary connection between cultural heritage and human rights further necessitates protection of the right of access by the members of a group, individually or collectively, as a human right.[130] The essential question is how international law will rectify these continuing deprivations as present violations of both international humanitarian law and international human rights law.

[127] In recognition both of the harm done and the difficulty of true repair, the ICC awarded Mali and UNESCO €1 as symbolic reparations. Al Mahdi was held liable for €2.7 million for damage to the historic structures, economic losses, moral harm, and individual reparations, to be paid from the Trust Funds for Victims. UNESCO, 'Mausoleums destroyed in Timbuctu: the International Criminal Court holds Ahmad Al Mahdi liable for 2.7 million euros of damage' (18 August 2017) <www.unesco.org/new/en/culture/themes/single-view/news/mausoleums_destroyed_in_timbuktu_the_international_criminal/> accessed 11 July 2021.

[128] Kristin Hausler, 'The UN Security Council, the Human Rights Council, and the Protection of Cultural Heritage' in Anne-Marie Carstens and Elizabeth Varner (eds), *Intersections in International Cultural Heritage Law* (OUP 2020) 202, 221 (hereafter Hausler, 'The UN Security Council'). The destruction of cultural heritage during armed conflict is now also recognized as a threat to world peace and security, as stated in UN Security Council Resolution 2347. ibid, 218–20; UNSC Res 2347 (24 March 2017) UN Doc S/RES/2347.

[129] OHCHR, 'Report of the independent expert in the field of cultural rights' (n 116) para 14. She noted that disconnection can occur for several reasons, including through preservation and safeguarding programmes, which 'should not be implemented at the expense of individuals and communities who, sometimes for the sake of preservation purposes, are displaced or given limited access to their own heritage'. ibid. Human rights violations may also occur when cultural heritage elements are placed in storage or displayed in institutions, sometimes preventing access and use or preventing deterioration which may be a necessary part of a cultural or religious tradition. ibid, para 16. This subject will be discussed further in chapter 7.

[130] Francioni, 'Culture, Heritage and Human Rights' (n 94) 7.

5.3.3 Human Remains and Burial Goods

Human remains and burial goods are a particular category of tangible cultural heritage and deserve special treatment because of their considerable sensitivity.[131] The crucial connection between Indigenous peoples and their land makes the disposition of human remains an even more significant issue for them. The excavation and collection of human remains are a common practice among archaeologists and anthropologists. Over the course of the nineteenth century, large quantities of contemporary and archaeological human remains were collected and curated by museums as part of the goal of classifying and determining racial classifications.[132] The European colonial powers collected human remains from colonized areas of the world often for use in studies to prove racist ideologies, as discussed in chapter 2, without the free, prior, and informed consent of the peoples, most often Indigenous peoples, to whose ancestors the remains belonged.[133] Some government authorities, such as the US government, operating within their own territories collected human remains of Indigenous and minority groups.[134] Often these collections were formed and studied in the stated interest of science,[135] although

[131] Dorough and Wiessner, 'Indigenous Peoples and Cultural Heritage' (n 103) 415. Human remains are included within the definition of 'cultural items' in the Native American Graves Protection and Repatriation Act, 25 USC § 3001(3). Human remains are also often discovered in context with burial goods, which are easily classified as cultural objects, placed in museum collections, and studied by forensic anthropologists and archaeologists. Human remains are therefore included in this discussion of the disposition of cultural objects.

[132] Myra Giesen and Liz White, 'International Perspectives towards Human Remains Curation' in Myra Giesen (ed), *Curating Human Remains: Caring for the Dead in the United Kingdom* (Boydell Press 2013) 13, 14–15. Burial objects are often collected by looters for the market, as well as by scientists for study. Although many would view them as *extra commercium*, human remains are still sold, even on the internet. See Shawn Graham, Damien Huffer, and Jeff Blackadar, 'Towards a Digital Sensorial Archaeology as an Experiment in Distant Viewing of the Trade in Human Remains on Instagram' (2020) 3 Heritage 208–27.

[133] Free, prior, and informed consent is a principle developed uniquely with respect to Indigenous peoples' rights to use of their traditional lands. It is recognized in ILO No 169 Indigenous and Tribal Peoples Convention (1989), Article 16, UNDRIP, Article 32(2), and the Convention on Biodiversity, Article 8(j).

[134] Chip Colwell, 'The Long Ethical Arc of Displaying Human Remains' (*Atlas Obscura*, 16 November 2017), <www.atlasobscura.com/articles/displaying-native-american-remains> accessed 10 May 2021; Rebecca Tsosie, 'Indigenous Peoples and Epistemic Injustice: Science, Ethics and Human Rights' (2012) 87 Washington Law Review 1133; Ryan M Seidemann, 'Bones of Contention: A Comparative Examination of Law Governing Human Remains from Archaeological Contexts in Formerly Colonial Countries' (2004) 64 Louisiana Law Review 545, 555–58 (hereafter Seidemann, 'Bones of Contention'); Honor Keeler, 'Indigenous International Repatriation' (2012) 44 Arizona State Law Journal 703, 734–37 (hereafter Keeler, 'Indigenous International Repatriation'). Indigenous groups have argued that they should have a distinct status from that of minority groups based on their different historical circumstances and continuing 'colonial' occupation, particularly by settler States. Vrdoljak, 'Self-Determination' (n 101) 71–74.

[135] For discussion of the range of scientific studies and evidence that can be derived from studies of human remains, see Seidemann, 'Bones of Contention' (n 134) 550–53. Treatment, display, and study of human remains should include mummies, particularly from countries such as Egypt and Peru. These are frequently featured in museum collections throughout Europe and North America. However, these displays have not typically elicited calls for repatriation or concerns with violations of human rights. Colwell, 'The Long Ethical Arc' (n 134).

these studies were used to claim differences and establish inferiority among races based on cranial and other morphologies.[136] The disposition of these remains needs to be considered in the context of some of the most fundamental of human rights, the right to the free exercise of religion, the right to dignity and respect for the dead, and associated rights.[137] While it is unlikely that a deceased person would be considered to have human rights, the rights of the deceased's descendants, community, or other representative would have rights in the treatment of their ancestors' remains.[138]

Within the common law system, human remains are not considered to be subject to ownership and a right of possession exists only among the next-of-kin for the limited purpose of burial to ensure respectful treatment.[139] Despite this, human remains were collected through both trade and robbing of burials among many of the formerly colonized and Indigenous groups such as in the United States,[140] New Zealand,[141] Canada, and Australia. Furthermore, despite some changes, Western museums have been remarkably reluctant to return human remains to lineal kin

[136] Seidemann, 'Bones of Contention' (n 134) 557–58; Keeler, 'Indigenous International Repatriation' (n 134) 735–38. See also chapter 2, section 2.4.3.

[137] For example, ICCPR, Article 27; UNDRIP, Article 12; European Convention on Human Rights, Articles 8 and 9 (adopted 4 November 1950, entered into force 3 September 1953); UNTS 222, Article 9. See Eric Hemenway, 'Finding Our Way Home' in Sangita Chari and Jaime MN Lavallee (eds), *Accomplishing NAGPRA* (Oregon State University Press 2013) 83, 84.

[138] Kevin Chamberlain, 'We Need to Lay our Ancestors to Rest—The Repatriation of Indigenous Human Remains and the Human Rights Act' in Ruth Redmond-Cooper (ed), *Heritage, Ancestry and Law: Principles, Policies and Practices in dealing with Historical Human Remains* (Institute of Art and Law 2015) 60, 64–65, 67–68, 73 (discussing whether under Article 8 of the European Convention on Human Rights a museum's retention of Indigenous human remains violates an Indigenous group's right to its way of life and culture); Edward Halealaha Ayau, 'The Responsibility to Restore the Ancestral Hawaiian Foundation through Repatriation and Reburial' in Deutscher Museumsbund (ed), *Guidelines: Care of Human Remains in Museums and Collections* (Deutscher Museumsbund 2021) 124, 126 (explaining the significance of the integrity of ancestors' final resting places and their restoration as a 'sacred duty').

[139] Hugh Y Bernard, *The Law of Death and Disposal of the Dead* (Oceana Publications 1979) 16 (citing 2 William Blackstone, Commentaries, 429); Norman Palmer, 'Relinquishment, Remembrance and Repose: Models for the Domicile of Human Remains' in Ruth Redmond-Cooper (ed), *Heritage, Ancestry and Law: Principles, Policies and Practices in Dealing with Historical Human Remains* (Institute of Art and Law 2015) 1, 24–38; Charlotte Woodhead, 'Care, Custody and Display of Human Remains: Legal and Ethical Obligations' in Myra Giesen (ed), *Curating Human Remains: Caring for the Dead in the United Kingdom* (Boydell 2013) 31, 32–33 (citing UK and Australian law). See also *Guidelines for the Care of Human Remains in Scottish Museum Collections* (Museums Galleries Scotland 2011) 32–33 <www.museumsgalleriesscotland.org.uk/media/1089/guidelines-for-the-care-of-human-remains-in-scottish-museum-collections.pdf> accessed 10 May 2021. German law is in accord. Carola Thielecke and Michael Geissdorf, 'Legal Provisions for Dealing with HumanRemains in Museums and Collections' in *Guidelines: Care of Human Remains in Museums and Collections* (Deutscher Museumsbund 2021) 96, 101.

[140] For example Margaret B Bowman, 'The Reburial of Native American Skeletal Remains: Approaches to the Resolution of a Conflict' (1989) 13 Harvard Environmental Law Review 147, 149 (estimating that American museum collections included approximately 300,000 human remains); Jack F Trope and Walter R Echo-Hawk, 'The Native American Graves Protection and Repatriation Act: Background and Legislative History' (1992) 24 Arizona State Law Journal 35, 40.

[141] Robert K Paterson, 'Taonga Maori Renaissance: Protecting the Cultural Heritage of Aotearoa/New Zealand' in James AR Nafziger and Ann M Nicgorski (eds), *Cultural Heritage Issues: The Legacy of Conquest, Colonization, and Commerce* (Martinus Nijhoff Publishers 2009) 107, 121–22.

and descendant communities, particularly in the international context, again retaining the remains in the furtherance of their proclaimed scientific value.

5.3.3.1 Intra-State Repatriation of Human Remains and Cultural Items

Repatriation of human remains can take place either internally within a State to Indigenous groups and minority groups or internationally. Primary examples of legislation enacted to achieve domestic repatriation are the Native American Graves Protection and Repatriation Act (NAGPRA) in the US[142] and the Aboriginal and Torres Islander Strait Heritage Preservation Act in Australia.[143]

In the United States, prior to adoption of NAGPRA, burials were protected by a patchwork of state laws that criminalized the desecration of or interference with human gravesites and cemeteries. However, these protections often did not apply to Native American burials as these were unmarked or not located in a recognized graveyard.[144] Adopted in 1990, NAGPRA, which is often viewed as civil rights legislation, had as its core purpose the recognition of the dignity and respect with which Native American human remains should be treated. NAGPRA establishes a tripartite structure for the treatment of human remains, associated and unassociated funerary goods, sacred objects, and objects of cultural patrimony. The last category is significant for recognizing a communal or group right to cultural objects, something that has been resisted in other countries.[145]

NAGPRA addresses the disposition of human remains and other cultural items discovered on federal or tribal land after 1990,[146] recognizing ownership or control in a pecking order of: lineal descendants; the tribe on whose tribal land the remains were discovered; the tribe with the closest cultural affiliation, or the tribe whose claim to the land where the remains were discovered has been recognized by a final judgment of the Indian Claims Commission or the US Court of Claims.[147] The second aspect of NAGPRA imposes an obligation on museums and institutions that receive federal funding to create inventories (for human remains and associated burial goods) and summaries (for unassociated burial goods, sacred objects, and objects of cultural patrimony) and make these cultural items available

[142] 25 USC §§ 3001–3013. The United States has also enacted the National Museum of the American Indian Act, which applies specifically to this museum within the Smithsonian Institution. 20 USC §§ 80q-15 (2015).

[143] Aboriginal and Torres Strait Islander Heritage Protection Act 1984 (Cth), s 4 (Austl).

[144] For example *Charrier v Bell* 496 So 2d 601 (La Ct App 1986); *Wana the Bear v Community Construction, Inc* 180 Cal Rptr 423, 426–27 (Cal Ct App 1982); *Newman v State* 174 So 2d 479, 483 (Fla Dist Ct App 1965); *Town of Sudbury v Dept of Public Utilities* 351 Mass 214, 218 NE 2d 415 (1966).

[145] See the discussion in n 187.

[146] This accounts for approximately 40 per cent of the land mass of the United States. At least half of the US states have adopted NAGPRA-type statutes applying to burials discovered on state-owned and private land, while additional states have similar laws that apply only to state-owned land.

[147] 25 US.C § 3002(a). These provisions apply to both Indian tribes and Native Hawaiian organizations.

for repatriation.[148] The third aspect criminalizes, first, the knowing sale, purchase, use for profit, or transport for sale or profit of Native American human remains without the right of possession and, second, the knowing sale, purchase, use for profit, or transport for sale or profit of any Native American cultural items obtained in violation of NAGPRA.[149]

NAGPRA is likely the broadest and most effective legislation dealing with the repatriation of human remains and certain other types of cultural objects. However, it also has drawbacks. Despite its requirements, compliance and progress have been slow. NAGPRA does not apply to international repatriation of human remains as non-US tribes are not federally recognized and are therefore not eligible for repatriation.[150] Another drawback is the limitation imposed on NAGPRA's repatriation provisions established through judicial decision in *Bonnichsen v United States*.[151] The case involved the disposition of human remains discovered on federal land and which were determined to be between 8,320 and 9,000 years old. The court held that the remains, dubbed 'Kennewick Man', would only be classified as Native American under NAGPRA if the claimant tribes could establish a significant relationship between the remains and a presently existing tribe, people, or culture. Rejecting the evidence presented by the tribal claimants based largely on oral tradition, the court held that the tribes failed to establish such a relationship with the remains. The NAGPRA repatriation provisions therefore did not apply.

Scientific evidence later vindicated the oral tradition, which proved more reliable than the court was willing to credit it.[152] Nonetheless, the requirements that a

[148] 25 USC §§ 3003 (inventories of human remains and associated funerary objects); 3004 (summaries of unassociated funerary objects, sacred objects, and objects of cultural patrimony); 3005 (repatriation).

[149] 18 USC § 1170. NAGPRA defines 'right of possession' in part as 'possession obtained with the voluntary consent of an individual or group that had authority of alienation'. 25 USC § 3001(13).

[150] See n 147. The term 'Indian tribe' is defined as 'any tribe, band, nation or other organized group or community of Indians, ... which is recognized' by the federal government. 25 USC § 3001(7). This definition excludes non-recognized tribes, including all tribes located outside of the United States. The National Museum of the American Indian has more flexibility. It has made several voluntary repatriations to groups located outside of the United States and often takes a broader view of what is legislatively required. See National Museum of the American Indian, 'Repatriation' <https://americanindian.si.edu/explore/repatriation> accessed 10 May 2021. Some US museums have made international repatriations outside the scope of NAGPRA, in which case the US museum is not protected by NAGPRA's limitation on the potential liability of the museum for claims of breach of fiduciary duty, public trust, or violations of state law. 25 USC § 3005(f).

[151] 357 F3d 962 (9th Cir 2004). Disposition of culturally unidentifiable human remains and associated funerary objects is determined under 43 Code of Federal Regulations § 10.11. Because the case was not appealed to the Supreme Court, the *Bonnichsen* decision is binding precedent only within the Ninth Circuit, which includes the states of California, Oregon, Washington, Alaska, and Nevada; otherwise, the decision has only persuasive authority.

[152] Analyses of the skeleton's DNA established that Kennewick Man is closer to modern Native Americans and one of the claimant tribes 'than to any other population worldwide' and that 'based on genetic comparisons ... Kennewick Man shows continuity with Native Americans over at least the last eight millennia'. Morten Rasmussen and others, 'The Ancestry and Affiliations of Kennewick Man' (2015) 523 Nature 455 <www.nature.com/articles/nature14625> accessed 10 May 2021. The remains were subsequently turned over to the tribal claimants and reburied.

claimant tribe must establish a significant relationship to the human remains and that scientific evidence should be heavily privileged over Native forms of evidence, such as oral tradition, remain the applicable legal principles. This provides in practice a temporal limitation for the application of NAGPRA to a few hundred years before the date of contact with Europeans, while older remains will continue to be the purview of scientists and the perceived value of such remains will be for global history rather than for those who view themselves as descendants.[153]

Canada has no federal legislation, but the province of Alberta has enacted legislation that allows a First Nation to apply for the repatriation of a sacred ceremonial object that is 'vital to the practice of their sacred ceremonial traditions' from the Royal Alberta Museum or the Glenbow-Alberta Institute; the minister must agree to the repatriation unless 'repatriation would not be appropriate'.[154] Repatriation efforts in Canada have tended to focus on negotiations and agreements between First Nations and institutions rather than on broader legislative and legal mandates.[155]

Australia enacted the Aboriginal and Torres Strait Islander Heritage Protection Act in 1984. Its purpose is similar to the first aspect of NAGPRA in that it requires the repatriation of newly discovered human remains to the Aboriginal community.[156] The minister may also make a declaration to preserve or protect a specified object or an area from injury or desecration. For an area to be protected under a declaration it must be a significant Aboriginal area and it must be under threat of injury or desecration.[157] An object must be 'a significant Aboriginal object or the class of objects is a class of significant Aboriginal objects'.[158] A declaration must include provisions for the protection and preservation of the area or the object from injury or desecration.[159] A declaration with respect to an area can apply to burials, while a declaration with respect to an object can include human remains and burial objects, apparently regardless of who the current owner or possessor is, in which case human remains or an object may be transferred to Aboriginals (s 12(4)(a)). The minister needs to take into consideration the effect of a declaration on the 'proprietary or pecuniary interests of persons'.[160] Newly discovered human remains must be transferred to Aboriginals (s 21). A specific section of the Act

[153] D Gareth Jones and Robyn J Harris, 'Archaeological Human Remains: Scientific, Cultural and Ethical Considerations' (1998) 39 Current Anthropology 253, 254.

[154] First Nations Sacred Ceremonial Objects Repatriation Act, RSA 2000, c F-14 (1)(e), (2).

[155] For example, see Catherine Bell, 'Repatriation of Cultural Material to First Nations in Canada: Legal and Ethical Justifications' in James AR Nafziger and Ann M Nicgorski (eds), *Cultural Heritage Issues: The Legacy of Conquest, Colonization, and Commerce* (Martinus Nijhoff Publishers 2009) 81.

[156] Aboriginal and Torres Strait Islander Heritage Protection Act 1984 (Cth), ss 20 and 21 <www.legislation.gov.au/Details/C2005C00228> accessed 10 May 2021.

[157] ibid, s 10. The minister may also make an emergency declaration for an area that 'is under serious and immediate threat of injury or desecration'. ibid, s 9. Significance of both areas and objects is determined in 'accordance with Aboriginal tradition'. ibid, s 4.

[158] ibid, s 12.

[159] ibid, s 11 (areas), s 12 (objects).

[160] ibid, s 12(1)(c).

that applies to Victoria is more expansive. In addition to similar provisions that apply to newly discovered remains, the minister is empowered to negotiate with a university, museum, or other institution for the return of human remains to the Aboriginal community.[161]

An issue not addressed by these legislative efforts is the ownership and control of the intellectual property and other materials, such as scientific data, archival materials, and photographs, produced through the study of the human remains and burial, sacred, and cultural objects located in museum and other institutional collections. Honor Keeler points out that the World Intellectual Property Organization has acknowledged that Indigenous traditional knowledge, genetic resources, and traditional cultural expressions are 'economic and cultural assets of Indigenous and local communities and their countries'.[162] The products of research undertaken without free and informed consent of the relevant descendant or cultural community should be subject to return to these groups or used only with their permission.

5.3.3.2 International Repatriation of Human Remains

Indigenous groups located within both settler States and formerly colonized States have sought repatriation of human remains that are housed in the museums and institutions of the former colonial powers, but such efforts have met with mixed results. There is no binding international instrument that deals with the question of international repatriation of human remains and Indigenous sacred and cultural objects. The closest such instrument is the UN Declaration on the Rights of Indigenous Peoples, which states, in Article 12, that: 'Indigenous peoples have the right to ... repatriation of their human remains [and] States shall seek to enable the access and/or repatriation of ceremonial objects and human remains in their possession through fair, transparent and effective mechanisms developed in conjunction with Indigenous peoples concerned.'[163] Other provisions of the Declaration include as violations the display of Indigenous remains and cultural objects without proper free, prior, and informed consent from Indigenous peoples.

[161] ibid, s 21X.

[162] Keeler, 'Indigenous International Repatriation' (n 134) 750. The Intellectual Property Issues in Cultural Heritage (IPinCH) project, based at Simon Fraser University in British Columbia, studied the relationship among material culture, traditional cultural knowledge, and heritage research <www.sfu.ca/ipinch/> accessed 10 May 2021. For discussion of intellectual property rights in the context of repatriation of Indigenous remains and cultural objects, see Mathilde Pavis and Andrea Wallace, 'Response to the 2018 Sarr-Savoy Report' (2019) 10 Journal of Intellectual Property Information Technology and Electronic Commerce 115.

[163] Although the United States, New Zealand, Australia, and Canada originally voted against the Declaration, each country has subsequently changed position. Keeler, 'Indigenous International Repatriation' (n 134) 708. The Declaration is non-binding and applies to both intra-state and international repatriations. Wiessner suggests that it has reached the status of customary international law. Wiessner, 'The Cultural Rights of Indigenous Peoples' (n 96) 130.

Consent is also required for the use of such remains and cultural objects in scientific research and to produce other materials.[164]

The international repatriation movement suffers from several significant obstacles. First is the lack of a legally enforceable international instrument, which leaves consideration of repatriation to voluntary negotiations. Another is the difficulty of tracing the provenances and proveniences, and therefore ancestral and cultural affiliations, of human remains that were collected over several hundred years and were exchanged among museums, often with a loss of identifying information.[165] Third, particularly British and French museums are, in general, prohibited from removing any items, including human remains, from their collections.[166] The changes in legislation that have been achieved only permit deaccessioning from museum collections, rather than requiring repatriation. Repatriation is subject to additional negotiations and agreements that have so far yielded modest results.

Australia and New Zealand have been particularly active in attempting to repatriate Indigenous human remains from UK museums. The Working Group on Human Remains, chaired by Norman Palmer, was established in 2001, following the 2000 Prime Ministerial Joint Statement on Aboriginal Remains between Australia and the United Kingdom.[167] The Working Group Report noted that about half of the 61,000 human remains dated between 1500 and 1947 and held in UK institutions originated outside of the United Kingdom. While some institutions were willing to return human remains that had been requested, others, such as the British Museum, asserted that they were not able to do so under legislative provisions prohibiting removal of items from collections. This led to amendment of the Human Tissue Act in 2004 to allow the deaccessioning of human remains from nine national museums so long as the remains are those of a person who died less than 1,000 years before enactment.[168]

The 2005 Guidance for the Care of Human Remains in Museums assists museums to establish best practices for the care and repatriation of human remains

[164] Article 15; Keeler, 'Indigenous International Repatriation' (n 134) 777–78.

[165] Keeler, 'Indigenous International Repatriation' (n 134) 740–45.

[166] See Marie Cornu and Marc-André Renold, 'New Developments in the Restitution of Cultural Property: Alternative Means of Dispute Resolution' (2010) 17 IJCP 1, 8–9. This restriction applies to only some UK museums but does apply to the British Museum. In addition, UK museum collections and deaccessioning policies are subject to more general restrictions, such as those imposed by a donor, by general charities and corporations law, and by a museum board's fiduciary obligations. Arts Council England, 'Restitution and Repatriation: A Practical Guide for Museums in England' (2022) 28–30. Voluntary restitutions pursuant to ethical guidelines are discussed further in chapter 6.

[167] Report of the Working Group on Human Remains <https://plone.unige.ch/art-adr/cases-affaires/17-tasmanian-human-remains-2013-tasmanian-aboriginal-centre-and-natural-history-museum-london/working-group-on-human-remains-report-14-november-2003> accessed 10 May 2021.

[168] Human Tissue Act 2004 c 30, s 47. Similarly, it required an act of Parliament to allow deaccessioning of artworks stolen during the Holocaust so that they could be returned to the descendants and heirs of Nazi victims. Holocaust (Return of Cultural Objects) (formerly known as Holocaust (Stolen Art) Restitution) Act 2009, ch 16 <www.legislation.gov.uk/ukpga/2009/16/pdfs/ukpga_20090016_en.pdf> accessed 10 May 2021. This Act was set to expire after ten years, but that time period was subsequently extended for an additional ten years.

rooted in an ethical framework and in light of the 1998 Human Rights Act. This guidance, while not legally binding, bears some similarities to the provisions of NAGPRA. Priority for repatriation is given to genealogical descendants. If the claimant is a cultural community, the community is expected to establish 'continuity of belief, customs or language' and a 'clear demonstration of a continuity of association between the claimant and the remains will be of great importance in dealing with any claim'.[169] Similar to the *Bonnichsen* decision, the Guidance sets a presumption that claims will be for remains between 100 and 300 years old and claims for remains more than 500 years in age 'are unlikely to be considered'.[170] The justification is that this time period corresponds to the period of UK colonial expansion but also that it is unlikely that a close genealogical link can be made between living people and older remains and that 'it is very difficult to demonstrate clear genealogical, cultural or ethnic continuity far into the past'.[171] Despite these limitations, UK museums have repatriated human remains to tribal and other Indigenous groups in the United States, Australia, and New Zealand.[172]

Between 1904 and 1908, Germany carried out a genocide against the Indigenous Herero and Nama people of Namibia. At the same time, it sent skulls back to Germany for eugenics research. In response to requests made in 2011 for repatriation of Namibian human remains from the Charité Hospital in Berlin, in 2013, the German Museums Association published 'Recommendations for the Care of Human Remains in Museums and Collections' with a new guidance published in 2021.[173] Human remains were repatriated from German institutions between 2011

[169] Department of Culture, Media and Sport, 'Guidance for the Care of Human Remains in Museums' (2005) 26–27 <www.gov.uk/government/publications/guidance-for-the-care-of-human-remains-in-museums> accessed 20 July 2021.

[170] ibid, 27.

[171] ibid.

[172] These repatriations include seventeen Tasmanian aboriginal remains that were held at the Natural History Museum returned through a mediation process (after initial litigation in Tasmania to prevent the further study of the remains). Norman Palmer, *Art, Adventure and Advocacy: Contracts, Claims and Controversies in the World of Cultural Property* (Institute of Art and Law 2015) 60–61 (hereafter Palmer, *Art, Adventure and Advocacy*). The Natural History Museum returned remains of thirty-seven Indigenous Australians in 2019, as well as twenty-two remains of Torres Strait Islanders, also in 2019. Madeleine Keck, 'London's Natural History Museum Returns Remains of Indigenous Australians after 100 Years' (*Global Citizen*, 29 March 2019) <www.globalcitizen.org/en/content/museum-return-aboriginal-remains-to-australia/?template=next> accessed 20 July 2021; Natural History Museum returns Human Remains to Torres Strait Islands <www.returningheritage.com/natural-history-museum-returns-human-remains-to-torres-strait-islands> accessed 20 July 2021.

[173] Deutscher Museumsbund e.V. 'Recommendations for the Care of Human Remains in Museums and Collections' (2013) <www.museumsbund.de/publikationen/recommendations-for-the-care-of-human-remains/> accessed 10 May 2021; Deutscher Museumsbund, *Guidelines: Care of Human Remains in Museums and Collections* (Deutscher Museumsbund 2021) (with discussion of Australian Aboriginal and Torres Strait Islander People, the Native Hawaiian organization Hui Malama I Na Kupuna O Hawai'i Nei, and Namibian remains); Larisa Förster and Sarah Fründt, 'Editorial' in Larisa Förster and Sarah Fründt (eds), *Human Remains in Museums and Collections. A Critical Engagement with the 'Recommendations for the Care of Human Remains and Collections' of the German Museums Association* (21 Historisches Forum 2017) 3. Guidelines issued in 2003, the 'Recommendations for the care of specimens made from human tissue in collections, museums and public spaces', addressed

and 2014 to Namibia, Australia, New Zealand, and Paraguay and from Austria to South Africa in 2012.[174] In 2018, Germany returned an additional twenty-five remains to Namibia and subsequently returned Indigenous human remains to Hawaii.[175]

Similar to the law with respect to UK national museums but broader in scope, the French *Code du patrimoine* states that the collections of public museums are inalienable.[176] Therefore, human remains cannot be removed from these collections. Nonetheless, the French Parliament adopted specific legislation in two circumstances to allow repatriation of human remains. One instance involved the remains of Sarah Baartman, who was brought from South Africa to London in 1810 and put on public display. After her death, her remains were brought to the French National Museum of Natural History where a plaster cast was made, and parts of her remains were preserved. These were on display until 1974. In 1994, Nelson Mandela asked for the remains to be returned. Finally, in 2002 legislation was adopted that applied only to her remains, removing them from the collection of the National Museum of Natural History and ordering their return to South Africa.[177]

A second case involved preserved tattooed heads (*mokomokai*), which have great cultural and religious significance for the Maori people of New Zealand. The tattooing of bodies and faces is a long cultural tradition among the Maori, especially warriors. The heads with their tattooed flesh of distinguished warriors and wise leaders were often preserved after death and were 'regarded with great

collections holding remains from the Nazi era and did not confront 'racist research in colonial times'. ibid, 4. The 2021 guidelines are discussed in chapter 6, section 6.4.

[174] ibid.

[175] BBC, 'Germany returns skulls of Namibian genocide victims' (*BBC News*, 29 August 2018) <www.bbc.com/news/world-africa-45342586> accessed 20 July 2021. In 2021, Germany acknowledged the genocide and agreed to pay $1 billion in aid for development projects in Namibia to be paid over thirty years. However, hundreds of additional human remains are still in Germany. Franziska Boehme, 'Germany acknowledged colonial atrocities in Namibia as genocide. Victims' groups want more' (*Washington Post*, 9 June 2021) <www.washingtonpost.com/politics/2021/06/09/germany-acknowledged-colonial-atrocities-namibia-genocide-victims-groups-want-more/> accessed 20 July 2021. Bremen's Übersee Museum returned eight Indigenous human skulls to Hawaii while museums in Berlin, Jena, and Göttingen returned additional human remains. 'Germany: Bremen museum returns human skulls to Hawaii' (*DW*, 8 February 2022) <www.dw.com/en/germany-bremen-museum-returns-human-skulls-to-hawaii/a-60706108> accessed 15 September 2022.

[176] Article L 451–55. While objects that were donated as a gift or bequest cannot be deaccessioned for any reason, Article L 451–57, other objects may be deaccessioned with the authorization of the Commission scientifique nationale des collections. Mathilde Roellinger, 'The French Experience of Repatriation of Human Remains' in Ruth Redmond-Cooper (ed), *Heritage, Ancestry and Law: Principles, Policies and Practices in dealing with Historical Human Remains* (Institute of Art and Law 2015) 151, 153 (hereafter Roellinger, 'The French Experience').

[177] France Law No 2002-323 of 6 March 2002, on the restitution by France of the remains of Saartje Baartman to South Africa, Official Journal of 7 March 2002. See Caroline Renold, Alessandro Chechi, Marc-André Renold, 'Case Sarah Baartman – France and South Africa' (*ArThemis* January 2013) <https://plone.unige.ch/art-adr/cases-affaires/sarah-baartman-2013-france-and-south-africa> accessed 10 May 2021; Roellinger, 'The French Experience' (n 176) 154.

veneration and respect',[178] while the heads of enemy chiefs were preserved as war memorials. Beginning as early as 1770, a trade in the heads of enemy chiefs developed with British traders. About 200 *mokomokai* are known to have been traded between 1770 and 1831, when the trade was outlawed, although it continued for much longer. These heads were then sold on to collectors and museums in other countries, including France, Germany, and the United States.[179] The trade contributed to the demise of the cultural practice of tattooing as individuals with desirable tattoos might be killed specifically for the purpose of selling their heads to traders.

In 2002, the Museum of New Zealand Te Papa Tongarewa initiated a programme of achieving the return of Maori heads from foreign collections.[180] The Museum of the City of Rouen had one Maori head, which was on display until 1974. The City voted to repatriate the head in 2007, based on the principle of dignity. However, the national Minister of Culture determined that the City did not have authority to remove an item from the Museum's collection in violation of the inalienability provisions of the *Code du Patrimoine*. The Court of Appeal of Douai gave precedence to the nonalienability rule of museum collections over rules protecting human remains and their dignity, considering 'human remains firstly to be cultural goods before being regarded as *human* remains'.[181] In 2010, the French legislature adopted a provision declaring that all Maori human remains were no longer part of the public collection of French museums.[182] The head from the Rouen Museum, along with nineteen others, was returned to the New Zealand ambassador in a ceremony at the Quai Branly Museum in Paris.[183] Numerous other Maori heads and other human remains have been returned to the Te Papa Tongarewa Museum of New Zealand, which then returns the remains to the appropriate tribe after studies have been conducted to determine affiliation.[184] Although the legislation

178 Ngahuia Te Awekotuku, 'More than Skin Deep: Ta Moko Today' in Elazar Barkan and Ronald Bush (eds), *Claiming the Stones, Naming the Bones: Cultural Property and the Negotiation of National and Ethnic Identity* (Getty Publications 2002) 243–54, 245 (quoting T Steel, 'Maori Preserved Heads of New Zealand' (1891) 8 Victorian Naturalist 105).

179 Brigit Katz, 'Preserved Maori Head Returns to New Zealand' Smithsonian Magazine (16 July 2018) <www.smithsonianmag.com/smart-news/german-museum-returns-preserved-maori-head-new-zealand-180969634/> accessed 10 May 2021.

180 Raphael Contel, Anne Laure Bandle, and Marc-André Renold, 'Tête Maori de Rouen' (*ArThemis*, March 2012) <https://plone.unige.ch/art-adr/cases-affaires/tete-maorie-de-rouen-2013-france-et-nouvelle-zelande> accessed 10 May 2021.

181 Roellinger, 'The French Experience' (n 176) 155.

182 Loi No 2010-501 of 18 May 2010 visant à autoriser la restitution par la France des têtes maories à la Nouvelle-Zélande et relative à la gestion des collections.

183 UNESCO, 'Maori Heads Return to New Zealand from France after 200 years' (3 April 2012) <www.unesco.org/new/en/member-states/single-view/news/maori_heads_return_to_new_zealand_from_france_after_200_yea/> accessed 10 May 2021.

184 'The repatriation of Maori and Moriori remains' <www.tepapa.govt.nz/about/repatriation/repatriation-maori-and-moriori-remains> accessed 10 May 2021. New Zealand has recovered Maori remains from Argentina, Australia, Canada, Denmark, England, France, Germany, Ireland, the Netherlands, Norway, Scotland, Switzerland, Sweden, the United States, and United Kingdom. Keeler, 'Indigenous International Repatriation' (n 134) 754; Palmer, *Art, Adventure and Advocacy* (n 172) 60. In 1988, the auction of a Maori head by Bonham's was prevented when a New Zealand court granted letters

that resolved the repatriation of the Maori remains was broader than that involving the remains of Sara Baartman, the French approach is problematic in comparison to the British approach. The French approach requires the enactment of specific legislation to allow the repatriation on an individual basis of each group of human remains.

The reluctance of French authorities to grant broadly to human remains the dignity and respect accorded to living humans under French law was echoed in the refusal to view Native American sacred objects as religious objects and therefore *extra commercium*. A Paris auction house held several auctions of dozens of Hopi and other Native American sacred and cultural items between 2013 and 2016. The Hopi tribe attempted to sue to stop the sales, but the French courts held that the tribe did not have standing. In a decision in which the universalistic nature of high art prevailed over the interests of the community, the courts also held that the objects were no longer 'sacred' but rather had become works of art so that French law prohibiting 'immoral' sales did not apply. The Hopis argued that the tribe as a whole was the owner of the sacred objects, but French law does not recognize this form of collective property. The plaintiffs also could not clearly establish that the objects were stolen; the auction house claimed they had been acquired in the 1930s and 1940s. Neither US domestic law (NAGPRA and the American Indian Religious Freedom Act[185]) nor international law (UNDRIP and the 1970 UNESCO Convention[186]) were considered to apply.[187] The US Congress enacted the Safeguard Tribal Objects of Patrimony Act in late 2022 to impose export restrictions on certain categories of Native American cultural items and thereby provide greater protection to Native American cultural objects in other countries. In particular, the act adopts methods, such as export controls, that are more likely to be recognized by foreign courts.[188]

of estate administration for the unknown deceased individual to the President of the New Zealand Maori Council. ibid, 61–62.

[185] 42 USC § 1996 (1978).

[186] UNESCO Convention on the Means of Prohibiting and Preventing the Illicit Import, Export and Transfer of Ownership of Cultural Property (adopted 14 November 1970, entered into force 24 April 1972) 823 UNTS 231 (1970 UNESCO Convention).

[187] Laetitia Nicolazzi, Alessandro Chechi, and Marc-André Renold, 'Case Hopi Masks—Hopi Tribe v. Néret-Minet and Estimations 7 Ventes aux Enchères' ArThemis (2015), https://plone.unige.ch/art-adr/cases-affaires/hopi-masks-2013-hopi-tribe-v-neret-minet-and-estimations-ventes-aux-encheres> accessed 10 May 2021; Marie Cornu, 'About Sacred Cultural Property: The Hopi Masks Case (2013) 20 IJCP 451; Angela R Riley and Kristen A Carpenter, 'Owning Red: A Theory of Indian (Cultural) Appropriation' (2016) 94 Texas Law Review 859, 901–03. The auction of one item, an Acoma shield, was averted in May 2016 when evidence was presented that the shield was stolen, and a US district court issued a warrant asking for recovery of the shield. Allison Meier 'US Judge Approves Warrant for Acoma Shield Listed for Sale by Paris Auction House' (*Hypoallergic*, 7 September 2016) <https://hyperallergic.com/321130/us-judge-approves-warrant-for-acoma-shield-listed-for-sale-by-paris-auction-house/> accessed 10 May 2021.

[188] Public Law No 117-258.

In comparison to Australia and New Zealand, the US and Canadian governments have taken a minimal role in supporting the claims of Native American tribes and First Nations for international repatriation. Nonetheless, there have been several cases of successful repatriations of cultural items. The Kelvingrove Museum in Glasgow returned a Ghost Dance Shirt to the Wounded Knee Survivors Association. The tribe argued that NAGPRA did not create new rights but rather reaffirmed the existing rights of a Native American tribe in the cultural items that belonged to the descendants and tribes of the victims of the Wounded Knee massacre, thus illustrating the reach of NAGPRA beyond its technical legal confines.[189] Several Crowfoot cultural items were returned to the Siksika Nation in Canada by the Royal Albert Memorial Museum and Art Gallery in Exeter (UK) in 2022.[190] Despite these successful repatriations, thousands of Indigenous human remains languish in institutional collections in Europe, particularly in the United Kingdom, France, and Germany, and some requests for repatriation of human remains have been denied.[191]

5.4 International and Regional Conventions and the Regulation of Trade in Cultural Objects

The growth of the international market in cultural objects following the Second World War led to the development of an international legal regime to restrain the market's more detrimental aspects, while encouraging international movement through means that do not endanger the integrity and context of cultural heritage. At the same time, with the end of colonialism, the new countries sought legal means to conserve at home what remained of their heritage, after so much had been lost to the colonial powers, while expecting that the new treaty regime emobided inj the 1970 UNESCO Convention would provide an avenue for recovering what had been lost. The newly independent States were disappointed in this treaty regime in that it failed to provide a remedy and means of restitution for cultural artefacts taken during nineteenth-century colonialism and neo-imperialism, what may be

[189] Sam Maddra, 'The Wounded Knee Ghost Dance Shirt' (1996) 8 Journal of Museum Ethnography 41, 55; Keeler (n 134) 764. For discussion of how NAGPRA affects the status of Native American human remains held in UK collections, see Myra J Giesen, 'Native American Human Remains in UK Collections: Implications of NAGPRA to consultation, repatriation, and policy development' in ME Lewis and M Clegg (eds), *Ninth Annual Conference of the British Association for Biological Anthropology and Osteoarchaeology* (Archaeopress 2009) 123.

[190] 'Native American Crowfoot Regalia Returns from Exeter to its Homelands' (*the American*, 25 May 2022) <www.theamerican.co.uk/pr/ne-Native-American-Regalia-Returned-From-Exeter-Museum-to-Siksika-Nation> accessed 11 September 2022.

[191] Javier Pes, 'It's Not Just Art That Indigenous People Are Fighting to Reclaim from Museums. They Want Their Ancestors' Remains Back, Too' (*Artnet news*, 29 November 2018) <https://news.artnet.com/market/its-not-just-art-that-indigenous-peoples-want-back-from-museums-they-want-their-ancestors-human-remains-too-1397737> accessed 10 May 2021.

termed historical appropriation.[192] This section turns now to regulation of the general art market through the international legal regime.

5.4.1 The 1970 UNESCO and 1995 UNIDROIT Conventions

The goal of the 1970 UNESCO Convention is to regulate the trade in a broad range of cultural objects through public international law, to encourage nations to protect their cultural heritage *in situ*, and to provide an international mechanism for recognition of different countries' export controls with respect to cultural objects. Article 1 of the 1970 UNESCO Convention defines cultural property as 'property which, on religious or secular grounds, is specifically designated by each State as being of importance for archaeology, prehistory, history, literature, art or science' and which belongs to one of eleven enumerated categories. The specific designation requirement has caused difficulties in effective implementation of the Convention and has been variously interpreted by different States Parties. At the same time, by allowing each State to specifically designate what it considers important, the Convention privileges the role of the State over the roles of both the international community and local communities and groups.

In considering whether listing of object types that are subject to export control satisfies the 'specific designation' requirement of Article 1, a Canadian court held that the categorization of cultural objects for the purpose of export control by a State Party constitutes designation.[193] The Bolivian Decree, which was at issue in the case, restricted the export of the category of textiles. The court held that the listing of export categories satisfied the designation requirement in light of the difficulty posed by a specific designation requirement, stating:

> [T]he appellant's submission that, to 'specifically designate' cultural property something more was required of Bolivia than what was specified in the Decree, is not tenable. It would not be possible for a nation to create an itemized list of every piece of property to be protected.... Textiles that are cultural property reveal valuable information regarding ethnic groups and their religious practices.[194]

This approach has not as yet been judicially evaluated in other destination or transit market States. A requirement of designation by category or type rather than documentation in an inventory or on a list is very effective for dealing with the

[192] Sarah Van Beurden, 'The Art of (Re)possession: Heritage and the Cultural Politics of Congo's Decolonization' (2015) 56 Journal of African History 143, 143–44. This subject will be considered in chapter 7, section 7.2.2. The specific application of the international treaty regime to the contemporary looting of archaeological sites is considered in chapter 4.

[193] *R v Yorke* [1998] 166 NSR (2d).

[194] ibid, 150.

problem of undocumented cultural objects. This method of satisfying the designation requirement has been adopted by several market States including Germany.[195]

To most ratifying States, the core provision of the Convention is Article 3, which makes illicit the import, export, and transfer of ownership of cultural objects contrary to the Convention's provisions and those provisions adopted by States pursuant to the Convention. According to Patrick O'Keefe, this means that States Parties shall not permit the import of objects whose export from another State Party was illegal.[196] In enacting domestic implementing legislation for Article 3, most market States have adopted reciprocal import restrictions making it illegal to import cultural objects that were exported from their country of origin (or discovery) in violation of an export control adopted under the Convention.[197] This means that such countries do not need to enact additional import restrictions or take any other action in crisis situations.

In contrast, Switzerland and the United States utilize a reactive approach, requiring that other States Parties enter into a supplemental bilateral agreement for their export controls to be recognized. Switzerland implements Article 3 and so its import restrictions apply to a broad range of cultural materials. The Swiss Federal Council also has the flexibility to respond to crisis situations without the need for a request from the affected State, by imposing import restrictions on an emergency basis under Article 9 of the Convention.[198] The United States imposes import restrictions under Article 9, which applies only to archaeological and ethnological objects.[199]

The Convention imposes obligations on both market States and States with rich cultural resources. These obligations represent the obverse of restraints on the

[195] Germany, Act on the Protection of Cultural Property (Cultural Property Protection Act—KGSG) 31 July 2016, BGBl I, 2016, 1914; Federal Government Commissioner for Culture and the Media, 'Key Aspects of the new Act on the Protection of Cultural Property in Germany' (September 2016), 7. <www.bundesregierung.de/Content/DE/_Anlagen/BKM/2016/2016-09-23-kulturgutschutz-informationen-englisch.pdf?__blob=publicationFile&v=2> accessed 10 May 2021. The US legislation explicitly removes the specific designation requirement but also uses a category approach, Convention on Cultural Property Implementation Act, 19 USC §§ 2601–2604 (hereafter CCPIA).

[196] Patrick J O'Keefe, *Protecting Cultural Objects: Before and After 1970* (Institute of Art and Law 2017) 135–38.

[197] For examples, see Canada, Cultural Property Export and Import Act, RSC 1985, c C-51, s 37(2); Germany, Act on the Protection of Cultural Property (Cultural Property Protection Act—KGSG) 31 July 2016, BGBl I, 2016, 1914. See also Robert Peters 'The Protection of Cultural Property: Recent Developments in Germany in the Context of New EU Law and the 1970 UNESCO Convention' (2016) 2 SAACLR 85, 96–97 (hereafter Peters 'The Protection of Cultural Property'); Patty Gerstenblith, 'Implementation of the 1970 UNESCO Convention by the United States and Other Market Nations' in Jane Anderson and Haidy Geismar (eds), *The Routledge Companion to Cultural Property* (Routledge 2017) 70.

[198] Federal Act on the International Transfer of Cultural Property (Cultural Property Transfer Act) (20 June 2003), Article 7. The United States can impose emergency import restrictions only after a State has requested a bilateral agreement. CCPIA § 2603.

[199] CCPIA §§ 2602–2603. However, the United States prohibits the import of cultural objects that were documented in the inventory of a 'museum or religious or secular public monument or similar institution' and stolen after the date when both the United States and the other country had ratified the convention. ibid, § 2607.

market in illegally obtained cultural objects—that countries rich in these resources have an obligation to protect their own sites and museums, to police their borders, and to educate their people about the values in conserving their cultural heritage. These obligations more specifically include establishing a government agency or service that will assist in the preparation of laws for the regulation of cultural objects, establish a national inventory of protected property, promote scientific and technical institutions and museums, and supervise archaeological excavations (Article 5); establishing a licensing system for the export of cultural objects (Article 6), and requiring dealers to maintain information on the origin, supplier, description, and price of items sold (Article 10).[200]

In 1995, the UNIDROIT Convention on Stolen or Illegally Exported Cultural Objects was finalized.[201] While the 1970 UNESCO Convention as a public international law instrument operates on a State-to-State basis, the UNIDROIT Convention functions within a private law framework. The UNIDROIT Convention provides that stolen cultural objects should, in most circumstances, be returned to the original owner and illegally exported objects to the country of origin. It was devised to appeal more to the civil law nations by requiring that fair and reasonable compensation be paid to a good faith possessor.[202]

To be eligible for compensation, the possessor must have 'neither [known] nor ought reasonably to have known that the object was stolen and can prove that it exercised due diligence when acquiring the object'.[203] In evaluating the possessor's due diligence and circumstances of the acquisition, the Convention lists a range of factors to consider, including the price, the character of the parties involved in the transaction, whether the possessor consulted a register of stolen objects, other available documentation, and any other steps that a reasonable person would have taken.[204] Particularly in the realm of antiquities, additional factors should be taken as indicating likelihood of theft or illegal export, including origin in areas known to have been looted on a massive scale, such as Iraq, Syria, Libya, Yemen, and

[200] The obligation to maintain records of art market transactions is being imposed in the European Union, the United Kingdom, and the United States by subjecting such transactions to anti-money laundering regulations. For example Directive (EU) 2018/843, Article 1(1)(c) (amending Art 2(1)(3) of Directive (EU) 2015/849 to subject persons trading in or storing in free ports artworks worth more than €10,000 to anti-money laundering regulations).

[201] UNIDROIT Convention on Stolen or Illegally Exported Cultural Property (adopted 24 June 1995, entered into force 1 July 1998) 34 ILM 1322 (hereafter 1995 UNIDROIT Convention). See Lyndel V Prott, Commentary on the UNIDROIT Convention (2nd edn, Institute of Art and Law 2021).

[202] Article 4(1). Article 3(2) of the Convention adopting a version of State ownership is discussed in chapter 4, section 4.3.2.4.

[203] Article 4(1). Article 6 has parallel provisions for the possessor of an illegally exported object. Manlio Frigo points out that the UNIDROIT Convention reversed the burden of proof so that the current possessor needs to establish due diligence, rather than engaging in a presumption of good faith, and entitles the good faith possessor only to monetary compensation rather than the right to retain the object. Manlio Frigo, 'Codes of Ethics' in Francesco Francioni and Ana Filipa Vrdoljak (eds), *The Oxford Handbook of International Cultural Heritage Law* (OUP 2020) 787, 804–05. These changes should facilitate return or restitution.

[204] Article 4(4).

Afghanistan; the presence of soil, mud, or straw on the object; and certain classes of antiquities that are known to have been the subject of large-scale looting, such as cuneiform tablets, cylinder seals, and coins.[205]

5.4.2 European Union Import and Export Restrictions

Since 1992 the European Union has regulated the export of cultural goods by requiring an export licence from the competent Member State.[206] The Council Directive on the Return of Cultural Objects Unlawfully Removed from the Territory of a Member State requires EU Member States to return cultural objects that have been unlawfully removed from another Member State.[207] However, this left unregulated the import of cultural objects from non-EU Member States into the European Union with the exception of cultural goods imported from Iraq[208] or Syria.[209]

In 2019, the European Union adopted the Regulation on the Import of Cultural Goods to deal with the problem of trafficking of cultural materials imported into the European Union from non-EU Member States.[210] In Articles 3–5, the Regulation sets out the requirements, depending on the category of cultural goods, for an importer to obtain an import licence from the EU State through which the cultural goods are introduced into the European Union or to make an importer

[205] See chapter 4, section 4.2.1.

[206] Council Regulation (EC) 116/2009 of 18 December 2008 on the export of cultural goods [2009] OJ L39/1 (Reg 116/2009) Article 2(2). The Council Regulation was originally adopted in 1992 as Council Regulation (EEC) 3911/92 of 9 December 1992 on the export of cultural goods and was restated in 2008. A competent Member State is defined as either the State 'in whose territory the cultural object in question was lawfully and definitively located on 1 January 1993' or 'in whose territory it is located following either lawful and definitive dispatch from another Member State, or importation from a third country, or re-importation from a third country after lawful dispatch from a Member State to that country'.

[207] Council Directive 93/7/EEC of March 1993 was recast as Directive 2014/60/EU with several substantial modifications: elimination of the annex with age or financial thresholds, thereby allowing each Member State to define its national cultural property; extension of the time limit to three years in which Member States must substantiate their claim for return; improving administrative cooperation among the Member States by using the Internal Market Information System; setting minimal standards for the issuance of an EU export licence; and shifting of the burden of proof so that a possessor must demonstrate due diligence in order to receive compensation as a good faith purchaser when relinquishing a cultural object. The Directive's due diligence provisions correspond to those in the 1995 UNIDROIT Convention. Peters, 'The Protection of Cultural Property' (n 197) 94–95.

[208] Council Regulation (EC) 1210/2003 of 7 July 2003 concerning certain specific restrictions on economic and financial relations with Iraq and repealing Regulation [2003] OJ L169/6.

[209] Council Regulation (EU) 1332/2013 of 13 December 2013 concerning restrictive measures in view of the situation in Syria and amending Regulation (EU) 36/2012 concerning restrictive measures in view of the situation in Syria [2013] OJ L335/3.

[210] Regulation (EU) 2019/880 of the European Parliament and of the Council of 17 April 2019 on the introduction and the import of cultural goods [2019] OJ L151/1 (EU Import Regulation). For more detailed discussion of the Regulation, see Robert Peters, 'New Perspectives Beyond State Sovereignty and Territoriality in the Protection of Cultural Heritage' in Anne-Marie Carstens and Elizabeth Varner (eds), *Intersections in International Cultural Heritage Law* (OUP 2020) 364.

statement. Article 3 sets out the general principle that the import of cultural goods, which were removed from the territory of the country where they were created or discovered in breach of the laws and regulations of that country, is prohibited. An import licence is required for the types of cultural goods listed in Annex B and includes (1) products of archaeological excavations and discoveries on land and underwater (including regular and clandestine discoveries) and (2) elements of artistic or historical monuments or archaeological sites that have been dismembered (Art 4). To fall under this requirement, the objects must be at least 250 years old, but there is no minimum financial threshold.[211] All other categories of cultural objects, defined as cultural objects that are more than 200 years old and with a value above the minimum financial threshold of €18,000 per item (Annex, Part C) do not require an import licence but, rather, an importer statement (Art 5).

When applying for an import licence, the importer must provide evidence that the goods have been exported from their country of creation or discovery in accordance with the laws and regulations of that country or that the country does not have such laws or regulations (Art 4(4)). However, as an alternative, the importer may present evidence that the goods have been legally exported from an intermediary country where they have been located for more than five years and for purposes other than temporary use, transit, re-export, or transshipment. This exception allows legal export from an intermediary country which, like the United States, may not have export restrictions to be a proxy for legal export from the country of origin or discovery. This exception allows cultural objects to be laundered through such intermediaries so that they can be imported legally into the EU. However, this exception applies only if the country of creation or discovery cannot be reliably determined or if the cultural goods were exported from the country of creation or discovery before 1972 (Art 4(4)). The first basis for the exception may provide a significant loophole as it is often difficult to determine the country of modern discovery as ancient cultures and modern territorial boundaries often do not coincide. This basis will also encourage cultivation of ignorance as it will be easier to import a cultural object if the country of creation or discovery is not known. The licence or importer statement is also waived if the cultural goods are being imported for the purpose of safekeeping 'with the intent to return those goods, when the situation so allows' (Art 3(4)(b)). This last provision allows for the import of cultural goods under the First Protocol of the Hague Convention without need for an export licence from the country of origin.[212]

The exit of the United Kingdom from the European Union creates challenges in applying the EU Regulation because of the differential treatment of Northern

[211] The age requirement provision seems to be modelled on the US implementation of the 1970 UNESCO Convention that requires archaeological materials to be at least 250 years old, 19 USC § 2601(2)(C)(i)(II), although this requirement is not a part of the Convention itself.

[212] See section 5.2.2.3.

Ireland. The United Kingdom revoked the EU Regulation for Great Britain but left it in place in Northern Ireland.[213] However, cultural goods can enter Great Britain without the need to comply with the Regulation's requirements and then enter Northern Ireland, again without compliance. From Northern Ireland, cultural goods can then move on to the EU, particularly through the Republic of Ireland, as there are no customs checks, tariffs, or other paperwork for goods moving between Northern Ireland and the Republic of Ireland.[214] While additional legislation to control imports is unlikely, it may be equally challenging to resolve this inconsistency and method for evading the EU Regulation through additional enforcement measures taken in Great Britain.[215]

5.4.3 UN Security Council Resolutions

The patchwork quilt of ratifications and implementation of the 1970 UNESCO Convention and of the 1995 UNIDROIT Convention and the limited provisions of the 1954 Hague Convention regime translate into an international treaty regime that is weak in controlling the movement of illegally obtained cultural objects and often still weaker for the purpose of achieving restitution of illegally removed cultural objects even within for cultural objects illegally removed within the effective time period of these international agreements. The international community determined that the existing legal regime is insufficient to meet recent emergency threats to cultural heritage and, in particular, the threat to international security through trafficking in movable heritage. As a result, on two occasions the United Nations Security Council took the unprecedented step of adopting resolutions requiring its Member States to restrict the import of cultural objects outside of the existing treaty regime and bypassing the ratification and implementation process of international treaties.

The first United Nations Security Council Resolution to address specifically the status of cultural objects was Resolution 1483 adopted on 22 May 2003 in the wake of the looting of the Iraq Museum in Baghdad and of other cultural sites and institutions during the United States-led invasion of Iraq.[216] The Resolution applied to

[213] Fionnuala Rogers, 'Following the UK's Repeal of the EU Import Regulation in Great Britain, will Northern Ireland become a gateway to Europe for illicit cultural property?' Policy Brief No 9 The Antiquities Coalition 4-5 <https://thinktank.theantiquitiescoalition.org/following-the-uks-repeal-of-the-eu-import-regulation-in-great-britain-will-northern-ireland-become-a-gateway-to-europe-for-illicit-cultural-property-recommendations-for-the-uk-to-mitigate/> accessed 4 March 2022 (hereafter Rogers, 'Following the UK's Repeal').

[214] Northern Ireland Protocol <www.gov.uk/government/publications/the-northern-ireland-protocol> accessed 4 March 2022.

[215] Rogers, 'Following the UK's Repeal' (n 213) 7–10.

[216] UNSC Res 1483 (22 May 2003) UN Doc S/RES/1483 para 7. National and regional provisions adopted pursuant to this Resolution include: Emergency Protection for Iraqi Cultural Antiquities Act of 2004, Pub L No 108-429, 118 Stat 2434, §§ 3001–3003 (United States); Iraq (United Nations Sanctions) Order 2003, SI 2003/1519, s 8 <www.legislation.gov.uk/uksi/2003/1519/contents/made> accessed 10

objects reasonably suspected of being illegally removed after 1990, not just those that were established to have been removed illegally. The types of objects to which the trade restrictions applied track the definition of cultural property in Article 1 of the 1970 UNESCO Convention and include: 'cultural property and other items of archaeological, historical, cultural, rare scientific, and religious importance'.[217] This was the first time that States were required to prohibit import and trade in cultural objects for the purpose of return, not as a matter of their specific consent to be bound to a treaty provision but through membership of the United Nations.

The Security Council took a similar approach in 2015 with respect to Syria after indications that the Islamic State of Iraq and the Levant had orchestrated large-scale looting of sites and thefts from institutions to provide a stream of income to fund its terrorist activities and armed conflict, although there is considerable debate as to the extent of funding ISIL realized from these activities. Upon recommendation of the ISIL (Da'esh) and Al- Qaida Sanctions Committee and Monitoring Team,[218] the Security Council adopted Resolution 2199, reaffirming the commitment of Resolution 1483 to prevent trade in cultural materials illegally removed from Iraq after August 1990 and calling for new prohibitions on trade in cultural materials illegally removed from Syria after March 2011.[219] This Security Council Resolution

May 2021 (United Kingdom); Council Regulation (EC) 1210/2003 of 7 July 2003 concerning certain specific restrictions on economic and financial relations with Iraq and repealing Regulation (EC) 2465/96 [2003] OJ L169/6, Article 3 <http://eur-lex.europa.eu/legal-content/EN/TXT/PDF/?uri=CELEX:32003R1210&rid=1> accessed 10 May 2021 (European Union); Ordonnance instituant des mesures économiques envers la République d'Irak RS 946.206, art 1a, modified 28 May 2003 <www.admin.ch/opc/fr/classified-compilation/19900200/index.html#a1a> accessed 10 May 2021 (Switzerland).

[217] In order to comply with Security Council Resolutions 1483 and 2199 (see n 219 below), the import restrictions implemented for Iraq and Syria by the United States, although applied under Article 9 of the 1970 UNESCO Convention, redefined 'archaeological and ethnological material' as the broader term of 'cultural property'. The import restrictions adopted by the United States for Iraq and Syria therefore apply to all cultural property as defined by Article 1 of the 1970 UNESCO Convention. Pub L No 108-429, 118 Stat 2434, § 3002(b) (Iraq); Pub L 114-151, 130 Stat 369, § 3(d)(2) (Syria). This represented a significant shift in the scope of import restrictions imposed by the United States for undocumented cultural objects.

[218] The Al-Qaida and Taliban Sanctions Committee was originally established in 1999, pursuant to Security Council Resolution 1267. The 1267 Sanctions Regime, monitored by the ISIL (Da'esh), Al-Qaida and Taliban Monitoring Team, is the only sanctions regime that applies to transnational non-State actors who constitute a global, regional, or local threat or an evolving and asymmetric threat using unconventional methods and weapons.

[219] UNSC Res 2199 (12 February 2015) UN Doc S/RES/2199, paras 15–17. <unscr.com/en/resolutions/doc/2199> accessed 1 November 2017 (hereafter UNSC Res 2199). The Resolution has been implemented by the European Union, Council Regulation (EU) 1332/2013 of 13 December 2013 amending Regulation (EU) 36/2012 concerning restrictive measures in view of the situation in Syria, Article (4) adding Article 11c, Annex XI; the United Kingdom as a criminal provision, The Export Control (Syria Sanctions (Amendment)) Order 2014, SI 2014/1896, para 2 (inserting Article 12A) <www.legislation.gov.uk/uksi/2014/1896/made> accessed 10 May 2021; Switzerland, *Verordnung über Massnahmen gegenüber Syrien* (Ordinance on Sanctions against Syria) revised on 17 December 2014, Article 9A, para 1 <www.admin.ch/opc/de/official-compilation/2015/45.pdf> accessed 10 May 2021; and United States, Protect and Preserve International Cultural Property Act, Pub L 114-151, 130 Stat 369 (2016).

marked a significant change in how the international community perceives theft and looting of movable cultural objects based on the recognition that such objects could be sold onto the international market to provide funding for armed conflict and terrorist activity. Regardless of whether Article 4 and the Protocols of the Hague Convention applied, Resolutions 1483 and 2199 cured a defect in the Hague Convention in that the initial illegality of the taking of cultural objects now attached to and followed those objects onto the market and into States not involved in the conflict.

In March 2017, the UN Security Council adopted Resolution 2347, which focuses almost exclusively on the theft, looting, and movement of cultural objects from Syria and Iraq.[220] As with UNSC Resolution 2199, this Resolution was largely motivated by data indicating that the theft, looting, and sale onto the international market of cultural objects were sources of income to ISIL and that cultural objects had become intertwined with trafficking networks and other forms of cross-border movement of contraband goods, such as drugs and weapons.[221] The Resolution is largely aspirational but also expresses a general concern with terrorism and its financing through international networks and the specific role in terrorism finance of the looting of archaeological sites and thefts from cultural institutions, whether directly or indirectly orchestrated by terrorist groups.

These Security Council Resolutions represent an evolution towards an approach based on the securitization of cultural heritage, particularly movable heritage. Yet they are insufficient. They are reactive in nature and are targeted to specific countries.[222] Therefore, like the domestic legislation of some market countries (such as that of the United States in implementing the 1970 UNESCO Convention), the Resolutions do not prepare us to deal with the *next* crisis—especially if the next crisis does not share a link with funding of armed conflict and international terrorism or if the situation has not captured the world's attention through the media. When taken together, the three Resolutions constitute a striking acknowledgement by the international community that the existing treaty regime is inadequate to prevent trade in cultural objects illegally removed from areas of armed conflict.

This inadequacy is the result of a failure to impose strict requirements for ratification and implementation of treaties and to link sufficiently the armed conflict treaties (the 1954 Hague Convention and Protocols) with those treaties that aim to

[220] UNSC Res 2347 (24 March 2017) UN Doc S/RES/2347.

[221] See chapter 4, section 4.2.5. For a discussion of the relationship between organized transnational crime and trafficking of cultural objects, see Janet Blake, 'Trafficking in Cultural Property: Where Cultural Heritage Law and the International Fight against Organized Crime Coincide' in Anne-Marie Carstens and Elizabeth Varner (eds), Intersections in Cultural Heritage Law (Routledge 2020) 157, 165–70. The Council of Europe Convention on Offences relating to Cultural Property (adopted 19 May 2017) (2017) CETS 22 (Nicosia Convention) establishes criminal offences and other measures related to cultural property. Blake, ibid, 175–80.

[222] For discussion of these failures, see Neil Brodie, 'Syria and its Regional Neighbors: A Case of Cultural Property Protection Policy Failure?' (2015) 22 IJCP 317.

regulate the international market. As they are limited to circumstances of armed conflict and occupation, Article 4(3) of the Convention and the First Protocol do not make trafficking in an object removed in violation of these provisions illegal. The treaties that regulate the market should explicitly create an intersection among these treaty regimes[223] whereby an object illegally removed during armed conflict or occupation is illegal on the international market and in transit and destination countries. In this way, the initial illegality would attach to and remain with the object, rather than having the object enter into a different legal regime as it travels from country to country. It would also create an obligation of interdiction and restitution.

This situation also constitutes a failure as, while the link to terrorism finance was real enough in Syria and Iraq, Resolution 2347 indicates that the world is now less concerned with preserving cultural heritage for its own sake, for the sake of the local communities that produced the heritage or that live among the heritage, and broadly throughout the world (despite the Resolution's hortatory statements in that regard). Rather, the world community is moved to action to compensate for a weak treaty regime only when other criminal activity and funding of terrorism and armed conflict are specifically implicated. A good example of this failure is the lack of mechanisms for dealing with the similar crises that evolved in Yemen and Libya.[224] Thus inhibition of the trade and movement of illegally or inappropriately obtained cultural objects has become instrumental in the goal to achieve security, rather than being valued for the rights and interests that would be preserved.

It is not feasible for the Security Council to continuously adopt Resolutions on a country-by-country basis. Nor is it realistic for market and other States to adopt legislation on a country-by-country basis. Furthermore, given the haphazard nature of such Resolutions, as illustrated by the paralysis of the Security Council during the Russian invasion of Ukraine, and implementing legislation, this approach fails in the essential function of deterring the market through dampening demand. Reducing demand would, in turn, reduce the incentive to supply the market. Multilateral conventions exist to provide a uniform mechanism for carrying out stated objectives to resolve problems upon which the international community has reached consensus. Reliance on Security Council Resolutions to fulfil this function and to fill the lacunae that the current international treaty regime has created is doomed to fail within the broader scope of the goal of protecting cultural heritage and of returning tangible heritage to its rightful owners. The flexibility of deciding which conventions to ratify and how to implement them may be viewed as an essential tenet of national sovereignty. However, the use of Security Council

[223] See Article 11 of the 1970 UNESCO Convention (n 39). However, this provision does not seem to be part of the implementing legislation of many of the States Parties, especially the market countries. Some States, such as the United Kingdom, Germany, and the Netherlands, that have ratified and implemented the two Hague Convention Protocols have taken a more consistent approach to this issue.

[224] Neil Brodie 'Why Is No One Talking about Libya's Cultural Destruction?' (2015) 78 NEA 212.

Resolutions to control the market in movable cultural objects, perhaps ironically, may constitute a greater derogation from national sovereignty.

The move to protecting cultural heritage as a means towards providing security and ensuring peace is a useful mechanism, in the short term, for enacting international resolutions and national legislation to fill gaps in the web of protections that are intended to keep cultural objects within their original contexts and communities. This approach focuses on the instrumental value of protecting heritage, primarily for the benefit of States that see themselves as potential targets of terrorism. As Hausler points out, the Security Council does not seem to be taking sufficient notice of developments initiated by the Human Rights Council, which recognizes the destruction of cultural heritage as a violation of the rights to access and engage in one's culture.[225] A further step is needed to recognize that the illegal removal of cultural objects also constitutes a violation of the same human rights.

5.5 Conclusion

The international humanitarian treaties, the human rights treaties and instruments, the treaties that aim to regulate movement and trade in cultural objects, and other legal mechanisms discussed in this chapter and in chapter 4 provide a contemporary legal analysis for the question of where cultural objects removed during the twentieth and twenty-first centuries should be located and a legal basis for their return. Public international law treaties are limited in that, for the most part, they grant rights to States and not to communities or individuals. As will be discussed in chapter 7, they are further limited by time, in that they are not retroactive in nature, and by inconsistencies in ratification and implementation by individual States. This chapter also illustrates the relative paucity of interest among both international humanitarian law treaties and international human rights treaties in questions of transnational movement, often illegal, and of the return of movable cultural objects to their countries and communities of origin. Greater integration among these sources of law, so that an initial violation of a treaty obligation makes an object unsaleable on the market, and a more proactive approach to interdicting illegally obtained objects are needed. Finally, recognizing the broader human rights interests in the disposition of cultural objects, certainly human remains and burial and sacred objects but also more broadly, would provide a means for making a principle of restitution more generally and uniformly applicable and enforceable.

[225] Hausler, 'The UN Security Council' (n 128) 221.

6

Beyond the Law: Ethical Considerations

6.1 Introduction

The previous chapter outlined the development of the law at both the international and domestic levels that aims to prevent illegal removal of cultural objects and that determines when such objects should be returned to their places of origin. However, these legal doctrines produce a patchwork quilt of relevant law and gaps in response to the question of where cultural objects should be located. These gaps are further exacerbated and projected into the present through such doctrines as nonretroactivity, as will be discussed in chapter 7. One way to fill these gaps is through the development of ethical policies and codes of voluntary conduct that, within a professional association, can require or encourage certain behaviours, which the law does not sufficiently address.

A code of ethics is a set of 'fundamental principles, rules, and guidelines based on the values and ethical standards to which the professionals of the relevant sector and/or organization are held'.[1] Individual actors, institutions, and organizations make voluntary decisions in cases where the law, by itself, does not fully accomplish a particular policy goal. While the law is the starting point in setting a minimal threshold of appropriate conduct, a code of ethics and professional conduct sets a higher standard than what is required by the law. A code of ethics may also establish best practices, which may later be explicitly incorporated into legal rules or indirectly incorporated as indicating what constitutes reasonable conduct and industry standards for a participant in that industry. Codes are often enacted in a horizontal manner and typically are without a strong enforcement mechanism or any enforcement at all,[2] but their purpose is to instil a higher standard so as to earn the trust and confidence of the public and other more specific audiences. For example, the Code of Ethics of the American Alliance of Museums states that 'legal standards are a minimum. Museums and those responsible for them … must

[1] Manlio Frigo, 'Codes of Ethics' in Francesco Francioni and Ana Filipa Vrdoljak (eds), *The Oxford Handbook of International Cultural Heritage Law* (OUP 2020) 787, 787 (hereafter, Frigo, 'Codes of Ethics'). The Smithsonian Institution's policy on Shared Stewardship and Ethical Returns recognizes that unethical acquisition includes objects that were stolen but also those whose legality is less clear, such as objects taken under duress or otherwise removed without consent of the owner. 'Smithsonian Adopts Policy on Ethical Returns' (3 May 2022) <www.si.edu/newsdesk/releases/smithsonian-adopts-policy-ethical-returns> accessed 5 May 2022.

[2] Frigo (n 1), 787–90.

Cultural Objects and Reparative Justice. Patty Gerstenblith, Oxford University Press. © Patty Gerstenblith 2023.
DOI: 10.1093/oso/9780192872104.003.0006

take affirmative steps to maintain their integrity so as to warrant public confidence. They must act not only legally but also ethically.'[3]

An important element in evaluating a code of ethics is whether its provisions are cast as rules or standards. Standards are more flexible, leave more to the individual judgement of association members, and have more exceptions so that they cannot be described as establishing clear rules for acceptable conduct.[4] In the cultural heritage sphere, voluntary actions may be taken to fill gaps that result from reliance solely on the law as a means to determine the proper disposition of cultural objects. Perhaps the most important function of a code of ethics in this context is a shift in the burden of proof regarding the legitimacy of an object's background. Other gaps result from time-bound restraints that severely curtail restitution efforts, as will be discussed in chapter 7. However, the effectiveness of codes in this regard is limited as well, as their reach back in time is constrained in the case of archaeological artefacts to 1970 and to cultural objects taken during the Holocaust. As a result, most codes do not address the disposition of cultural objects removed during earlier periods of colonialism and violence.

This discussion does not aim to be comprehensive but rather focuses on prominent examples of the codes of ethics that have been adopted to address questions of the restitution of cultural objects to the individuals, communities, and States from which they were removed without consent. In particular, it describes voluntary approaches that have been taken with undocumented works that newly appear on the market or that are problematic because of their background in periods of mass theft, such as the Holocaust, or during colonialism, including the treatment of Indigenous human remains and cultural items. In doing so, criteria may be identified that should guide the development of codes or guidelines of ethical conduct. These criteria should include that an object was legally and ethically acquired and possessed; that the intrinsic values of the object (authenticity and cultural and historical values) are preserved and apparent; and that the original and subsequent contexts of the object are known and, to the fullest extent possible, preserved and intact. Ethical principles can inform determinations of the location of cultural

[3] American Alliance of Museums, AAM Code of Ethics for Museums (1993, amended 2000) <www.aam-us.org/programs/ethics-standards-and-professional-practices/code-of-ethics-for-museums/> accessed 21 July 2021 (hereafter American Alliance of Museums, Code of Ethics). The American Alliance of Museums (AAM) is the largest museum association in the United States. Its membership spans many categories of museums, including natural history museums, state and local museums, historic house museums, and zoos, as well as art museums. See also United Kingdom, Museum Association Code of Ethics for Museums 'Application of the Code' <www.museumsassociation.org/campaigns/ethics/code-of-ethics/> accessed 21 July 2021 (hereafter, United Kingdom, Museum Association Code of Ethics).

[4] Duncan Kennedy articulated the distinction between rules and standards in the context of private law. However, the distinction is applicable to voluntary codes of conduct, although these lack the enforcement mechanism of law. Duncan Kennedy, 'Form and Substance in Private Law Adjudication' (1976) 89 HLR 1685, 1687–89.

objects, focusing on reuniting objects with their original contexts and descendant communities.

6.2 General Codes of Conduct

Many of the codes of conduct and guidelines discussed here pertain to museums. Museums have particular obligations to the public.[5] The largest museum association is the International Council of Museums (ICOM), with over 30,000 individual and museum members representing the global museum community. Primary emphasis is placed on the ability of a museum to obtain title to any object that it acquires, whether by purchase, gift, loan, bequest, or exchange, for its collection.[6] The ICOM Code also requires that an object has not been illegally exported from its country of origin or any intermediate country, even if it was owned legally.[7] The ICOM Code acknowledges the vagaries resulting from changes in the legal status of objects as they move through different jurisdictions by stating that '[e]vidence of lawful ownership in a country is not necessarily valid title'.[8] Three issues have raised particular ethical concerns for museums in terms of both their existing collections and possible new acquisitions: whether works were stolen during the Holocaust and whether archaeological artefacts are the products of recent site looting. The third issue is collections of Indigenous human remains and cultural items.[9]

A contrast to the museum codes is that presented by the code of the Confédération Internationale des Négociants en Oeuvres d'Art (CINOA), a confederation of thirty-two art and antiques dealer associations in twenty-one countries. Its brief Code of Ethics is presented as a way of preventing enactment of legislation that would restrict and be harmful to the market. The Code requires compliance with current law, including with respect to objects 'clearly established to have been imported illegally under applicable national law' but requiring compensation from a country requesting return in the amount of the purchase price for

[5] Museums in the United States are typically incorporated under state statutes as not-for-profit organizations and recognized as charitable organizations under the federal Internal Revenue Code, 26 USC § 501(c)(3). They obtain favoured tax status as charitable institutions through their dedication to the purpose of furthering public education and science; this status, in turn, benefits the institution's donors. Except in the case of the Smithsonian Institution and state and local museums, most museums in the United States are private institutions, unlike many of their counterparts in other countries.

[6] International Council of Museums, ICOM Code of Ethics s 2.2 <https://icom.museum/en/resources/standards-guidelines/code-of-ethics/> accessed 7 July 2021 (hereafter 'ICOM Code of Ethics for Museums'). The ICOM Code of Ethics was first adopted in 1986 and revised in 2004.

[7] ibid, s 2.3.

[8] ibid, s 2.2. See also Frigo, 'Codes of Ethics' (n 1) 790–91.

[9] In the United States, this last issue has been handled primarily through the Native American Graves Protection and Repatriation Act, 25 USC §§ 3001–3013. US museums may therefore perceive there is less need to address Native American remains and cultural items through codes of ethics.

good faith acquisition, when permitted under local law.[10] The market professional should consult registers and databases of stolen property and should not participate in transactions that can be linked to money-laundering operations.[11] The only international instrument mentioned is the Convention on International Trade in Endangered Species.[12] This code presents as ethical requirements regulations that, for the most part, recite applicable law.

Another approach is taken by the Maastricht Code of Conduct for The European Fine Art Fair (TEFAF), which sets out best practices for a 'diligent art trade'. It requires that its participants follow the rules and regulations of the Netherlands and of international conventions.[13] The fair organizers cooperate with Dutch national and local law enforcement, and a vetting committee with a scientific research team vets all objects in advance of the fair. If it is 'thought that an object might have been' obtained illegally, law enforcement is notified. The code of conduct does not establish requirements that exceed the scope of the law, but it sets up enforcement mechanisms through its cooperation with law enforcement that exceed the parameters of most ethical codes of conduct.

6.3 Codes of Conduct with Respect to Cultural Works Looted during the Holocaust

Throughout the 1990s it became increasingly clear that many cultural objects had not been restored to their original owners at the end of the Second World War. The Washington Conference Principles on Nazi-Confiscated Art, adopted in 1998, called for identification of artworks that had not been restituted, the opening of records and archives, and additional resources to be devoted to provenance research. 'Just and fair' solutions should be found to the problem of the disposition of artworks that had not been restituted.[14] Still dissatisfied with efforts to recover and return property looted during the Holocaust, the Czech Republic and six institutions sponsored the 2009 Prague Holocaust Era Assets conference with representatives

10 CINOA 'Code of Ethics' <www.cinoa.org/cinoa/codeofethics> accessed 21 July 2021, para 1.

11 ibid, paras 3 and 4.

12 ibid, para 2. The codes of ethics of the Art Dealers Association of America and the Comité Professionnel des Galeries d'Art do not address the disposition of cultural objects. See, respectively, ADAA Code of Ethics and Professional Practices <https://artdealers.org/about/code-of-ethics-and-professional-practices> accessed 21 July 2021; Code de déontologie des galleries d'art (2016) <www.comitedesgaleriesdart.com/sites/default/files/atoms/files/code_deontologie_galeries_d_art_cpga.pdf> accessed 21 July 2021. See also Tessa Solomon, A New Code for Ethical Collecting Calls on the Art Market to Do Better by Transparently Working with Dealers' Artnews, 1 March 2022 <www.artnews.com/art-news/market/ethics-code-art-collecting-1234620606/> accessed 4 March 2022.

13 Maastricht Code of Conduct <www.tefaf.com/code-of-conduct> accessed 22 September 2022.

14 US Department of State Office of the Special Envoy for Holocaust Issues, 'Washington Conference Principles on Nazi-Confiscated Art' (1998) <www.state.gov/washington-conference-principles-on-nazi-confiscated-art/> accessed 7 July 2021.

of forty-six nations. This conference produced the Terezin Declaration which, with respect to cultural objects and artworks, called for additional support for intensified systematic provenance research and urged all stakeholders to facilitate 'just and fair solutions' and to resolve claims based on the facts and merits.[15] This last point raises the issue of whether current possessors, particularly museums, should rely on the technical defences, such as the statute of limitations, adverse possession, and equitable defense of laches, rather than adjudicating claims based on the underlying merits of ownership and rightful possession.

In Europe, where the major museums are often government institutions, the national governments undertook the responsibility to determine which cultural objects should be returned to their original owners or those claiming from them. Many European countries established a commission to review claims and determine whether return was appropriate.[16] These determinations are the product of neither a judicial determination nor a code of ethical practice. Perhaps because decisions on restitution are made by government commissions, museum codes of ethics do not explicitly address this issue. For example, the UK Museum Association makes no direct reference to Holocaust looted art.[17]

In the United States, however, most museums are private, non-government entities, although obligated to fulfil a public purpose. Each museum therefore has the right to determine how to respond to a claim and is not subject to direct government regulation in matters of collections management. The American Alliance of Museums (AAM) and the Association of Art Museum Directors (AAMD) each developed a set of principles to guide museums in the restitution of works currently in their collections and to assist them in avoiding the acquisition of works that had not been returned to their original owners or their heirs following the Second World War. Both guidelines call on museums to search their existing collections and to scrutinize works offered as new acquisitions. If a museum determines that a work in its collection was illegally confiscated and not returned, the museum should make this information public; if a 'legitimate claimant comes forward, the museum should offer to resolve the matter in an equitable, appropriate, and mutually agreeable manner'.[18] A 2001 addendum to the 1998 AAMD report called for museums to publicly disclose the results of the provenance research

[15] 'Terezin Declaration' Holocaust Era Assets Conference (30 June 2009) <www.holocausteraassets.eu/program/conference-proceedings/declarations/> accessed 7 July 2021.

[16] For a list of national commissions, see The Central Registry of Information on Looted Cultural Property 1933–1945 <www.lootedart.com/infobycountry> accessed 7 July 2021.

[17] The Code states that a museum should '[r]eject any item for purchase, loan or donation if there is any suspicion that it was wrongfully taken during a time of conflict, stolen, illicitly exported or illicitly traded . . .' United Kingdom, Museum Association Code of Ethics (n 3) 'Stewardship of Collections', s 2.5.

[18] Report of the AAMD Task Force on the Spoliation of Art during the Nazi/World War II Era (1933–45) s II.D.2 <https://aamd.org/sites/default/files/document/Report%20on%20the%20Spoliation%20of%20Nazi%20Era%20Art.pdf> accessed 21 July 2021 (hereafter AAMD, 'Task Force on Spoliation of Art'). The membership of the AAMD consists of the directors of approximately 200 art museums in Mexico, Canada, and the United States.

conducted on works in their collections 'created before 1946, transferred after 1932 and before 1946, and which were or could have been in continental Europe during that period, giving priority to European paintings and Judaica'.[19] These guidelines apply to works of art on loan, but these are subject to a lower level of scrutiny.[20]

With respect to a museum's reliance on technical or procedural bars to a claim, the AAM's Guidelines Concerning the Unlawful Appropriation of Objects during the Nazi Era provide that 'in order to achieve an equitable and appropriate resolution of claims, museums may elect to waive certain available defenses'.[21] Despite these provisions, museums have often used these technical defences, which pose a significant obstacle to restitution claims. In 2015, the World Jewish Restitution Organization issued a Report Concerning Current Approaches of United States Museums to Holocaust-Era Art Claims. The Report criticized major US museums for asserting 'defenses such as the statute of limitations, to avoid resolving on the facts and merits claims by Holocaust victims and their heirs . . . by avoiding any adjudication of the substance of those claims'.[22]

In 2016, Congress went a step further in enacting the Holocaust Expropriated Art Recovery Act, which preempted 'any defense at law relating to the passage of time'.[23] However, this legislation left in place the equitable defences, such as laches, and museums have continued to rely on such defences. For example, in *Zuckerman v Metropolitan Museum of Art*, the Metropolitan Museum successfully used laches to defeat a claim for the restitution of Picasso's *The Actor* to the estate of its pre-war owners.[24] Thus, despite museums' stated ethical principle of resolving claims for recovery of artworks stolen during the Holocaust based on substantive legal merits, these claims often continue to be resolved through technical defences without a determination of proper ownership and without the historical background of presumptions applicable to sales under duress, as adopted in the London Declaration of 1943.[25]

[19] ibid, 'Addendum'. The Nazi-Era Provenance Internet Portal Project maintains a searchable list of museum objects that fit these criteria. <www.nepip.org/> accessed 21 July 2021 (hereafter, Nazi-Era Provenance Internet Portal Project). The AAMD maintains a registry on Resolutions of Claims for Nazi-Era Cultural Assets <https://aamd.org/object-registry/resolution-of-claims-for-nazi-era-cultural-assets/browse> accessed 21 July 2021.

[20] ibid, s II.F.

[21] AAM, 'Unlawful Appropriation of Objects during the Nazi Era' Guidelines, <www.aam-us.org/programs/ethics-standards-and-professional-practices/unlawful-appropriation-of-objects-during-the-nazi-era/> accessed 21 July 2021. This encouragement reduces the likelihood that museum trustees will be viewed as breaching their fiduciary obligations if they choose to waive the technical defences.

[22] World Jewish Restitution Organization, 'Report Concerning Current Approaches of United States Museums to Holocaust-Era Art Claims' (25 June 2015) <https://wjro.org.il/cms/assets/uploads/2015/12/ReportMuseums.pdf> accessed 7 July 2021.

[23] Pub L 114-308, 130 Stat 1524, 114th Congress, 2015–17, § 5(a).

[24] *Zuckerman v Metro Museum of Art*, 928 F3d 186 (2nd Cir 2019). The lower court had rejected the plaintiff's claim because the plaintiff had failed to establish the elements for voiding a contract on the basis of economic duress. 307 F Supp 3d 304, 318–20 (SDNY 2018).

[25] Inter-Allied Declaration against Acts of Dispossession Committed in Territories under Enemy Occupation or Control. United States Diplomatic Papers Vol 1 (1943) <https://history.state.gov/historicaldocuments/frus1943v01/d456> accessed 7 July 2021. See chapter 5, n 9.

6.4 The 1970 UNESCO Convention as an Ethical Standard

Another particularly fraught category of cultural objects is recently acquired archaeological objects. In recognition of the significance of the Convention on the Means of Prohibiting and Preventing the Illicit Import, Export and Transfer of Ownership of Cultural Property ('the 1970 Convention'),[26] many professional associations and institutions have adopted some form of what might be termed 'the 1970 standard'.[27] This standard refers to archaeological artefacts that are documented outside their country of modern discovery (or country of origin) before 1970 or are known to have been legally excavated and, if no longer within the country of origin, legally exported after 1970 and legally imported into the country in which the object is currently located.

Application of the 1970 standard, as with the law itself, depends on the provenance and provenience of an archaeological artefact.[28] While use of the 1970 standard focuses on the length of the provenance given for an object, the more important question may be the degree of certainty or objectivity, in other words the quality, of a stated provenance.[29] Therefore, the ability to trace provenance back to a certain point in time, such as 1970, in default of being able to determine the object's findspot, forms the fulcrum of the voluntary codes and guidelines that are considered here.

While the date of 1970 has no legal significance, it is sometimes viewed as a proxy for both authenticity and legality. However, use of the 1970 standard does not establish authenticity as forgeries predate 1970.[30] Similarly, the date of 1970 does not

[26] Convention on the Means of Prohibiting and Preventing the Illicit Import, Export and Transfer of Ownership of Cultural Property (adopted 14 November 1970, entered into force 24 April 1972) 823 UNTS 231.

[27] For the distinction between rules and standards, see n 4 above. Because the use of 1970 as an ethical guideline has many exceptions and variations, this is better denominated a standard. Some ethical guidelines use the date of 1970, others use the date of 1972 when the Convention entered into force, and some use 1973, depending on when a particular association or institution adopted the standard. Nonetheless, the standard will be referred to here as the '1970 standard' for ease of explanation.

[28] Rosemary A Joyce, 'From Place to Place: Provenience, Provenance, and Archaeology' in Gail Feigenbaum and Inge Reist (eds), *Provenance: An Alternate History of Art* (Getty Research Institute 2012) 50, 51–53; Patty Gerstenblith, 'Provenience and Provenance Intersecting with International Law in the Market for Antiquities' (2020) 45 North Carolina Journal of International Law 457, 466–69. See also chapter 4, n 10.

[29] Jane A Levine, 'The Importance of Provenance Documentation in the Market for Ancient Art and Artifacts: The Future of the Market May Depend on Documenting the Past' (2009) 19 DePaul Journal of Art, Technology and Intellectual Property Law 219 (hereafter, Levine 'Importance of Provenance Documentation'). Brodie suggests that, while one might posit that a provenance to 1970 would increase market value thereby incentivizing the use of provenance data, the date of 1970 has relatively little effect on the market value of an antiquity. Neil Brodie, 'Provenance and Price: Autoregulation of the Antiquities Market?' (2014) 20 EJCPR 427 (hereafter Brodie, 'Provenance and Price').

[30] Christopher A Rollston, 'Forging History: From Antiquity to the Modern Period' in Matthew T Rutz and Morag M Kersel (eds), *Archaeologies of Text: Archaeology, Technology, and Ethics* (Oxbow Books 2014) 176 (discussing forged texts from antiquity to the present). Elizabeth Marlowe suggests that the 1970 standard is not useful in establishing authenticity but rather one needs to know the definitive findspot of an object. 'What We Talk About When We Talk About Provenance: A Response to Chippindale and Gill' (2016) 23 IJCP 217, 218–19. But see also Rosemary A Joyce, 'When is Authentic?

establish the legality of an object due to variations in applicable laws, their dates of enactment, particularly of State vesting laws, and the varying dates in ratification and methods of implementation of the 1970 UNESCO Convention. An object may satisfy the 1970 standard and yet not be legal if the object was discovered after the date that a State enacted an ownership law but before 1970.[31] On the other hand, an object may not satisfy the 1970 standard but be legal if the country had not ratified the 1970 Convention at the time the object was exported from that country and that country does not have a State ownership law. The situation is even more complex because the legal status of an object may change as it moves through time and space, crossing jurisdictional boundaries and with different applicable laws.

Nonetheless, the 1970 standard may be a useful tool to fill gaps left by these legal complexities. Perhaps the most significant tool is that the standard eliminates bars based on passage of time (back to the year 1970). The 1970 standard also alters the burden of proof. Unlike in most legal proceedings, where the burden of proof is placed on a claimant, the burden of establishing that an object meets the 1970 standard should fall on whoever is attempting to satisfy the ethical or professional standards to which that individual or institution is subject. If an artefact has a documented history back to 1970, any associated looting occurred more than fifty years ago, and its current acquisition is less likely to contribute a direct financial incentive to the contemporary looting of archaeological sites, although well publicized objects may provide an indirect incentive. Use of the 1970 standard may reduce the losses to our understanding of the past caused by site looting. However, the 1970 standard does not necessarily set a higher standard of conduct than what the law requires and for this reason, one may question whether the use of the date of 1970 represents an effective or valid approach based on ethics.

6.4.1 Professional and Scholarly Associations

The Archaeological Institute of America (AIA), the largest American archaeological organization, adopted a resolution in 1973 stating that its Annual Meeting would not serve as the place of initial announcement or scholarly presentation of an antiquity acquired after December 1973 that cannot be shown to have left its country of origin before that date.[32] In 1978, the same policy was applied to

Situating Authenticity in the Itineraries of Objects' in Alex Geurds and Laura van Broekhaven (eds), *Creating Authenticity: Authentication Processes in Ethnographic Museums* (Sidestone Press 2013) 39, 41 (stating that '[t]hings with long histories in known collections often pass a test of authenticity more easily than those that emerged only recently').

[31] For example, Iraq: Antiquities Law No 59 of 1936, Article 3; Turkey: Decree on Antiquities (Asar-ı Atika Nizamnamesi) of 10 April 1906; Turkish Civil Code No 753, Article 697 (1926).

[32] Naomi Norman, 'Editorial Policy on the Publication of Recently Acquired Antiquities' (2005) 109 American Journal of Archaeology 135–36, 135.

publications in the American Journal of Archaeology (AJA). As Naomi Norman, a later editor of the AJA explained, '[t]he clear intent of the policy was not to enhance the market value or importance of these objects by giving them the imprimatur of the AIA by publishing them for the first time in the *AJA*'.[33] While the AIA has modified these policies over time, their substance has remained largely the same.

Other professional organizations have adopted codes of ethics or professional practice that require members to avoid enhancing the commercial value of undocumented archaeological objects, but these codes do not specifically reference the date of 1970.[34] The European Association of Archaeologists forbids its members from any association with the illegal trade in antiquities, but the publication policy forbids publication only where the material was 'knowingly obtained illegally from unprovenanced sources'.[35] Other professional organizations refer to the 1970 UNESCO Convention but without setting a clear line as to how they will deal with publications and presentations at their scholarly meetings of material that does not meet the 1970 standard.[36]

The American Society of Overseas Research (ASOR) adopted a policy in 2015 that largely echoes that of the AIA. Both the AIA and ASOR policies derogate from the provisions by allowing publication of an object that does not meet the 1970 standard whose 'publication or announcement serves primarily to emphasize the degradation of archaeological heritage'.[37] However, as an organization whose members include both field archaeologists and text scholars working in the Eastern Mediterranean and Mesopotamian regions, ASOR and other scholarly associations that are composed of text scholars have faced particularly strong opposition to the application of the 1970 standard to textual and epigraphic materials.[38]

33 AIA Code of Ethics (adopted 29 December 1990 and amended); Code of Professional Standards (adopted 29 December 1997 and amended) <www.archaeological.org/about/governance/policies/> accessed 20 July 2021.

34 Society for American Archaeology, 'Principles of Archaeological Ethics' (1996) <www.saa.org/career-practice/ethics-in-professional-archaeology> accessed 4 March 2022.

35 European Journal of Archaeology Publications Ethics Policy, s 6 <www.e-a-a.org/EAA/About/EAA_Codes/EAA/Navigation_About/EAA_Codes.aspx?hkey=714e8747-495c-4298-ad5d-4c60c2bcbda9#EJAethics> accessed 20 July 2021.

36 College Art Association, 'Statement on the Importance of Documenting the Historical Context of Objects and Sites' (adopted 2 May 2004) <www.collegeart.org/guidelines/context> accessed 20 July 2021.

37 ASOR, 'Policy on Professional Conduct' (adopted 18 April 2015, and amended in 2017 and 2019) s III.E.4 <www.asor.org/about/policies/conduct.html> accessed 20 July 2021 (hereafter ASOR 'Policy'). ASOR also addresses the status of excavations in occupied territory, permitting the publication of results of excavations carried out in occupied territory only when the 'research is required strictly to safeguard, record or preserve the archaeological heritage of the occupied territory' or with consent of the competent national authorities. ibid, s III.E.7.

38 For a survey of the publication policies of scholarly journals regarding textual materials, see John F Cherry, 'Publishing Undocumented Texts: Editorial Perspectives' in Matthew T Rutz and Morag M Kersel (eds), *Archaeologies of Text: Archaeology, Technology, and Ethics* (Oxbow Books 2014) 227. See also Patty Gerstenblith, 'Ethical Guidelines for Publishing Ancient Texts' in Neil Brodie, Morag M Kersel, and Josephine M Rasmussen (eds), *Variant Scholarship* (Sidestone Press forthcoming).

Some text scholars believe that they can derive much historical information from a text without knowing its findspot,[39] that such texts are considerably more difficult to forge,[40] and that the information that can be gleaned should not be ignored in the interest of preserving archaeological context.[41] They also do not seem to be concerned with the legality of the objects that they handle. As the cuneiform scholar Aage Westenholz wrote: 'Though undeniably a part of illicit trade merchandise, objects with inscriptions are indeed different from other "works of art" – they are not easily faked, and they hold information more or less independent of their archaeological context.'[42] David Owen of Cornell University and other scholars have published extensive collections of cuneiform texts in the *Cornell University Studies in Assyriology and Sumerology* series from unlocated sites in southern Iraq, including Garšana and Iri-Saĝrig, which is the source of many of the cuneiform texts acquired by the Hobby Lobby Stores and subsequently forfeited.[43] Invoking the rescue narrative, Owen described his publication project as 'the most productive tablet rescue, preservation, and publication program in the history of Assyriology',[44] rather than as ancillary to an extensive looting operation.

[39] For a refutation that an archaeological findspot is not important in the study of texts, see Christopher A Rollston, 'Navigating the Epigraphic Storm: A Palaeographer Reflects on Inscriptions from the Market' (2005) 68 NEA 69

[40] A significant number of papyrus fragments, purporting to be Dead Sea Scrolls, surfaced on the market after 2002 and have now been accepted as forgeries, including several purchased by Hobby Lobby and donated to the Museum of the Bible. A Journey for the Truth: Investigating the Recent Dead Sea Scrolls Fragments <https://museumofthebible.org/dead-sea-scroll-fragments> accessed 10 July 2020. For forged Biblical inscriptions of the Iron Age, see Christopher A Rollston, 'Non-Provenanced Epigraphs I: Pillaged Antiquities, Northwest Semitic Forgeries, and Protocols for Laboratory Tests' (2003) 10 Maarav 135. For the so-called 'Gospel of the Wife of Jesus', see Ariel Sabar, 'The Unbelievable Tale of Jesus's Wife' (*The Atlantic*, July/August 2015) <www.theatlantic.com/magazine/archive/2016/07/the-unbelievable-tale-of-jesus-wife/485573/> accessed 20 July 2021. For forged cuneiform texts, see Erle Leichty, 'A Remarkable Forger' (1970) 12/3 Expedition <www.penn.museum/sites/expedition/a-remarkable-forger/> accessed 30 March 2022.

[41] See, for example, David I Owen, 'Censoring Knowledge: The Case for the Publication of Unprovenanced Cuneiform Tablets' in James Cuno (ed), *Whose Culture? The Promise of Museums and the Debate Over Antiquities* (Princeton University Press 2009) 125; John Boardman, 'Archaeologists, Collectors, and Museums' in James Cuno (ed), *Whose Culture? The Promise of Museums and the Debate Over Antiquities* (Princeton University Press 2009) 107; Aage Westenholz, 'Illicit Cuneiform Tablets: Heirlooms or Stolen Goods?' in Alexandra Kleinerman and Jack M Sasson (eds), *Why Should Someone Who Knows Something Conceal It?* (CDL Press 2010) 257 (hereafter, Westenholz, 'Illicit Cuneiform Tablets'). These critics refer to restrictions on publication of unprovenanced materials as 'censorship'.

[42] Westenholz, 'Illicit Cuneiform Tablets' (n 41) 260.

[43] For example, David I Owen and Rudolf H Mayr, *The Garšana Archives* (CUSAS 4, CDL Press 2007); Marcel Sigrist and Tohru Ozaki, *Tablets from the Irisaĝrig Archive* (CUSAS 43, 1st edn, Eisenbrauns 2020). For the Hobby Lobby forfeitures, see chapter 4.

[44] David I Owen, *Cuneiform Texts Primarily from Iri-Saĝrig/Āl-Šarrākī and the History of the Ur III Period* (NISABA 15, CDL Press 2013) 352. The competing arguments concerning publication of unprovenanced texts are further discussed by Tero Alstola, *Judeans in Babylonia: A Study of the Deportees in the Sixth and Fifth Centuries BCE* (vol 109 Culture and History of the Ancient Near East, Brill 2020) 34–43; Neil Brodie, 'Cuneiform Exceptionalism? Justifying the Study and Publication of Unprovenanced Cuneiform Tablets from Iraq' in Naomi Oosterman and Donna Yates (eds), *Crime and Art: Sociological and Criminological Perspectives of Crimes in the Art World* (Springer 2021) 103, 109–12; Abdul Salam Taha, 'The Role of Academics in Enabling the Illicit Antiquities Market: The Damage to

These publications demonstrate the difficulty of enforcing policies on the activities of individual scholars, particularly policies that deny only the place of first publication. Text scholars seem to have no difficulty finding publishers willing to serve as the place of first publication, after which the texts are deemed acceptable for publication by the major academic and scholarly organizations.

The ASOR publication policy is unique in that it has a specific exception that allows publication of cuneiform texts that do not comply with the 1970 standard.[45] This exception was initially adopted in 2004 in the wake of the looting of the Iraq Museum and the subsequent widespread looting of sites in southern Iraq and in response to pressure from cuneiform scholars. The policy was extensively revised in 2015. In explaining the reasons for this exception, the ASOR policy, perhaps somewhat ironically, includes the looting that had occurred in Iraq since the early 1990s 'on a truly massive scale'.[46] However, additional restraints are placed on the use of the cuneiform exception: the author of a publication must note in a prominent manner the lack of archaeological provenience, and the author must certify to ASOR that the 'owner of the artifact' will return the tablet to the country of origin or that its title has been ceded to the country of origin or to 'some other publicly-accessible repository, if return to its country of origin is not feasible'. This last provision seems intended to ensure the rights of the country of origin of the texts and that the artefacts will be returned upon request,[47] although ceding title to a repository does not accomplish this purpose. Nonetheless, some scholarly and academic organizations composed primarily of text scholars have moved to adopt a variant of the 1970 standard.[48]

6.4.2 Museum Policies

6.4.2.1 Early Policies: Individual Museums

The Southwest Museum in Los Angeles formulated what is likely the first museum policy on the acquisition of looted antiquities in 1937.[49] This policy allowed for

Iraq's Cultural Heritage' in Lorenzo Kamel (ed), *Collapse and Rebirth of Cultural Heritage: The Case of Syria and Iraq* (Peter Lang 2020) 129.

45 ASOR 'Policy' (n 37) ss E.5–6.

46 ibid.

47 ibid, s E.6. In contrast, the 2004 policy required that any materials were accessioned into the collection of the Iraq Museum before publication was allowed. These restraints have been sufficiently potent that the exception has rarely been used.

48 For example, the Society of Biblical Literature (SBL) follows the ASOR policy, see SBL Policy Manual, 'SBL Policy on Scholarly Presentation and Publication of Ancient Artifacts' (2020) 97 <www.sbl-site.org/assets/pdfs/Policy_Manual.pdf> accessed 20 July 2021; 44 Bulletin of the American Society of Papyrologists, 'ASP Resolution Concerning the Illicit Trade in Papyri' (adopted 1 August 2007) 289–90 <https://quod.lib.umich.edu/b/basp/0599796.0044.001/00000289> accessed 20 July 2021.

49 Brian I Daniels, 'A History of Antiquities Ownership in the United States, 1870–1934' (Unpublished PhD Dissertation, University of Pennsylvania 2013) 148.

the acquisition of archaeological objects only if they were discovered accidentally, scientifically collected, or 'known not to have been gathered contrary to law'.[50] The policy recognized that '[t]he only way to stop the pot-hunter is to deprive him [sic] of his market. That market consists principally in museums and in other institutions of learning and research.'[51]

Three museums took the lead in the early 1970s in adopting policies that applied some formulation of the 1970 standard. The University of Pennsylvania Museum of Anthropology and Archaeology announced in April 1970 that it would not purchase any object unless it was accompanied by a full provenance, including legality of export.[52] In 1978, the Penn Museum adopted a more stringent policy that it would not acquire by any means an object known or suspected to be illegally exported from its country of origin nor would it permit museum staff to authenticate such an object. Further, the museum would not lend objects to museums or departments that acquired or to exhibitions that included illegally acquired objects. Harvard University adopted a policy in 1971 'forbidding the acquisition or exhibition of any object looted or illegally exported from its country of origin and specifying that museum staff must seek reasonable assurance that an object is not so tainted before it is acquired or borrowed'.[53]

The Field Museum adopted the 1970 standard in 1971, offering the justification that '[d]angerously large quantities of primitive and ancient artifacts are now being stolen or looted—at times in a quasi-legal fashion—smuggled, and sold at high prices. If this market continues to operate at its present scale and in its present rapacious manner, it will quite soon succeed in obliterating large segments of the cultural heritage of mankind.'[54] Similar to the earlier policy adopted by the Southwest Museum, which was concerned primarily with objects illegally excavated within the United States, this part of the Field Museum's policy also applies to objects 'reasonably believed to have been illegally or unscientifically excavated within the United States'.[55]

[50] FW Hodge, 'Pot-Hunting: A Statement of Policy' (1937) 3(2) American Antiquity 184.

[51] ibid.

[52] Penn Museum, 'The Pennsylvania Declaration' (1980) 22(3) Expedition 3 <www.penn.museum/documents/publications/expedition/PDFs/22-3/The%20Pennsylvania.pdf> accessed 7 July 2021.

[53] Harvard University, 'The Art of Ownership' (1998) *John Harvard's Journal* <www.harvardmagazine.com/sites/default/files/html/1998/05/jhj.html> accessed 7 July 2021. The journalist, Walter V Robinson, raised questions about whether the Arthur M Sackler Museum, one of the Harvard University Art Museums, was following this policy when, in the late 1990s, it acquired and exhibited several artefacts from the dealers Robert Hecht and Robert Guy, including a bronze figure owned by the collectors Leon Levy and Shelby White. Walter V Robinson and John Yemma, 'Harvard museum acquisitions shock scholars', *The Boston Globe* (Boston, 16 January 1998) A1.

[54] Field Museum, 'Policy Statement Concerning Acquisition of Antiquities, Curator' (1971) 14(4) Museum Journal 232.

[55] ibid, 234.

6.4.2.2 Museum Association Guidelines

ICOM's Code of Ethics adopts a position that is stronger than the 1970 standard, requiring conformity with all national, local, and international laws.[56] The ICOM Code deals directly with the underlying problem of looting of archaeological sites, stating museums should not acquire objects if 'there is reasonable cause to believe their recovery involved unauthorised or unscientific fieldwork, or intentional destruction or damage of monuments, archaeological or geological sites'.[57] It is broader than the 1970 standard in that it requires the museum to make every effort to ensure that any object, whether to be acquired by purchase, gift, loan, or bequest, was not 'illegally obtained in, or exported from its country of origin or any intermediate country in which it might have been owned legally' even if exported before 1970.[58]

The Museums Association based in the United Kingdom requires museums to 'reject any item ... if there is any suspicion that it was wrongfully taken during a time of conflict, stolen, illicitly exported or illicitly traded'.[59] These policies apply to purchases, gifts, bequests, and loans.[60] Despite legal restrictions imposed on deaccessioning by some museums, the policy expects museums to 'deal sensitively and promptly with requests for repatriation both within the UK and from abroad'.[61] However, the policy does not specifically call for restitution. The main museum organizations based in the United States, the AAM and AAMD, for many years did not have policies that specifically addressed the acquisition of archaeological material from foreign countries. Primarily concerned with the looting of archaeological sites within the United States, the AAM had adopted a policy in 1925 that called on museums to 'carefully scrutinize the titles to objects offered for sale and refuse to acquire those obtained through vandalism'.[62] While addressing the problem of site looting through its mention of vandalism, the AAM policy did not refer specifically to the problem of the international trade in looted archaeological materials.

In the early years of the twenty-first century, it became apparent that American museums had been acquiring poorly provenanced archaeological materials while large-scale looting of archaeological sites was ongoing. In 1995, Italian and Swiss authorities raided the warehouses of an Italian dealer, Giacomo Medici, in Geneva.[63] These warehouses revealed thousands of documents and artefacts with

[56] 'ICOM Code of Ethics for Museums' (n 6) s 7.
[57] ibid, s 2.4.
[58] ibid, s 2.3.
[59] United Kingdom, Museum Association Code of Ethics (n 3) 'Stewardship of collections', s 2.5.
[60] ibid, s 2.4
[61] ibid, s 2.7.
[62] American Alliance of Museums, 'A Code of Ethics for Museum Workers' (1926) 3 <http://babel.hathitrust.org/cgi/pt?id=mdp.39015059682297;view=1up;seq=9> accessed 7 July 2021.
[63] Peter Watson and Cecilia Todeschini, *The Medici Conspiracy: The Illicit Journey of Looted Antiquities from Italy's Tomb Raiders to the World's Greatest Museums* (PublicAffairs 2006).

strong evidence of recent looting. This evidence indicated that museums, dealers, and private collectors had knowingly traded in and acquired recently looted archaeological objects. These revelations led to the indictment in Italy of Marion True, the curator of the Getty Villa, for allegedly conspiring to deal in antiquities stolen from Italy. Italy also brought pressure on numerous US museums to return archaeological artefacts that had been looted from Italy. Based in part on the clarification given in the *Schultz* decision of the status of archaeological objects subject to foreign State vesting laws as stolen property,[64] several museums returned more than one hundred artefacts to Italy.[65] When returning these objects, most of these museums entered into cultural property agreements with Italy, allowing the objects that had been sent to Italy to return to the US museum on a rotating basis. While the objects were in Italy, Italy loaned different objects to the US museum.[66]

These events played a central role in changing the policies of US museums for the collecting of antiquities. In 2004, the AAMD adopted a policy that, in making an acquisition, the museum was to consider 'whether the work of art has been outside its probable country or countries of origin for a sufficiently long time that its acquisition would not provide a direct, material incentive to looting or illegal excavation'.[67] The recommended period of time was ten years. The policy thus allowed a museum to acquire an antiquity that a smuggler or intermediary held in a market or transit country for as little as ten years after which its background was 'laundered' and the AAMD policy allowed a museum to acquire the object. As a result, the policy did little to deter the looting of archaeological sites.

Recognition of the failure of this rolling ten-year approach and the ongoing pressure from Italy and other countries of origin led the AAM and AAMD each to adopt a new policy in 2008. The AAM policy adopted the 1970 standard, requiring that objects without pre-1970 provenance have documentation of legal

64 *United States v Schultz* 178 F Supp 2d 445 (SDNY 2002), affd, 333 F3d 393 (2nd Cir 2003).

65 For more discussion of these restitutions, see chapter 4, section 4.3.2.1. Medici was convicted of dealing in stolen antiquities. The indictments of True and the dealer Robert Hecht were ultimately dropped due to expiration of the Italian statute of limitations. Bruce Weber, 'Robert Hecht, 92, Antiquities Dealer, Dies' *New York Times* (New York, 10 February 2012) A18.

66 Italy loaned the Moregine Treasure, a set of silver found near Pompeii, to the Metropolitan Museum, when it returned the Morgantina silver set looted from Morgantina on Sicily. Two *kantharoi* or drinking cups among the Moregine objects were over a hundred years old when they were buried and likely had been made in Alexandria, Egypt. The Met, Important Antiquities Lent by Republic of Italy on View at Metropolitan Museum (10 February 2010) <www.metmuseum.org/press/news/2010/important-antiquities-lent-by-republic-of-italy-on-view-at-metropolitan-museum> accessed 7 July 2021. See Laetitia La Follette, 'The Trial of Marion True and Changing Policies for Classical Antiquities in American Museums' in Laetitia La Follette (ed), *Negotiating Culture: Heritage, Ownership, and Intellectual Property* (University of Massachusetts 2013) 38, 64–71 (listing objects returned to Italy from US museums); Claire L Lyons, 'Museums as Sites of Reconciliation' in James AR Nafziger and Ann M Nicgorski (eds) *Cultural Heritage Issues: The Legacy of Conquest, Colonization, and Commerce* (Martinus Nijhoff Publishers 2009) 421, 425–26 (hereafter, Lyons, 'Museums as Sites of Reconciliation').

67 Association of Art Museum Directors, 'New Acquisitions of Archaeological Material and Works of Ancient Art' <https://aamd.org/object-registry/new-acquisitions-of-archaeological-material-and-works-of-ancient-art/more-info> accessed 20 July 2021.

export from the country of origin and legal import into the United States.[68] The policy allows exceptions when full documentation is not available, but the museum 'should be transparent about why this is an appropriate decision in alignment with the institution's code of ethics and those of the field'. As with the guidelines for Holocaust era artworks in museum collections, the AAM policy calls on museums to examine objects already in their collections and to continue research on those objects for which provenance is not complete or certain. However, the AAM does not seem to have an enforcement mechanism for its policy against individual museums.

The AAMD 2008 policy, which was amended in 2013, adopts the 1970 standard but allows its member museums to acquire a nonconforming object under liberal circumstances.[69] The 2008 guidelines articulated two grounds for acquiring nonconforming objects: (1) where the museum, based on provenance research, could make an 'informed judgment' that the object was exported from its country of origin before 1970 or exported legally after 1970, and (2) where 'cumulative facts and circumstances', including prior displays and publications of the work, allowed the museum to make an 'informed judgment' to acquire the work consistent with the AAMD's Statement of Principles.[70] In 2013, in response to donor dissatisfaction with the 2008 policy, the AAMD added two more categories of exceptions to include situations in which a donor had indicated the intent to make a gift to the museum or had donated a fractional interest before 2008.[71] If the museum discovers additional information through ongoing provenance research or if information is brought to the museum's attention as to another party's right to ownership, the museum should initiate the return of the work to that party.[72]

If the museum decides to proceed with a nonconforming acquisition, it should 'carefully balance the possible financial and reputational harm... against the benefit of collecting, presenting, and preserving the work in trust for the educational benefit of present and future generations'.[73] These two considerations both relate

[68] American Alliance of Museums, 'Standards Regarding Archaeological Material and Ancient Art' (2008) <www.aam-us.org/programs/ethics-standards-and-professional-practices/archaeological-material-and-ancient-art/> accessed 7 July 2021 (hereafter AAM, 'Standards Regarding Archaeological Material and Ancient Art').

[69] AAMD, 'Guidelines on the Acquisition of Archaeological Material and Ancient Art, Statement of Principles' (revised 2013) <https://aamd.org/sites/default/files/document/Guidelines%20on%20the%20Acquisition%20of%20Archaeological%20Material%20and%20Ancient%20Art%20revised%202013_0.pdf> accessed 20 July 2021 (hereafter AAMD, 2013 Guidelines on the Acquisition of Archaeological Material and Ancient Art Guidelines).

[70] ibid, s III.F.1–2.

[71] ibid, s III.F.3–4. The 2013 exceptions are: (1) where the work was acquired by gift or bequest and the work was on long-term loan to the museum before 2008, the donor had executed a written instrument prior to 2008 indicating an intent to donate or bequeath the work to the museum, or the museum had an expectation before 2008 that the work would be given by gift or bequest and that expectation was memorialized in some form; and (2) where the museum had acquired a fractional interest in the work by gift, bequest, or purchase before 2008.

[72] ibid, s III.I.

[73] ibid, s III.F.

to the museum's *own* situation. The policy does not call on museums to examine the harms to the archaeological record, and thereby to the museum's educational mission, and to the rights of the country of origin, or the possible incentivization of future looting that the acquisition may cause. In addition, museums are required to post nonconforming objects acquired after 2008 on an online object registry with available provenance information and an explanation of how the acquisition comports with the AAMD guidelines.[74] The AAMD policy applies only to works of art and archaeological objects created 'in antiquity' and leaves it to each museum to define the term.[75]

The object registry for archaeological objects and works of ancient art seems to have been based, at least in part, on the registries of artworks stolen during the Holocaust.[76] In the latter case, the registries give public notice of the work's location, thus furthering the goal of restitution. However, in the case of nonconforming archaeological objects, rather than facilitating restitution, the registry may have the opposite effect. The registry may give actual or constructive notice to interested parties of the location of these nonconforming works, thus effectively triggering the accrual of a cause of action for recovery and initiating the statutory limitations period. Any later claim may be time-barred. Furthermore, to the extent that use of the registry enables acquisition of a nonconforming and possibly recently looted antiquity, the guidelines are not an effective deterrent to the market with its detrimental consequences, as discussed in chapter 4. In the case of artworks looted during the Holocaust, the detriment is the continuing dispossession of the rightful owners, and the registry can help to alleviate this harm by giving notice to potential claimants. However, in the case of poorly provenanced archaeological objects, there are two detriments—deprivation of the rightful owner and harm to the archaeological record. The latter is an ongoing phenomenon, which is not alleviated

[74] AAMD Object Registry: Registry of New Acquisitions of Archaeological Material and Works of Ancient Art <https://aamd.org/object-registry/new-acquisitions-of-archaeological-material-and-works-of-ancient-art/browse> accessed 20 July 2021.

[75] An AAMD survey of museum practice indicated the use of the following dates to define the end of antiquity for nine cultures: Greek and Roman art (*c* 476 or 527 CE); Egyptian art (641 CE); Chinese art (221 BCE, 220, 618, or 907 CE); Japanese art (710, 710, 645, or 1185 CE), Korean art (668, 676, or 918 CE); Indian (South Asian) art (320 CE); Southeast Asian art (*c* 800, 500, 1462 CE, as well as other dates); Ancient Near Eastern art (313, 622, 644, 651, or 700 CE); Art of the Americas (time of European conquest, *c* 1492–1550 CE). <https://aamd.org/sites/default/files/document/Antiquity%20Definitions%20Memo.pdf> accessed 20 July 2021. While these dates are tied to historical events, the event chosen to mark the end of 'antiquity' varies considerably among museums.

[76] Nazi-Era Provenance Internet Portal Project (n 19) lists close to 30,000 objects from 179 participating museums. La Follette points out that the registry of objects possibly looted during the Holocaust is far more extensive and gives more provenance information than is given for antiquities on the AAMD Registry. Laetitia La Follette, 'Looted Antiquities, Art Museums and Restitution in the United States since 1970' (2016) 52(3) Journal of Contemporary History 669, 673–74. One explanation (among several) is that the AAM and AAMD guidelines with respect to Holocaust-looted art require museums to search their existing collections and not only new acquisitions, as is the case with antiquities.

and may be encouraged through museum acquisitions of nonconforming archaeological objects.

A difficulty in evaluating the extent of compliance with the 1970 standard is the lack of transparency among museums. Although some museums post their acquisitions policies online,[77] others do not. Because museums do not announce which objects they decline to acquire because they do not conform to the 1970 standard and many do not publish with provenance all the objects that they do acquire, it is not possible to determine the true extent of compliance with the 1970 standard. Museums should be required by legislation to engage in greater transparency by making public their acquisitions policy and all recent acquisitions with full provenance information.[78]

Studies of the object registry have concluded that museums are interpreting the exceptions to the 1970 standard quite liberally and that, for the most part, they are not engaging in a process of provenance documentation scrutiny that would allow them to formulate 'an informed judgment' that the object complies with the 1970 standard. As Laetitia La Follette has noted, '[m]ost museums still tend to emphasize the first life (the moment of creation), which leads them to treat all antiquities the same, be they scientifically excavated or undocumented'.[79]A statistical study of the objects on the AAMD registry as of late 2017 drew two preliminary conclusions: first, that these nonconforming objects did not have a long provenance history that could be traced back close to 1970, and, second, most of the acquisitions did not rely on high quality provenance information.[80]

In the considerable majority of post-2008 acquisitions by AAMD member museums there could not have been a basis in objectively verifiable provenance documentation for a museum, in its 'informed judgment', to conclude that the object was outside of its country of modern discovery before 1970.[81] In almost half of

[77] See, for example, J Paul Getty Museum Collection Policy (revised policy approved 15 September 2019), s V.C.3 <www.getty.edu/about/governance/pdfs/acquisitions_policy.pdf> accessed 20 July 2021; Museum of Fine Arts Boston Acquisitions and Provenance Policy <www.mfa.org/collections/provenance/acquisitions-and-provenance-policy> accessed 20 July 2021.

[78] The policy of the Museum of Fine Arts Boston states: 'In order to ensure transparency and aid potential claimants, all accessioned objects will be posted on the Museum's website and on other applicable databases . . .' ibid. Such a disclosure requirement would be justified by the significant benefits that accrue to a museum through its status as a charitable organization and the favourable tax treatment of donations.

[79] Laetitia La Follette, 'The Impact of the 1970 UNESCO Convention on Unprovenanced Etruscan Artifacts in the United States' in Alexandra Carpino and others (eds) *Collecting and Collectors from Antiquity to Modernity* (Archaeological Institute of America 2018) 75, 76.

[80] Patty Gerstenblith, 'Provenances Real, Fake and Questionable' (2019) 26 IJCP 285.

[81] ibid, 299–302. The study examined approximately 1,100 entries on the Object Registry. Only 235 (approximately 22 per cent) had provenance information (based on provenance documentation of any type) that predates 1970, even though the Guidelines call for museums to have reached an informed judgement that the objects they acquire were outside of their country of origin before 1970. Ninety-eight objects had an earliest provenance date between 1971 and 1980, indicating a degree of substantial compliance with the 1970 standard, while 172 objects have an earliest provenance date between 1981 and 1989. The year with the largest number of earliest provenance dates is 1990 with 114 objects, reflecting some of the Bourne collection acquired by the Walters Art Gallery in Baltimore in 2009. For discussion of the problematic aspects of the Bourne collection, see ibid, 298–99.

these acquisitions, the object does not have an objectively verifiable provenance that predates 2008 or that, in many cases, predates the acquisition itself. This means that at the time the museum acquired the object, the object was previously unknown or only minimally known and might therefore be the product of recent site looting. This evidence refutes the notion that the AAMD's adoption of the 1970 standard would stand as a bulwark between the looting of an archaeological site, on the one hand, and museum acquisitions or acquisitions by collectors that would later be donated to museums, on the other.

A second challenge in evaluating compliance with the 1970 standard is the quality of the provenance information on which museums rely in determining whether a possible acquisition complies with the standard. Given the ubiquitous nature of false provenance information that may accompany authentic but illegal antiquities and the self-interest of the donor or seller, presumably the primary source of provenance information, evaluation of the information relied upon by museums is an important component in assessing the extent of compliance. Compliance with an acquisition guideline is only as good as the quality of the provenance documentation upon which an acquisition depends. While the field of provenance research with respect to artworks looted during the Holocaust has developed with funding, publications, internet resources, and workshops to train researchers, provenance research methodology with respect to archaeological artefacts has not yet seen comparable development. As Jane Levine, former Worldwide Compliance Counsel at Sotheby's, has commented:

> [a] credible and documented provenance, or ownership history, stands as a kind of buffer zone at the intersection between an antiquities market that could function legally and legitimately, and the dirty and largely illegal business of site looting .... A higher standard of care in due diligence research provides the best mechanism to distinguish between objects that are legal to sell ... and objects that are the products of recent and ongoing looting and destruction of sites.[82]

Levine further questions whether the market has arrived 'at an accepted consensus surrounding the *type* of documentation and the nature of the evidence that buyers and sellers will accept as proof of ownership history'.[83]

Levine offers a hierarchy of types of provenance documentation. The highest level of documentation consists of '[r]eliable, credible written invoices showing the historical chronology of the transfers of the object, or published proof of exhibition in books or catalogues ....'[84] She suggests that provenance research should be conducted much like an investigative inquiry—whether contemporaneously created

[82] Levine, 'Importance of Provenance Documentation' (n 29) 221.
[83] ibid, 229 (emphasis in original).
[84] ibid.

documents, such as insurance records, letters, or family photographs, are available and whether lower quality evidence, such as verbal accounts, are acceptable. She also points out that the authenticity of some forms of evidence, particularly verbal accounts, should be judged against the backdrops of reliability, potential financial gain, self-interest, and availability or lack of objective corroborating evidence.[85]

An example of the difficulty of applying the 1970 standard to museum acquisitions and unreliable provenance documentation is the purchase by the Metropolitan Museum of Art of the gold coffin of an Egyptian priest, Nedjemankh (Figure 6.1). The museum purchased the coffin in 2017 in reliance on an export licence dated to 1971. Because it was accompanied by an export licence, the export would have seemed legal, and the museum would not have placed the acquisition on the AAMD object registry. However, an investigation by the New York County District Attorney's Office revealed that the export licence was a forgery and that the coffin had been looted from Egypt in 2011 and was part of an extensive international smuggling ring.[86] A more careful inspection of the export licence would have shown the forgery, as it gave an incorrect name for the country at the time of the supposed export.

The US museum community posited that acceptance of the 1970 standard, despite the inconsistencies in its implementation, would mean that countries of origin would not bring claims to recover objects that had left their country before 1970.[87] Yet in a few cases, countries of discovery have brought claims, such as Turkey's claim for the gold treasure purchased by the University of Pennsylvania Museum of Anthropology and Archaeology in 1966, which was resolved with the objects given on permanent loan to Turkey.[88] Another pre-1970 return was a marble relief excavated on Thasos in Greece in 1911 and stolen from an excavation storeroom soon after. J Paul Getty purchased it in 1955; the Getty Trust returned it in 2006.[89] These cases illustrate that artefacts taken illegally before 1970 should also be returned as a matter of fairness and justice, even when these objects fall outside of the ethical policies.[90]

Another difficulty with application of the 1970 standard is that museums increasingly engage in long-term loans of cultural materials from both private collectors and institutions. However, it is unclear whether the AAM and AAMD policies apply to loans, thus potentially presenting a significant gap in applicability

[85] ibid, 231–32.

[86] 'Manhattan D.A.'s Office Returns Ancient Gold Coffin to Egypt' (25 September 2019) <www.manhattanda.org/manhatta-das-office-returns-ancient-gold-coffin/> accessed 21 July 2021.

[87] AAMD, Introduction to the Revisions to the 2008 Guidelines, 2013 Guidelines on the Acquisition of Archaeological Material and Ancient Art Guidelines (n 69).

[88] George F Bass, 'A Hoard of Trojan and Sumerian Jewelry' (1970) 74(4) American Journal of Archaeology 335; C Brian Rose, 'Beyond the UNESCO Convention: The Case of the Troy Gold in the Penn Museum' (2017) 5(1) JEMAHS 87.

[89] Lyons, 'Museums as Sites of Reconciliation' (n 66) 425.

[90] Lyons commented: 'The case of the Thasos relief shows that when there is reasonably sound evidence of an illegal transaction, there should be no statute of limitations for making restitutions.' ibid.

Figure 6.1 Lid of the coffin of Nedjemankh, priest of Heyrshef, Egypt, 150–50 BCE. Returned to Egypt 2019, now in the National Museum of Egyptian Civilization

of the 1970 standard. The AAMD guidelines specifically define an acquisition to include purchase, gift, bequest, and exchange but do not mention loans. In 2006, the AAMD had adopted guidelines stating that long-term loans should be evaluated under the criteria for acquisitions. However, this guideline cites the specific applicable guideline adopted in 2004 for acquisition of archaeological materials. Therefore, one should conclude that the AAMD does not apply later adopted guidelines to long-term loans.[91] Borrowing works of art for a long

[91] AAMD, 2013 Guidelines on the Acquisition of Archaeological Material and Ancient Art Guidelines (n 69) s I.A. AAMD, 'Report of the AAMD Subcommittee on Incoming Loans of Archaeological Material and Art' (2006) Guideline II (D). The provisions of the AAM policy are less precise, but the policy refers only to 'new acquisitions'. AAM, 'Standards Regarding Archaeological Material and

Figure 6.2 Rock Crystal Ewer, Egypt, Fatimid, late tenth–eleventh century. Keir Collection, Dallas Museum of Art

term[92] allows the museum to study and display the object. The loan may also substitute for an outright acquisition, particularly as a lender may be paid a fee for the

Ancient Art' (n 68). This contrasts with the AAM and AAMD guidelines concerning works of art that may have been looted during the Holocaust, which explicitly apply to loans. See AAMD, 'Task Force on Spoliation of Art' (n 20) s II.F (Incoming Loans). However, the AAMD policy sets a lower threshold of provenance research for loans of works possibly looted during the Holocaust than for acquisitions.

[92] There is no agreed definition of how long a long-term loan is. However, travelling special exhibits typically remain in a single location for less than a year (and often only about three to four months) and travel to several venues.

loan and the terms of loan agreements are generally not publicly available. As long-term loans become more prevalent with museums treating them as de facto substitutes for acquisitions, the line between a loan and an acquisition becomes blurred and particularly loans from private collections require greater scrutiny.

One example is the loan to the Dallas Museum of Art of a large private collection of Islamic art, known as the Keir collection. The loan is for fifteen years, which may be extended, and consists of almost 2,000 objects spanning 1,300 years (Figure 6.2).[93] Although not paying any loan fees, the Museum is conferring value by storing the objects and creating a new exhibition space for the collection, as well as conserving, studying, and publishing it. The flexibility that the Dallas Museum is granted in dealing with the collection extends to lending to other institutions. In the United States, objects on loan receive two legal advantages. The State Department may grant immunity from seizure to objects entering the United States on loan but not to objects entering permanently.[94] Similarly, objects imported temporarily for exhibit are exempt from the import restrictions imposed under the Convention on Cultural Property Implementation Act.[95] The use of long-term loans allows museums to take advantage of loopholes in the application of the 1970 standard as well as loopholes created by legal provisions.

6.4.3 Codes of Conduct among Market Participants

While dealers, auction houses, and private collectors are not bound by museum policies, it was assumed that the adoption of such policies by museums would have an indirect effect on the higher-end collector and therefore also on the market. Such a collector would want to know before acquiring an object that it could ultimately be donated to a museum. By refusing to acquire objects without a pre-1970 provenance or refusing to pay a premium based on a possible future tax benefit, private collectors would place pressure on dealers and auction houses to also comply with the 1970 standard. Some market observers therefore posited that antiquities with a pre-1970 provenance would command higher prices at auction,[96] thus providing a self-regulating mechanism, although this effect has been disputed.[97]

93 Randy Kennedy 'Dallas Museum Lands a Rich Trove of Islamic Art' (*New York Times* 3 February 2014) <https://www.nytimes.com/2014/02/04/arts/design/dallas-museum-lands-a-rich-trove-of-islamic-art.html?_r=0> www.dma.org/press-release/dallas-museum-art-receives-one-world-s-leading-private-collections-islamic-art> accessed 11 July 2023.

94 22 USC § 2459.

95 19 USC § 2611(1).

96 For example Souren Melikian, 'Antiquities, With a Proven Record, Drive Auction Market' (*New York Times*, 14 June 2013) <www.nytimes.com/2013/06/15/arts/15iht-melikian15.html> accessed 21 July 2021.

97 Brodie, 'Provenance and Price' (n 29). Some have also suggested that the presence on the market of lower priced antiquities may serve as a way of encouraging new collectors to enter the antiquities field. Patrick J O'Keefe, *Trade in Antiquities: Reducing Destruction and Theft* (Archetype 1997) 66–69.

In 1999, UNESCO promulgated its International Code of Ethics for Dealers in Cultural Property.[98] In general, the Code states that traders should not import, export, or transfer ownership of property when they have 'reasonable cause to believe it was stolen, illegally alienated, clandestinely excavated or illegally exported'.[99] Traders who have reasonable cause to believe the object was involved in illegal conduct will not assist further in any transaction.[100] The Code was to be enforced by a body to be nominated by participating dealers, but it is not clear whether this body was established or whether any complaints have come before it. As O'Keefe noted, 'traders do not seem to have responded to it'.[101]

6.5 Human Remains and Indigenous Sacred and Cultural Objects

Most codes of ethics recognize that human remains require respect and special treatment reflecting their nature, but the codes are often vague as to what that treatment should be. The ethical statements of the World Archaeological Congress, the Vermillion Accord on Human Remains (1989) and the Tamaki Makau-rau Accord on the Display of Human Remains and Sacred Objects, have had a significant impact on the profession of anthropology by requiring respectful treatment of human remains and restricting their display. In particular, these statements emphasize the need for consultation with affected communities; equal treatment regardless of origin, race, religion, nationality, custom, and tradition; and negotiation to reach mutually acceptable agreements as to disposition.[102]

The ICOM Code of Ethics for Museums reflects the influence of the statements of the World Archaeological Congress. The ICOM Code states that: '[r]esearch on human remains and materials of sacred significance must ... take into account the interest and beliefs of the community, ethnic or religious groups from whom the objects originated, where these are known.'[103] Display of these sensitive materials should also be limited by similar concerns for the beliefs of the communities from which they originated and such materials 'must be presented with great tact and

[98] UNESCO, International Code of Ethics for Dealers in Cultural Property (1999) CLT/CH/INS-06/25 rev <https://unesdoc.unesco.org/ark:/48223/pf0000121320> accessed 21 July 2021 (hereafter, UNESCO, International Code of Ethics). Patrick J O'Keefe, *Protecting Cultural Objects: Before and After 1970* (Institute of Art and Law 2017) 46–48, 79–90 (hereafter O'Keefe, *Protecting Cultural Objects*).

[99] UNESCO, International Code of Ethics (n 98) Article 1.

[100] ibid, Articles 3 and 4.

[101] O'Keefe, *Protecting Cultural Objects* (n 98) 89–90.

[102] World Archaeological Congress, 'The Vermillion Accord on Human Remains' (1989) and 'The Tamaki Makau-rau Accord on the Display of Human Remains and Sacred Objects' (2005) <https://worldarch.org/code-of-ethics/> accessed 21 July 2021. For an overview of relevant policies, see Christian Lenk, 'Ethical Principles for Collections containing Human Remains' in Deutscher Museums Bund (ed), Guidelines for Care of Human Remains in Museums and Collections (2021) 110, 114.

[103] International Council of Museums, 'ICOM Code of Ethics for Museums' (n 6) s 3.7.

respect for the feelings of human dignity held by all peoples'.[104] Requests for removal of such materials from display and requests for return should be 'addressed expeditiously with respect and sensitivity'.[105] While recognizing the particular interests of communities and ethnic and religious groups from which remains originated, the ICOM Code permits the collection of human remains and sacred materials.[106]

As discussed in chapter 5, the United States and Australia have confronted the issue of repatriation of human remains, burial objects, and sacred and cultural objects through legislation. The National Museum of Australia has a policy for Non-Australian Indigenous Human Remains under which the Museum does not generally collect human remains but may act as a custodian of remains; it seeks to identify the correct communities or custodians for the remains; it conducts research only with the written free, prior, and informed consent of the relevant community; it treats associated grave goods in the same manner; and it returns ancestral human remains to appropriate communities on request without placing any restrictions on communities to whom ancestral remains are returned.[107]

Canada does not have federal legislation regulating the disposition of human remains in museum collections. The Museums Association's Ethics Guidelines, without referring specifically to Indigenous human remains or funerary objects, state that museums should be 'committed to the return of human remains, directly associated funerary objects and culturally sensitive objects when requested by communities or groups with a demonstrable claim of historical relationship'.[108] The Guidelines also direct that requests for restitution be given 'immediate and serious consideration' but that requests will be resolved by each museum on a case-by-case basis. The Guidelines do not address the curation or study of human remains and sensitive objects, stating that '[w]here appropriate, museums could assist in the reinterment of (archaeological) human osteological material by assisting local reburial committees or other community groups'.[109] Otherwise, the code specifies that the museum should carry out research and other activities 'in a manner acceptable to the originating community'.[110] The Guidelines set a high standard of

[104] ibid, s 4.3.
[105] ibid, s 4.4.
[106] ibid, s 2.5.
[107] National Museum Australia, 'Non-Australian indigenous human remains policy' (2020) ss 3–4 <www.nma.gov.au/about/corporate/plans-policies/policies/non-australian-indigenous-human-remains> accessed 21 July 2021.
[108] Canadian Museums Association, 'Ethics Guidelines' (2006) Guideline E.4.4 <www.ethicscodescollection.org/detail/83df8b9f-6fe3-436c-b15c-3a11878c2e34> accessed 4 March 2022 (hereafter 'Guidelines'). Unlike the US court decision in *Bonnichsen et al v United States* 357 F3d 962 (9th Cir 2004), where the court rejected reliance on oral histories, the Guidelines direct museums to respect oral history and traditional knowledge concerning culturally significant objects and human osteological material'. ibid, Guideline C.3.
[109] ibid, Guideline G.
[110] ibid.

legal compliance requiring that museums 'avoid even the remotest suspicion of compliance in any illegal activity' and that museums notify law enforcement of any suspected illegal activity.[111]

The Additional Guidance of the UK Museums Association directs individual museums to develop their own policy with respect to acquiring, holding, disposing of, and repatriating human remains and for consulting with 'source communities'.[112] Legal requirements for handling older human remains are few. Therefore, the ethical obligations that derive from the Department of Culture, Media and Sport (DCMS) Guidance for the Care of Human Remains in Museums issued in 2005 are more significant for setting standards of conduct.[113] The Human Tissue Act permits but does not require deaccessioning and return of human remains.[114] Human remains can be displayed so as long as it is done in a way that does not outrage public decency and the display provides 'a material contribution to a particular interpretation ....'[115] The Guidance adopts consultation as the principle governing the treatment of human remains.[116] The Guidance sets out five ethical principles: (1) nonmaleficence (do no harm), (2) respect for diversity of belief, (3) respect for the value of science, (4) solidarity, and (5) beneficence.[117] While acknowledging that decisions about return of human remains must be made on a case-by-case basis, the Guidance sets out detailed principles and procedures for responding to claims taking into consideration such factors as rights of possession; cultural and religious values of individuals and communities and strength of their relationship to the remains; cultural, spiritual, and religious significance of the remains; and the scientific, educational, and historical importance of the material.[118]

The policy of the National Museum of Ireland is worth noting for its details concerning acquisition, care, deaccessioning, and research of human remains.

[111] ibid, Guideline C.2.

[112] Museums Association, Additional guidance to the Code of Ethics 2(c) Human Remains <www.museumsassociation.org/campaigns/ethics/code-of-ethics/> accessed 21 July 2021.

[113] Department for Culture, Media and Sport, 'Guidance for the Care of Human Remains in Museums' (Oct 2005) <https://webarchive.nationalarchives.gov.uk/+/http://www.culture.gov.uk/images/publications/GuidanceHumanRemains11Oct.pdf> accessed 21 July 2021 (hereafter Department of Culture, Media, and Sport 'Guidance'). See Charlotte Woodhead, 'Care, Custody and Display of Human Remains: Legal and Ethical Obligations' in Myra Giesen (ed), *Curating Human Remains: Caring for the Dead in the United Kingdom* (Boydell 2013) 31, 31.

[114] Human Tissue Act 2004 c 30, s 47.

[115] Department for Culture, Media and Sport, 'Guidance' (n 113) s 2.7.

[116] ibid, s 1.2. Consent is the principle governing disposition of remains that are less than one hundred years old. In the case of older human remains, consent is 'problematic' particularly because UK legislation does not recognize that human rights can be exercised by groups, restricting human rights to individuals. ibid.

[117] ibid. The principle of respect for diversity of belief is explained as demonstrating 'humility and modesty regarding one's own opinions, and shows respect for individuals, cultures, groups and communities. The principle requires decision-makers to give consideration to the cultural and historical backgrounds, beliefs and values relevant to all parties concerned.' ibid. The principle of solidarity focuses on cooperation and consensus, recognizing that 'we all have a shared humanity and an interest in furthering common goals and tolerating differences that respect fundamental human rights.' ibid.

[118] ibid, part 3.

It includes a particularly sensitive approach to the display of human remains, which takes 'into account the interests and beliefs of members of the community, ethnic or religious groups from whom the objects originated'.[119]

In contrast to the approach taken by the UK Museums Association, the German Museum Association sets no chronological or geographic limits to the human remains to which its policy applies.[120] The guidelines suggest examining the contexts of injustice, such as during colonialism and the Holocaust, in which human remains may have been collected, what would constitute legitimate consent, and determining the community of origin. Establishing a context of injustice provides the particularly relevant circumstances in which museums and collections should no longer continue to retain human remains; remains not from a context of injustice may be considered for return when the remains or objects are of 'special significance' to those to whom the remains would be returned.[121] The guidelines specify that determinations should be made 'in light of today's ethical standards', rather than relying on standards extant at the time the remains were collected. This is a rejection of an approach based on nonretroactivity of contemporary ethical standards for evaluating past conduct.[122] The practical guidance gives extensive detail not only about collecting, storage, exhibition, and deaccessioning of human remains but also about when, under what circumstances, and how research may be conducted on remains, and when the research may be published.[123] In addition, extensive detail is given as to how to respond to requests for repatriation. In cases where a claim does not have a legal basis, the institution should consider an ethical–moral basis. Public institutions are constrained in returning deaccessioned items only in circumstances where there is a legal basis to do so. However, the practical guidance acknowledges a broad consensus that human remains taken during a colonial context may be returned on a purely moral or ethical basis. Copies of documentation and archival materials should also be repatriated, but relevant information should be retained by the institution, with the question of whether the institution can continue to use the information to be decided by an agreement.[124]

The IZIKO Museums in South Africa adopted a policy in 2005 that addresses the acquisition, documentation, storage, and study of human remains in their collections, although the policy is constrained by the National Heritage Resources Act.[125] IZIKO Museums is an umbrella organization of twelve museums and

[119] National Museum of Ireland Human Remains Policy (2019) 4, para 3.
[120] Deutscher Museums Bund, Guidelines Care of Human Remains in Museums and Collections (2021) 14–15.
[121] ibid, 15–21.
[122] ibid, 21.
[123] ibid, 35–42.
[124] ibid, 52–57.
[125] Policy on the Management of Human Remains in IZIKO Collections, in Jeremy Silvester, Museums Association of Namibia, Report on the Human Remains Management and Repatriation Workshop (13–14 February 2017) 18–22.

historical houses in South Africa, which hold human remains taken from Namibia during colonialism and the genocide of the early twentieth century. The Policy on the Management of Human Remains in IZIKO Collections provides parameters for restitution to descendant communities of unethically collected[126] human remains and burial goods that were directly associated with human remains. Unlike human remains collected in other circumstances, because of the relatively recent date of these takings and the use of archival materials, these remains can often be identified with specific, known individuals or, in default, associated with specific communities and locations.

In the United States, one of the main purposes of the Native American Graves Protection and Repatriation Act (NAGPRA) is to require museums to provide information to Native American tribes about the museums' holdings and to repatriate them when lineal descent or cultural affiliation is identified.[127] As a result, the ethical guidelines of the US museum associations do not consider this issue in detail. For example, the AAM Code of Ethics states: 'the unique and special nature of human remains and funerary and sacred objects is recognized as the basis of all decisions concerning such collections.'[128]

While not addressing human remains, the AAMD released a Report on the Acquisition and Stewardship of Sacred Objects in 2006.[129] The Report distinguishes between religious works, which express religious ideas, and sacred objects, which were 'created for use in ritual or ceremonial practice of a traditional religion'. According to the Report, museums, as secular institutions, are not in a position to identify sacred objects but rather should do so through consultation with Indigenous and traditional religious leaders.

The AAMD Report suggests that its members should exceed NAGPRA's requirements by consulting with non-federally recognized tribes and tribes in other countries. On the other hand, the Report refers to the narrow definition given to 'sacred objects' under NAGPRA as 'specific ceremonial objects which are needed by traditional Native American religious leaders for the practice of traditional Native American religions by their present-day adherents'.[130] The Report views such a narrow definition as necessary for art museums to be able to carry out their

[126] The policy defines as 'unethical' the 'Collecting of human remains solely for the purposes of racial study' and 'Collecting without appropriate consent, human remains from recent graves of individuals who were known in life, or were from known communities'. Ethical collecting of remains is the 'taking custody' of accidentally discovered remains and '[l]egitimate intervention at the request of a community in areas where burial places are at risk'. ibid, paras 2.10 and 2.11.

[127] 25 USC §§ 3003 (requiring detailed inventories for human remains and associated funerary objects); 3004 (requiring less detailed summaries for unassociated funerary objects, sacred objects, and objects of cultural patrimony).

[128] American Alliance of Museums, Code of Ethics (n 3).

[129] Association of Art Museum Directors, Report of the AAMD Task Force on the Acquisition and Stewardship of Sacred Objects' (2006) <https://aamd.org/sites/default/files/document/Sacred%20Objects%20Guideline%2008.06.pdf> accessed 21 July 2021.

[130] 25 USC § 3001(3)(C).

mission in terms of acquisition, preservation, and presentation to the general public. The Report also calls on museums to find ways of reconciling their own principles (such as conservation requirements) with religious dictates and to consult with Indigenous religious leaders to determine whether a sacred object can be acquired 'without damaging the society's central religious beliefs'. Finally, the Report encourages museums to use sensitivity in determining how to display sacred objects that are already in their collections and to accord equal treatment and respect in the interpretation and presentation of different religions.

The Authentic Tribal Art Dealers Association (ATADA), an international association of dealers, auction houses, museums, and collectors, focuses on primarily Native American tribal arts.[131] The ATADA statement of 'Trade Practices, Ethics, and Guarantees' requires that its members do not trade in objects until they have established 'to the best of their ability that such objects were not stolen from excavations, architectural monuments, public institutions, tribal communities, or private property'.[132] The members also agree not to trade items 'known to be of current sacred, communal use to Native American tribal communities'; this obligation does not regard objects made for commercial purposes or for individual use by Native American artisans 'as sacred or ceremonial, regardless of age'.[133] Finally, ATADA also condemns illegal removal of artefacts from tribal or federal lands. These provisions seem to be a restatement of existing legal requirements rather than an attempt to set a higher standard of conduct.[134]

6.6 Conclusion

Approaches based on ethical principles to the particularly problematic areas of artworks stolen during the Holocaust, archaeological artefacts looted from sites, and Indigenous human remains and sacred objects seem, for the most part, to be unsatisfactory. Applicable law leaves many gaps and varies significantly among different countries. Ethical codes and principles adopted by many of the stakeholders—academics, academic institutions, professional associations, museums, museum associations, and market professionals—should close those gaps. Ethical codes should do so by requiring conduct that surpasses what the law requires and

[131] ATADA <https://atada.org/bylaws-policies> accessed 21 July 2021.

[132] ATADA, 'Bylaws & Policies', s 4.

[133] ibid, s 5. This distinction seems to be an attempt to interpret narrowly NAGPRA's definition of sacred cultural items, which must be needed 'for the practice of traditional Native American religions by their present day adherents'. It similarly interprets narrowly the definition of cultural patrimony, which must have 'ongoing historical, traditional, or cultural importance central to the Native American group or culture itself, rather than property owned by an individual Native American'. 25 USC § 3001(3)(C) and (D).

[134] 18 USC § 1170 (criminalizing trading in Native American cultural items obtained in violation of NAGPRA).

restricting interactions with cultural objects that may not be demonstrably illegal but whose background indicates that they may be the product of illegal activity.

Perhaps of greater significance is that, with the possible limited exception of ethical principles based on the 1970 standard, there is little consistency among ethical codes and virtually no enforcement mechanisms among the associations. These codes of ethics and professional conduct are also limited in their application. The codes dealing with artworks looted during the Holocaust are limited to a particular category of artworks and sacred objects. Codes dealing with antiquities apply only to objects possibly obtained illegally after 1970 and do not reach back in time to the period of colonialism and other periods of violence. The 1970 standard ignores the legal mechanisms, particularly State vesting laws, that were in place earlier, often significantly predating 1970. Further, the 1970 standard applies generally only to new acquisitions and has applied only occasionally to objects already in the collection of a museum. It is therefore a limited mechanism for restitution. The codes that deal with human remains and sacred or burial objects have the potential to reach back further in time, with the German Museums Association adopting this approach. In contrast, the UK's DCMS Guidance applies only to remains that are more than one hundred years old. As seen in the discussion in chapter 5, section 5.3.3, the number of human remains that have been returned is relatively small, other than where such repatriation is required by law.[135] As we turn in the next chapter to the even more fraught topic of the disposition of cultural objects expropriated in a more distant past, primarily through colonialism and other forms of violence, the need for a stronger and more encompassing framework with justifications rooted in broader concerns for achieving justice through restitution is clear.

[135] Between 1992 and 2013, US museums and federal agencies repatriated over 48,000 sets of human remains and one million associated funerary objects under NAGPRA. Jason Corcoran Roberts, 'Unwinding Non-Native Control Over Native America's Past: A Statistical Analysis of the Decisions to Return Native American Human Remains and Funerary Objects under the Native American Graves Protection and Repatriation Act, 1992–2013' (2016) 38 University of Hawai'i Law Review 337, 338.

7
Historical Appropriations: Of Time and Reparative Justice

7.1 Introduction

The mantra to decolonize museums has come to signify many things and to encompass disparate actions that museums can take to move past their origins as a beneficiary of colonialism, armed conflict, and political and economic imperialism. Here the question of decolonizing the museum refers to one specific aspect—whether the return of cultural objects taken during periods of armed conflict, colonialism, and empire can contribute to achieving redress and justice. Decolonization is 'the repatriation of Indigenous land and life', which were taken from Indigenous peoples through extractive colonialism. In the case of Indigenous peoples, cultural objects are closely associated with the land. Restitution of cultural objects is a part of decolonization through the return of cultural objects, which is a facet of returning life.[1]

The restitution of cultural objects to their communities, both original and descendant, often falls outside of legal strictures and the boundaries set by contemporary voluntary and ethical guidelines of conduct. This chapter therefore turns to proposing a methodology for the return of cultural objects from where they were taken without the consent of local communities and States. This methodology focuses, in particular, on those objects removed before the current treaty regime was adopted over the course of the twentieth century, as discussed in chapter 5, and those objects to which contemporary ethical codes and voluntary guidelines also do not apply, as discussed in chapter 6. Passage of time and characterization of the ownership status of historically appropriated objects present significant obstacles, and it is therefore unlikely that the countries and communities of origin will succeed in such claims through the existing legal system. However, these obstacles are the product of political actions that set arbitrary limits and that can be reversed through political decisions and voluntary steps. This endeavour requires a rebalancing to increase focus on State and community interests in the location of movable cultural objects in comparison to universalist interests. A new paradigm may

[1] Eve Tuck and K Wayne Yang, 'Decolonization is not a metaphor' (2012) 1/1 Decolonization: Indigeneity, Education & Society 1, 21. The application of decolonization to other forms of restitution may not fit this definition and is not discussed here.

Cultural Objects and Reparative Justice. Patty Gerstenblith, Oxford University Press. © Patty Gerstenblith 2023.
DOI: 10.1093/oso/9780192872104.003.0007

resolve these conflicting claims to the tangible cultural remains of the past. In turn, these questions raise issues of the deeper meaning of cultural heritage and the role that objects play in constituting history, memory, and heritage for communities and States.

7.2 The Problem of Time

The disposition of cultural objects removed during nineteenth-century and early-twentieth-century colonialism, imperialism and armed conflict raises the challenge of the 'perennial issue of *time and law*' and, in particular, the necessity to 'live and work *within time*'.[2] Yet in his opinion in the Preah Vihear Temple case, Judge Cançado Trindade asserted that courts need to refrain from being strictly limited by time. Time raises three obstacles to restitution: the bar on legal claims through the passage of time; the failure to project contemporary law back in time through the non-retroactivity principle; and the willingness to project past infirmities in the law forward to the present, particularly the double standard that became engrained in international law during the nineteenth century. These bars based on passage of time pose obstacles to the return of historically appropriated cultural objects and attempts to correct historical injustices.

7.2.1 Bars Based on Passage of Time

Bars to claims based on passage of time typically arise in private litigation in which the claimant attempts to recover stolen property. In common law countries, a thief cannot transfer title to stolen property, but the owner's claim may be barred through passage of time based on statutes of limitation, equitable defences, or adverse possession doctrine.[3] The UNIDROIT Convention grafts onto time bars a discovery rule that runs from the time a claimant learns the location of the object or identity of the possessor. This discovery rule applies where the object forms 'an integral part of an identified monument or archaeological site, or belong[s] to a public collection' (Art 3(4)). It also applies to 'a sacred or communally important cultural object belonging to and used by a tribal or indigenous community ... as

[2] Request for Interpretation of the Judgment of 15 June 1962 in the case concerning the Temple of Preah Vihear *(Cambodia v Thailand)* (Judgment) [2013] ICJ Rep 281 Separate Opinion of Judge Cançado Trindade, para 62.

[3] Patty Gerstenblith, 'Statutes of Limitation and Other Legal Challenges to the Recovery of Stolen Art' in Saskia Maria Hufnagel and Duncan Chappell (eds), *The Palgrave Handbook on Art Crime* (Palgrave Macmillan 2019) 271, 271–79 (hereafter Gerstenblith, 'Statutes of Limitation'). In the United States, state courts have molded these doctrines to delay the accrual of a cause of action until the original owner has a reasonable opportunity to learn the facts necessary to bring a claim. ibid, 274–76.

part of that community's traditional or ritual use' (Art 3(8)).[4] Nonetheless, even this flexibility is often insufficient to enable the original owner or community to bring a claim for restitution. That it might have been impossible for a colonized or subjugated people to bring a claim in the courts of the colonizing State rarely factors into the legal calculation of the time period that should be allowed before a claim is barred. This problem is exacerbated in civil law jurisdictions where a claim may be barred by the good faith purchaser doctrine, as well as prescription.[5]

Solutions to the problem of time limits on recovery claims can be found when the political will is present, which has occurred in the United States with respect to cultural objects stolen during the Holocaust.[6] In 2016 and in fulfilment of obligations under the Washington Conference Principles, Congress enacted the Holocaust Expropriated Art Recovery (HEAR) Act. This legislation abrogated any defence at law relating to passage of time for Holocaust recovery claims brought within ten years from enactment and within six years after actual discovery (defined to mean knowledge) of the identity and location of the property and of a possessory interest in the claimant.[7] The preemption applies to claims based on 'Nazi persecution' defined to mean 'any persecution of a specific group of individuals based on Nazi ideology by the Government of Germany, its allies or agents, members of the Nazi Party, or their agents or associates' between 1 January 1933 and 31 December 1945. The preemption applies to a broad range of cultural objects, including paintings, drawings, prints, lithographs, engravings, books, archives, musical instruments and manuscripts, sacred and ceremonial objects, and objects of Judaica.

However, much of the efficacy of the HEAR Act was negated by the Second Circuit Court of Appeals, which held in *Zuckerman v Metropolitan Museum of Art* that, based on the legislative history of the HEAR Act, the equitable defence

[4] UNIDROIT Convention on Stolen or Illegally Exported Cultural Objects (adopted 24 June 1995, entered into force 1 July 1998) 34 ILM 1322 (hereafter 1995 UNIDROIT Convention). See Lyndel V Prott, *Commentary on the UNIDROIT Convention* (2nd edn, Institute of Art and Law 2021); Patrick O'Keefe, 'Using UNIDROIT to Avoid Cultural Heritage Disputes: Limitation Periods' in James AR Nafziger and Ann M Nicgorski (eds), *Cultural Heritage Issues: The Legacy of Conquest, Colonization, and Commerce* (Martinus Nijhoff Publishers 2009) 389, 391–400.

[5] The differences in applicable law between civil law and common law jurisdictions also raise questions of conflicts and choice of law doctrines. Gerstenblith, 'Statutes of Limitation' (n 3) 279–85.

[6] US institutions have been criticized for their reliance on procedural or technical defences to recovery of artworks looted during the Holocaust. World Jewish Restitution Organization, 'Report Concerning Current Approaches of United States Museums to Holocaust-Era Art Claims' (25 June 2015) <https://wjro.org.il/cms/assets/uploads/2015/12/ReportMuseums.pdf> accessed 7 July 2021. Other defences, particularly based on foreign sovereign immunity and the act of state doctrine, may also bar claims of original owners and their successors.

[7] Pub L 114-308, 130 Stat 1524, s 5(a). California had previously enacted two statutes preempting the state's statute of limitations in Holocaust art recovery cases. The first was held unconstitutional. *Von Saher v Norton Simon Museum of Art at Pasadena*, 592 F3d 954, 960–68 (9th Cir 2010). Among its provisions, the California statute defined duress as 'a threat of force, violence, danger, or retribution against an owner ... sufficient to coerce a reasonable person of ordinary susceptibilities to perform an act that otherwise would not have been performed or to acquiesce to an act to which he or she would otherwise not have acquiesced'. AB 2765, codified as s 338(c)(3)(C)(iv).

of laches was not preempted and so could still bar a claim.[8] Although the Second Circuit noted Congress' goals in enacting the HEAR Act of achieving uniformity and just and fair resolutions, perpetuating availability of the laches defence means that uniformity will not be achieved. It will hinder the return of artworks taken during the Holocaust, and, by allowing current possessors to continue to rely on technical defences, it undermines resolution of claims on a substantive basis, a key element to achieving a just and fair resolution. Despite this undermining of its applicability, the HEAR Act provides a precedent for removing the obstacle posed by the passage of time, when the legislative body is prompted to enact ameliorative legislation. It remains an important precedent for the actions that can be taken to rectify the past once the political will to do so becomes sufficiently strong.

In European countries, a dispute that involves artworks looted during the Holocaust and now located in a national museum is often resolved through an art claims commission established for this purpose rather than through private litigation.[9] These claims commissions bypass technical defences and represent a political decision to return at least some of the looted artworks, regardless of what technical bars may exist. Despite the general proposition that collections of United Kingdom and French institutions cannot be deaccessioned, both countries have enacted legislation to allow deaccessioning for the purpose of the return of artworks stolen during the Holocaust[10] and of human remains.[11] Although not involving bars based on time, these political actions effectuate a policy of restitution in these specific circumstances. A broader step was taken through political action regarding claims for the return of cultural objects in museum collections when the 2022 UK Charities Act, applicable in England and Wales, amended the 2011 Charities Act. This amendment expands the ability of museums, including those created by statute, to seek permission from the Charity Commission, Attorney General, or

[8] 307 F Supp 3d 304 (SDNY 2018), aff'd on other grounds, 928 F3d 186, 195–97 (2nd Cir 2019). On the non-preemption of laches, see the Senate Report accompanying S 2763 <www.congress.gov/congressional-report/114th-congress/senate-report/394> accessed 12 August 2021. The court concluded that the plaintiff's delay in attempting to recover a well-known publicly held painting was unreasonable. The court assumed that prejudice, one of the required elements for a laches defence, caused to the Metropolitan Museum of Art was obvious and therefore did not need to be analysed, stating the prejudice is 'evident on the face of Zuckerman's complaint'. 928 F3d 190.

[9] See The Central Registry of Information on Looted Cultural Property 1933–1945 <www.lootedart.com/infobycountry> accessed 7 July 2021.

[10] Holocaust (Return of Cultural Objects) (formerly known as Holocaust (Stolen Art) Restitution) Act 2009, ch 16. This provision was to expire after ten years but was extended for an additional ten years. Earlier French legislation allowed deaccessioning of fifteen paintings that were looted during the Holocaust. Loi No 2022-218 du 21 février 2022 relative á la restitution ou la remise de certains biens culturels aux ayants droit de leurs propriétaires victims de persecutions antisémites.The French National Assembly subsequently modified the cultural heritage code to allow public institutions to return Nazi-looted objects in their collections, eliminating the need for individual legislation to be enacted in each case. Tessa Solomon, 'France Passes Law Allowing Museums to Restitute Nazi-Looted Artworks' (*ARTnews* 3 July 2023) https://www.artnews.com/art-news/news/france-passes-law-museums-restitute-nazi-looted-artworks-1234673197/ accessed 11 July 2023.

[11] Human Tissue Act 2004, c 30, s 47; Loi No 2010-501 of 18 May 2010 visant à autoriser la restitution par la France des têtes maories à la Nouvelle-Zélande et relative à la gestion des collections.

a court to make transfers of property pursuant to a moral obligation (s 16) and to transfer lower value property without the need for permission (s 15).[12] This removes an obstacle to returns and opens the possibility of more returns from these institutions of objects taken during colonialism and imperialism.

7.2.2 Bars Based on Non-Retroactivity

A second obstacle to the recovery of historically appropriated cultural objects is the principle of non-retroactivity (*tempus regit actum*). Actions are judged by the law in effect at the time of the action and not the law in effect at the time a dispute arises. This principle applies equally to treaty obligations with respect to any act or fact that occurred before ratification, unless a different intention is established.[13] As a defence against retroactive provisions, during debate on a UN General Assembly Resolution in 1973, the colonial and settler States pushed back on the idea that colonialism was to blame for the large-scale removal of artefacts. Instead, the States blamed the victims and the art market, thus producing a weakened resolution on restitution of colonial plunder.[14] In response to explicit acknowledgement of the problem of non-retroactivity in the 1970 UNESCO Convention,[15] in 1978 UNESCO established the Intergovernmental Committee for Promoting the Return of Cultural Property to the Countries of Origin or its Restitution in case of Illicit Appropriation.[16] However, the Committee has had few concrete successes.[17]

[12] Charities Act 2022, c 6, ss 15–16. However, these amendments may be changed to limit the applicability of moral bases for deaccessioning of cultural objects such as the Parthenon Sculptures and Benin objects.

[13] Vienna Convention on the Law of Treaties (opened for signature 23 May 1969, entered into force 27 January 1980) 1155 UNTS 331, 8 ILM 679, Article 28; Ana Filipa Vrdoljak, *International Law, Museums and the Return of Cultural Objects* (CUP 2006) 207–08 (hereafter Vrdoljak, *International Law*); Andreas von Arnauld, 'How to Illegalize Past Injustice: Reinterpreting the Rules of Intertemporality' (2021) 32(2) EJIL 401, 403 (hereafter von Arnauld, 'How to Illegalize Past Injustice'); Francesco Francioni, 'Custom and General Principles of International Cultural Heritage Law' in Francesco Francioni and Ana Filipa Vrdoljak (eds), *The Oxford Handbook of International Cultural Heritage Law* (OUP 2020) 531, 532. Francioni discusses whether custom can fill the gaps left by problems with treaty ratifications. The 1995 UNIDROIT Convention (n 6) is non-retroactive, Article 10(1), (2), but it explicitly does not legitimize any earlier illegal transaction nor prevent a claim under remedies outside of the Convention, Article 10(3).

[14] Sarah Van Beurden, 'The Art of (Re)possession: Heritage and the Cultural Politics of Congo's Decolonization' (2015) 56 Journal of African History 143, 157 (hereafter Van Beurden, 'The Art of (Re) possession'). See also Bénédicte Savoy, *Africa's Struggle for its Art: A History of a Postcolonial Defeat* (Princeton University Press 2022) 29-34.

[15] UNESCO Convention on the Means of Prohibiting and Preventing the Illicit Import, Export and Transfer of Ownership of Cultural Property (opened for signature 14 November 1970, entered into force 24 April 1972) 823 UNTS 231 (hereafter 1970 UNESCO Convention). Effectiveness of the 1970 UNESCO Convention also suffers from the patchwork quilt of ratifications and different methods of implementation.

[16] 'Return & Restitution' Intergovernmental Committee <https://en.unesco.org/fighttrafficking/icprcp> accessed 24 June 2021; Vrdoljak, *International Law* (n 15) 211–17.

[17] Lyndel V Prott, 'Strengths and Weaknesses of the 1970 Convention: An Evaluation 40 Years after its adoption' (2012) <www.unesco.org/new/en/culture/themes/illicit-trafficking-of-cultural-property/

The archaeologically and culturally rich formerly colonized countries of origin were disappointed that they were not able to recover their cultural objects at the time of independence. This disappointment indicates a fundamental disagreement between former colonizers and the formerly colonized as to what independence, self-determination, legitimate means of acquisition, and decolonization mean.[18] The formerly colonized countries continue to be frustrated with the current legal framework, which fails them in cases of historical appropriation. This frustration has been expressed in a push to revise the 1970 UNESCO Convention or to add a protocol that would make the Convention's provisions and requirements for restitution retroactive. This has met considerable resistance, particularly among the Western European and North American countries where most of the artworks appropriated through conquest and colonialism reside.[19] UNESCO's failure to hold meetings of the Convention's States Parties until 2011[20] and to establish Operational Guidelines until 2015 exacerbated the situation.[21] For the moment, the countries seeking change have agreed to follow a course of pursuing clearer and more vigilant enforcement of the 1970 UNESCO Convention, as it exists, to deal with the problems of contemporary theft and illegal export rather than one of amendment to deal with the problems of historical appropriation. This path recognizes the reality of the greater power of the countries that hold these objects, because any suit must be brought in their courts of law and any amendment or protocol to the 1970 UNESCO Convention would have to be ratified and implemented by the legislatures of these 'possessing' countries. Much work can be done with the Convention as it exists, but it remains ineffective for historically appropriated objects.

Despite the strong position on non-retroactivity of legal instruments, some countries have chosen as a result of their political process to make aspects of their laws partially retroactive. Australia enacted implementing legislation, the *Protection of Movable Cultural Heritage Act 1986*, before becoming a State Party in 1989 to the 1970 UNESCO Convention.[22] This legislation is perhaps unique among

meeting-of-states-parties/40th-anniversary-of-the-1970-convention-2011/> accessed 12 August 2021 (hereafter Prott, '1970 Convention Evaluation').

[18] Van Beurden, 'The Art of (Re)possession' (n 14) 143–44; Andrzej Jakubowski, *State Succession in Cultural Property* (OUP 2015) 117–18 (hereafter Jakubowski, *State Succession*).

[19] Prott, '1970 Convention Evaluation' (n 17) 8–9.

[20] UNESCO, '40th Anniversary of the 1970 Convention' <www.unesco.org/new/en/culture/themes/illicit-trafficking-of-cultural-property/meeting-of-states-parties/40th-anniversary-of-the-1970-convention-2011/> accessed 12 August 2021.

[21] UNESCO, 'Operational Guidelines for the Implementation of the Convention on the Means of Prohibiting and Preventing the Illicit Import, Export and Transfer of Ownership of Cultural Property' (UNESCO, Paris, 1970) <www.unesco.org/new/en/culture/themes/illicit-trafficking-of-cultural-property/operational-guidelines/> accessed 12 August 2021.

[22] Protection of Movable Cultural Heritage Act 1986 (No 11, 1986) <www.legislation.gov.au/Details/C2016C01056> accessed 12 August 2021. See also Patrick J O'Keefe, *Protecting Cultural Objects Before and After 1970* (Institute of Art and Law 2017) 200–01.

the States that have ratified the 1970 UNESCO Convention in that its import controls apply to all illegally exported cultural objects, if the export control violated is one 'relating to cultural property' regardless of when the object was illegally exported from its country of origin.[23] Germany provides another example in that it ratified the 1970 UNESCO Convention in 2007 but revised its implementing legislation in 2016. This legislation[24] requires evidence of legal export from another State Party to the Convention if the object was exported after 2007.[25]

Partial retroactive application is found in the legislation of several States Parties implementing the First Protocol to the 1954 Hague Convention.[26] In 2007, Germany[27] and the Netherlands[28] enacted legislation applying to objects removed illegally from occupied territory after the date when the respective country ratified the First Protocol (1967 for Germany and 1959 for the Netherlands) rather than 2007 when the implementing legislation was adopted. The United Kingdom, which ratified and adopted implementing legislation for the First Protocol in 2017,[29] took a still broader approach. The statute's prohibition on dealing in illegally exported cultural property applies to objects illegally exported any time after 1956, when the First Protocol went into effect and more than sixty years before the United Kingdom became a State Party,[30] but it applies only to objects that enter the United Kingdom after the legislation went into effect.[31]

Other examples may raise questions of retroactive application in circumscribed cases. UN Security Council Resolution 1483, adopted in May 2003, called on UN Member States to prohibit the import or trade in cultural artefacts illegally removed from Iraq after August 1990,[32] based on an earlier resolution that imposed economic and trade sanctions on Iraq.[33] Similarly, UN Security Council

[23] Protection of Movable Cultural Heritage Act 1986, s 14(1)–(2). The import controls apply to any cultural object that is imported into Australia after the effective date of the legislation. Such an object is subject to forfeiture and a person who knowingly violates the import prohibition commits an offence.

[24] Act on the Protection of Cultural Property (Cultural Property Protection Act—KGSG) 31 July 2016, BGBl I, 2016, 1914.

[25] Federal Government Commissioner for Culture and the Media, *Key Aspects of the New Act on the Protection of Cultural Property in Germany* (September 2016) <www.bundesregierung.de/Content/DE/_Anlagen/BKM/2016/2016-09-23-kulturgutschutz-informationen-englisch.pdf?__blob=publicationFile&v=2> accessed 12 August 2021. In the absence of documentation, it is presumed that cultural objects were unlawfully exported from the relevant State Party after 2007.

[26] Protocol for the Protection of Cultural Property in the Event of Armed Conflict (adopted 14 May 1954, entered into force 7 August 1956) 249 UNTS 358.

[27] Transformation Act of 25 April 2007; Act of 18 May 2007 Implementing the UNESCO Convention of 14 November 1970 on the Means of Prohibiting and Preventing the Illicit Import, Export and Transfer of Ownership of Cultural Property (Implementation Act) 18 May 2007, BGBl I, 2007, 757, Article 4.

[28] Cultural Property Originating from Occupied Territory (Return) Act, Stb 2007, 123, currently codified as Sections 6.9–6.15 of the Act of 9 December 2015, Relating to the Combining and Amendment of Rules Regarding Cultural Heritage (Heritage Act 2016).

[29] Cultural Property (Armed Conflicts) Act 2017 (United Kingdom).

[30] ibid, ss 16(2) and 17(2).

[31] ibid, s 21.

[32] UNSC Res 1483 (22 May 2003) UN Doc S/RES/1483, para 7.

[33] UNSC Res 661 (6 August 1990) UN Doc S/RES/661.

Resolution 2199, adopted in February 2015, called for a prohibition on trade in cultural artefacts illegally removed from Syria after the beginning of the conflict in March 2011.[34] The use of retroactivity here has less clear legal basis than in the case of Iraq in that trade in all goods from Syria had not previously been prohibited.

7.2.3 The Double Standard of Nineteenth-Century International Law

A third time-based obstacle to the recovery of cultural objects is that the international legal system that emerged during the nineteenth century recognized only the European States as beneficiaries of international law.[35] The international legal system evolved to protect the territorial and economic interests of the colonizing powers, while ignoring the rights of the colonized. With their loss of territorial sovereignty, colonized peoples also lost any rights to the resources within their territory, including their cultural objects. This differential treatment set the stage for legalization of the removal of cultural objects from their places of origin to Europe, as this was viewed as only moving objects internally within the States' own territories and therefore not implicating international legal principles.

Over the course of the nineteenth century, beginning with the British insistence that the French return cultural objects taken from within Europe by Napoleon and ending with the adoption of the 1899 and 1907 Hague Conventions,[36] the norm developed within Europe that cultural objects should not be removed during armed conflict and, if they were removed, they should be returned at the end of the conflict. Yet this norm did not apply to appropriations from outside of Europe. This discriminatory legal system operated against the Indigenous and colonized peoples who were excluded from the protections against seizure of cultural objects which international law recognized for European and North American States.

This discriminatory standard is projected forward into the present through incorporation of the principles of non-retroactivity and extinguishment of a claim through passage of time. The modern States in Africa, Asia, and Latin America are at a significant disadvantage in attempting to reclaim their heritage because these takings were not considered illegal under nineteenth century (European) law. The formerly colonized States are at a further disadvantage as they are forced to litigate their claims in the courts of the countries where these objects are currently located

[34] UNSC Res 2199 (12 February 2015) UN Doc S/RES/2199, paras 15–17.

[35] Vrdoljak, *International Law* (n 13) 46–67.

[36] Convention (IV) Respecting the Laws and Customs of War on Land and its Annex: Regulations concerning the Laws and Customs of War on Land (open for signature 18 October 1907, entered into force 26 January 1910) 187 CTS 227; Hague Convention (II) with Respect to the Laws and Customs of War on Land and its Annex: Regulations concerning the Laws and Customs of War on Land (adopted 29 July 1899, entered into force 4 September 1900) 187 CTS 429.

and which are not likely to negate their own legal principles or disadvantage their cultural institutions.[37] While in principle victims of violations of international humanitarian law and of human rights law are entitled to a remedy,[38] the factors outlined here mean that, as a practical matter, it has been virtually impossible to recover historically appropriated cultural objects.

This projection forward perpetuates the colonial system and allows it to continue to dictate the present location of cultural objects whose removal in the past was effectuated through colonialism, imperialism, and armed conflict. Appropriations that were considered legitimate under the legal rules of colonialism and imperialism will continue to be considered legitimate, thus replicating past power structures in the present.[39] To observe the literal dictates of non-retroactivity and the other time-based bars means that we continue to perpetuate in the present this double standard imposed on the non-European world by the colonial powers in these circumstances of fundamental inequality. Thompson shifts the analysis by concluding that if an action, such as the taking by the British of cultural objects from Ethiopia during military conquest, is wrongful today, then it was also wrongful in the past.[40] Even Merryman, in arguing against retroactive application of contemporary legal principles to determine the status of the Parthenon Sculptures in the British Museum, acknowledged that an exception would be justified 'in the most unusual circumstances'.[41] The atrocities committed by the colonial powers would seem to constitute just such a circumstance to justify restitution of cultural objects to the peoples and communities from whom they were often taken through violence and other exertions of power. The decision whether to abrogate these time bars is largely a political one that can be reversed when sufficient political will to do so is present.

[37] In *Odyssey Marine Exploration, Inc v The Unidentified Shipwrecked Vessel* 657 F3d 1159 (11th Cir 2011), a salvage company based in the United States recovered some 600,000 silver and gold coins and other artefacts from a historic shipwreck, the *Nuestra Senora de Las Mercedes*, a Spanish ship that was carrying cargo from South America to Spain and sank in international waters, west of the Straits of Gibraltar. Odyssey Marine brought the cargo to the United States where the US government sought to forfeit the cargo and return it to Spain. Peru claimed that it was entitled to the gold and silver that Spain had taken from its territory through colonialist exploitation. The US court rejected Peru's claims on the ground that Spain was entitled to sovereign immunity in a US court and that Peru would have to seek redress from a court in Spain, despite the severe obstacles that Peru would face there. ibid, 1182.

[38] Ana Filipa Vrdoljak, 'Cultural Heritage, Transitional Justice, and Rule of Law' in Francesco Francioni and Ana Filipa Vrdoljak (eds), *The Oxford Handbook of International Cultural Heritage Law* (OUP 2020) 169, 184–86 (hereafter Vrdoljak, 'Cultural Heritage').

[39] Von Arnauld, 'How to Illegalize Past Injustice' (n 13) 403–04.

[40] Janna Thompson, 'Cultural Property, Restitution and Value' (2003) 20(3) Journal of Applied Philosophy 251, 254 (hereafter Thompson, 'Cultural Property, Restitution and Value').

[41] John Henry Merryman, 'Thinking about the Elgin Marbles' (1985) 83 Michigan Law Review 1881, 1897.

7.3 The Cultural Heritage Debate in Contemporary Context

Despite the historical circumstances of armed conflict and colonialism during which cultural objects were removed, and despite the moral justifications for restorative justice through reparations, arguments persist as to why these objects should not be returned. These arguments, most often made by Western museums and, to a lesser extent, private collectors, display a remarkable degree of continuity with the justifications for the initial takings of these objects. Before turning in the last section to how reparations should be accomplished, this section looks at the contemporary formulation of these arguments for retention.

7.3.1 The Rescue Narrative Revisited

The primary justification for the removal of cultural objects and for their retention is embodied in the 'rescue narrative'. The same justifications used by the British for acquiring and retaining the Elgin collection appeared in the French artists' petition to Napoleon to bring to Paris as many artworks as possible: superiority of the new cultural centre (whether Paris or London) based on military and political strength as well as belief in their superior intellectual, scientific, and cultural sensibilities; status as the rightful inheritor of the past (whether Rome or Athens); the need to rescue the artworks from their original owners who fail to appreciate them; and the benefits that will be granted not only to the new owners but to all humanity through the act of appropriation. Thomasson observes that the essential arguments over appropriation and restitution are fundamentally the same today as they were in the great age of removal during the late eighteenth and nineteenth centuries.[42]

Dominique-Vivant Denon, the artist and diplomat who accompanied Napoleon's expedition to Egypt and later became the director of the Louvre, was quoted as stating 'they have no eyes to see them with, France will always prove by her superiority in the arts that the masterpieces were better here than elsewhere'.[43] The remains in Athens were described in 1811 as 'dangerously neglected: this was a perilous location "where they were daily suffering destruction, where one half of them had been pounded into lime for mortar, and the other half gradually approaching the same usage"'.[44] According to the rescue narrative, the damage caused by the removal of pieces by Europeans, the vagaries of transport back to northern

[42] Frederik Thomasson, 'Justifying and Criticizing the Removals of Antiquities in Ottoman Lands: Tracking the Sigeion Inscription' (2010) 17 IJCP 493, 510 (hereafter Thomasson, 'Justifying and Criticizing').

[43] Timothy Webb, 'Appropriating the Stones: The "Elgin Marbles" and English National Taste' in Elazar Barkan and Ronald Bush (eds), *Claiming the Stones, Naming the Bones: Cultural Property and the Negotiation of National and Ethnic Identity* (Getty Research Institute 2002) 51, 81 (hereafter Webb, 'Appropriating the Stones').

[44] ibid, 81–82.

Europe, and the subsequent damage caused during the Duveen cleaning episode and from the atmospheric conditions in London[45] all pale in comparison to what would have happened had the Sculptures been left *in situ*.

The rescue narrative is dependent upon the assumption that the local inhabitants who lived among antiquities did not care about them, did not care for them, or, even worse, engaged in their destruction. This concept is, however, belied by a detailed study of the appropriation of a less famous antiquity, the Inscription of Sigeion.[46] British and French diplomats made several attempts to remove the stele, but they were thwarted by the local inhabitants who did not wish it to be removed. Even though the 'Greeks ... were extremely averse to their being taken away', Elgin ultimately succeeded after calling upon the chief admiral of the Ottoman navy, the local governor, the commander of the British mission, and a detachment of British officers and soldiers.[47] The stele and an accompanying bas relief were the first objects to become part of Elgin's collection, although the stele is now located in the basement of the British Museum.

When local inhabitants objected to the removal of ancient artefacts, the Europeans dismissed their objections as either the product of superstition and pagan religious practices or greed.[48] Dyfri Williams, former Keeper of Greek and Roman Antiquities at the British Museum, perpetuated this trope, when he wrote in 2002 that the attachment of local Athenians to the Acropolis sculptures was not 'engendered by any scientific sense of the sculptures' importance or even a sense of "national heritage"... '.[49] Conversely, some European observers were critical of the removals carried out by the British and the French for destroying the original contexts of the objects they appropriated and the changes to the objects when they were placed in museums. These objectors included the Swedish diplomat Johan David Åkerblad, who decried the loss of documented context; Jacob Berggren, the chaplain of the Swedish legation in Constantinople; and the French theorist Quatremère de Quincy, who condemned Napoleon's appropriations.[50]

[45] See chapter 3, section 3.2.4.

[46] Thomasson, 'Justifying and Criticizing' (n 42).

[47] ibid, 498–99 (quoting William Wittman, *Travels in Turkey, Asia Minor, Syria, and Across the Desert into Egypt During the Years 1799, 1800, and 1801, in Company with the Turkish Army and the British Military Mission* ... (London 1803) 65–66). As with the removal of the Parthenon Sculptures, this occurred at a time when Britain was assisting the Ottomans in repelling the French invasion of Egypt and Syria. ibid, 498.

[48] ibid, 499–503. The local inhabitants were thus despised, either for wanting to sell and thereby reap monetary reward, or for refusing to sell, in which case the refusals were attributed to their superstitions. ibid, 502.

[49] Dyfri Williams, '"Of Publick Utility and Publick Property": Lord Elgin and the Parthenon Sculptures' in Athéna Tsingarida and Donna Kurtz, *Appropriating Antiquity, Saisir l'Antique. Collections et collectionneurs d'antiques in Belgique et en Grande-Bretagne au XIXe siècle* (Le Livre Timperman 2002) 103, 139–40 (hereafter Williams, 'Of Publick Utility').

[50] Thomasson, 'Justifying and Criticizing' (n 42) 505–08. Jacob Berggren commented that 'it is better like certain countries to be without *Museums* ...'. Or, as Thomasson put it, these observers did not criticize the individuals, but rather 'the system, that is, collections and museums'. Thomasson, 'Justifying and Criticizing' (n 42) 508.

The rescue narrative is frequently used today to justify acquisition through the market of cultural objects that typically are unprovenanced or poorly provenanced and likely the product of recent thefts and site looting, even when the purchaser acknowledges that the purchase price may be used to fund terrorism, armed conflict, and other crimes.[51] Hardy compares the antiquities market to the purchases by British and American collectors of artworks that the Nazi regime removed from German museums during the 1930s. Collectors justified these acquisitions, even when they knew that Germany would use the proceeds to acquire armaments, as Germany would otherwise destroy the artworks.[52] The purchaser utilizes the rescue narrative as a way of distracting from, justifying, or neutralizing the illegal aspects of the activity.[53] However, by allowing looters to monetize the products of site looting and thefts, purchasers encourage the production of more objects through continued looting and thefts, demonstrating that rather than rescuing objects, purchasers are continuously putting more cultural objects at risk and, at times, may *create* the market and market demand for certain types of objects.[54] The act of claimed rescue in order to save objects and knowledge does, in fact, destroy both objects and knowledge.

7.3.2 The Universal or Encyclopedic Museum

As discussed in chapter 2, section 2.2, in the second half of the eighteenth century, the justification based on the universal or encyclopedic museum for collecting and retaining works from throughout the world developed. The concept is as vibrant today as it was close to three hundred years ago. However, it has never been clear what the terms 'universal' and 'encyclopedic' museum mean or whether these terms are synonymous. One interpretation, likely more prevalent at the time of the origin of the concept, is that it describes a museum that is universally open to the public and not restricted to the monarchy, aristocrats, or the Church, as the antecedents of the modern museum frequently were.[55] Today, the term is used more in

[51] Samuel Andrew Hardy, '"Conflict Antiquities" Rescue or Ransom: The Cost of Buying Back Stolen Cultural Property in Contexts of Political Violence' (2021) 5 IJCP 5 (hereafter Hardy, 'Conflict Antiquities').

[52] ibid, 5–6.

[53] Neutralization techniques are denial of responsibility, denial of injury, denial of the victim, condemnation of the condemners, and an appeal to higher loyalties. Simon RM Mackenzie, *Going, Going, Gone: Regulating the Market in Illicit Antiquities* (Institute of Art and Law 2005) 203. Taha summarizes statements of cuneiform scholars who justify their publication of unprovenanced texts through variations of the rescue narrative. Abdul Salam Taha, 'The Role of Academia in Enabling the Illicit Antiquities Market: The Damage to Iraq's Cultural Heritage' in Lorenzo Kamel (ed), *Collapse and Rebirth of Cultural Heritage: The Case of Syria and Iraq* (Peter Lang AG 2020) 129, 135, 140–41. All these techniques of neutralization are seen at play in the antiquities market, but the appeal to a higher loyalty embodies the rescue narrative by portraying the act of 'rescue' as superior to any other factor.

[54] Hardy, 'Conflict Antiquities' (n 51) 14.

[55] Bénédicte Savoy, '1815: Musées d'Europe année?' in Patrick Boucheron (ed), *Histoire mondiale de la France* (Seuil 2017) 453, 456 (hereafter Savoy, '1815').

Figure 7.1 View of the Acropolis Museum, Athens.

the 'encyclopedic' sense that a museum's collection would represent objects collected from throughout the world,[56] a form of collecting that could only be made possible through empire, colonialism, and economic imperialism.

At the time of the 2004 Olympics held in Athens the British Museum was sufficiently apprehensive about calls for return of the Parthenon Sculptures that the Museum thought it necessary to ask the major art-collecting museums of the world to issue the Declaration on the Value of the Universal Museum. To these museums, the possibility of the restitution of the Parthenon Sculptures brings into question the status and future of all art-owning and acquiring institutions in Europe and North America. Eighteen museums, many of which do not have collections of ancient art and antiquities and are therefore unaffected by this particular issue, supported the British Museum.[57] The justifications of the universal museum presented

[56] Neil MacGregor, 'To Shape the Citizens of "That Great City, the World"' in James Cuno (ed), *Whose Culture? The Promise of Museums and the Debate over Antiquities* (Princeton University Press 2009) 39 (hereafter MacGregor, 'To Shape the Citizens').

[57] The Declaration was signed in 2002 and is printed in full in James Cuno, 'View from the Universal Museum' in John Henry Merryman (ed), *Imperialism, Art and Restitution* (CUP 2006) 15, 34. The eighteen museums that originally signed the Declaration were the Art Institute of Chicago; Bavarian State Museum, Munich (Alte Pinakothek, Neue Pinakothek); State Museums, Berlin; Cleveland Museum of Art; J Paul Getty Museum; Solomon R Guggenheim Museum; Los Angeles County Museum of Art; Louvre; Metropolitan Museum of Art; Museum of Fine Arts, Boston; Museum of Modern Art; Opificio della Pietre Dure, Florence; Philadelphia Museum of Art; Prado Museum; Rijksmuseum; State Hermitage Museum; Thyssen-Bornemisza Museum; Whitney Museum of American Art. The British Museum signed later.

in this Declaration fit well with the philosophical approach of the Association of Art Museum Directors (AAMD), which was wrestling with adopting an appropriate policy for acquisitions of ancient art and archaeological remains first in 2004 and then again in 2008 with additional changes in 2013.[58] Many American museums were at the beginning of a flood of negative publicity and restitutions to Italy and Greece. The completion a few years later of the new Acropolis Museum posed an additional threat to the British Museum's retention of the Sculptures in London (Figure 7.1).

The Declaration posited three principles. First, it reiterates the non-retroactivity principle, not only from a strictly legal perspective, but also from an asserted ethical or moral perspective. The Declaration argues that the collecting practices of the past should not be judged by today's standards. Second, the Declaration argues that museums 'provide a valid and valuable context for objects that were long ago displaced from their original source'. One cannot deny that the museum provides a context for objects in its collection, but this does not answer the question of which context—a museum or the object's original and communal context—should be given priority when one must choose among an object's multiple contexts.

The Declaration's third point is that the placement of cultural objects in a museum allows people from throughout the world to appreciate the culture that produced the object—that, for example, Greek sculpture is admired and is considered to have universal value because it has been placed in universal museums throughout the world. The Declaration posits that objects also derive value from their juxtaposition with objects from diverse cultures.[59] However, the Declaration pays little attention to how objects were obtained or their loss of context and accompanying scientific knowledge. In this case, value derived from juxtaposition with similarly decontextualized objects becomes limited to their immanent elements, that is, their aesthetic value, with much of their historical, cultural, and scientific values lost.

The Declaration's reference to Enlightenment ideals embodied in the concept of the universal museum seems oddly out of touch with contemporary developments and changes in how the role of the museum should be understood. The Declaration perpetuates a Eurocentric approach to what is important about the representations of cultures from different parts of the world. We need to consider the Enlightenment ideal of the universal museum in a modern context, in which

[58] See chapter 6, section 6.4.

[59] James Cuno, former director of the Art Institute of Chicago and later President of the J Paul Getty Trust, and Neil MacGregor, former director of the British Museum, are unclear as to whether the purpose of juxtaposition is to show the similarities among objects of different cultures or to show their differences. James Cuno, 'Introduction' in James Cuno (ed), *Whose Culture? The Promise of Museums and the Debate over Antiquities* (Princeton University Press 2009) 1, 17–29; MacGregor, 'To Shape the Citizens' (n 56) 42. MacGregor acknowledged that the modern role of the encyclopedic museum, which he also calls the Enlightenment museum, is to involve diaspora communities in the presentation of their cultural past while also lending to other museums. In turn, people throughout the world can share in and learn from the experience of the encyclopedic museum. ibid, 53.

the multiplicity of ethnicities and cultural identities calls into question whether there is an objective perspective to representing the world's myriad of cultures presented in only a small number of institutions.

Folarin Shyllon asserted that the purpose of museums is to illustrate the differences among cultures but that these differences must be appreciated within a broader diverse cultural context. 'We would surely all be the poorer ... if we could not by travel come upon, not just different works of art, but also a sense of being in a wholly different culture, a different artistic world.'[60] Universality or the global perspective is one way of looking at cultural heritage, but heritage must be viewed through the lenses of States and local communities as well. Museums need to pay attention to how these objects were acquired—whether through armed conflict, political and economic imperialism, or illegal trafficking—and, more importantly today, how they continue to be retained. The formation of museums that can represent the national and local cultures has significant benefits that are lost if we look only to the universal character of museums. 'Universal' museums can no longer be restricted to the centres of Western Europe, North America, and a few other locations. Existing museums must be reconfigured and new 'universal' museums reborn into a variety of locations, representing a multiplicity of cultures and histories. The 'universal' museum must also be one that returns ownership, possession, and control to the communities and States from which cultural objects were removed so that the creators and their descendants can determine the disposition, display, interpretation, and curation of these objects, whether in a museum or elsewhere.

The invocation of universality in the Declaration is primarily a defence against claims of restitution. It is suggested that 'the objects were co-opted into communicating messages of imperial, white, male and national superiority'.[61] Another way of looking at the legitimacy of these museums in claiming the mantle of universality is to recognize that they have done so unilaterally and without the consent of those whose cultural objects were forcibly removed and of whose cultures the universal museums consider themselves to be the arbiter and interpreter. These museums cannot serve the citizens of the world when the citizens did not consent to these actions.

7.3.3 National Identity

Another argument against restitution is that appropriated cultural objects have become part of the national identity of the States where they are currently located.

[60] Folarin Shyllon, 'Unraveling History: Return of African Cultural Objects Repatriated and Looted in Colonial Times' in James AR Nafziger and Ann M Nicgorski (eds), *Cultural Heritage Issues: The Legacy of Conquest, Colonization, and Commerce* (Martinus Nijhoff Publishers 2009) 159, 166 (hereafter, Shyllon 'Unraveling History').

[61] Mark O'Neill, 'Enlightenment Museums: Universal or Merely Global' (2004) 2(3) Museums and Society 190, 197 (hereafter O'Neill, 'Enlightenment museums').

While the past physical and metaphysical attachment of these objects to their places and communities of origin are obvious, the States in which these cultural objects currently reside now claim them as part of their national cultural heritage. As Claire Lyons wrote:

> As the physical evidence of individual and collective pasts, archaeological heritage is esteemed by communities that locate their historical identity in its material expressions. These communities can include indigenous people, ethnic groups, the countries in which the heritage originates, and countries that claim the patrimony of others' pasts to define their political institutions and national character.[62]

Many societies and communities look to a time in the past when they were the dominant political force within their geographic sphere and attempt to recreate that time of dominance through the physical remains found on their land. On the Acropolis of Athens, the archaeological and historical remains of the later periods are to a large extent removed, particularly the later accretions on the Parthenon itself. The buildings are carefully restored to their state during the fifth century BCE, the time of the pinnacle of artistic, as well as military and political, power of Athens. Thus, these remains become a reminder and a symbol of the past glory, political achievements, and cultural transcendence of Periclean Athens. Lyons commented:

> Based, however loosely, on the remains of the past, political narratives are legitimated by ancestral achievements and are made to appear the result of an inevitable evolutionary process. The physical record may coincide with the way that myths of origin are formulated, or it may be diverted for various political, religious, and psychological ends.[63]

Communities and national groups are entitled to their own narrative of their past. If contemporary Greeks see themselves as inheritors of ancient Greek culture, it is not for the people of other nations to reject this. Similarly, the contemporary peoples of Africa have a right to their cultural connection to the past. However, communities and States have been deprived of many of the physical cultural remnants of their past and are therefore unable to reconstruct these as part of their historical or cultural memory. As Sarr and Savoy note, 'the absence of cultural heritage can render memory silent'.[64]

[62] Claire L Lyons, 'Objects and Identities: Claiming and Reclaiming the Past' in Elazar Barkan and Ronald Bush (eds), *Claiming the Stones, Naming the Bones: Cultural Property and the Negotiation of National and Ethnic Identity* (Getty Research Institute 2002) 116, 116.

[63] ibid.

[64] Felwine Sarr and Bénédicte Savoy, 'The Restitution of African Cultural Heritage. Toward a New Relational Ethic' (2018) 35–37 (hereafter Sarr and Savoy, 'The Restitution of African Cultural Heritage').

These uses of the past to define present national identities are matched in the countries that currently possess the remains of others' pasts. Institutions in the possessing countries often criticize the countries of origin when the latter wish to use the remains of the past as part of a project of building national identity and unity. Yet the possessing countries have used these remains for the same purpose and resist restitution for the same reason.[65] While the Parthenon Sculptures in the British Museum have embodied different myths and motives over the past two centuries, today they are claimed as an inalienable part of the British national heritage. As Webb wrote, quoting in part from Ian Jenkins, 'the English are the descendants of the Greeks and ... London has succeeded Athens as the defender of Western freedom.... "Waterloo became England's Battle of Marathon and acquisition of the Elgin Marbles by the British Museum was hailed as confirmation of the ancient claim that liberty and the arts rise and fall together"'.[66] The possessing States assert that incorporation into the national heritage gives them a superior right to retention of cultural objects.

Once an ancient object is incorporated into the cultural fabric of the possessing State, its disposition and export may be limited. Permanent export of cultural objects from the United Kingdom may require an export licence.[67] The purpose of the export licensing system is to retain cultural goods deemed to be of outstanding national importance, which is determined under the Waverley criteria.[68] In an example of incorporation into British national heritage, when the Egyptian statue of Sekhemka from the Old Kingdom period (2650–2150 BCE) was put up for auction, its export was initially denied (Figure 7.2). The Second Marquess of Northampton, Spencer Joshua Alwyne Compton, acquired the sculpture between 1849 and 1850 and donated it to the Northampton Museum and Art Gallery later in the nineteenth century.[69] It 'was arguably the finest piece of non-royal sculpture from Old

[65] For example James Cuno, *Who Owns Antiquity? Museums and the Battle over Our Ancient Heritage* (Princeton University Press 2008) 121–45 (hereafter Cuno, *Who Owns Antiquity?*).

[66] Webb, 'Appropriating the Stones' (n 43) 78. Similar attitudes were expressed during the Parliamentary debate on the acquisition of the Marbles. ibid, 78–81; see also O'Neill, 'Enlightenment museums' (n 61) 192–93.

[67] UK Export Licensing for Cultural Goods: Procedures and Guidance for Exporters of Works of Art and Other Cultural Goods (2021).

[68] If the Reviewing Committee on the Export of Works of Art and Cultural Interest finds that the object for which export permission has been requested fits one or more of the Waverley criteria, its export can be prohibited temporarily while a museum or other public institution attempts to raise the funds to purchase the object at a fair market price. The three Waverley criteria are: whether the object is closely connected with British history and national life; whether it is of outstanding aesthetic importance; and whether it is of outstanding significance for the study of some particular branch of art, learning, or history. Frances Wilson, 'UK Export Controls and National Treasures' (2019) 5 SACLR 197–99.

[69] Christie's Auction Catalogue, 'The Exceptional Sale 2014' (10 July 2014) <www.christies.com/lotfinder/ancient-art-antiquities/an-exceptional-egyptian-painted-limestone-statue-5812479-details.aspx> accessed 12 August 2021. The auction catalogue gives an extensive description of the Northampton family's acquisition of the sculpture, its interest in the arts, and its gifts to the Northampton museum. The price realized at auction was £15,762,500, approximately three times the presale estimate range. There was some question as to who owned the sculpture and so the proceeds were shared by the Marquis of Northampton and the Northampton Borough Council.

Figure 7.2 Statue of Sekhemka, Egypt, Old Kingdom period (2650–2150 BCE)

Kingdom Egypt (age of the pyramids) anywhere in the world, and there was not a single object of this quality, form and date housed in a UK collection (public or private)'.[70]

The Reviewing Committee on the Export of Works of Art and Objects of Cultural Interest decided that the statue met the Waverly criteria, based, in part, on its association with British national life or history. The criterion does not require that the work was created within the United Kingdom but applies to objects associated with an important person, location, or event, including whether it has been part of a collection of great historical significance. The Committee explained that the sculpture satisfied this criterion because '[t]he statue reflected the 19th century British engagement with Egypt, the role of the landed elite in shaping Britain's understanding of the ancient world and the historiography of collections of ancient art ... It had, since the late nineteenth century, been an integral part of the public museum display in Northampton',[71] although it had not been on display for four years before the sale.[72] The British thus view the sculpture as integral to British history and national life through the role of the British aristocracy in appropriating the cultural remains of the Mediterranean region. Britain, a major art-collecting and art-importing nation for over three hundred years, has incorporated these works into its national identity based on Britain's pattern of appropriation and acquisition.

Similarly, the UK placed a temporary export ban on a finial from the octagonal throne of Tipu Sultan, who was defeated in 1799 by British forces protecting the commercial interests of the East India Company. Following the Sultan's defeat, the British army's Prize Agents dismembered the throne.[73] Among the reasons for the temporary export ban were: it is a rare example of eighteenth century South Indian goldsmiths' work and an outstanding example of the quality and 'expertise of Tipu's goldsmiths and jewellers', it is an 'important symbolic object in Anglo-Indian history', and it is important for the study of 'royal propaganda' and British imperial and military history.[74] In another move of incorporation, the French government transferred supervision of colonial collections from the Ministry of Colonies to the Ministry of Culture and the Direction des Musées de France.[75] By

[70] Reviewing Committee on the Export of Works of Art and Objects of Cultural Interest, note of case hearing on 12 November 2015: The Statue of Sekhemka, Case 14 (2014–15).

[71] ibid, 2.

[72] 'Egyptian statue Sekhemka sells for nearly £16m' (*BBC News*, 10 July 2014) <www.bbc.com/news/uk-england-northamptonshire-28257714> accessed 12 August 2021. A satisfactory purchase offer was not made for the statue and an export licence to the US was later granted. 'Northampton Council Sekhemka statue "now in US"' (*BBC News*, 15 October 2016) <www.bbc.com/news/uk-england-northamptonshire-37552316> accessed 12 August 2021.

[73] Department of Digital, Culture, Media & Sport '18th-Century Tipu Sultan Throne Finial worth £1.5 million at risk of leaving UK' (12 November 2021) Press Release <www.gov.uk/government/news/18th-century-tipu-sultan-throne-finial-worth-15-million-at-risk-of-leaving-uk> accessed 8 February 2022.

[74] ibid.

[75] Sarr and Savoy, 'The Restitution of African Cultural Heritage' (n 64) 18–19.

being incorporated into museums, these collections became considered part of the French cultural patrimony and therefore subject to the legal rules prohibiting alienation of patrimonial objects.

These assertions of national identity by the former colonial States become a justification for refusing to return cultural objects to their countries and communities of origin. The denigration of countries of origin for viewing cultural objects as part of their national identity constitutes hypocrisy when the possessing countries, with far less claim historically and culturally to appropriated cultural objects, do the same. The objects that were removed may have lost some of their connections to their original contexts, in particular when deracinated objects are transformed into works of universal art by being placed in museums. While the process of re-establishing these cultural, historical, and traditional connections may be challenging, the objects can be reintegrated into the contemporary cultural life of these countries and communities with a reconstruction of memory and a 're-socialization' or reconnection of the objects with contemporary communities.[76]

7.4 The Right to Reparations

7.4.1 Justice through Reparations

The framework for consideration of reparations consists of: (1) establishing an obligation to correct an historical injustice; (2) establishing an appropriate form of 'correction' (ie reparation); and (3) establishing an appropriate means of reparation (ie restitution and other forms of compensation and acknowledgement as may be appropriate).[77] In establishing an obligation to correct an historical injustice, four elements may be analysed. The first of these is the extreme violence and exploitation that were utilized in the process of establishing colonial and imperial spheres of dominance by the different European powers. The discussion in chapter 3 of the expropriation of cultural heritage in Africa and Asia illustrates the exploitation and extraction of natural and cultural resources through armed conflict. This violence was often perpetrated with the goal of pursuing geopolitical and economic advantage through the establishment of trade routes and extraction of favourable trade concessions.

The usurpation of cultural resources led to a second factor—the enrichment of the European colonial powers through the cultural and artistic legacy that they

[76] ibid, 31–33.

[77] Vrdoljak, 'Cultural Heritage' (n 40) 186–87; Erich Hatala Matthes, 'Repatriation and the Radical Redistribution of Art' (2017) 4(32) Ergo 931, 935 (hereafter Matthes, 'Repatriation'). Matthes uses repatriation as the form of achieving reparation. However, repatriation refers specifically to the return of cultural objects to sovereigns and is not the only form of restitution. Therefore, the more generic term 'restitution' will be used here, unless return to a sovereign is specifically intended.

gained, and the equivalent losses imposed on the countries and communities of origin. These cultural objects were an economic resource to the European States and stimulated artistic and industrial development. For example, the appearance of Yuanmingyuan objects in the United Kingdom spurred industrial design and production that assisted it in trade competition. The third element is the disparity in international law that developed over the course of the nineteenth century allowing acceptance of conduct against non-Europeans that was not tolerated among the European States at the end of the Napoleonic Wars and during both World Wars. This double standard should not be perpetuated through our contemporary view of the disposition of cultural objects.

The fourth element derives from viewing cultural heritage through a human rights framework, as suggested in chapter 5, section 5.3. While initially focusing on intentional destruction of cultural heritage, international cultural heritage law has evolved towards encompassing the relationship between cultural heritage and human rights.[78] Appropriation of objects and dismemberment of immovable heritage, similarly to destruction, separate people and communities from their heritage, thereby denying them the right to access and to engage with their culture.[79] Emphasis on the universality of cultural heritage implies that the location of cultural objects does not matter and has contributed to the divorce between peoples and their heritage. The human right to enjoy and access culture establishes the obligation to repair this break in particular through restitution of movable cultural objects.

While the Special Rapporteur in the Field of Cultural Rights referred to such actions as storage or display in museums and conservation and preservation measures as separating people from their heritage, the placement of objects in distant countries constitutes an even greater physical and spiritual separation. The close link of colonialism, imperialism, and appropriation with the ongoing nature of the violations is evidenced by the fact that the museums of the former colonial powers disproportionately hold cultural objects appropriated from the specific regions that these powers had colonized. Thus, the contemporary deprivation of cultural objects is clearly associated with the continuing after-effects of colonialism.[80] For

[78] Elisa Novic, *The Concept of Cultural Genocide: An International Law Perspective* (OUP 2016) 96 (hereafter Novic, *The Concept of Cultural Genocide*). As Judge Cançado Trindade noted in his separate opinion in the Preah Vihear Temple case, the International Court of Justice has 'endorsed the ongoing *humanization* of international law'. Request for Interpretation of the Judgment of 15 June 1962 in the Case concerning the Temple of Preah Vihear *(Cambodia v Thailand)* (n 4) [2013] Separate Opinion of Judge Cançado Trindade [2013], para 62.

[79] Human Rights Council (17th Session) 'Report of the independent expert in the field of cultural rights, Farida Shaheed' (21 March 2011) A/HRC/17/38, paras 14 and 16; Francesco Francioni, 'Culture, Heritage and Human Rights: An Introduction' in Francesco Francioni and Martin Scheinin (eds), *Cultural Human Rights* (Martinus Nijhoff Publishers 2008) 1, 7.

[80] The sub-Saharan countries whose cultures are most extensively represented in French collections are the former colonies of France. Sarr and Savoy, 'The Restitution of African Cultural Heritage' (n 64) 46–47.

example, Sarr and Savoy demonstrate, in their diachronic study of when objects entered European museums, that the considerable majority of objects originating from Cameroon entered the Musée du quai Branly between 1885, the date of the Berlin conference, and 1960, the date of independence.[81]

The deprivation of cultural objects tends to be analysed as something that occurred in the past, and possible remedies are therefore thought to be barred by time and the non-retroactivity principle. However, the contemporary presence of cultural objects in European and North American museums and private collections means that this deprivation continues today. It therefore constitutes an ongoing and present violation of the human rights of the descendants and communities from whom the cultural objects were taken. As Sarr and Savoy note:

> The extraction and deprivation of cultural heritage and cultural property not only concerns the generation who participates in the plundering as well as those who must suffer through this extraction. It becomes inscribed throughout the long duration of societies, conditioning the flourishing of certain societies while simultaneously continuing to weaken others.[82]

This current nature of the harm and injury establishes a vital element of the obligation to correct a present injustice with its roots in an historical injustice.

Matthes places restitution within a framework of the right to distributive justice[83] in recognition of the fact that cultural objects, although they may be denominated as public goods, are not available to all on an equal basis, as a practical matter and given inequalities of wealth and access. Rather, they are concentrated in a few museums in a few countries. Cultural objects should be redistributed throughout the world as a means of complying with the human right to access culture and cultural heritage and of achieving true universality. In this respect, universality is based on the original meaning of the universal museum as a place accessible to all[84] and relates here to the right of all people to have access to and possession of cultural objects. However, while redistribution may serve the ethical goal of a redistribution of artistic wealth, by itself it does not accomplish reparation, which requires remedying the past wrong done to a specific community or nation.[85]

[81] ibid, 47–58. Some 'diversification' of acquisitions occurred after the date of independence for the different African States. These post-independence acquisitions are likely attributable to donations from former colonial officers and administrators and their families or from circulation through the market.

[82] ibid, 8.

[83] Matthes, 'Repatriation' (n 77) 940.

[84] Savoy, '1815' (n 55) 456. Even in Neil MacGregor's vision of the obligation of a universal museum to share its cultural artefacts, objects would only be loaned, not necessarily to their countries or communities of origin, and communities and countries of origin would have limited control over exhibitions and curatorial decisions. MacGregor, 'To Shape the Citizens' (n 56) 53–54.

[85] Matthes acknowledges the conflict between redistribution and correcting historical injustices, particularly, in his example, with the case of Indigenous objects. In order to right some of the historical injustices done to Indigenous peoples, cultural objects should primarily be returned to them, even though this may not serve the redistribution purpose. Matthes, 'Repatriation' (n 77) 942–44.

7.4.2 Principles of Reparative Justice Applied: Reparations Design

The second step is to determine the means of fulfilling the obligation to correct the historical injustice. While one may respond to the large-scale appropriations of cultural objects by concluding that all objects should be returned, a theoretical basis for doing so and particularly a methodology for doing so are necessary. Ending the ongoing violation of the rights of descendants and descendant communities and compensating for past harm need to be achieved through reparations based on a broad governmental response of the former colonial powers and other States that benefited directly or indirectly from colonialism.[86] Reparations, including the material aspects, is central to achieving justice. The purpose of reparations is to eliminate the consequences of the illegal act and return to the prior circumstances.[87] The primary elements of reparations schemes describe well the application of reparations in this context: (1) payment in cash or in kind to a large group of claimants; (2) wrongs that 'were substantially permissible under the prevailing law when committed'; (3) present law bars a legally compulsory remedy for the past wrong (due to factors previously enumerated such as bars based on passage of time); and (4) payment 'justified on backward-looking grounds of corrective justice, rather than forward-looking grounds such as the deterrence of future wrongdoing'.[88] Posner and Vermeule further define reparations as occurring in the circumstance where the entities that pay the compensation and those that receive it are not the original parties who committed or suffered the harm.[89]

Posner and Vermeule point out that there are two possible moral bases for awarding reparations: one is based on wrongful harm caused by one group to another group, leading to compensation, and the second is that one group was unjustly enriched by another group, leading to restitution.[90] Both justifications apply to appropriation of cultural objects through colonialism, imperialism, and armed conflict. Reparations based on unjust enrichment may be the easier theory to apply[91] when the governments that appropriated the cultural objects still possess

[86] Reparations are intended 'to eliminate, as far as possible, the consequences of the illegal act and to restore the situation that would have existed if the act had not been committed'. Emanuela-Chiara Gillard, 'Reparation for violations of international humanitarian law' (2003) 851 (85) IRRC 529, 531 (hereafter Gillard, 'Reparation').

[87] Vrdoljak, 'Cultural Heritage' (n 38) 186; Novic, *The Concept of Cultural Genocide* (n 78) 192. Novic points out that, particularly in the case of Indigenous peoples, it may not be possible to return to their prior circumstances, in which case transformative justice is required. ibid, 193.

[88] Eric A Posner and Adrian Vermeule, 'Reparations for Slavery and Other Historical Injustices' (2003) 103(3) Columbia Law Review 689, 691 (hereafter Posner and Vermeule, 'Reparations for Slavery').

[89] ibid, 691–92. The literature on restorative or reparative justice is extensive and is only touched on briefly in this discussion.

[90] Posner and Vermeule, 'Reparations for Slavery' (n 88) 698.

[91] ibid, 700–02.

the same objects. If the objects have been transferred, often through sale, to other entities, compensation theory may apply more appropriately.[92] Both the restitutionary and compensatory theories may require individuals who are not directly responsible to provide reparations.[93]

Questions of whether individuals, who are not blameworthy, are asked to pay and of recipients, who were not the victims, often arise in the context of reparations.[94] However, in the case of cultural objects taken during colonialism, these questions are not as obtrusive or may be resolved under 'ethical collectivism'.[95] The primary wrongdoers were the governments of the colonial States and, particularly to the extent that national museums are the current possessors, it is the governments that will bear the costs of reparations to the descendants or descendant communities of the original victims. Reparations paid to the State of the descendant community also fits the paradigm of reparations based on membership in a group.[96] Reparations to descendants and descendant communities would be made not only for the initial injustice but also for the continuing injustice of separation of people from their cultural heritage. Therefore, making reparations to present individuals, communities, and States fits within the rubric of restorative justice and is compensating present-day victims in their own right, as well as in their role as representatives of past victims.[97]

Policy design of reparations here is based on three prongs: apology or acknowledgement, restitution, and compensation, which includes additional damages and other forms of relief.[98] Reparative justice may be promoted by 'undoing' the effects of the theft, pillage, and expropriation of cultural objects, often carried out in particularly egregious circumstances during wartime, armed conflict, colonialism,

[92] The museums of the former colonial powers may argue that they are entitled to an 'offset' for the value of the conservation and preservation measures that they expended on the cultural objects. The question of offset is discussed later, but offset is clearly not a justification for the retention of the objects themselves.

[93] Posner and Vermeule, 'Reparations for Slavery' (n 88) 704–05.

[94] Matthes, 'Repatriation' (n 77) 936–37. People who had no control over wrongdoing may nonetheless feel a moral taint and may be motivated to take actions, such as through reparations, to remove the taint. Posner and Vermeule, 'Reparations for Slavery' (n 88) 709–11

[95] Posner and Vermeule, 'Reparations for Slavery' (n 88) 706–07. See also Novic, *The Concept of Cultural Genocide* (n 78) 202.

[96] Posner and Vermeule, 'Reparations for Slavery' (n 88) 698–99.

[97] According to Matthes, a transfer of victimization can be based on either a 'harm argument' or an 'inheritance argument'. Both arguments would be applicable to the types of historical injustices considered here. Matthes, 'Repatriation' (n 77) 937.

[98] Gillard, 'Reparation' (n 86) 531. Vrdoljak lists the forms of reparation as: restitution, compensation, rehabilitation, satisfaction, and guarantees for non-repetition, including material and symbolic reparation. Vrdoljak, 'Cultural Heritage' (n 40) 187. Onyekachi Wambu lists the eight 'Rs': recognition and acknowledgment; remembrance; restoration of dignity; restitution of physical artefacts and human remains; financial and psychological reparations and healing; physical and mental reconnections; physical human return; holistic reconstruction of African societies. Onyekachi Wambu, 'Why Africa's stolen treasures must be returned' (*NewAfrican*, 17 September 2020) <https://newafricanmagazine.com/23909/> accessed 24 March 2022 (hereafter Wambu, 'Why Africa's stolen treasures').

genocide, or ethnic cleansing.[99] In this case, the harm is based principally on the deprivation not of property alone or its monetary value but rather on the deprivation of cultural, historical, traditional, spiritual, and religious values and connections. To create the circumstances for re-establishing these connections and values and because of the unique nature of the harm, reparations should primarily take the form of restitution of the objects themselves.[100] The nature of cultural heritage objects as part of the inheritance of future generations means that reparations are premised on the right to recover the tangible objects, regardless of the passage of time.[101] Nonetheless, there are circumstances that may call for payment of monetary reparations, primarily to fully compensate for the unjust enrichment garnered by the appropriators, in addition to restitution.[102]

Reparations through restitution also provides the basis for 'reflection on history, memories, and the colonial past', the origins of the Western museum, the meaning of cultural heritage, and 'the nature and quality of relations between people and nations'.[103] Restitution allows the creation of a new relationship between the formerly colonized and the former colonizers. Masurovsky calls for a 'decentering of a discourse whereby the host institution is no longer the purveyor of a system of ideas and values that has enabled and justified cultural crimes ... [N]ew forms of dialogue must be conceptualized, practiced, and implemented between the hosts of the displaced objects, the aggrieved parties, and the mediating institutions—a new social contract of cultural rights'.[104]

Returns of cultural objects that were stolen or otherwise extracted from victims of Nazi Germany, including those objects still located in German cultural institutions and institutions of collaborator States, are often not resolved on the basis of

[99] United Nations Declaration on the Rights of Indigenous Peoples, UNGA, A/RES/61/295 (13 September 2007) Article 11(2) (redress through restitution of cultural, intellectual, religious, and spiritual property taken without free, prior, and informed consent or in violation of their laws, traditions, and customs); Article 12 (right to repatriation of human remains and ceremonial objects). Elazar Barkan, 'Amending Historical Injustices: The Restitution of Cultural Property—An Overview' in Elazar Barkan and Ronald Bush (eds) *Claiming the Stones, Naming the Bones: Cultural Property and the Negotiation of National and Ethnic Identity* (Getty Publications 2002) 16–46.

[100] Vrdoljak, 'Cultural Heritage' (n 38) 187; Sarr and Savoy, 'The Restitution of African Cultural Heritage' (n 64) 29. This contrasts with most reparations which more typically take the form of cash payments, affirmative action (which is likely unique to the United States as a form of reparation), and apologies. Posner and Vermeule, 'Reparations for Slavery' (n 88) 725–26. Compensation as a primary form of reparation is necessary where the cultural heritage has been destroyed rather than appropriated.

[101] Thompson, 'Cultural Property, Restitution and Value' (n 40) 254.

[102] Vrdoljak, 'Cultural Heritage' (n 38) 187 (discussing the Yemen National Dialogue Conference Outcomes Document of 2014 that calls for restitution of expropriated books, manuscripts, and other cultural objects and compensation for war damage and to reacquire antiquities that were smuggled out of the country).

[103] Sarr and Savoy, 'The Restitution of African Cultural Heritage' (n 64) 29. Sarr and Savoy also raise the difficulties of restituting objects that have themselves been changed during the time of their exile or separation from their original contexts. Some have become works of art, ethnographic objects, or 'mere' witnesses of history. ibid, 30.

[104] Marc Masurovsky, 'A Comparative Look at Nazi Plundered Art, Looted Antiquities, and Stolen Indigenous Objects' (2020) 45 North Carolina Journal of International Law 497, 524–25.

reparations but rather on questions of method of acquisition and property rights, despite recognition in the Washington Conference Principles and other statements that such cultural objects should be returned regardless of technical legal barriers.[105] The right to repatriation for Native Americans and Native Hawaiian organizations is also premised on the failure of the current possessor institution or federal agency to have acquired title,[106] although the Native American Graves Protection and Repatriation Act (NAGPRA) is seen as a means of rectifying past wrongs and is often described as civil rights and human rights legislation.[107] The apparent anomaly of these situations seems to indicate a failure to sufficiently tie the appropriation of cultural objects to the underlying harms that were done in both these historical cases and are viewed, instead, as primarily disputes about property titles and rights.

7.4.3 Means of Reparation

In 2016, the Benin Minister of Foreign Affairs formally requested the return of all objects taken during the French colonization of Benin (at that time, the kingdom of Dahomey).[108] This request was rejected on the grounds that objects in French museums were part of the national patrimony and therefore were inalienable. However, in November 2017, in a speech at the University of Ouagadougou, French President Macron pledged the return within five years of cultural heritage objects taken during colonialism to countries of Africa on either a permanent or temporary basis. This was part of his announcement that France would no longer attempt to exert military, political, or commercial influence over its former colonies in Africa. Most of these artefacts are held in the Musée du Quai Branly, while others are scattered through numerous other French museums. Macron commissioned a report by Felwine Sarr and Bénédicte Savoy; the report was published a

[105] ibid, 498, 506; US Department of State Office of the Special Envoy for Holocaust Issues, 'Washington Conference Principles on Nazi-Confiscated Art' (1998) <www.state.gov/washington-conference-principles-on-nazi-confiscated-art/> accessed 7 July 2021; see also chapter 6, section 6.2. Compensation paid to Israel by Germany is a different form of reparations. Posner and Vermeule, 'Reparations for Slavery' (n 88) 698.

[106] Native American Graves Protection and Repatriation Act, 25 USC §§ 3001–3013, § 3002; C Timothy McKeown, *In the Smaller Scope of Conscience: The Struggle for National Repatriation Legislation, 1986–1990* (University of Arizona Press 2012) 164 (quoting Senator John McCain).

[107] Jack F Trope, 'The Case for NAGPRA' in Sangita Chari and Jaime M N Lavallee (eds), *Accomplishing NAGPRA: Perspectives on the Intent, Impact, and Future of the Native American Graves Protection and Repatriation Act* (Oregon State University Press 2013) 19, 28–29; C Timothy McKeown, '"The Secretary Shall": Actual and Apparent Delegation of NAGPRA's Implementation Responsibilities' in Sangita Chari and Jaime M N Lavallee (eds), *Accomplishing NAGPRA: Perspectives on the Intent, Impact, and Future of the Native American Graves Protection and Repatriation Act* (Oregon State University Press 2013) 55, 78.

[108] Valeria Kosta-Kostritsky, 'Rate of return—is France's commitment to restitution waning?' (*Apollo*, 4 January 2021) <www.apollo-magazine.com/french-restitution-africa-benin-senegal/> accessed 12 August 2021 (hereafter Kosta-Kostritsky, 'Rate of return').

year later in November 2018.[109] The report called for the return from French institutions of all cultural objects taken during colonialism.

Macron subsequently promised to return twenty-six cultural objects taken from Benin in 1892 during the sack of the Abomey Palace and one object to Senegal. The French Parliament enacted a law to allow the deaccessioning of these objects from the French collections in December 2020, but during the debate, it was stated that this was not 'an act of repentance or reparation' and it was not 'calling into question the universal mission of French museums'.[110] The objects were returned in 2021 and are intended to be exhibited in a new museum being built in Benin with loans and grants of €35 million from France, indicating that France will continue to exert control over Benin's cultural affairs.[111] The loan will create a significant indebtedness on the part of Benin to the French government.[112] The question of the return of additional cultural objects from France remains unsettled with parts of the government and French society opposed and this issue being regarded as politically sensitive.[113]

Since the time of Macron's Ouagadougou speech, there have been numerous announcements of the intent to return artefacts taken during colonialism, yet relatively few have been returned. Some of the returned objects were stolen more recently or are returns from non-government institutions. The largest return to date is an agreement between the Stiftung des Preussischer Kulturbesitz and Nigeria's Commission for Museums and Monuments for the return of 512 Benin objects from the Ethnologisches Museum of the Staatliche Museen zu Berlin to Nigeria.[114] A large collection of objects stolen by the British from Maqdala in

[109] Sarr and Savoy, 'The Restitution of African Cultural Heritage' (n 64). The Sarr and Savoy report was followed in 2023 by a report by Jean-Luc Martinez, 'Patrimoine partagé: universalité, restitutions et circulation des oeuvres d'art (Ministère de la Culture 27.04.2023) <https://www.culture.gouv.fr/fr/Espace-documentation/Rapports/Remise-du-rapport-Patrimoine-partage-universalite-restitutions-et-circulation-des-aeuvres-d-art-de-Jean-Luc-Martinez> accessed 11 July 2023 (hereafter Martinez, 'Patrimoine partagé'). This report called for legislation to facilitate restitution in three areas—Holocaust-looted cultural objects, human remains and cultural heritage. The legislation concerning Holocaust-looted cultural objects was adopted shortly later. See above n 10. See also Elaine Velie, 'Understanding France's New Restitution Guidelines' (*Hyperallergic* 4 May 2023) <https://hyperallergic.com/819941/understanding-frances-new-restitution-guidelines/> accessed 11 July 2023 (hereafter, Velie 'Understanding France's New Restitution Guidelines')..

[110] Quoted by Kosta-Kostritsky, 'Rate of return' (n 108).

[111] Amah-Rose Abrams, 'France Has Returned 26 Objects Stolen from an Ancient Palace in Benin' (*ArtNet News*, 9 November 2021) <https://news.artnet.com/art-world/france-returns-looted-items-benin-2032238> accessed 8 February 2022.

[112] The requirement to establish Western-style museums in the formerly colonized countries may constitute a means to prevent or postpone restitution. It is also a reflection of the remaking of formerly colonized countries in the image of the former colonial powers, including the projection of heritage 'upon non-Western cultures within the context of colonialism and shaped by colonial collecting and displaying practices'. Van Beurden, 'The Art of (Re)possession' (n 14) 145.

[113] Kosta-Kostritsky, 'Rate of return' (n 108); Martinez, 'Patrimoine partagé' (n 109); Velie, 'Understanding France's New Restitution Guidelines' (n 109).

[114] About a third of the objects will remain in Berlin on loan for ten years for display at the Humboldt Forum; the loan may be renewed. Two objects were transferred previously. Stiftung Preussischer Kulturbesitz, '514 Berlin Benin bronzes return to Nigerian ownership' (8 August 2022) www.preussischer-kulturbesitz.de/en/news-detail/article/2022/08/25/512-berliner-benin-bronzen-wieder-nig

1868 were returned to Ethiopia after being purchased by a private donor.[115] The Smithsonian Institution returned twenty-nine Benin works to Nigeria as part of a larger agreement for long-term loans, shared exhibitions, and collaborative educational programs.[116]

European institutions and politicians have at times proposed loans as an alternative to permanent restitution.[117] Loans achieve circulation of cultural objects, which is seen as a means of fulfilling the mission of the universal museum. In some cases, objects are loaned back to the country of origin, but the Western institution retains title.[118] However, this is typically an unsatisfactory solution in that acceptance of a loan by a country of origin may mean acknowledging legitimate title in the European or US museum or private collector. From an historical and restitutionary perspective, title should be recognized in the community or country of origin and then the owner can choose whether to lend objects back to the European or US institution, as it wishes. Sarr and Savoy see loans as a temporary solution while French law is changed to allow permanent deaccessioning and ultimately restitution without any stipulations or conditions.[119]

Sarr and Savoy suggested that all objects that will be returned should first be digitized and that all archival and other documentary materials held by French institutions and the government should be made open with free access to all.[120] However,

erianisches-eigentum.html accessed 15 September 2022. The museum has been a part of the Benin Dialogue Group since 2010. The Netherlands has announced the return of 472 objects to Indonesia and six to Sri Lanka that were looted during colonialism. Teresa Nowakowski, 'The Netherlands Repatriates Nearly 500 Looted Artifacts to Sri Lanka and Indonesia' (*Smithsonian Magazine* 11 July 2023) <https://www.smithsonianmag.com/smart-news/netherlands-repatriation-sri-lanka-indonesia-180982514/> accessed 12 July 2023.

115 Martin Bailey, 'Maqdala treasures looted by British troops returned to Ethiopia in "largest single restitution"' (*The Art Newspaper*, 10 September 2021) <www.theartnewspaper.com/news/maqdala-ethiopia-ambassador> accessed 24 September 2021. The director of the Victoria and Albert Museum is seeking the loosening of restrictions on deaccessioning from British museums so that the museum can return the Asante gold regalia to Ghana. Martin Bailey, 'V&A likely to return looted Asante gold treasures to Ghana' (*The Art Newspaper*, 12 September 2022) www.theartnewspaper.com/2022/09/12/va-raises-real-prospect-of-return-of-asante-treasures-to-ghana accessed 15 September 2022. Arts Council England published a manual that explains the process for resolving restitution claims by museums and the sources and content of various restrictions on alienability. Arts Council England, 'Restitution and Repatriation: A Practical Guide for Museums in England' (2022).

116 Smithsonian News Release, 'Smithsonian Returns 29 Benin Bronzes to the National Commission for Museums and Monuments in Nigeria' <www.si.edu/newsdesk/releases/smithsonian-returns-29-benin-bronzes-national-commission-museums-and-monuments> accessed 19 October 2022. A complaint filed by the Restitution Study Group to prevent the Smithsonian Institution from repatriating this corpus of Benin bronzes was dismissed for lack of subject matter jurisdiction, lack of standing, and mootness. *Farmer-Paellmann v Smithsonian Inst* 2023 US Dist LEXIS 115133 (DDC 2023).

117 MacGregor, 'To Shape the Citizens' (n 56) 53.

118 One such example is the 'Trojan gold' artefacts that were acquired by the University of Pennsylvania Museum of Anthropology and Archaeology in the 1960s. The objects have been placed on permanent loan with Turkey although the university retains title. C Brian Rose, 'Beyond the UNESCO Convention: The Case of the Troy Gold in the Penn Museum' (2017) 5(1) JEMAHS 87.

119 Sarr and Savoy, 'The Restitution of African Cultural Heritage' (n 64) 28–29.

120 ibid, 67–68.

this constitutes another means of denying agency to the countries and communities of origin, grants control over the digital resources to Western institutions, and implicates a range of issues involved in the open access of digital resources.[121] As Pavis and Wallace note, 'attempts to truly decolonize French institutions of African Material Cultural Heritage must carry through to the treatment of archival and digital materials, including those remaining in France. Digital heritage today is as important as material heritage and should be thoughtfully considered and fully integrated within future restitution policies and collections management'.[122] As will be discussed later, the archives and other records of the colonial administrations should be made available to the governments and communities of the formerly colonized States, but whether and how these are made publicly accessible should be subject to their determination.

7.4.3.1 Apology

As a first step in reparations, Posner and Vermeule suggest that an apology should serve as the legal basis for liability in order to make the apology credible.[123] Apologies are relatively rare with respect to actions taken during colonialism and even rarer with respect to the extensive appropriation of cultural objects effectuated during this time period. The reason for this reluctance is, as Posner and Vermeule noted, that an admission of any sort of guilt would raise the question of liability and undermine the legitimacy of the holdings of their national institutions. Nonetheless, in 2016, Macron referred to colonization as 'a crime against humanity, a true example of barbarism. And it is an example of this past history that we must have the courage to confront by earnestly apologizing to those toward whom we have committed these acts.'[124]

Despite these acknowledgements, while the French Parliament was debating the change in the law to allow repatriation of the objects to Benin, it was careful to avoid any statement that might resemble an apology or call into question the legitimacy of French acquisitions during colonialism and the legitimacy of the universal museum.[125] This attention to terminology so as not to imply acceptance of guilt or responsibility for the actions and effects of colonialism was similarly displayed as Belgium debated return of cultural objects to the Congo in 1973. Any return was a 'gift' and not 'restitution' to avoid an implied admission of guilt.[126]

121 Mathilde Pavis and Andrea Wallace, 'Statement: Response to the 2018 Sarr-Savoy Report' 10 (2019) JIPITEC 115.

122 ibid; Martinez, 'Patrimoine partagé' (n 109) 67-69 (discussing the status of archives and library materials and the special case of Senegal).

123 Posner and Vermeule, 'Reparations for Slavery' (n 88) 731; von Arnauld, 'How to Illegalize Past Injustice' (n 13) 422.

124 Sarr and Savoy 'The Restitution of African Cultural Heritage' (n 64) 1–2.

125 Kosta-Kostritsky, 'Rate of Return' (n 108).

126 Van Beurden, 'The Art of (Re)possession' (n 14) 158.

In addition to Macron's statement, one of the few apologies for past conduct during colonialism was the eventual apology that Germany offered to the Herero and Nama people of Namibia. This came in the context of an acknowledgement of the genocide that Germany perpetrated against these Indigenous groups and in the restitution of human remains taken to Germany for the purpose of conducting eugenics research.[127] However, for the most part, the former colonial powers have resisted any acknowledgement that colonialism and the deprivation of cultural objects were wrongful and the need for an apology. In fact, the former colonial powers seem to take the position both that they did nothing wrong in appropriating cultural objects and that if there is any blame, that blame should fall on the Indigenous peoples and on the art market, which became a convenient target particularly following adoption of the 1970 UNESCO Convention.[128]

7.4.3.2 A Proposed Paradigm of Restitution

Folarin Shyllon quotes John Merryman as saying, 'there is little agreement on the criteria for deciding whether a particular object ... should be returned or kept, or whether some other disposition of the object is desirable'.[129] Even as restitutions have increased, efforts have been made to establish criteria for which objects should be returned. Sarr and Savoy argue for return of all objects from French museums to the formerly colonized countries and enactment of a general law that would permit the necessary deaccessioning of these objects, although they acknowledge that the process would need to occur in stages.[130] They categorize the objects based on the circumstances of their appropriation, including as spoils of war, acquisition by exploratory or scientific missions, and gifts from private collectors, often former colonial administrators, diplomats, or their families.[131] Within the range of gradual restitution, the process would begin with restitution of objects whose histories and method of appropriation are well known and whose restitution has long been requested, such as the objects and regalia taken during the sack of Abomey in 1892.[132] The second phase would involve creation of inventories, sharing of digital content, workshops, and establishment of joint commissions. The third phase, which would be open-ended in its time frame, would involve a long-term process of restitution

[127] Alma Nankela and Jeremy Silvester, 'A Namibian Experience: The Contentious Politics of Repatriation of Human Remains and Sacred Objects' in Deutscher Museums Bund, Guidelines Care of Human Remains in Museums and Collections (2021) 129. In 2021, Germany acknowledged the genocide and agreed to pay $1 billion in aid for development projects in Namibia to be paid over thirty years. However, hundreds of additional human remains are still in Germany. Franziska Boehme, 'Germany acknowledged colonial atrocities in Namibia as genocide. Victims' groups want more' (*Washington Post*, 9 June 2021) <www.washingtonpost.com/politics/2021/06/09/germany-acknowledged-colonial-atrocities-namibia-genocide-victims-groups-want-more/> accessed 20 July 2021.

[128] Van Beurden, 'The Art of (Re)possession' (n 14) 157.

[129] Shyllon, 'Unraveling History' (n 60) 167.

[130] Sarr and Savoy, 'The Restitution of African Cultural Heritage' (n 64) 44.

[131] ibid, 50–59.

[132] ibid, 63–66.

of remaining objects.[133] The more recent Martinez report proposes nine criteria for restitution. These include: a request must be brought by the country of origin or with the consent of the country of origin; consideration of whether the method of acquisition was illegal or otherwise illegitimate; and a consideration of contextual elements, including that there can be no financial compensation for reparations. The category of human remains would receive special treatment. Referring to the limits under UK law, the report proposes that return of human remains would be limited to those that post-date 1500 CE.[134]

In an extensive study of the British taking of objects from Benin during the Punitive Expedition of 1897, Dan Hicks argues that the method by which a cultural object was removed should be used to establish a new typology, which he labels a 'necrography'.[135] Rather than focusing on types of objects, he suggests that we need to focus on 'the different forms that "acquisition" through which colonial material culture came to western museums has taken'.[136] He sets out seven types of takings: (1) looting with violence; (2) physical anthropology collecting of human remains; (3) missionary and other confiscations of objects of belief and religion; (4) archaeological collections; (5) scientific collections of natural history specimens; (6) ethnographic collecting; and (7) objects obtained through barter, purchase, and commissioning.[137]

Acknowledgement, recognized through apology, is one way of righting an historical injustice. However, von Arnauld suggests that negotiation as a means of achieving reparation is more effective. The 'duty to enter into negotiation ... has the advantage of actively including the victims in the reparation process'.[138] This process allows the victims to re-establish their collective memory and therefore their identities as part of a collective.[139] The role of cultural objects in this process is significant. Therefore, a purely procedural remedy that allows this recreation of identity only through narrative is not sufficient, especially where the tangible objects whose deprivation was a substantial part of the injury are still available for

[133] ibid, 66–69.

[134] Martinez, 'Patrimoine partagé' (n 109) 54-62.

[135] Dan Hicks, *The Brutish Museums: The Benin Bronzes, Colonial Violence and Cultural Restitution* (Pluto Press 2020) 238–39 (hereafter Hicks, *The Brutish Museums*).

[136] ibid, 238.

[137] ibid, 239. While Hicks explains his typology as based on the method of acquisition, some of his typology is based on the type of object rather than method of acquisition. Sarr and Savoy further point out that it is not always possible to determine the method of appropriation, in part because of the inconsistent provenance information given in museum records. Sarr and Savoy, 'The Restitution of African Cultural Heritage' (n 64) 50. The Smithsonian adopted a policy of Shared Stewardship and Ethical Returns based on '[t]he manner in which a collection was originally acquired and the context of its acquisition ... Circumstances demonstrating unethical acquisition may include items that were stolen, taken under duress or removed without consent of the owner.' 'Smithsonian Adopts Policy on Ethical Returns' (3 May 2022) www.si.edu/newsdesk/releases/smithsonian-adopts-policy-ethical-returns accessed 5 May 2022.

[138] Von Arnauld, 'How to Illegalize Past Injustice' (n 13) 424.

[139] ibid, 422.

restitution. The narrative and re-establishment of identity explain why this is a demand-led process that allows for recognition of the dignity and identity of the victims.

There are several facets and nuances to the design of a restitution paradigm. In cases where there is an enforceable legal claim for restitution or where ethical guidelines mandate such return, then those principles would prevail. This paradigm is intended to fill the gaps that neither the law nor ethics can resolve and thereby provide redress necessary to repair the harm that was done. The paradigm proposed here uses fairly simple categories of types of objects based primarily, but not exclusively, on their role in society before their removal and their potential role after return in reconstituting communities. The goal is to avoid imposing cultural categories on non-Western cultures and to negate the classifications assigned by Western art historical and museological concepts. Where determinations of cultural or other significance need to be made, these should be made by the individuals, communities, and States from which these objects were removed.

The first step is for Western museums to create inventories or summaries, modelled on the provisions of the Native American Graves Protection and Repatriation Act,[140] with a centralized portal, similar to the Nazi Era Provenance Internet Portal.[141] While restitution would be a demand-led process in that communities and States should take the lead as to what will be returned, it is necessary for the possessing institutions to make knowledge of their collections available and to encourage or invite requests for restitution through a process of consultation. Whether these databases would be publicly available needs to be decided in consultation with descendant communities and States as there may be concerns with issues such as cultural privacy and secrecy.[142] The inventories would incorporate as much information as can be gathered concerning the place from which the objects were taken, the date, and the circumstances. In the case of some objects, this process may be relatively simple because scholars and museum professionals have already done the work[143] or the object is sufficiently famous that its history has not been lost through the appropriation process. In other cases, identification may

[140] 25 USC § 3003 (inventory for human remains and associated funerary objects); 25 USC § 3004 (summaries for unassociated funerary objects, sacred objects, and cultural patrimony).

[141] <www.nepip.org/> accessed 11 July 2023.

[142] Sarah K Harding, 'Value, Obligation and Cultural Heritage' (1999) 31 Arizona State Law Journal 291, 313–15.

[143] A digital catalogue of over 5,000 Benin objects launched in 2022. 'Digital Benin' <https://digitalbenin.org/> accessed 10 November 2022. Sarr and Savoy have listed objects from sub-Saharan Africa in French museums and conclude that 70,000 of the 90,000 relevant objects are in one museum, the Musée du Quai Branly-Jacques Chirac. These are more accessible because of their documentation. Sarr and Savoy, 'The Restitution of African Cultural Heritage' (n 64) 45–46. In 2022, Belgium gave an inventory of some 84,000 cultural objects to the Democratic Republic of Congo as a first step towards restitution. 'Belgium gives DR Congo inventory of looted artefacts' (*France24*, 17 February 2022) <www.france24.com/en/live-news/20220217-belgium-gives-dr-congo-inventory-of-looted-artefacts> accessed 18 February 2022.

pose more challenges. The work to establish these identifications and lost histories should be done collaboratively and equally with the knowledge and experience of the local and descendant communities.

The second step is to establish a temporal basis for presumptions concerning legitimacy of removal. With the exception of human remains and burial objects, for which a presumption of improper removal would be irrebutable, a rebuttable presumption of improper removal would apply to any cultural objects removed after the time of Napoleon's cultural appropriations. Although we may trace restitution of cultural objects to 1815, the requirement of restitution applied to objects taken as early as Napoleon's campaigns in Italy, such as works taken from Parma in 1796 and the San Marco horses and Veronese's *Wedding at Cana* taken from Venice in 1797.[144] Therefore, the norm to refrain from taking cultural objects, in what may be considered circumstances of unjust acquisition,[145] and the obligation to return those taken should apply to objects taken after 1796.[146]

Legal norms should be interpreted within their contemporary cultural context.[147] While perhaps the majority of Europeans approved of these large-scale removals, there were always voices in Europe that objected to these appropriations: the objections of Quatremère de Quincy and his fellow petitioners opposing Napoleon's depredations, Byron's objections to Elgin's taking of the Parthenon's sculptures, objections from Swedish diplomats,[148] Victor Hugo's objection to the looting of the Yuanmingyuan Palace, and objections to the colonial conduct of Germany and Belgium in Africa. The local communities often protested these forcible removals. These objections indicate that there was not

[144] Alex Greenberger, 'The Louvre's Looted Renaissance Masterpiece' (*ARTnews*, 10 May 2021) <www.artnews.com/art-news/news/veronese-wedding-feast-at-cana-plunder-book-review-1234592381/> accessed 8 February 2022. This requirement of restitution of works appropriated during the Napoleon wars provides the 'point of entry' for determining when an obligation of restitution arose. Von Arnauld uses the Berlin Conference and the 1899 and 1907 Hague Conventions as 'points of entry' for broader colonial behaviour that was viewed as violating ethical-legal principles. 'How to Illegalize Past Injustice' (n 13) 409. However, these later dates are not appropriate to determine the 'point of entry' for the obligation of restitution, a history and precedent for which existed at an earlier date.

[145] Matthes, 'Repatriation' (n 77) 936.

[146] A much more recent date of 1970 is often suggested for determining improper removal of cultural items, particularly archaeological artefacts, based on adoption of the 1970 UNESCO Convention. UNESCO Convention on the Means of Prohibiting and Preventing the Illicit Import, Export and Transfer of Ownership of Cultural Property (opened for signature 14 November 1970, entered into force 24 April 1972) 823 UNTS 231 (hereafter 1970 UNESCO Convention). While the date of 1970 has little legal significance, as discussed in Chapter 6, adoption of the Convention provided notice to individuals who acquired objects after 1970 that their acquisitions would be in jeopardy. However, some removals before 1970 would be illegal under contemporary law. Sarr and Savoy, 'The Restitution of African Cultural Heritage' (n 64) 60–61, argue for a presumption of improper removal before 1960, the end of colonialism for many African States.

[147] Cover argues that law (*nomos*) needs to be understood in light of contemporary cultural expressions, such as through literature. Robert M Cover, 'Foreward: Nomos and Narrative' (1983) 97(4) Harvard Law Review 4, 17–18.

[148] Thomasson, 'Justifying and Criticizing' (n 42) 498–99.

a unanimous contemporary consensus as to the morality of these actions or of international law.[149]

Objects removed after this time would be presumed to have been transferred involuntarily or by someone without authority to transfer the cultural object. The Guideline established by the German Museumsbund sets out three categories where consent for appropriation in colonial contexts would need scrutiny: acquisitions carried out without consent of owners, guardians or descendants, such as through grave robbing, theft, and looting; acquisitions in which the donors were put under pressure or compulsion or where they acted out of desperation; and acquisitions in which consent was given by persons not entitled to give or refuse consent.[150] The current possessor would have the opportunity to rebut a presumption of nonconsensual transfer by establishing that the transfer was freely made, with the consent or under the authority of the individual or community that had authority to transfer the cultural object. The types of objects for which it may be possible to rebut the presumption of improper removal would primarily be objects made for the market. Because it is a rebuttable presumption, the burden of proving that the object was created for the market would be on the current possessor. It would also be necessary to establish that the seller had authority to sell, and that the sale was for a fair price.[151]

7.4.3.2.1 Human Remains and Burial Objects

Human remains would be considered per se inalienable and therefore any human remains collected in the past would be subject to return upon request. In the Anglo-American common law system, ownership rights in human remains and associated burial goods are not recognized, other than for the limited purpose of ensuring proper burial.[152] Despite this, human remains were collected through robbing of

149 Von Arnauld urges the use of non-legal voices, including those of literature as part of the law and literature movement, to determine a broader view of what was acceptable conduct, regardless of the technical status of such conduct under international law. Arnauld, 'How to Illegalize Past Injustice' (n 13) 410–13. In focusing on the German and Belgian colonial atrocities, which postdated adoption of the 1899 and 1907 Hague Conventions, von Arnauld is more easily able to argue that this conduct was a violation of contemporary *lex lata*. ibid, 415. However, many of the examples of colonial and imperial expropriations discussed here predated these conventions.

150 Deutscher Museumsbund, Guidelines Care of Human Remains in Museums and Collections (2021) 18.

151 Sarr and Savoy describe purchases of ethnographic materials by French ethnographic missions during the 1930s and, in particular, the considerably below market prices paid with as much as a 300-fold discrepancy. Sarr and Savoy, 'The Restitution of African Cultural Heritage' (n 64) 56. Such acquisitions, often accompanied by military and other power displays, are more accurately described as forced purchases or requisitions. ibid. However, Sarr and Savoy would exempt such ethnographic collections from restitution requests if there is 'explicit evidence or information witnessing' the full consent of those who possessed the objects. ibid, 57–58.

152 Hugh V Bernard, *The Law of Death and Disposal of the Dead* (Oceana Publications 1979) 16 (*citing* 2 William Blackstone, Commentaries, 429).

burials of Indigenous groups in the United States,[153] New Zealand,[154] Canada, Australia, and elsewhere. Museums and governments show their greatest willingness to make restitutions and repatriations with respect to human remains.[155] As discussed in chapter 5, section 5.3, the United Kingdom and France changed their laws to allow international repatriation of human remains, although in the case of France, these changes were narrow. Both these limits on deaccessioning and the loosening or elimination of these limits present examples of the political choices that determine what will be returned.

The United States enacted the Native American Graves Protection and Repatriation Act in 1990. It applied to newly discovered human remains and other cultural items but also to remains and cultural items that were recovered before NAGPRA's enactment and are housed in federal agencies and US institutions, including museums and universities, that receive federal funding.[156] In part, the justification for applying NAGPRA to human remains that had been acquired before NAGPRA's enactment was based on the principle that there are no ownership rights in human remains. One drawback of the NAGPRA scheme is that it distinguishes between associated and unassociated burial items; this distinction would not be maintained in this proposal, and any cultural item originally placed in a burial would qualify for the same treatment as human remains. NAGPRA applies to five categories of cultural items: human remains; associated funerary objects; unassociated funerary objects; sacred objects; and objects of cultural patrimony. Associated funerary objects are 'objects that, as a part of the death rite or ceremony of a culture, are reasonably believed to have been placed with individual human remains either at the time of death or later ...' and the objects and human remains are in the control or possession of the Federal agency or museum.[157]

A restitution scheme based to some extent on the NAGPRA priority[158] could be adapted to the international context. The first priority would be given to lineal descendants who claim the remains of an ancestor. In the absence of a lineal

[153] For example Margaret B Bowman, 'The Reburial of Native American Skeletal Remains: Approaches to the Resolution of a Conflict' (1989) 13 Harvard Environmental Law Review 147, 149(estimating that American museum collections include approximately 300,000 human remains).

[154] Robert K Paterson, 'Taonga Maori Renaissance: Protecting the Cultural Heritage of Aotearoa/New Zealand' in James AR Nafziger and Ann M Nicgorski (eds), *Cultural Heritage Issues: The Legacy of Conquest, Colonization, and Commerce* (Martinus Nijhoff Publishers 2009) 107, 121–22.

[155] Sarr and Savoy, The Restitution of African Cultural Heritage (n 64) 17.

[156] 25 USC §§ 3001–3013. The application of NAGPRA to cultural items and humans remains collected before its enactment is another example of retroactive effect, similar to those discussed earlier in this chapter.

[157] 25 USC § 3001(3)(3)(A). Unassociated funerary objects share the same definition, but the human remains and objects are not in the possession or control of the same federal agency or museum. 25 USC § 3001(3)(3)(B). Associated funerary objects are subject to the stricter requirements for creating inventories and giving notice to the culturally affiliated Native American tribe or Native Hawaiian organization, whereas unassociated funerary objects are subject to the less stringent requirements of summaries. 25 USC §§ 3003–3004. It is not intended that NAGPRA would or should apply literally to objects from other Indigenous groups, but these definitions can be used as guidance.

[158] 25 USC § 3002.

descendant, a descendant community would represent the line of the ancestor. Finally, Indigenous groups that are culturally affiliated with the remains, inhabit the same territory, or have some other claim as a representative or an institution that is designated by the community would also have a cognizable claim.[159]

7.4.3.2.2 Objects with Cultural, Religious or Historical Ties

Objects with cultural, religious, spiritual, or historical ties to a community are typically not alienable by an individual or subgroup of the community.[160] Catherine Bell explains the difficulty of defining when cultural objects are inalienable:

> Repatriation efforts in Canada, as elsewhere, are part of a broader movement of decolonization and reparation of past injustice. Within this context, certain material may be considered so integrally related to group identity that it takes on characteristics of community property, even if it was not considered to be so at the time of removal. Refusal to return may represent a continuation of oppression.[161]

Many of the cultural objects removed from Africa during the nineteenth and first half of the twentieth centuries would fall into this category.[162] The violence and armed conflict that often accompanied these removals provide an additional justification for return. Sacred sculptures, often considered to be living gods, have been

[159] Karolina Kuprecht addresses the question of the adaptability of NAGPRA's standards to the repatriation of Indigenous peoples' cultural property to other countries and on an international scale. Karolina Kuprecht, *Indigenous Peoples' Cultural Property Claims: Repatriation and Beyond* (Springer 2013) 68–73. Implementation of NAGPRA, even with respect to human remains, has not been entirely effective. While a 2022 Government Accountability Office report noted that between 1990 and 2020, federal agencies repatriated 91.5 per cent of the culturally affiliated human remains in their collections, more than 116,000 culturally unaffiliated Native American human remains are still in these collections. US Government Accountability Office, 'Native American Issues: Federal Agency Efforts and Challenges Repatriating Cultural Items' GAO-22-105685 <www.gao.gov/products/gao-22-105685> accessed 8 February 2022. For disposition of culturally unidentifiable human remains, see 43 Code of Federal Regulations § 10.11.

[160] Definitions of these object types could track those of NAGPRA: 'sacred objects' are defined as 'specific ceremonial objects which are needed by traditional Native American religious leaders for the practice of traditional Native American religions by their present-day adherents'. Cultural patrimony means 'an object having ongoing historical, traditional, or cultural importance central to the Native American group or culture itself, rather than property owned by an individual Native American, and which, therefore, cannot be alienated, appropriated, or conveyed by any individual regardless of whether or not the individual is a member of the Indian tribe or Native Hawaiian organization and such object shall have been considered inalienable by such Native American group at the time the object was separated from such group'. 25 USC § 3001 (C) and (D).

[161] Catherine Bell, 'Repatriation of Cultural Material to First Nations in Canada; Legal and Ethical Justifications' in James AR Nafziger and Ann M Nicgorski (eds), *Cultural Heritage Issues: The Legacy of Conquest, Colonization, and Commerce* (Martinus Nijhoff Publishers 2009) 81, 87.

[162] For example the *vigango* funerary statues taken from the Mijikenda people of Kenya. Stephen E Nash, 'A Curator's Search for Justice' (*Sapiens*, 14 May 2020) <www.sapiens.org/column/curiosities/vigango-repatriation/> accessed 24 March 2022.

returned to sanctuaries and temples in Nepal, Sri Lanka, India, Cambodia, and elsewhere in Asia as further examples of this category.[163]

Determinations of significance may appear to raise obstacles. How much significance an object carries to a particular people or nation will be judged differently depending on who is doing the judging.[164] There are cases of cultural discontinuities, but these were often created by the colonial powers either through massacres or through artificial constructs of identities and imposed national borders that sought to divide people and communities. But cultural objects are also a positive force for the construction of identities and, in light of the disruptions imposed by colonialism and conflict, communities from whom these objects were taken should be able to make these determinations of significance, in an act of cultural independence, for themselves. Outsiders, particularly Western collecting institutions, should not impose these determinations on them.

7.4.3.2.3 Integral Monuments

Another category of cultural artefacts that should be readily subject to repatriation claims would be works of art and architectural remains that were at one time part of, attached to, or integrated into structures. As parts of immovable structures, these objects were never intended to be sold onto a market or made into movable objects. The case for repatriation here is strong, particularly where the original structure might be reconstituted. However, there are examples where such reintegration is not possible, usually because of the damage done to the structure in the process of removal. Nonetheless, it may be possible to recontextualize such objects, bringing them closer to their original contexts.

An outstanding example of this is the Parthenon Sculptures.[165] These were created as, and were intended to be, an integral part of a unified structure. Many of the aspects of the display of the sculptures in the British Museum do not accord with the intent of the artists and creators. The sculptures are displayed indoors in artificial light, rather than outside under the Mediterranean sun. They are placed close to eye-level rather than atop the structure. Particularly jarring is the display of the frieze, which is turned in on itself rather than turning out towards the viewer. The disassociation between the original vision of the creators for the structure and its sculptures and the present state of dismemberment has become a

[163] For example Angelica Villa, 'Following Activists' Calls, Rubin Museum to Return Looted Nepalese Artifacts' (*ARTnews*, 11 January 2022) <www.artnews.com/art-news/news/rubin-museum-returns-looted-artifacts-nepal-1234615404/> accessed 8 February 2022.

[164] For example, James Cuno believes that archaeological materials taken from China, Turkey, or Iraq bear little relationship to the modern people of these nations and that ancient cultural objects should therefore not be returned to these countries. Cuno, *Who Owns Antiquity?* (n 65).

[165] This is not based on 'Parthenon exceptionalism' as Elizabeth Marlowe has coined the phrase. She rightly rejects the justification for restitution on the basis that the Parthenon is so exceptional in terms of its beauty or importance that it becomes a unique case. As she points out, the principle of reunification would apply to other examples. Elizabeth Marlowe, 'From Exceptionalism to Solidarity: The Rhetoric of the Case for the Parthenon Sculptures' Return' (2022) 41 CAELJ 125, 129-50.

strong justification for its reunification. Objection may be made that the sculptures cannot be returned to the structure, and, at this time, the sculptures remaining in Athens have also been removed for their safekeeping. However, the damage done to the structure by Elgin's agents is much of the reason for the inability to return the sculptures to their original placement. The British should not be allowed to benefit from the harm that Elgin inflicted. A modern museum has been constructed with ample views of the Acropolis and the Parthenon, allowing for a degree of recontextualization. Placement in the museum under these conditions provides a strong second-best disposition close to the original cultural context.

The objects removed from the Yuanmingyuan Palace in China are another example, although they did not constitute a single physical structure nor were they taken from a single monument. Nonetheless, the objects in the palace complex can be viewed as a single collection. Restitution of these objects poses a challenge because the objects are widely dispersed, and many are in private collections, making it difficult to trace the provenances of the specific objects.[166] However, the largest intact collection consists of those objects of the highest quality that were specially selected for Emperor Napoleon III and Empress Eugénie; this collection is now located in the Chinese Museum at the Fountainebleau Palace in France.[167] This collection could be offered for repatriation to China. Other Yuanmingyuan objects occasionally appear on the market, and they could be purchased by governments, particularly the United Kingdom and France, for the purpose of repatriation.

7.4.3.2.4 Representative Collections

Some countries whose cultural heritage was subject to appropriation through colonialism, armed conflict, and imperialism present a striking illustration of the need for restitution of representative collections to the countries of origin. According to Sarr and Savoy, a significant proportion of the material culture of sub-Saharan Africa is located outside of Africa.[168] These countries may not be able to acquire

[166] Nick Pearce, 'From the Summer Palace 1860' in Louise Tythacott (ed), *Collecting and Displaying China's "Summer Palace" in the West: The Yuanmingyuan in Britain and France* (Routledge 2018) 38, 41–46; Christine Howald and Léa Saint-Raymond, 'Tracing Dispersal: Auction Sales from the Yuanmingyuan loot in Paris in the 1860s' (2018) 2 JAMS 1 <www.fokum-jams.org/index.php/jams/article/view/30/92> accessed 24 March 2022.

[167] Vincent Droguet, 'Empress Eugénie's Chinese Museum at the Chateau of Fontainebleau: An Unusual Décor in the "House of the Ages"' in Louise Tythacott (ed), *Collecting and Displaying China's "Summer Palace" in the West: The Yuanmingyuan in Britain and France* (Routledge 2018) 138, 143–46; Greg M Thomas, 'Yuanmingyuan on Display: Ornamental Aesthetics at the Musée Chinois' in Louise Tythacott (ed), *Collecting and Displaying China's "Summer Palace" in the West: The Yuanmingyuan in Britain and France* (Routledge 2018) 149, 151.

[168] Sarr and Savoy 'The Restitution of African Cultural Heritage' (n 64) 3. While the reliability of this statistic has been questioned, Alain Godonou estimated that 90–95 per cent of sub-Saharan Africa's heritage is located outside of Africa and contrasts this situation with that of Egypt, Greece, and other countries that retain significant amounts of their heritage, although they have suffered considerable deprivations as well. ibid. Others estimate a lower amount at 80–90 per cent. Wambu, 'Why Africa's stolen treasures' (n 98).

on the market when cultural objects are sold by the descendants of those who appropriated them during military and other expeditions of the European colonial powers. There may also be cultural and legal reasons for not acquiring on the market, even if a country or community is able to do so, as this may constitute an acknowledgement of the legitimacy of the title of the appropriator. These challenges of participating in the market provide additional reasons for restitution.

7.4.3.2.5 To Whom Should Cultural Objects be Returned?

The question may arise of to whom cultural objects should be returned.[169] Treaty law, embodied in the First Protocol to the 1954 Hague Convention and the 1970 UNESCO Convention, incorporates a traditional principle based on territoriality that cultural objects should be returned to the place from which they were removed, often considered to be the State within which that territory is located. The 1954 First Protocol states that an object removed illegally from occupied territory should be returned to that territory at the end of the occupation. This establishes the basic norm of territoriality—that an object should be returned to the place where it was last located before its illegal removal, even if it had previously been illegally removed from a different location.[170] The territoriality principle also determines where movable cultural objects should be located following State succession. In most cases, the successor State will have rights to cultural objects from that territory; in some exceptions, the question of significance may determine a different result.[171]

As has been apparent throughout, cultural heritage must be viewed through three perspectives: the global or universalistic, the State, and the local community. When restitution is made pursuant to an international treaty, restitution is typically made to the corresponding State because these are State-to-State instruments, regardless of the prior location of the cultural objects. In a dispute as to whether Scythian gold objects, which were on loan to Dutch museums at the time of the Russian annexation of Crimea in 2014, should be returned to the national government of Ukraine or to the museums in Crimea which had loaned the objects, the

[169] See also Patty Gerstenblith, 'The Disposition of Movable Cultural Heritage' in Anne-Marie Carstens and Elizabeth Varner (eds) *Intersections in International Cultural Heritage Law* (OUP 2020) 17, 43–52.

[170] The Horses of San Marco in Venice are a paradigmatic example. Their original location is unknown, but they were in Constantinople by the early fourth century, plundered and taken to Venice in 1204 during the Fourth Crusade, and then taken to Paris by Napoleon. The French were required to return the horses to Venice in 1815. Return to Istanbul does not seem to have been considered. See Charles Freeman, *The Horses of St. Mark's* (Overlook 2004); Andrew McClellan, *Inventing the Louvre: Art, Politics, and the Origins of the Modern Museum in Eighteenth-Century Paris* (CUP 1994) 122–23, 149. While this may reflect a Eurocentric approach and reinforces the nineteenth-century principle that international laws applied only to European countries, Vrdoljak, *International Law* (n 13) 47–50, it also fit the pattern that artworks taken during armed conflict are returned to the place from which they were last taken.

[171] Jakubowski, *State Succession* (n 18) 324–26.

Dutch courts held that the objects should be returned to the national government. This decision was based on the ownership of the objects by the Ukrainian Museum Fund, rather than by the individual museums or the regional government.[172] Once cultural objects are returned, the receiving State would determine the disposition of the cultural objects, in particular whether they are placed in a national or regional institution or transferred to a cultural group. However, this means that cultural objects may not be placed with the local or descendant community. Placement and ownership of the objects may be determined under national law, such as where national law recognizes religious foundations as the owners of religious or sacred objects. In such cases, the cultural objects would be returned to the religious foundation.[173]

When restitution is made outside of treaty law, there is an opportunity for greater flexibility, thereby creating the option of return directly to a community of origin or descendant community. This would seem particularly desirable when the community is Indigenous or of a religious or ethnic minority whom the State may not recognize or to whom the State may not wish to give greater deference through restitution of cultural objects, which may be seen as reinforcing a cultural group's claim to sovereignty or independence. While an unwillingness to do so implicates many of the human rights issues discussed in chapter 5, in particular the rights of Indigenous groups and the right to access and engage in one's culture, the issue may not be one that can be entirely resolved. However, the restituting entity may have greater leverage when the restitution occurs as a voluntary action.

7.4.3.3 Reparations Beyond Restitution

Restitution of cultural objects is presumed to be the most appropriate form of reparations.[174] Cultural objects are often unique and have a close connection to the people and communities who are descended from the original victims of the injustice. However, additional reparations in the form of compensation might be required to make the victims whole or to facilitate restitution. Monetary compensation may be appropriate if the cultural object was destroyed or significantly damaged so that it requires conservation or repair. In some cases, monetary compensation might be chosen in place of restitution, but this would be open to the free choice of the recipient.

Monetary compensation would be needed for the loss of artistic and industrial production that would have resulted from the presence of cultural and artistic wealth in the formerly colonized countries and as an offset to the unjust

[172] *Tavrida Central Museum and others v Ukraine* (High Council, Civil Chamber) 22/00270 (9 June 2023). This result may also be justified by the status of Crimea as occupied territory.

[173] For example Egypt Law No 117 of the Year 1983 concerning the Issuance of Antiquities' Protection Law, Article 6 (stating that '[a]ll antiquities are considered to be public property—except for [charitable and religious endowments] . . .').

[174] Matthes, 'Repatriation' (n 77) 938.

enrichment the colonial powers realized. One often thinks primarily of the revenue lost through the absence of tourism.[175] However, many of these appropriations had the purpose or effect of inspiring and improving domestic European production and led to new phases of artistic and industrial creativity and design inspired by the appropriated objects. Both Napoleon and the seventh Earl of Elgin had the explicit motive of inspiring domestic French and English artistic and craft production through copying of molds and, more explicitly, observation of the appropriated artworks.[176] The Yuanmingyuan artworks, although not taken for this purpose, inspired British industrial design. While denigrating the Chinese 'major' arts as not conforming with the European cultural hierarchy, English designers and artists were admonished to copy the 'minor' arts of Yuanmingyuan, particularly enamel and cloisonné, and the use of colour.[177] Sarr and Savoy noted that the presence of African art in Europe sparked a 'spectacular cultural production ... (from Picasso to the Surrealists via the German Expressionists)'.[178] The loss of opportunities from these deprivations should also be compensated. Along similar lines compensation for loss of other forms of economic resources, such as through tourism and the economic activity that tourism engenders, would be justified.[179]

The scheme developed here of reparations will require funding. To the extent that the cultural objects are held by national institutions of the Western colonial and imperial powers, these institutions and States should provide the funding as an additional form of reparations. Where the cultural objects are held by private collectors or by non-governmental institutions, both direct funding through grants and indirect funding through tax incentives should be provided to encourage returns. There may also be circumstances where a State should exercise the power of eminent domain or similar authority to take the cultural object for the purpose of return and pay compensation to the current possessor. This approach should be applied to human remains, burial objects, and sacred objects, which should not remain in private possession outside of the descendant community, if the community seeks their return.

The last issue to be considered is the ownership and uses of intellectual rights in the information and products derived from study of these cultural objects and human remains. Different determinations need to be made with respect to records, research, and information that has already been derived, on the one hand,

[175] Wambu, 'Why Africa's stolen treasures' (n 98).

[176] Williams, 'Of Publick Utility and Publick Property' (n 49) 104–05.

[177] Kate Hill, 'The Yuanmingyuan and Design Reform in Britain' in Louise Tythacott (ed), *Collecting and Displaying China's "Summer Palace" in the West: The Yuanmingyuan in Britain and France* (Routledge 2018) 53, 58–59. The Yuanmingyuan objects in England and France also generated artistic styles based on 'orientalism' and 'chinoiserie'.

[178] Sarr and Savoy, 'The Restitution of African Cultural Heritage' (n 64) 14.

[179] Among the greatest tourist attractions at the British Museum are the Parthenon Sculptures and the Rosetta Stone. Although the British Museum does not charge admission fees, other museums do, and cities such as London and Paris benefit economically from the tourism industry. See also Wambu, 'Why Africa's stolen treasures' (n 98).

and research that may be conducted in the future, on the other. Archival and digital records of colonial administrations, records of the cultural objects, and the results of research already conducted should be returned or at least freely shared with the formerly colonized States and descendant communities. With respect to research conducted on human remains, a parallel may be found in medical experiments on human subjects that have been carried out under extremely egregious circumstances, including the Holocaust[180] and the Tuskegee experiment.[181] The question of whether the information garnered from the human experiments during the Holocaust may be used is still debated with no clearly accepted answer.[182] In some cases, human remains collected in the nineteenth and early twentieth centuries involved similarly egregious circumstances where people were killed for their remains or remains were collected from the battlefield immediately after the death of the individual. Whether the research from these studies should continue to be used is similarly unresolved, but if it does continue, this should be done only with consent of the descendants of the individuals or the consent of the descendant community of which the individual was a member.

NAGPRA never resolved what should happen with the information derived from research conducted by museums and educational institutions on human remains and cultural objects that were later repatriated. The results of such studies should be given to the descendant communities so that they can utilize these results in whatever ways they see appropriate, including a determination of what further use may be made. At a minimum, researchers should be denied any intellectual property rights in research products so that these products are freely available to descendant communities.[183] However, this information should not be made publicly available without the consent of those communities. A parallel to this approach may be found in the Anti-Bootlegging provisions of the US Copyright Act.[184] This provision prohibits the fixation of sounds and images of a live musical performance in a copy or phonorecord without the consent of the performers and imposes the possibility of both civil and criminal penalties. By prohibiting fixation under these circumstances, the legislation denies the recorder copyright rights in

[180] Not only were experiments carried out on humans during the Holocaust, but the medical profession assisted in devising means of carrying out the genocide and mass murder. Tessa Chelouche, 'Teaching Hard Truths about Medicine and the Holocaust' (2021) 23(1) AMA Journal of Ethics E59–63 <https://journalofethics.ama-assn.org/article/teaching-hard-truths-about-medicine-and-holocaust/2021-01> accessed 27 January 2022.

[181] Centers for Disease Control and Prevention, The US Public Health Service Syphilis Study at Tuskegee, <www.cdc.gov/tuskegee/timeline.htm> accessed 27 January 2022. This study does not seem to have resulted in any scientifically useful information.

[182] See Lynn Gillam, 'Is it ethical to use data from Nazi medical experiments?' (*The Conversation*, 10 June 2015) <https://theconversation.com/is-it-ethical-to-use-data-from-nazi-medical-experiments-39928> accessed 27 January 2022.

[183] While there is no copyright or other intellectual property rights in underlying data, authors would have rights in the aggregation of data, photographs, and publications. Such rights might limit the ability of descendant communities and States to access and use this information.

[184] Copyright Act, 17 USC §1101.

the recording. The same logic should be applied to research conducted on cultural materials that were taken without the consent of the individuals and communities that produced the cultural object and without the consent of countries of origin that are the owners of illegally removed archaeological materials.

With respect to future research, museums should make and retain records of objects that have been returned. These collecting histories are important for future research and, in some cases, may assist in other claims for return.[185] Records of human remains and sacred objects may require special handling involving traditional secrecy, confidentiality, and possible human rights violations. Where descendants or the community of origin is known with reasonable certainty, research should not be conducted without their consent. But the *presence* of objects and human remains in collections should be made public in the interest of transparency and to further research and possible returns. Future research may be conducted pursuant to agreements between the holding institution and descendants, the communities of origin, or State. Such research may present opportunities for knowledge restitution through both transfer of information and the training of future generations from those communities and States. This would enable communities and States of origin to conduct such research and to participate on an equal basis in future knowledge production.

7.5 Conclusion

Obstacles to restitution are based primarily on the passage of time: bars to legal recovery through statutes of limitation, equitable defences, and prescription; the principle of non-retroactivity of newer legal instruments (*tempus regit actum*), and the projection forward to the present day of the double standard engrained in nineteenth-century legal rules concerning disposition of cultural objects. Western institutions and collectors continue to use the same justifications, particularly the rescue narrative and universality, for their retention of cultural objects as justified the initial removals of cultural objects during the nineteenth and early twentieth centuries. However, by examining the principles derived from human rights instruments and instruments pertaining to Indigenous groups, the argument is built that these cultural objects must be subjected to a tripartite scheme of reparations based on apology, restitution, and other forms of compensation.

The scheme proposes a methodology for determining a priority among objects to be returned. Central to this methodology is the use of an irrebutable presumption of illegitimacy with respect to human remains and burial objects and a rebuttable presumption of illegitimacy for other cultural objects placed on the current

185 For example Deutscher Museumsbund, Guidelines Care of Human Remains in Museums and Collections (2021) 57.

possessor. The current possessor would have the burden to establish the legitimacy of acquisitions during colonialism, imperialism, and armed conflict at any time from the Napoleonic Wars of the 1790s. Additional reparations would be provided through monetary compensation and the transfer of intellectual property rights and products that resulted from studies of cultural objects that were removed without consent.

This volume has taken an historical view of the legal and moral underpinnings for determining where cultural objects should be located and when they should be returned to owners and their descendants, communities, and States. This study began with the three strands that defined the origins in the late eighteenth and early nineteenth centuries of the contemporary questions as to where cultural objects should be located. The first strand focused on the effects of armed conflict exemplified by the Napoleonic depredations in Europe and the precedent established for the return of cultural objects at the end of the Napoleonic Wars. This precedent is used to set a timeline for a presumption that cultural objects removed after that time are subject to a requirement of return, unless the current possessor can establish legitimacy based on freely given consent from the person, community or institution with authority to give consent. The second strand is the development of universal or encyclopedic museums and the third is the development of archaeology as a science. Both of these contributed to expansions of knowledge but also constituted justifications for the taking to and retention of cultural objects in what were the European centres of power during the nineteenth century.

The third chapter examined takings of cultural objects over the course of the nineteenth century: the Parthenon Sculptures taken through British diplomatic authority backed up by military power in Britain's relationship with the Ottoman Empire; the looting and destruction by British and French forces of the Yuanmingyuan Palace as part of armed conflict carried out to assert trade and economic dominance in China; and the looting and destruction in Benin and elsewhere in Africa to protect the extractive activities of European powers and to thereby perpetuate their dominance, wealth, and political authority. These examples were only three of the episodes of looting over the course of the nineteenth century that could be considered. These episodes are united in the continuation of the mantras of the rescue narrative, unworthiness of the current inhabitants to possess cultural objects, and universal museums as justifications for these removals. They are also united by the role that military power, economic exploitation, and the desire to maintain favourable trade positions played in enabling these large-scale removals of cultural objects by the European colonial and imperial powers from throughout the world. The nineteenth century also saw the development of international law premised on the notion that international law granted to and determined rights among the European and a few other States to limit cultural looting or to require restitution at the end of a conflict. However, international law did not apply or protect rights against looting in the colonized regions, thus establishing a discriminatory system.

The fourth chapter followed chronologically and turned to the second half of the twentieth and early twenty-first centuries. While the market in cultural objects has existed since antiquity, beginning in the mid-twentieth-century, market perpetuation and supply became an additional motive for the looting and removal of cultural objects. The role of the market is particularly pernicious in the context of archaeological site looting because of the losses to knowledge and our ability to reconstruct the past that results from the unscientific removal of archaeological artefacts. The chapter considers and evaluates the *sui generis* legal doctrines, international conventions, and bilateral agreements that have developed to discourage the market in undocumented artefacts and thereby stem these destructive activities.

Chapter 5 presented an analysis of the legal regimes that developed over the course of the twentieth century to limit the theft and looting of cultural objects and to mandate return of such objects under certain circumstances. The first part of the chapter considered the law of armed conflict as it developed primarily in the 1954 Hague Conventions and Protocols to prohibit the taking of movable cultural objects during armed conflict and occupation. However, this legal regime is criticized for its failure to make illegally taken objects uniformly illegal on the market in countries that are not party to the conflict. The second part of the chapter examined international human rights instruments, particularly as they apply to the rights of Indigenous groups to the return of human remains and burial objects. The chapter then evaluates the two conventions formulated to regulate the contemporary movement of cultural objects outside of armed conflict, the 1970 UNESCO Convention and the 1995 UNIDROIT Convention. The following chapter turned to the different voluntary codes of conduct and professional ethics that are intended to set higher standards than the law and thereby fill the gaps left by the law. These codes are adopted by museum associations, individual museums, trade groups, and academic and scholarly associations but do not in many cases set a higher standard than what the law requires.

The legal rules discussed in chapter 5 and the ethics and professional codes discussed in chapter 6 provide means of discouraging thefts and looting through disincentivizing the market and requiring returns of improperly removed cultural objects. However, even at their optimal operation, they apply only to thefts and looting that occurred in the twentieth century. The ethical and professional codes are of limited usefulness in that they apply primarily either to artworks looted during the Holocaust or to archaeological artefacts removed illegally after 1970. Thus, despite the developments of the legal regime and professional codes of conduct, many gaps remain even among contemporary examples of looting and theft. Furthermore, these principles do not extend back to apply to removals in the late eighteenth and nineteenth centuries.

The last chapter therefore examined first the oft-stated inability of these legal and ethical rubrics to extend back to the nineteenth century through the principles of bars based on the passage of time, non-retroactivity of laws and international conventions, and a willingness to perpetuate into the present the past discriminatory treatment engrained in international law. It also examined the contemporary formulations of the rescue narrative and the role of the universal museum that are used as defences against claims of return and to justify retention often in the institutions that benefited from the nineteenth-century appropriations. The chapter and this study concluded with a justification for the need to adopt a scheme of reparations based on discussions in previous chapters and then a detailed analysis of how such a scheme would operate. Based on three elements—apology, return, and additional compensation—the scheme would establish an irrebutable presumption of illegitimate acquisition for human remains and burial objects and a rebuttable presumption for other cultural objects whereby the current possessor would need to establish legitimate acquisition based on free and informed consent from a person, community, or State that had authority to give consent. These presumptions would apply to any cultural objects removed from parts of the world subject to colonialism, imperialism, or armed conflict from the time of the Napoleonic Wars. Issues of additional monetary compensation to carry out the restitutions and disposition of intellectual property rights and products are also considered as part of the reparations scheme.

Determining the disposition of movable cultural objects through historical and legal analysis is an essential element in achieving reparation for the appropriations that have been imposed on many communities over the past two centuries. Adoption of such a reparations scheme as is proposed here would be a significant step in repairing the harms to people and to their cultural heritage perpetrated throughout many parts of the world by European and other Western States through colonialism, armed conflict, violence, and economic and political imperialism. This repair is a necessary step in reconnecting communities and States to their heritage to foster the flourishing of their identities and connections to their cultural past. A rebalancing of the interests between universalism on the one hand and States and communities on the other would also be promoted, as well as a greater understanding of cultural objects through the contextualized knowledge that would result. Reparations through restitution can thus become a means of building cultural relations, honouring the State's and community's interest in cultural heritage, achieving true cultural universalism, and increasing contextual understanding of the past.

Index

For the benefit of digital users, indexed terms that span two pages (e.g., 52–53) may, on occasion, appear on only one of those pages.

Figures are indicated by *f* following the page number